D1593158

Pierre Monteux, Maître

Monteux with the score that made him famous, Boston, 1951. Photo by Lenscraft Studio Inc., courtesy of the Boston Symphony Orchestra Archives

Pierre Monteux, Maître

by John Canarina

with a foreword by Sir Neville Marriner

Amadeus Press, LLC
Pompton Plains • Cambridge

Published in 2003 by
Amadeus Press, LLC
512 Newark Pompton Turnpike
Pompton Plains, New Jersey 07444, U.S.A.

Amadeus Press
2 Station Road
Swavesey
Cambridge CB4 5QJ, U.K.

Printed in China

Library of Congress Cataloging-in-Publication Data

Canarina, John, 1934–
    Pierre Monteux, maître / by John Canarina ; with a foreword by Sir Neville Marriner.
        p.   cm.
    Includes bibliographical references, discography, and index.
    ISBN 1-57467-082-4
    1. Monteux, Pierre, 1875–1964. 2. Conductors (Music)—France—Biography.
    I. Title.

ML422.M72 C36 2003
784.2'092—dc21
[B]

2002040871

Contents

Photographs follow page 128

Dedicated,
with affection,
to Nancie, Claude, and Denise

Foreword

by Sir Neville Marriner

"Because of a certain reticence, I have never known my fellow-men as I should." This was Monteux in reflective mood in later years—still unaware of his influence on his professional fellow-men, or if he guessed, still too modest to identify it.

Perhaps only his students wholly appreciated his pragmatic philosophy, his economical intensity, his comprehensive musicianship, and his remarkable experience. "I saw the first electric light in Paris, the first automobile, first cinema, first *avion*—so many firsts"—too modest to list *L'après-midi d'un faune, Daphnis et Chloé, Petrouchka*, and *Sacre du printemps*. Just typical of the "Maître" who converted the title Maestro to a symbol of affection.

"Young conductors talk too much. I don't know if it's a nervous reaction or if they feel the need to show their erudition." So said Monteux, and I have already talked too much. Read the book, and share the gratitude all musicians feel for a great example of the conductor's art.

Preface

Composers may not consciously write for posterity, but posterity is the ultimate judge of their worth, and the great ones survive. The performing arts are, unfortunately, more transitory. While recordings may be permanent, public demand for them gradually decreases as the artists involved recede into history. New artists, new versions of the same repertoire, and new recording and playback techniques replace the old. It is only natural that people buy records by performers they can see and hear in the flesh, or at least on television. Of course, the further an artist disappears into the past, the more he or she becomes a historic, even legendary figure, and there is then a new demand for the reissued recordings.

In my student years, the conductors I could see and hear in the flesh (and occasionally on television), and whose records I bought, were Ernest Ansermet, Sir Thomas Beecham, Leonard Bernstein, Guido Cantelli, Antal Doráti, Herbert von Karajan, Serge Koussevitzky, Rafael Kubelík, Erich Leinsdorf, Igor Markevitch, Dimitri Mitropoulos, Pierre Monteux, Charles Munch, Eugene Ormandy, Paul Paray, Fritz Reiner, Artur Rodzinski, William Steinberg, Leopold Stokowski, George Szell, Arturo Toscanini, Bruno Walter, and quite a few more. I did not feel compelled to purchase recordings by Willem Mengelberg and Felix Weingartner, who had already passed from the scene, or by Wilhelm Furtwängler and Otto Klemperer, who did not perform in New York while I was growing up. (These omissions have since been rectified.)

In my circle, and a few others as well, the consensus was that the greatest of these was Toscanini. There was also—notwithstanding the individual merits of the others—one maestro who was ranked just a notch below Toscanini. That was Pierre Monteux. It was my good fortune to have been able to study with him for seven summers at his conducting school in Hancock, Maine, and to see him conduct many times in New York, at Tanglewood, and elsewhere. It fascinates me to realize that I am only one person removed from the great musical events in which Monteux participated early in the twentieth century.

Strangely enough, very little has been written about Pierre Monteux, in contrast to the many books and articles about Bernstein, Furtwängler, Karajan, and

Toscanini. Perhaps it is difficult to write about Monteux for the simple reason that there was very little about him that was controversial, even though he was involved in at least one great controversy not of his making. Toscanini, for example, was a stronger and more volatile personality, making headlines in spite of himself and achieving performances of greater intensity. Monteux was more easy-going, his music-making more relaxed, but exciting all the same. Where Toscanini terrorized orchestras, Monteux cajoled them, although he was not always the "benevolent papa" he became in later years. Orchestras loved to play for him and audiences loved to hear and see him, perhaps as much for his distinctive portly figure and walrus mustache as for anything else. What Toscanini and Monteux had in common was the basic integrity of their approach to the score, a selflessness and humility in the service of the composer that allowed the music to unfold with a natural feeling of inevitability. As for Monteux and his extremely wide repertoire, he was the only French conductor in my experience who consistently gave convincing performances of German music, especially Brahms, often surpassing those of German conductors.

For many years the sum of writing about Pierre Monteux in book form was two volumes written by his wife Doris, although the first of these, *Everyone Is Someone*, was written under the name of the Monteuxs' pet poodle, Fifi. As such, it was reviewed favorably in *The New York Times* by Harold C. Schonberg's dog, Zipper. The second, *It's All in the Music*, Doris wrote under her own name. Both books, especially the first, are written in a rather cute style and are surprisingly devoid of specific information, though much of the second purports to be told in Monteux's own words. Even his daughter Nancie has said, concerning the Monteux quotes in the book, "My father never talked like that."

Nevertheless, in the present volume I have relied on these quotes when no other source was available. It was very tempting to quote Monteux's remarks in a visual version of his inimitable French accent. I decided against this, however, for fear of becoming cutesy myself. In only a few brief instances have I tried to reproduce his accent. Readers who heard Monteux speak are free to imagine it in the quotes.

In 1999 a third book about Pierre Monteux appeared, though only in France and in French: *Pierre Monteux*, by Jean-Philippe Mousnier. A paperback, it is part of a series on French musicians that the author began the year before with a volume on Paul Paray. While Mousnier's book contains useful information, it is not entirely free of errors and mentions nothing about Monteux's family life. Nor does Doris Monteux, for that matter, say anything about it. Relying on her book and Mousnier's, one would have no idea that Monteux had been married twice before and that he was the father of several children.

Following the example of Anthony Tommasini in his admirable biography of Virgil Thomson, I have written in the first person when describing events in which I participated or at which I was present, or when expressing an opinion. While my admiration of and respect and affection for Pierre Monteux will no doubt become evident in what follows, I have tried to present a balanced picture of his life and work, not an exercise in hagiography. Where my research uncovered warts, they are exposed.

In addition, Monteux, among the great conductors, had one of the most wonderful senses of humor, comparable only to that of Sir Thomas Beecham, though Monteux rarely uttered his humorous remarks publicly. Where appropriate, I have tried to show this side of Monteux as well.

To all his work Pierre Monteux brought not only his profound musical understanding and flawless conducting technique, but also his personal warmth, geniality, and humanity. To have studied with and enjoyed the friendship of this beloved *maître* will always remain one of the most cherished experiences of my life.

J. C.

Acknowledgments

$\mathbf{M}$any people contributed to the assembling of what you are about to read. First and foremost I wish to thank the members of the Monteux family, beginning with Nancie Monteux-Barendse, who lives in the home where her parents, Pierre and Doris Monteux, once resided, and which contains a vast storehouse of Monteux information in the form of programs, photographs, letters, documents, and other memorabilia. At least it did until Nancie generously allowed me to cart much of it away to my own home, where I could sift through it. (By the time these lines are read, that material will have been returned to its rightful place.)

Pierre Monteux's son and daughter, Claude Monteux and Denise Lanese, have been most kind and helpful in sharing their memories with me. A grandson, also named Claude Monteux, has been virtually my Paris research assistant, guiding me to the proper archive or library, assisting me while I was there, and continuing to unearth information once I had left. Nancie's son, Henry Barendse, contacted Amadeus Press on my behalf and without my knowledge, lighting the spark that resulted in this book. Henry was also very helpful in bringing information to my attention. Pierre and Doris's niece, Ginia Davis Wexler, provided information not only about the Monteuxs, but also about her own family, headed by Meyer and Hilda Davis. To all of them, my most heartfelt thanks.

Thanks are also due the many former students of Pierre Monteux whom I interviewed or at least spoke with: Bernard Basescu, Charles Bruck, Anshel Brusilow, Michael Charry, George Cleve, John Covelli, Harry Ellis Dickson, Hubert Doris, Edwin Freeman, Erich Kunzel, Lorin Maazel, Sir Neville Marriner (who has generously contributed the foreword to this book), Francis Madeira, Gordon Peters, Jonathan Sternberg, Adrian Sunshine, and David Zinman. Though not a student of Monteux, the conductor Max Rudolf was his friend and colleague at the Metropolitan Opera and graciously shared his memories with me.

I am also grateful to the following, who gladly spoke with me about Monteux: Kathryna Barone, Martin Bookspan, Dorothy Carroll, Robert Commanday, Philippe Entremont, Marius Flothuis, Peter Francis, Morton Gould, Carle Gray,

14

Henry Greenwood, Adolph (Bud) Herseth, Roland Kohloff, Hugh Maguire, Jean O'Meara, Earl Bernard Murray, Adeline Peake, John Pfeiffer, Sanford (Sandy) Phippen (my virtual Hancock research assistant), Michael Rosenker, Gunther Schuller, Thomas Slattery, and Beatrice Wernick.

Additionally, I wish to thank the following for graciously allowing me to quote from their writings or oral comments or from the writings of a deceased family member or associate: Amberson, Inc. (for the letter by Leonard Bernstein), Nancie Monteux-Barendse, Robert Craft, Joel and Timothy Creston, Ernest Fleischmann, Donal Henahan, Jacqueline Landowski, Vera Leinsdorf, Sanford Phippen, André Previn, Michael Stern, the Estate of Virgil Thomson (Robert Cornfield), Ginia Davis Wexler, and David Zinman.

I also thank the following publications and publishers for permission to quote from their material: Alfred A. Knopf (for excerpts from *Stravinsky: A Creative Spring* by Stephen Walsh); *The Boston Globe*; the *Boston Herald*; *Commentary*; the *Daily Mail* (London); *The Dallas Morning News* (for the quotation from *The Dallas Times Herald*); the *Express* (London); *Financial Times*; *The Guardian* (London); Harper Collins Publishers (for *The Bluebird of Happiness* by Alan Levy and Jan Peerce); *The Nation*; *The New Criterion*; the *New York Post*; *The New York Times*; *Notes: Quarterly Journal of the Music Library Association*, vol. 27, no. 3 (March 1971): 461–68; the Orion Publishing Group Ltd. (for *Diaghilev* by Richard Buckle, published by Phoenix); Presidio Press (for *The San Francisco Symphony* by David Schneider); Random House, Inc. (for *Mother Is Minnie* by Sophie Guggenheimer Untermeyer and Alix Williamson); the *San Francisco Chronicle*; *The San Francisco Examiner*; and *The Times* and *Sunday Times* (London).

Every effort has been made to contact the relevant persons, heirs, publishers, and publications for purposes of permission. No negative responses have been received. However, in some cases there have been no responses at all, which has resulted in the adoption of the philosophy that "no news is good news."

The archives of symphony orchestras and other arts organizations were important sources of information, and I wish to thank the following: Gemeentearchief, Amsterdam (J. H. Giskes); the Boston Symphony Orchestra (Bridget Carr and Barbara Perkel); the Chicago Symphony Orchestra (Brenda Nelson-Strauss and Frank Villella); the Cleveland Orchestra (Carol Jacobs); the London Philharmonic Orchestra (Edmund Pirouet); the London Symphony Orchestra (Libby Rice); the Los Angeles Philharmonic Orchestra (Steve Lacoste); the Metropolitan Opera Association (Robert Tuggle and John Pennino); the Minnesota Orchestra (Paul Gunther); the New York Philharmonic (Barbara Haws and staff); the Philadelphia Orchestra (Joanne Barry); the Royal Concertgebouw Orchestra (Truus de Leur, joint artistic director); the San Francisco Performing Arts Library and Museum (Lee Cox and staff); the Vienna Philharmonic (Otto Strasser); the respective staffs of the Bibliothèque de l'Arsenal, the Bibliothèque Nationale, and the Bibliothèque Gustav Mahler, all in Paris; the Archives of the City of Paris and the Archives of the Paris Opera; and the staffs of Cowles Library, Drake University; the Ellsworth, Maine, Public Library; the Historical Society of the Town of Hancock, Maine (Lois Crabtree Johnson); and the New York Public Library for the Performing Arts. I would also like to thank Marilea Chase of Drake University's College of Arts and Sciences for dealing so patiently with my innumerable faxes.

Three people read my preliminary manuscript; I thank Martin Bookspan, Richard Freed, and Misha Rosenker for their many invaluable suggestions concerning clarity, the appropriateness of certain comments I had made, the proper placing of diacritics, and many other aspects of the book. Richard Freed became, in fact, my indefatigable pre-editor. For supplying me with the few out-of-print Monteux recordings I did not already possess, my thanks go to Henry Fogel and David Hamilton, while the latter and Dennis Rooney receive my appreciation for suggestions pertaining to the discography. Last, and far from least, I wish to thank Eve Goodman, editorial director of Amadeus Press, for her faith in this project and for her valuable assistance in the development of it, and my editor, Barbara Norton, for inimitably providing the finishing touches.

J. C.

29 May 1913

As the reedy, somewhat sleazy high-pitched sound of what might be a bassoon resonates from the orchestra pit, soon to be joined by other wind instruments quietly playing in mild cacophony, a feeling of unrest begins to spread over the assembled audience, most of whom have come to watch rather than listen. A loud high-pitched muted trumpet adds to the general confusion. For two minutes, silence from the crowd.

The tones subside, and again there is that strange-sounding instrument from the opening, the player straining to produce the notes. Boos and catcalls begin to be heard, first from the gallery, then from the lower floors. In a moment loud, repeated, oddly pulsating string chords, eight horns adding their irregular accents. Further shouts of dismay. Bedlam in the auditorium. Fist fights break out between those who approve of the proceedings and those who do not. At first this derision is directed at the dancers, but the musicians producing these strange and discordant sounds are soon the principal target of anger and ridicule. Various objects are tossed in their direction, yet the orchestra continues to play. The police are called in.

Incredibly, this din, this confusion, much worse than the performance that incited it, continues for the better part of half an hour, disrupting a historic musical and choreographic event. The dancers can barely hear the orchestra; the choreographer shouts the beats from the wings; and the composer, fearful of bodily harm, escapes through a backstage window. Through it all, the imperturbable conductor continues to direct his musicians, even though at times he cannot hear them at all—he keeps track of where they are in the score by watching the players, where their bows are placed at any given moment, which wind instruments are playing or not playing—players he has already led through seventeen rehearsals. Since the work being performed contains some of the loudest music ever written up to that time, as well as the most complex, the audience's achievement in drowning out most of it is truly impressive. A final crashing chord and it is all over, save for additional protests mixed with applause. The most significant event in twentieth-century music is now history.

And what of that imperturbable conductor, that little round man with the large moustache? How did he come to be involved in this *scandale*? The event, the *scandale*, was, of course, the world premiere of Igor Stravinsky's *Rite of Spring*. The date was 29 May 1913. The conductor was Pierre Monteux.

.

CHAPTER 1

Early Years

The ancestors of Pierre Monteux can be traced at least to the time of the Spanish Inquisition—Sephardic Jews who arrived in France from North Africa by way of Spain. Little is known about them, save that they settled in a city called Sète in Languedoc, in the south of France, on the Mediterranean coast near Marseilles. Most likely the original settlers were fishermen. Today Sète is still the first port of fishermen on the Mediterranean and a port for passengers to and from North Africa. Eventually some of the ancestors moved to the village of Monteux, also in southern France, from which they adopted the family name.

The nearest large city to Monteux is Carpentras, which in earlier times had allowed Jews to settle in a corner of the city. For lack of space, their buildings extended upward, with exterior staircases. Later the city would provide the setting for Darius Milhaud's opera *Esther de Carpentras*. Located five kilometers southwest of Carpentras, Monteux is today a town of some four thousand inhabitants, its ancient walls well preserved. Its principal attraction is the ruins of an old chateau in which Pope Clement V once resided.

A useful book called *Les Juifs du Midi* (*The Jews of the South of France*), by Danièle and Carol Iancu, provides a history of Jewish settlers in France's Midi region. The earliest possible ancestor of Pierre Monteux mentioned is one Mosse de Monteux, a surgeon who settled in Aix in 1489. In 1637 we find, in Carpentras, Rabbi Abraham de Monteux and his sons Isaac, Mordecai, and Ain; and in 1775, Benjamin de Monteux. Many others are mentioned through the years, including a poet, Saul ben Joseph de Monteux. In 1826 there were eleven Monteux families in the region. That at least one member of the Monteux family was a rabbi is probably responsible for the mistaken belief, held by many of his students, that Pierre's father was a rabbi, when he was, in fact, a shoe salesman.

Gustave Elie Monteux, son of Cadet Jassé Monteux and Rousse Mosse Monteux, was born in 1835 in the town of Entraigues, near the provençale city of Aix, also in the Carpentras area. Extremely handsome, he had a reputation in the family that endures to this day as a roué who had many mistresses and who enjoyed writing poetry about beautiful women. He is also remembered as an amateur billiards champion who always had great ideas for making a fortune, ideas that never came to fruition. Gustave did, however, succeed in establishing himself in the shoe business in Marseilles.

In 1860 Gustave married Clémence Rebecca Brisac. Eight years his junior, she was a native of Marseilles and a graduate of its music conservatory. Clémence was slightly less than five feet tall and rather plump, which perhaps explains the physical appearance of her most famous son, though he at least stood five feet five inches in height.

By 1864 two boys, Paul and Émile, had joined the family, and Gustave and Clémence decided to move to Paris. It was thought that the French capital would be a better place for Clémence to pursue her musical interests, and it was not long before she established herself as a teacher of piano, both privately and at an exclusive girls' school. Gustave, meanwhile, had no difficulty in transferring his salesmanship to Paris. He was not, however, a success, failing with one shoe shop after another. It was during this time that his interest in billiards grew (probably a contributing factor to the failing shops), and he soon became the champion player of Paris, a title he held for twenty years. When people would congratulate Clémence on her husband's championships, for which she had little patience, she would reply that it was because he spent more time at the cafés than anywhere else. Meanwhile, in 1866, a daughter, Marguerite, had arrived. Eight years were to pass before the appearance of son Henri in 1874.

At three o'clock in the afternoon on 4 April 1875, Clémence gave birth to Pierre Benjamin Monteux in the family home at 16 rue de la Grange Batelière, in Paris's ninth arondissement. In the following year, yet another son, André, was born. At the time of Pierre Monteux's birth, Hector Berlioz had been dead only six years; Claude Debussy was thirteen years old; Maurice Ravel was exactly four weeks old; Johannes Brahms was forty-two and had not yet produced his First Symphony; and the birth of Igor Stravinsky was seven years in the future.

Early exposure to his mother's piano playing and teaching brought out Pierre's natural gift for music, but it was with a violin rather than a piano that he began his music lessons. He was given his first instrument at the age of six through the kindness of a cousin, Félix Bloc, who would soon marry Pierre's sister Marguerite. He displayed genuine talent on this half-size violin, and by the time he was nine, lessons at the Paris Conservatory were being seriously considered. Gustave, however, did not approve of this plan, and it was only after much persuasion by Clémence, Bloc, and Pierre's brother Paul, who was already playing the violin in Paris cafés, that he relented. (Paul would eventually become a conductor of light music in cafés and theaters, such as La Cigale de Paris. After Pierre had established himself as a conductor, Paul billed himself as Paul Monteux-Brisac to avoid confusion, for the newspapers often printed concert listings with only the first-name initial and surname of the conductor. Had he not, there would have been two conductors called "P. Monteux.")

After a successful audition at the conservatory, Monteux began his violin studies, first in the preparatory class of Jules Garcin and later with Henri Berthelier; meanwhile he also observed the classes of Lambert Massart and Martin Marsick, whose students at that time included Georges Enesco, Carl Flesch, Fritz Kreisler, and Jacques Thibaud. Among his other teachers were Charles Lenepveu for counterpoint, fugue, and composition; and Albert Lavignac for harmony and theory (his name is known and dreaded by music students the world over who have had to deal with his solfège books in multiple clefs). When he was fourteen, Monteux began playing in the little orchestra of the Folies Bergères, an experience to which he credited his great sense of rhythm and, perhaps of equal importance, his introduction to the pleasures of women.

A year later, Monteux decided to transfer his instrumental allegiance to the viola, firstly because he was attracted to the mellow sound of the instrument, and secondly because he felt he would have more and better employment opportunities as a violist. As the Paris Conservatory did not offer viola classes, he sought out one of its professors, the composer Benjamin Godard (1849–1895), to help him. It was at Godard's home that Monteux had his first experiences playing the viola in chamber music ensembles, an activity that was to remain a lifelong love for him. In fact, he played with Godard in the first performance of Camille Saint-Saëns's (1835–1921) Septet, with the composer at the piano. Monteux did not neglect the violin, however, and graduated from the conservatory in 1896 with first prize on that instrument, quite an achievement when one remembers who his fellow students were.

Among Monteux's fellow students at the Conservatory was a young man named Alfred Cortot (1877–1962), who would become one of the greatest pianists of the first half of the twentieth century, especially noted for his performances of Frédéric Chopin and Robert Schumann, as well as of French music. Cortot and Monteux became good friends; Monteux even organized and conducted a small orchestra of fellow students to accompany Cortot in a program of concertos, which they performed in Paris and on a short tour to neighboring towns.

The composition lessons with Lenepveu resulted in Monteux's writing several short pieces for voice, for piano, and for clarinet, as well as a more substantial string quartet. Meanwhile, at the age of sixteen Monteux, already a veteran player, left the Folies Bergères to do a bit more freelance work. At the same time, he continued composing under Lenepveu's supervision and, in 1892, produced an amusing little piano polka with a title in solfège syllables, *Sol, fa, si, la, si, ré*. When said quickly in French, it becomes *Sol facile à cirer*—"Floor easy to polish." Monteux orchestrated this polka in response to an invitation to conduct one of his works at a charity ball. Standing for the first time in front of a professional orchestra, directing his own composition, he then and there determined to become a conductor, an ambition that, according to Monteux, he had harbored since the age of twelve.

Realizing that it was a bit premature to be recognized as a conductor, Pierre continued playing the viola and composing. When he was seventeen years old he was informed by a friend, Lucien Capet, concertmaster of the Lamoureux Orchestra in Paris and leader of the Capet Quartet, of a vacancy for viola in the Geloso Quartet, a prestigious French string quartet of that time in which Capet played second violin. The leader, Albert Geloso, at first thought Monteux too young for the post, but after hearing his audition Geloso enthusiastically engaged him on the spot.

Programs for the Geloso Quartet show that on 20 January 1894, with Monteux as violist, three of its members performed Gabriel Fauré's Piano Quartet No. 2 in G minor with the composer at the keyboard. Later the same year the group presented its annual cycle of "the last great quartets of Beethoven" for the Beethoven Foundation, started in 1889 by Fritz Schneklud, the quartet's cellist, and Camille Chevillard, who played a Beethoven piano sonata on each program. In 1899 Chevillard (1859–1923) became the conductor of the Lamoureux Orchestra, with which he would give the world premiere of Debussy's *La mer* in 1905.

So here we have Pierre Monteux as quite a busy young man, still a minor living at home, a full-time student at the conservatory, rehearsing at least three times a week and performing with a professional string quartet, accepting freelance engagements as time permitted, writing and orchestrating his compositions, teaching young violin and viola students, and now entertaining thoughts of conducting. One would think that he had little time for social activities. Yet while at the conservatory he had met Victoria Barrière, a vivacious fellow student from Bordeaux, also born in 1875. She was a very fine pianist who had already won the conservatory's first prize in piano at the age of twelve, competing not merely among her age group but with all the piano students at the institution. A courtship ensued, and in 1893, at the age of eighteen, Pierre and Victoria married. No one in either newlywed's family approved of this union, primarily because they were thought to be too young, and secondarily because Victoria was a Catholic and Monteux a Jew.

The Monteuxs did pronounce Victoria *très jolie*, though her vivacity was soon found to include a fiery temper that often manifested itself in throwing whatever object might be at hand (though never at Pierre, fortunately). The marriage produced a son, Jean Paul, and a daughter, Suzanne. Jean Paul would become a jazz percussionist, touring Europe with Mistinguette and Josephine Baker and playing in Paris at the Moulin Rouge.

Programs for 1895 show that on 9 and 23 March and 6 April, Victoria and Pierre performed together the complete Beethoven Sonatas for Piano and Violin (as the composer himself designated them). Additionally, on 26 May the two presented a joint recital of their pupils. It is interesting to note that the printed program does not identify the pupils by surname, but only, for example, as "Marguerite P." or "Marcel C." Also of interest is that the program contained a Mélodie for viola and an Andante Religioso for four violins by one P. Monteux.

Meanwhile, in 1893, Monteux, only eighteen years old, had successfully auditioned for the position of principal violist of one of Paris's major orchestras, the

Orchestre des Concerts Colonne. (There is no better training for a prospective conductor than actually playing in an orchestra.) In the 1890s, and for some time thereafter, four symphony orchestras performed regularly in Paris (usually all four at once in different halls on Sunday afternoons); the others were the Orchestre de la Société des Concerts du Conservatoire (commonly known in English as the Paris Conservatory Orchestra—in spite of its name, not a student orchestra), the Orchestre des Concerts Lamoureux, and the Orchestre des Concerts Pasdeloup. The Colonne, Lamoureux, and Pasdeloup orchestras were named after their respective founders and principal conductors: Édouard Colonne (1838–1910), Charles Lamoureux (1834–1899), and Jules Pasdeloup (1819–1887). Originally a violinist, Colonne founded his orchestra in 1873; it played at first at the Odéon but soon moved to its permanent home at the Théâtre du Châtelet. The repertoire was largely French and German, with Colonne conducting almost all the concerts until his death. Occasionally he invited prominent German guest conductors, such as Felix Mottl, Hans Richter, Richard Strauss, and Siegfried Wagner, as well as the great Hungarian maestro Arthur Nikisch. In 1910 Gustav Mahler conducted the Paris premiere of his Second Symphony with the Colonne Orchestra.

As a young man Colonne had known Hector Berlioz, and he became a prime interpreter of his music. Each season of his concerts featured a Berlioz cycle, with the programs repeated several times. From the beginning he gave annual performances of *The Damnation of Faust*, including in 1896 in celebration of the fiftieth anniversary of its premiere, and he continued to present that great and demanding work every season. By the time of his death, he had given it 174 times.

The Damnation of Faust includes an aria for Marguerite, "Le roi de Thulé," that has an important part for a solo viola. Scanning the programs of the Colonne Orchestra's concerts after 1893, one notices that whenever that work is performed, in addition to a listing of the vocal soloists and chorus, the indication "alt solo, M. Monteux" also appears. Strangely, considering that virtually every major orchestral and choral work of Berlioz was given by Colonne, there appear to have been no performances of *Harold in Italy*, which features the viola prominently.

Another work for which Monteux's name appears as violist on several occasions is Gustave Charpentier's *Impressions d'Italie*, and on 13 January 1906 he was soloist in the premiere of *Thème varié* by Georges Hüe (1858–1948). Hüe had won the Prix de Rome in 1879 and in 1922 would be elected to the Académie des Beaux-Arts to take the place of Saint-Saëns, who had died the previous year.

Several notable events at the Colonne concerts took place in 1908, and Pierre Monteux took part in them all. On 19 January Debussy conducted the orchestra's first performance of *La mer*, on 23 February Serge Koussevitzky appeared as double bass soloist in transcriptions of Mozart's A major Violin Concerto (!) and Max Bruch's *Kol Nidre*, and on 8 March Victoria Monteux-Barrière was one of two pianists in Berlioz's *Fantasy on Shakespeare's "The Tempest"* for chorus, orchestra, and piano four hands.

Monteux would later recall that Debussy was impatient with conductors and other musicians who performed his works in what he considered to be an excessively delicate and "perfumed" style. He disliked the term "impressionism" as applied to his music and would insist that when he wrote *forte*, he wanted *forte*. "Impressionism" in music implies a subtle depiction of moods and emotions rather than an aurally graphic representation of the subject matter. Debussy would have none of this, though the term continued to be used to describe his music, in spite of his protestations. Monteux also remarked that the members of the Colonne Orchestra found it difficult to take seriously the strange (to them) sounds of *La mer*, even with the composer conducting and exhorting them. One member made a small boat out of music paper.

> With a slight push of the foot, it sailed on a wooden sea, from basses through the celli and violas, the length of the platform. This childish idea met with such success that there was soon a whole fleet of small ships made from all kinds of paper wending their hazardous ways through an ocean of legs, instruments and sound, as Neptune, conceived by Claude Debussy, thundered his way to the end. (D. Monteux 1965, 54)

Even after joining the Colonne Orchestra, Monteux continued for a time his work with the Geloso Quartet, which included tours of Belgium, England, Germany, Austria, Italy, and Switzerland. On a visit to Vienna the quartet met Johannes Brahms and played one of his string quartets privately for him. As Monteux recalled many years later, Brahms stated, at the conclusion, "It takes the French to play my music properly. The Germans all play it much too heavily." (Monteux also admitted that he did not then speak or understand German, nor did Brahms speak French; Brahms's remarks were relayed to him in translation.)

Monteux had the impression that Colonne did not like him very much, even though the conductor respected the young man as a violist and musician. Actually, according to Monteux, Colonne was an extremely disagreeable person who was never really kind or affectionate toward anyone in the orchestra. While he was an excellent musician, he had a rather inexpressive baton technique and could be extremely sarcastic during rehearsals (in which he was hardly alone among conductors of that and later periods). Still, Monteux felt he gained great insight into Berlioz's music through Colonne's understanding of the composer's scores.

It was in 1895, at the age of twenty, that Pierre Monteux made his first appearance as a conductor on a prestigious occasion, and an unscheduled appearance at that. In the palatial home of "one of the Princesses of the Boulevard St. Germain" (Monteux's description), a chorus and orchestra, with Monteux as a member, had been engaged to give a private performance of an early oratorio by Saint-Saëns, *La lyre et la harpe*, based on an ode of the same name by Victor Hugo. Saint-Saëns was to conduct, with a Parisian church organist playing the part many were sure the composer had written for himself.

At the rehearsal Saint-Saëns became increasingly dissatisfied with the organist, who was making one mistake after the other, especially after being exposed to the composer's sarcasm. When he had finally had enough, Saint-Saëns, in a fit of frustration, threw down his baton and shouted, "Is there anyone here able to conduct this work at sight?" A chorus from the orchestra replied, "Oui—Monteux!" (D. Monteux 1965, 45).

As Saint-Saëns took his place at the organ, the offender having been relieved of his duties, Monteux, not without trepidation, mounted the podium to begin conducting a demanding score he had never seen. It is in just such a situation that the training of the type offered at the Paris Conservatory, involving rigorous solfège, sight-singing, and sight-reading exercises, proves its worth, for Monteux had no difficulty in reading the score and leading the assembled forces. Saint-Saëns was pleased and the concert was a great success. Apparently, however, the princess was upset because she had engaged Saint-Saëns as the composer-conductor, not as the organist. Monteux received no additional fee from her, nor any words of appreciation.

Notwithstanding the princess's ingratitude, this event gave Monteux the confidence to audition for the post of assistant conductor of the Colonne Orchestra. He was selected by the members of the orchestra committee, even though Colonne told him, in no uncertain terms, that he had not voted for him and that Monteux should not expect to conduct any concerts. Colonne remained true to his word, though the assistant conductor's duties, such as they were, did include training the chorus for performances with the orchestra. Monteux knew that Colonne's wife felt him to be some sort of threat to her husband, for she had remarked during a committee meeting, "Keep an eye on the little Monteux. He seldom speaks, but he thinks a lot, nonetheless" (D. Monteux 1965, 49).

As Monteux put it:

> The truth of the matter is that I was bored to death by the long discussions of the committee on the placing in the programs of advertisements for Bon-Ton corsets, a face-powder called Poudre de Riz, Pinaud's Tonique, and what have you. So I sat and thought of my music, and of the notes I had written in my scores of the various ways Colonne exposed Berlioz's desires, all of which pleased me. (D. Monteux 1965, 50)

(Monteux's self-description is typical of what others would observe later on many social occasions, when he would appear to retreat from the conversations around him and become absorbed in his own thoughts, most likely musical ones.)

It is difficult to imagine the already roly-poly figure of Pierre Monteux as suitable for military life, and he would have been the first to say that he was not. Yet upon his graduation from the Paris Conservatory in 1896 he was eligible for national service, and in November of that year he duly presented himself to the Bureau of Registration for Military Service. As it happened, laureates from the *grandes écoles*, of which the conservatory was one, were exempt from the usual three years of service and were required to serve only ten months. Monteux was sent to Reims, where he "became the most pitifully inadequate soldier that the 132nd Infantry ever had." Soon the regiment's Colonel Jeannot, knowing of Monteux's background, sent for him and ordered Monteux to give him violin lessons. In fact, the violin proved useful to Monteux throughout his military stint, for he was asked to play at officers' parties, Christmas and Easter masses, and various other events.

Gymnastics were certainly not something at which Monteux excelled, to the consternation of his captain, who continually threatened him with disciplinary action for his poor performance in exercises. In one of these, when he was supposed to chin himself at the bar three times, Monteux succeeded in doing so only once. He jumped down to find Colonel Jeannot standing before him.

"I must say, Monsieur Monteux, you play the Meditation from *Thaïs* better than you work at gymnastics." The captain later informed him, "It's lucky for you the Colonel recognized you or I'd have flung you into prison!" (D. Monteux 1965, 63–65).

After the ten months of service, the requirement was to be called up every three years for two four-week periods and one of two weeks. We shall learn something of Monteux's later service in due course. Release from the army meant returning to the Geloso Quartet, the Colonne Orchestra, and the busy life of a Parisian musician, one who was now considered the city's premier violist.

Monteux did not limit his chamber music activity to his membership in the Geloso Quartet. On 27 April 1903 he took part in a concert devoted to music by Edvard Grieg in which the composer performed some of his *Lyric Pieces* for piano and accompanied the soprano Hilda Fjord in several of his songs. Monteux played Grieg's String Quartet in a quartet led by Johannes Wolff. There were also some programs in 1903 that were in the nature of family affairs—recitals by pupils of Monteux's mother, who was known as Madame Monteux-Brisac, in which Pierre and Victoria both participated, as did his brother Henri, who, having begun to establish himself in Paris as an actor, recited some poems.

Meanwhile, Victoria's abilities as a pianist meant that she was often away from home on a concert tour. This did not suit Pierre very well, nor did he appreciate the fact that she was apparently a bit of a flirt. As the marriage began to deteriorate, Gustave Monteux introduced Pierre to Germaine Benedictus, a piano pupil of Victoria's, whose family was descended from that of the Dutch philosopher Spinoza. Gustave liked her, but the rest of the Monteux family did not, especially Clémence, who was particularly displeased when Germaine, an avid tennis player, would come to the dinner table directly from a match, without changing clothes and drenched in perspiration. Monteux divorced Victoria on 18 August 1909 and married Germaine on 3 February 1910, when she was barely eighteen. Because of the experience of Victoria's absences when on tour, he was very adamant about Germaine's not making a career as a concert pianist. She did continue to perform, but not in major venues—only in local concerts in and around Paris for schools and music societies and in chamber music. Her style of playing has been likened to that of the great Brazilian pianist Guiomar Novaes (1895–1979), who was noted for the beauty of her tone and the delicate shadings of her playing, especially in the music of Chopin and Schumann. As a tennis player, Germaine eventually won several local tournaments in France before an injury halted her tennis career. Undaunted, she took up golf and excelled in that as well, with a seven handicap.

CHAPTER 2

Becoming a Conductor

Édouard Colonne's steadfast refusal to allow his assistant to conduct his orchestra meant Monteux had to look elsewhere for opportunities. One arose at Paris's Théâtre de l'Odéon. There he was engaged to conduct the orchestra for theatrical productions, which included Georges Bizet's incidental music for Alphonse Daudet's play *L'Arlésienne* and Gabriel Pierné's ballet *Ramuntcho*. Since this employment was not full-time, Monteux continued his work with the Colonne Orchestra as principal violist and assistant conductor. In addition, from time to time he could be found in the viola section of the Orchestra of the Opéra-Comique, for he still managed to find the time to do some freelance work, probably substituting for a colleague. It was as a freelance violist for the Opéra-Comique that he took part in the premiere of Debussy's masterpiece *Pelléas et Mélisande*.

In 1902 Monteux took a summer job as second concertmaster and assistant conductor of the Orchestra of the Casino in Dieppe, a seaside resort in Normandy on the English Channel especially noted for its casino, which in turn boasted a first-class orchestra composed of the best musicians from among numerous French ensembles, none of which had summer seasons. The conductor of the Dieppe Orchestra was Joseph Bordeau; the director of the casino, Isadore Bloch. In 1904, after Bordeau's death, Gabriel Marie was appointed principal conductor. Marie's name may be familiar to piano students, for he was the composer of a rather innocuous little piece called *La cinquantaine*. As if Colonne's animosity were not causing Monteux enough problems, he found that Marie detested him and was extremely unpleasant to Monteux whenever it was his turn to conduct the orchestra. It is difficult to know why the two men disliked him so intensely. Perhaps they perceived him as some sort of threat to their authority, or were disconcerted by his rather placid exterior.

Unwilling to continue in this atmosphere, Monteux went to Isadore Bloch to tender his resignation. Bloch, however, refused to accept it. He informed Monteux that the casino was planning to embark on a season of opera and that he, Monteux, was to be the conductor. Monteux was delighted to accept this offer and relished imagining Marie's disgust when he learned of it. As recounted by Monteux, it was quite an operatic repertoire that he conducted in Dieppe: *Faust, Carmen, Manon, Thaïs, La bohème, Tosca, Cavalleria rusticana, Pagliacci, Aida, Rigoletto, La traviata, Samson et Dalila,* and several others. The inclusion of Italian repertoire is notable, for Monteux was not later known as an exponent of Italian opera (though he did record *La traviata*). By 1906 Bloch had decided to change from opera to seasons of drama and comedy. However, he informed Monteux that Marie was leaving the casino, as the management and the musicians could no longer tolerate his temper tantrums, and that, beginning with the 1907 season, Monteux alone would be in charge of the concerts. Marie was later to remark that he had "plucked a superb fruit [the casino] only to find a miserable worm [Monteux, presumably] inside." Monteux's comment was, "Some worm, *hein?*" (D. Monteux 1965, 71).

With a fine orchestra at his disposal, Monteux was able to begin to put into practice all he had learned from his place in the first violist's chair of the Colonne Orchestra. First of all, through much repetition—and thanks to his excellent ear— he knew the standard repertoire from memory. Secondly, by observing at close range Colonne and the few guest conductors he engaged, Monteux knew very well what worked in a rehearsal and what did not; what kind of gesture produced the desired results and what kind failed to do so; and what behavior on the part of the conductor resulted in a good working atmosphere and what was self-defeating. In particular was he impressed with the work of Arthur Nikisch, whose self-effacing baton technique, coupled with a compelling pair of eyes, made him Monteux's idol as a conductor. (Monteux was not alone in his admiration for Nikisch. Among his contemporary colleagues, Sir Adrian Boult and Fritz Reiner both credited Nikisch with profoundly influencing their conducting styles.)

In later years Monteux enjoyed telling an anecdote about an incident that took place during his time in Dieppe. He received a letter from Saint-Saëns, then in his seventies but still a marvelous pianist, in which he expressed a desire to play the Robert Schumann concerto with the orchestra. His reason was that everyone performed the concerto too fast, and he wished to demonstrate how it should be done. Monteux readily agreed to Saint-Saëns's proposal, knowing that the composer was a popular figure in Dieppe, where a street is named after him (there is also a nearby town of the same name). Saint-Saëns then made two stipulations: He would accept no fee, and there must be no publicity—his name was not to appear in any announcements for the concert. It was summertime and he did not wish to perform in the heat in an overcrowded auditorium. To this last demand Monteux also agreed, for he knew what the outcome would be. After all, there had to be a rehearsal, and then everyone would know who the soloist was.

At the rehearsal Saint-Saëns played the first two movements of the Schumann concerto at normal tempos, then proceeded to play the finale, which is marked allegro vivace, at a much slower tempo than usual, what Monteux described as an andante moderato. Apparently this was the point Saint-Saëns wished to make.

The sweltering auditorium was packed for the concert, with Saint-Saëns receiving the greatest ovation of the season.

Among Monteux's duties as assistant conductor of the Colonne Orchestra (perhaps his only duty, for actually conducting the orchestra was not yet one of them) was training the chorus for its appearances with the orchestra. On several programs he is listed as the chorus master for performances of Beethoven's *Missa solemnis*. (The program for 12 November 1911, part of a Festival Beethoven, shows the *Missa* being generously preceded by the overture and a chorus from *King Stephen* and the First Piano Concerto, with Alfred Cortot as soloist. Today the approximately eighty-minute *Missa* is considered sufficient for an entire program.) One of Monteux's choral preparations was for the Paris premiere on 17 April 1910 of Gustav Mahler's Second Symphony, in which the soloists were the soprano Povla Frijsh and the mezzo-soprano Hélène Demellier. According to Monteux, Mahler "did nothing but rant and rave and did not see fit to thank me. He was a fine conductor, but very disagreeable." While in later years Monteux did conduct an occasional Mahler performance, that composer's music was really not to his taste. As he said, his "heart was not in it" (D. Monteux 1965, 69). For the program of 18 December 1910 he prepared the chorus for César Franck's *Hymne*, which received its French premiere, and Alexander Borodin's Polovtzian Dances from *Prince Igor*, and he conducted the chorus alone in Claude Debussy's a cappella work *Trois chansons de Charles d'Orléans*.

On 28 March 1910 Colonne died. As the orchestra had evolved into a cooperative organization, its members selected Gabriel Pierné (1863–1937) to succeed him. Today Pierné is remembered primarily as a composer, best known for the ballet *Cydalise* and for the oratorio *The Children's Crusade* as well as for his Concert Piece for Harp and Orchestra. A brief excerpt from *Cydalise*, the introductory "Entrance of the Little Fauns," lasting all of a minute and a half, is probably his single most-performed composition. But in 1910 Pierné was equally known as both composer and conductor. Few recall that he led the world premiere of one of the twentieth century's best-known ballet and concert scores.

In the spring of 1910 the famous Ballets Russes made its second visit to Paris, presided over by its remarkable impresario, Sergei Diaghilev (1872–1929). Though he was not a professional musician, Diaghilev has more than earned an honored place in the musical pantheon through his commissioning of works from the outstanding composers of the day, including Claude Debussy, Manuel de Falla, Maurice Ravel, and, above all, Igor Stravinsky, works that have long since become twentieth-century classics.

A local orchestra was engaged in each city in which the Ballets Russes performed, and in Paris it was the Colonne Orchestra. Because Pierné was that ensemble's principal conductor, it fell to him to lead most of the performances, including the world premiere of Stravinsky's *Firebird* on 25 June 1910 at the Paris Opéra. It is amusing to recall that Stravinsky was not Diaghilev's first choice to compose the music for this ballet. That honor was bestowed upon Anatoli Liadov

(1855–1914), known today principally as the composer of such orchestral minia-tures as *Kikimora* and *The Enchanted Lake*. A professor of composition at the St. Petersburg Conservatory, Liadov would doubtless have provided a subtly evoca-tive score but was an extremely slow worker, probably because of his well-known laziness. By the time Diaghilev was ready to hear some of the score, Liadov had not done much more than buy the music paper.

In turning to Stravinsky, Diaghilev began what was to be a remarkable col-laboration. They were to ballet what Wolfgang Amadeus Mozart and Lorenzo da Ponte were to opera. For its 1911 visit to Paris, the Ballets Russes was to present another Stravinsky world premiere, *Petrushka*, with choreography by Michel Fokine (1880–1942), who also had *The Firebird* to his credit. Again the Colonne orchestra was engaged, but Diaghilev had planned for the Russian Nikolai Tcherepnin (1873–1945) to conduct. Tcherepnin, respectively the father and grandfather of the composers Alexander and Ivan Tcherepnin, was also a com-poser; one of his ballet scores, *Narcisse*, was in the Diaghilev repertoire. As Tcherepnin could not be present for the purely orchestral rehearsals of *Petrushka*, Diaghilev asked Pierné if he would conduct them. Pierné's response was that since he had conducted the premiere of *The Firebird*, he would lead the preliminary rehearsals of *Petrushka* only if he could conduct the premiere as well—he was beyond the point of preparing an orchestra for someone else. But Diaghilev still wanted Tcherepnin.

Pierre Monteux, however, was not beyond that point. As the Colonne Orches-tra's assistant conductor, he was asked to take over those first rehearsals, to which he readily agreed. While the orchestra did not know what to make of the piece at the first rehearsal, laughing out loud at times (as orchestras are prone to do when confronted with unfamiliar music in a strange idiom), Monteux very quickly impressed Stravinsky both with his straightforward rehearsal technique and with his thorough knowledge of a complex score that he had first seen only a short time before. Monteux, in turn, was fascinated by "this slight, dynamic man, twenty-nine years of age, darting like a dragonfly from one end of the foyer to the other, never still, listening, moving to every part of the orchestra, landing at inter-vals behind my back, and hissing semi-voce instruction in my ear" (D. Monteux 1965, 79). When it came time for Tcherepnin to assume command, Stravinsky adamantly insisted to Diaghilev that only Monteux would conduct *Petrushka*, for he knew the piece better than anyone. Diaghilev had no choice but to acqui-esce, so Monteux, at the age of thirty-six, began his association with the Ballets Russes, even though, as he was later to say, up until that time he had had not the slightest interest in ballet.

While many of his contemporary colleagues, especially the Middle Europeans and the Italians, learned their craft in the opera house, it was as a ballet conduc-tor that Monteux first made his mark, his operatic experience in Dieppe notwith-standing (and Dieppe was not an important musical center). Ernest Ansermet and Efrem Kurtz are others whose careers began in ballet. Antal Doráti began in opera but came to prominence as a ballet conductor. Whether opera or ballet, the important point is that most of the major conductors of the twentieth century started out in a theater, where one is concerned with elements of performance beyond the orchestra. It was and still is the ideal route, though few take it today.

Meanwhile, in addition to *Petrushka*, Monteux was asked by Diaghilev to take over the conducting of the other ballets included on the program with it, *Scheherazade* and *Le spectre de la rose*. Both also had choreography by Fokine; the latter was set to Carl Maria von Weber's *Invitation to the Dance* in the orchestration by Berlioz. Diaghilev had asked Monteux to conduct a rehearsal of *Scheherazade* prior to making his decision. *Scheherazade* had always been a great favorite of Monteux's as a concert piece, but it was a work to which many people, the Rimsky-Korsakov family among them, objected as the basis of a ballet for which it was not intended. In later years Monteux himself would not approve of the choreographing of major works of the symphonic repertoire, such as Beethoven and Brahms symphonies, but *Scheherazade*, with its sumptuous scoring and exotic subject matter, was an early exception. Besides, he was not in a position to refuse.

On 13 June 1911 at the Théâtre du Châtelet, with the magnificent Vaslav Nijinsky in the title role, *Petrushka* scored a great success. The tormented puppet was to become Nijinsky's favorite part. Although his spectacular elevation and leap through the window at the end of *Le spectre de la rose* made his reputation, he wished to be remembered not for his gymnastics but for roles, such as the tragicomic figure of Petrushka, that gave him an opportunity to display his ability as an actor.

This particular program was given three more times. After that the company paid a visit to London, but because *Petrushka* was not in the repertoire for those performances (Diaghilev felt it was too advanced for the British public), Monteux returned to his place in the Colonne Orchestra. The following summer, Diaghilev asked Monteux if he would be the conductor for a tour beginning in the fall in London. Tcherepnin, perhaps unhappy at being denied the premiere of *Petrushka*, was no longer the company's principal conductor, and Diaghilev had decided on Monteux for this position. Although he initially had misgivings about ballet conducting, having spent his professional life thus far as a member of a serious quartet and a symphony orchestra and as a conductor of symphonic and operatic repertoire, the experience of directing such a work as *Petrushka* and collaborating with its composer had given him a more positive attitude about this area of his profession.

Before accepting Diaghilev's offer, however, Monteux had to request a leave of absence from the Colonne Orchestra, which his orchestral colleagues granted only grudgingly. It is ironic that men who had supported his assumption of the assistant conductorship and who obviously liked and respected him should have been so reluctant to grant his request. Perhaps they did not want him to advance his career that much. Orchestral musicians tend to be wary of colleagues who become conductors—the "enemy," as it were.

Diaghilev's tour began in London on 16 October 1911 with five weeks at the Royal Opera House, Covent Garden. Here he engaged Thomas (not yet Sir Thomas) Beecham's orchestra, modestly called the Beecham Symphony Orchestra (perhaps in emulation of Parisian orchestras). Monteux found it to be a very good ensemble and greatly enjoyed working with it. This experience was the beginning of Monteux's love affair with London and with British musicians, which was to reach its zenith in the final years of his life.

It was an extremely successful visit for the Ballets Russes, with the London public and critics thoroughly enjoying such favorites as *Les sylphides*, *Carnaval*, *Le spectre de la rose*, and *Scheherazade*. Monteux became unwittingly involved in an incident on the final night of the engagement, 9 December. As recounted by the English painter, stage designer, and art collector Charles Ricketts, on a generous program that included all four of the above-mentioned ballets, the first three received "thunderous applause," but the public was greatly affected by the tragic conclusion of *Scheherazade*.

> They put such beauty into their deaths that we became amorous of death.
> . . . The audience was cowed and applauded silently, one faded round of sound, whereupon that pimple of a French conductor struck up *God Save the King*, which of course suggests to the Britisher coats, hats and trains to the suburbs. (Buckle 1979, 213)

Buckle comments, "Poor Monteux doubtless knew that after an evening prolonged by an encore and applause, the orchestra were impatient to get away." Ricketts was able virtually by himself to restart the applause, which then continued for twenty minutes.

The tour itinerary was to have included Russia, to which Monteux was greatly looking forward; he felt that his conducting of Russian music would benefit from his studying it in its natural environment. Unfortunately, that portion of the tour had to be canceled because the theater in which the company was to perform had burned to the ground. Diaghilev had then to arrange hastily a new tour encompassing Vienna, Budapest, and Prague, as well as Berlin, which had already been scheduled.

While in Berlin Monteux received an urgent telegram from the Colonne Orchestra informing him that Gabriel Pierné had broken his foot in an accident and would be unable to conduct the concert of Sunday, 11 February 1912. Even though he was on leave of absence, as assistant conductor Monteux was obligated to return to Paris to substitute. With *his* assistant conductor, Désiré Inghelbrecht (1880–1965), taking over the ballet duties, Monteux hurried to Paris by train to begin rehearsals. Even considering that concert programs were longer at that time than they are today, the stamina of an orchestra and an audience for such a program as this, presumably selected by Pierné, is difficult to imagine. The soloist was the celebrated German pianist Emil von Sauer.

Beethoven: *Coriolan* Overture
Beethoven: Symphony No. 3 in E-flat major ("Eroica")
Beethoven: Piano Concerto No. 4 in G major
Pierre Kunc: *Au pied des Monts de Gavarnie* (first performance)
Liszt: Piano Concerto No. 1 in E-flat major
Strauss: *Don Juan*

(Pierre Kunc [1865–1941] was an organist and choir master in several different Parisian and provincial churches, as well as the composer of *mélodies*, two masses, and a *Symphonie pyrénéenne*.)

This was the only concert that Pierre Monteux conducted with the Colonne Orchestra during his seventeen-year tenure as assistant conductor. Though the public was enthusiastic, Monteux later recalled that the general consensus of the critics was that any member of the orchestra could have done as well as he, and it was hoped that Pierné would return soon. However, the anonymous critic of *Le monde musical* wrote on 15 February 1912 that Monteux's conducting was remarkably careful and composed, though not without animation and warmth. The reviewer noted that Monteux was able to balance sonorities perfectly and succeeded in allowing the winds to be heard clearly, whereas in previous performances they were frequently covered by the strings. Rarely had the critic heard the "Eroica" Symphony performed with such attention to detail and such perfection of execution.

On rejoining the company in Vienna, Monteux had, as he described it, "one of the few unpleasant experiences I have ever had with an orchestra" (D. Monteux 1965, 84–85). The Vienna State Opera House had been engaged, and *Petrushka* was on the schedule. For this, Stravinsky had insisted on the employment of the full Vienna Philharmonic. This orchestra was then (and still is) well steeped in the classical and romantic German and Austrian repertoire, with occasional forays into such exotic territory as Tchaikovsky and Dvořák. Thus the members were unaccustomed to and unprepared for such "dirty music"—their term—as *Petrushka*. They instantly rebelled, the string section with its own version of a strike. At the first performance all the strings played so softly that Monteux, who had developed a proprietary interest in this score, could barely hear them, while the woodwinds and brass played *fortissimo*. So angry was he that, in retaliation, he motioned to the strings to play even more softly and encouraged the brass, already at peak volume and obviously struggling to maintain it, to play still louder. The next day a delegation from the orchestra came to Monteux and insisted that their action should not have been interpreted as being against him, to which he replied that while that may have been so, in his country if part of a group strikes, they all strike.

At a subsequent rehearsal the entire orchestra played *pianissimo*, and the players became distressed when Monteux continually indicated that they were too loud. From the rear of the theater came Diaghilev's voice shouting that what they were playing was not *Petrushka*, but a funeral march. On hearing this, all the orchestra immediately rose, shaking their instruments menacingly and demanding an apology. Diaghilev, who had come forward to peer into the orchestra pit, knew that the Viennese musicians would not be able to understand French when spoken very quickly, and in a mixture of French and Russian, which they also did not understand, began insulting them in no uncertain terms, all in a calm and controlled voice accompanied by gracious gestures and pleasant facial expressions. The musicians accepted this "apology," and the rehearsal continued without further incident, though the remaining performances were far from inspired; as Monteux put it, "The great Vienna Philharmonic simply could not play Petrushka" (D. Monteux 1965, 85).

Two major events conducted by Pierre Monteux were the highlights of the Ballets Russes 1912 Paris season at the Théâtre du Châtelet. The first marked the debut of Nijinsky as a choreographer: his erotic treatment of Debussy's *Prélude à l'après-midi d'un faune*. This sensuous score, really the beginning of impressionism in music, had been premiered as far back as 1894, and Nijinsky had been working on a ballet to it for at least a year prior to its eventual unveiling on 29 May. He had in mind a new kind of choreography. Rather than rely on the traditions of classical ballet, as found in such works as *Swan Lake, Sleeping Beauty, Scheherazade, Carnaval*, and other pieces in which the dancing was a natural ingredient of the story line or stage setting, he wished to liberate the dancing, to transform it into an independent entity that would make sense even without the music.

Debussy had gladly given permission for the use of his music, but Nijinsky's scenario did not follow the action of Stéphane Mallarmé's poem, which had inspired the composition. Instead, it dealt frankly with the awakening of sexual feelings. The ballet's conclusion, with Nijinsky as the Faun performing a rather explicit movement suggesting orgasm, proved to be highly controversial with the Parisian public and press. Much booing could be heard on the first night, to Diaghilev's and Nijinsky's consternation, and the controversy continued for days with articles and letters pro and con in the newspapers. In the end the brouhaha delighted Diaghilev, for it helped sell tickets for the remaining performances. For the second performance, on 31 May, the police were called. However, Nijinsky modified his final gesture and, finding nothing offensive, they approved the ballet; it received two more performances.

As for the second major event, for three years Maurice Ravel, a slow and meticulous worker, had been occupied with a commission he had received from Diaghilev for a ballet on a Greek subject, again to be choreographed by Fokine. As the 1912 Paris season of the Ballets Russes was approaching, Ravel had not yet completed the score of *Daphnis et Chloé*, necessitating several postponements of the opening night. Meanwhile, however, he had extracted an orchestral suite (later known as the Suite No. 1) from the score, which was played in Paris by the Colonne Orchestra, Pierné conducting, on 2 April. Fokine was unhappy that a portion of the music of "his" ballet had been heard by the Parisian public before the entire work could be produced.

Ravel was in the habit of attending rehearsals of the Ballets Russes, in many of which *Scheherazade* was on the stage. According to Monteux, Ravel had heard the dramatic trombone and trumpet calls of the second movement so many times, with their dotted and triplet rhythms, that, as a joke, he incorporated a variant of them into the final Danse Générale of *Daphnis et Chloé*, where it is heard initially played by the violas and clarinets. The dancers had difficulty at first with the 5/4 meter of that final dance, which they solved by counting to the five syllables of "Ser-gei Dia-ghi-lev."

Additionally, Fokine was upset because *Daphnis* would have to follow *L'après-midi* in the schedule. He felt there would be lessened interest in his ballet after the uproar caused by Nijinsky's, of which Diaghilev now wanted to schedule more performances. In the end, with a final postponement to 8 June and the season closing on 10 June, *Daphnis et Chloé*, one of the greatest works of the twentieth century, received only two performances in its first presentation. Its brilliant and subtle orchestration enhanced by the addition of a wordless chorus, the ballet featured Nijinsky in the role of the shepherd Daphnis and the equally great Tamara Karsavina in that of the shepherdess Chloé. The critic Robert Brussel of *Le Figaro* wrote of the great acclamation with which the work was received and remarked that Ravel was too modest to share in the applause accorded Fokine and his colleagues.

In his brief ballet career, Pierre Monteux had already presided over the world premieres of two works that became twentieth-century classics (*Petrushka* and *Daphnis et Chloé*) as well as the premiere of a ballet version of an existing nineteenth-century classic (*Prélude à l'après-midi d'un faune*). This gave him a fine European reputation as a solid and dependable conductor, but one associated primarily with ballet. Now the greatest twentieth-century classic of all, the one with which he would forever be associated, was waiting in the wings.

CHAPTER 3

The Rite

W hen the Ballets Russes finished its 1912 Paris season, Monteux returned to his seat in the Colonne Orchestra and then to the podium for his summer concerts in Dieppe. On learning that Diaghilev wished to engage him for another tour that fall and winter, Monteux, who had by this time become very enthusiastic about working with him and his company, applied for another leave of absence from the Colonne Orchestra. This time the orchestra committee, along with Pierné, refused his request. Monteux was determined to go with Diaghilev, so he proffered his resignation to the committee, which informed him that he could not resign in September—June was the month for resignations. When he insisted, he was told that all the money in his pension fund account, the accumulation of seventeen years of savings, would be confiscated if he resigned at that time. Without any hesitation Monteux bid the Orchestre des Concerts Colonne *adieu*, perhaps with a less polite word.

At the beginning of 1913 the company was in Budapest, where the orchestra, with limited rehearsal time, had problems with *The Firebird*. Stravinsky, who had arrived on 4 January, was angered by the orchestra's sloppy performance and blamed Monteux, who then resigned. In a letter to Stravinsky dated 5 January, Monteux wrote:

My dear friend,

Appearances can be misleading. Underneath my cold and indifferent
exterior, I am so sensitive that a simple remark can sometimes make me
ill. Perhaps it seemed to you that I was indifferent to the criticisms you
addressed to me a while ago, but I was so stunned by them that I have just
sent my resignation to M. Diaghilev. You hold me responsible for having
played *Firebird* under bad conditions. But what can I do when my contract
with M. Diaghilev obliges me to conduct all performances required by him?
I can do only one thing: I can work without interruption, divide the orchestra, take one group and then the other separately, then rehearse all together
and, without a moment of rest, put all my heart and all my devotion into a

score that I love, at the same time trying, as a man who is an artist and who dreams only of art, to avoid the deadening weariness. In thanks, I receive criticisms from you, who are my friend, but who says that I am too weak because I did what I had to do. I cannot endure what I consider to be unjust, and I gave up my position. I have tried in this letter to justify myself in your eyes, since I was not able to do it in person, after the event. Believe, my dear friend, in my regrets at having received your censure, and accept the assurances of my keen sympathy and my profoundest feelings of admiration.

Pierre Monteux (Craft 1984, 51)

Stravinsky's reply, if any, has not survived, but in any case Diaghilev did not accept Monteux's resignation. (Monteux's reference to his "cold and indifferent exterior," while self-deprecating, nevertheless acknowledges the personal impression he occasionally made, for he did not possess the volatile temperament associated with conductors, particularly in those days.)

The Beecham Symphony Orchestra was again engaged for the Ballets Russes' February–March London season at Covent Garden. This time Diaghilev felt that London was ready for *Petrushka*. Though the first-night audience on 4 February was initially startled by it, the public soon warmed to the piece and gave it an enthusiastic reception, as did the press. Stravinsky, for his part, felt that the piece had never been performed better than by Beecham's orchestra. *L'après-midi* was also given, and while it received a few boos after the first performance, it, too, was generally well accepted without incident.

In Doris Monteux's book *It's All in the Music*, Pierre Monteux is quoted as saying, "During the London season I was called back to Paris, due to an important event in our family" (D. Monteux 1965, 88). It is curious that nowhere in the book is there any mention of either of Monteux's first two wives or of his children. If Germaine Monteux has been little mentioned in this book, it is because there are no records of Pierre's private life at that time. Did she travel with him on any of his tours with the Ballets Russes? Did she spend the summers with him in Dieppe? Did she remain in Paris the entire time, performing in her own musical events and playing tennis? None of this is known. However, the two must have spent some time together, for the "important event in our family" was the birth of Denise Monteux on 1 March 1913. On 5 March Monteux wrote to Stravinsky from Paris:

I have the pleasure of announcing to you and to Madame Stravinsky the birth of a daughter, Denise, on March 1. The little girl must like your music, because she took advantage of the only program that did not have a single one of your works on it and chose to come into the world at that time. This allowed me to leave London without doing any harm to your music! My wife and the baby are as well as can be expected, and they ask me to convey their best wishes to you and Madame Stravinsky. (Craft 1984, 51)

In spite of Monteux's remark about leaving London "without doing any harm to your music," Monteux's sudden absence resulted in Thomas Beecham himself conducting a performance of *Petrushka* and *Le spectre de la rose* without rehearsal and acquitting himself brilliantly. It was his orchestra, and his musical astuteness enabled him to conduct a complex score such as *Petrushka* virtually at sight.

Stravinsky has said that he conceived the idea for a new ballet while he was still composing *The Firebird*. "I had dreamed a scene of a pagan ritual in which a chosen sacrificial virgin danced herself to death" (Stravinsky and Craft 1962, 159). Thus was planted the seed for a ballet originally to be titled *The Great Sacrifice*. Stravinsky was later to remark that the musical ideas that came to him were so complex that he was not sure how to notate them exactly, which accounts for the piece's many metrical irregularities.

Prior to the 1912 Paris season, Diaghilev's company was in Monte Carlo, where Stravinsky joined them for more than two weeks to oversee rehearsals and performances of *The Firebird* and *Petrushka*. During this period Diaghilev came to Monteux, who was rehearsing in the theater, and furtively whispered to him that Stravinsky had written "an extraordinary new work" (D. Monteux 1965, 90) that they both wanted Monteux to hear that afternoon. Monteux, who thought that Stravinsky had written a lovely work more or less in the style of *The Firebird*, or perhaps something in the *Petrushka* vein, was thoroughly unprepared for the experience awaiting him.

Over the years Monteux must have been asked hundreds of times about the premiere of *Le sacre du printemps* (*The Rite of Spring*), what he thought when he first heard it or saw the score, what happened during the first performance, and so on. He would unfailingly reply with patience and good humor, even though he surely must have tired of describing it. One suspects that he had developed a standard response to the question. In Doris Monteux's book he tells of going with Diaghilev to a small rehearsal room in Monte Carlo's Théâtre du Casino to hear Stravinsky play the score on the piano. The passage is worth quoting here, because it is very similar to the description he was heard to give on numerous occasions:

The room was small and the music was large, the sound of it completely dwarfing the poor piano on which the composer was pounding, completely dwarfing Diaghilev and his poor conductor listening in utter amazement, completely dwarfing Monte Carlo, I might say. The old up-right piano quivered and shook as Stravinsky tried to give us an idea of his new work for ballet. I remember vividly his dynamism and his sort of ruthless impetuosity as he attacked the score. By the time he had reached the second tableau, his face was so completely covered with sweat that I thought, "He

will surely burst, or have a syncope." My own head ached terribly, and I
decided then and there that the symphonies of Beethoven and Brahms were
the only music for me, not the music of this crazy Russian! I must admit I
did not understand one note of *Le sacre du printemps*. My one desire was
to flee that room and find a quiet corner in which to rest my aching head.
Then my Director turned to me and with a smile said, "This is a masterpiece, Monteux, which will completely revolutionize music and make you
famous, because you are going to conduct it." And, of course, I did.
(D. Monteux 1965, 91)

If Monteux's first reaction to this music was as he described it—he a thoroughly trained and expert musician already familiar with Stravinsky's earlier
works—one should perhaps not censure the first-night audience too harshly for its
failure to understand the piece.

Monteux went on to say that he studied the score daily with Stravinsky at the
piano and continued to study it the following winter. What he did not mention
was the role he played in perfecting certain aspects of the orchestration. Having
already begun orchestral rehearsals two months before the premiere, Monteux
wrote to Stravinsky on 30 March 1913 a letter that "remains the most conse-
quential that the composer ever received from a musician" (Craft 1984, 49). Monteux began by saying that as he had not yet rehearsed in the Théâtre des Champs-
Elysées, he could not be sure of what the piece will sound like there, but it should
be comparable to *The Firebird* and *Petrushka*. He did, however, make a number
of observations and suggestions:

At 28, beginning with measure 5 (4-hand piano score, p. 22, first measure),
I do not hear the horns loudly enough (unless the rest of the orchestra
plays pp), and if I make a little crescendo, I do not hear them at all. At 37,
measures 3 and 4 (4-hand piano score, p.25, measure 3), it is impossible to
hear a single note of the flute accompanied by four horns and four trumpets
FF, and first and second violins, also FF. The first flute plays the theme
alone in the middle of all this noise. At 41, measures 1 and 2 (4-hand piano
score, p. 27, measure 1), you have, first the tubas, which, in spite of FF,
produce only a very weak sound; second, the seventh and eighth horns,
which one does not hear at all in the low register; third, the trombones,
which are extremely loud; fourth, the first six horns, which one hears only
moderately in comparison with the trombones. I have added the fourth
horn to the seventh and eighth, but without achieving an equilibrium for
the four groups. One hears:

1. mf
2. nothing
3. FF
4. FF

At 65, measure 3 (4-hand piano score, p. 39, measure 10), the first four horns have FF, but they play with mutes, and I can hear them only with difficulty. (Craft 1984, 53)

Monteux goes on to mention that there are some discrepancies in the brass parts concerning the use of mutes, and that "it is possible that the four passages I have listed will sound better when the orchestra is in place, though this would surprise me, because the proportions remain the same." The result of the letter was that Stravinsky made alterations in the scoring according to Monteux's suggestions. (One shudders to think that eventually some misguided authenticity-minded conductor may attempt to restore Stravinsky's first notations, so as to give us the composer's "original" conception.)

On 15 May 1913, two weeks before the premiere of *The Rite of Spring*, Monteux led another first performance for Diaghilev, that of Debussy's *Jeux* (Games), with choreography by Nijinsky (which Monteux thought "asinine" [D. Monteux 1965, 91]), a ballet ostensibly about tennis but more subtly about human relationships. While not exactly a failure, the work did not excite the public, but rather puzzled it. Two weeks later Debussy wrote to a friend:

Among recent pointless goings-on I must include the staging of *Jeux*, which gave Nijinsky's perverse genius a chance of indulging in a peculiar kind of mathematics. This fellow adds up triple crotchets with his feet, checks them on his arms, then suddenly, half-paralyzed, he stands crossly watching the music slip by. It's awful. It's even Dalcrozian—for I consider Monsieur Dalcroze as one of the greatest enemies of music and you can imagine what havoc his method can create in the mind of a young savage like Nijinsky! (Buckle 1979, 251)

(Émile Jaques-Dalcroze [1865–1950] is known for his exercises, called "eurhythmics," in which the rhythmic aspects of music are expressed through physical movements. This technique had a great influence on ballet.) Considered by many to be one of Debussy's greatest works, and certainly his most difficult orchestral score, *Jeux* has remained on the fringe of the repertoire. Monteux continued to perform it in concert from time to time, and today Pierre Boulez is its most distinguished champion.

The world premiere of *The Rite of Spring* on 29 May 1913 took place exactly one year after the ballet premiere of *L'après-midi*, in Paris's Théâtre des Champs-Elysées (which is, perversely, not on the Champs-Elysées), which had opened earlier that year.

Perhaps a word or two about how Diaghilev acquired the financing for his ballet company is appropriate here. Even after taking into account the rental of a theater, salaries for dancers and staff (including choreographers and scenic designers), and the engagement of an orchestra and a conductor, composers still have to be commissioned and the orchestral requirements of their scores met. Apparently no limit was placed on the composers as to instrumentation. *The Firebird* and *Petrushka*, in their original versions, require an extremely large orchestra, as does *Daphnis et Chloé*, which additionally calls for a chorus. *The Rite of Spring* uses the largest orchestration for a purely orchestral work ever required up to that time: two piccolos, three flutes, alto flute, four oboes, two English horns, E-flat clarinet, three B-flat clarinets, two bass clarinets, four bassoons, two contrabassoons, eight horns, piccolo trumpet in D, four trumpets in C, three trombones, two tubas, five timpani requiring two players, bass drum, tambourine, gong, triangle, antique cymbals, guiro (scratcher), and, as program annotators are fond of saying, the usual strings. Obviously someone had to pay for all that.

On a visit to Paris in 1906, Diaghilev had met the music publisher Gabriel Astruc, who was always interested in promoting new music and new ideas in music and who helped him to organize a festival of Russian music in 1907 as well as the succeeding visits by the Ballets Russes. Meanwhile, Diaghilev had been introduced to Countess Greffulhe, whose husband was an extremely rich banker. So powerful and influential was she in Parisian society that once Diaghilev had gained her confidence, he had no difficulty in meeting other wealthy and artistically minded bankers, countesses, and similar well-born people. They became the patrons for his various enterprises, including the Ballets Russes.

These patrons and their friends formed a large portion of the first-night audience for *The Rite of Spring*. They had come for a good evening's entertainment and, while *Petrushka* and *L'après-midi* might have provoked them a bit, entertainment was what Diaghilev usually provided in such works as *Scheherazade*, *Carnaval*, and the like.

Nijinsky was also the choreographer for *The Rite of Spring*, having won his spurs the year before as Debussy's Faun. In later years Monteux would blame Nijinsky for the scandal that occurred, feeling that the choreography was the weakest part of the production. Nijinsky's wife, Romola, in her biography of her husband, claims:

> Nijinsky found that Monteux had developed into an ideal conductor for ballet. He was musically very well qualified, but during the last year he had improved immensely his choreographic sense. Without changing the tempi, which would have been unmusical, he had the kind of sense to know how to conduct for dancing. (Nijinsky 1934, 193)

At the premiere, the music was thought strange and intimidating, but as so much of it was drowned out, it can hardly be considered a cause of the riot that accompanied it. While it is true that the initial reaction was against the dancers, then the musicians, in the end the confusion was so great that everyone was held responsible. Perhaps Nijinsky's choreography or Léon Bakst's decor was responsible, although rarely are stage settings the cause of tumult. But when the curtain went up, the audience was treated to the sight of the dancers with their knees bent, standing pigeon-toed, which is the exact opposite of classical ballet's first position. This immediate violation of one of ballet's basic principles may have ignited the audience's fuse, for the French like to think that they "own" ballet, much as Americans feel about jazz and Italians about opera.

In his admirably detailed biography of Stravinsky, Stephen Walsh speaks of "a sense of unease" before the first performance (as opposed to the public dress rehearsal the night before, which had passed without incident), "due partly to the complexity of the score, partly to a feeling that Nijinsky and his dancers were not wholly at one with the music or each other, partly perhaps to Diaghilev's own instinct that trouble was in the air" (Walsh 1999, 203). The dress rehearsal, which was only for *The Rite of Spring*, had been attended by musicians (including Debussy and Ravel), critics, and other cognoscenti. At the actual performance, which was part of a subscription series, *The Rite* was preceded by *Les sylphides* and followed by *Le spectre de la rose* and the Polovtzian Dances from *Prince Igor*, all traditional ballets that never failed to please an audience. In the midst of these, *The Rite* (subtitled *Pictures of Pagan Russia*) could not fail to provoke. Also, advance word was, according to Walsh, that "the new ballet was difficult, violent, and incomprehensible." He quotes the composer Florent Schmitt as saying, "These so-called 'society' people, unable to see, hear and feel for themselves, these grown-up children . . . could only respond to these splendors, so immeasurably remote from their feeble understanding, with the stupid hilarity of infants" (Walsh 1999, 203–4).

Murmurs of discontent could be heard soon after the start of the piece, that high-pitched, strained, and tortuous bassoon solo. (Stravinsky once said that if he had known how easy that solo would become for bassoonists, every ten years he would have raised it half a step.) Soon catcalls and other imprecations were heard along with the voices of those trying to quell the disturbance, each side fueling the other. It was a case of the elegant inhabitants of the stalls and the boxes versus the more enthusiastic crowd in the balconies. Shouts were heard of "À bas les greus du 16ème!" ("Down with the bitches of the sixteenth district!"—the wealthy and fashionable area of Paris). Punches were thrown, and cards were exchanged so that duels could be fought the next day. Complete mayhem reigned.

Through all this turmoil Monteux continued to conduct the orchestra, even though at times he could not hear the music at all. Stravinsky later recalled:

> I was sitting in the fourth or fifth row on the right and the image of Monteux's back is more vivid in my mind today than the picture of the stage. He stood there apparently impervious and as nerveless as a crocodile. It is still almost incredible to me that he actually brought the orchestra through to the end. I left my seat when the heavy noises began—light noise had started from the very beginning—and went backstage behind Nijinsky in the right wing. Nijinsky stood on a chair, just out of view of the audience, shouting

numbers to the dancers. I wondered what on earth these numbers had to do with the music, for there are no "thirteens" and "seventeens" in the metrical scheme of the score. (Stravinsky and Craft 1959, 47–48; 2002, 91)

Diaghilev was actually delighted with the chaos, stating that it was exactly what he wanted. (Cynics thought he himself had staged the riot.) According to Monteux the public reaction was the same at each performance, which surprised him, for Parisians usually think of themselves as genuine connoisseurs of the arts, especially savoring anything avant-garde. Perhaps Stravinsky's garde was a bit too avant for them. Naturally the newspapers had a field day, with reviews and articles pro and con.

Soon after their Paris season, Diaghilev and the company were in London for performances at the Drury Lane Theater. *The Rite of Spring* was given four times there, the first on 11 July. Diaghilev had planned to make cuts in the piece, but Monteux, whom Stravinsky had appointed his musical guardian, resisted. There were also difficulties with the orchestra, which disliked playing the work, causing Monteux to erupt in a rare display of temper before order could be restored. In the end, public reaction to *The Rite*, while mixed, was nevertheless polite when compared to that in Paris. Monteux felt that the Londoners were intent on showing the Parisians how much more sophisticated they were in appreciating music and ballet. Romola Nijinsky observed, "Even today, to dance or conduct *Sacre* is difficult, but in those days it was almost a superhuman effort" (Nijinsky 1934, 205). When it was all over, Monteux returned to the peace and quiet of Dieppe and his summer concerts there. He was now, at age thirty-eight, truly a famous conductor.

CHAPTER 4

Beyond *The Rite*

Having known and respected Monteux since virtually the beginning of his career, Camille Saint-Saëns quite naturally selected him to conduct the composer's farewell performance as a pianist. The date was 6 November 1913, the place, Paris's Salle Gaveau. Organized for the benefit of the Cercle National pour le Soldat de Paris, the program consisted mostly of works by Saint-Saëns himself—chamber music in which he played the piano, and pieces for organ, which he also played. Only two orchestral works were given: the violinist Jules Boucherit played the Introduction and Rondo Capriccioso, and Saint-Saëns performed a Mozart concerto, which the program lists simply as "Concerto *en si bémol*" (in B-flat). Concert presenters of that time were a bit lax in identifying pieces by Köchel or opus numbers, and there are four such concertos by Mozart (three among the mature works), but it is fairly safe to say that the work Saint-Saëns performed was the Concerto No. 15, K. 450, the same concerto with which he had made his debut on 6 May 1846 at the age of eleven. The orchestra on the farewell program is identified only as "Orchestre sous la direction de M. Pierre Monteux." (Most likely it was what we would call a pick-up orchestra.) The program also carried an excerpt from a letter of Saint-Saëns dated 12 October 1913: "You will observe that I have not played in a concert in Paris for a long time and that one will now hear me for the last time."

Monteux would continue to perform *The Rite of Spring* for the rest of his life. While he did not again conduct it for Diaghilev, he was responsible not only for the ballet premiere, but also for the work's first concert performance. At the beginning of 1914, Monteux began a series of symphony concerts at the Casino de Paris. (Casinos played a great part in his early career, but while the Casino de Dieppe was a true casino, with gambling the main attraction apart from the music, the Casino de Paris did not offer gambling; it was solely a presenter of concerts and entertainment.)

For the Concerts Monteux, as they were called, the orchestra of 110 musicians was that of the Théâtre des Champs-Elysées (perhaps augmented a bit), which had been assembled the year before by Gabriel Astruc. Considering that all the major Parisian orchestras gave concerts at the same time on Sunday afternoons (give or take a half hour), it says something for the pool of musicians in Paris that a first-class orchestra of such size could still be assembled for yet another Sunday afternoon series.

Among the members of that orchestra was the oboist Louis Speyer, who had been an extra oboist (that is, not a regular member of the ensemble, but one called in for works requiring more than the normal complement of players) with the Colonne Orchestra and thus had participated in the premieres of the Stravinsky and Ravel ballets with the Ballets Russes. Called for military service in World War I, he came to the United States in 1918 as a member of a French military band and soon became the English horn player of the Boston Symphony Orchestra, a post he held until his retirement in 1964.

The Concerts Monteux began on Sunday 1 February 1914 with a substantial program including both Berlioz's *Harold in Italy*, with Frédéric Denayer the solo violist, and Beethoven's Violin Concerto, with Monteux's old friend Lucien Capet as soloist. The second program, on 15 February, included the concert premiere of the orchestral version of Ravel's *Valses nobles et sentimentales*. (It had first been performed as ballet music on 22 April 1912, with Ravel himself conducting.)

For the third program, on 1 March, Monteux gave the concert premiere of *Petrushka* (for some reason a full three years after the ballet premiere), in which the all-important piano part was played by the Italian composer-conductor Alfredo Casella. The program also included Casella's orchestration of two marches by Schubert.

So successful was the *Petrushka* performance that Monteux repeated it on 15 March, again with Casella at the keyboard, after which he wrote to the composer: "You cannot have any idea how much this music gains by being played in concert! Every detail is heard and carries through the hall, and musicians who have heard it in the theatre find that they have never heard it so well! For you it has been a really considerable success" (Craft 1984, 58). Then, feeling that most of the disturbance at the premiere of *The Rite of Spring* had been aimed at Nijinsky's choreography and that the music, if given a chance to be heard on its own, would have "a colossal success," Monteux proposed to Stravinsky a concert presentation of the music. Stravinsky readily agreed, and on the afternoon of 5 April *The Rite* was played before a sold-out house, with all of musical Paris attending. Saint-Saëns sat in a box with Monteux's mother, who reported that he kept repeating, "Mais il est fou, il est fou!" ("But he is crazy, he is crazy!"), and became very angry, leaving in great indignation (D. Monteux 1965, 93).

Saint-Saëns's reaction notwithstanding, the concert was a spectacular success. The audience listened silently and applauded vehemently, and the critics proclaimed the work a masterpiece. Stravinsky was hoisted on the shoulders of audience members and carried out of the hall into the Place de la Trinité. There is no record of whether Monteux was similarly hoisted (doubtful), but it was certainly a triumph for him as well, not to mention his orchestra, which had played brilliantly. Years later Stravinsky was to recall: "At the end, the entire audience jumped to its feet and cheered. I came on stage and hugged Monteux, who was a river of perspiration; it was the saltiest hug of my life" (Stravinsky and Craft 2002, 92).

In a letter dated 5 April 1914, Stravinsky wrote to Monteux:

> I am happy to be able to give you here my impression of your performance of *Sacre du printemps*. To tell you that it was excellent is not sufficient, for you have merited this praise since the last Russian Season. But today I am touched to see you spontaneously placing your mastery in the service of works that, though obscure, seem to you to represent an artistic effort. And you do this voluntarily, without fear of the reactionary critics, who will attack you, perhaps openly. After such an artistic performance of my work, I also wish to express to you not only my own recognition, but also that of my French colleagues, who are aware of your comparable efforts and care [in behalf of their music]. I attach the greatest importance to the devoted and attentive collaboration of the remarkable artists of the orchestra whom you guide so intelligently in the interpretation of music of whose great difficulty I am well aware. It is precisely because I consider all of the instrumentalists to be equally important that I write difficult music for each of them. Once again, thank you for the most beautiful performance that I have had of the *Sacre du printemps*. (Craft 1984, 59–60)

Craft adds, "This was the *first* complete performance that Stravinsky had heard."

Monteux repeated *The Rite*, again to great acclaim, on 26 April, the final concert of the series (on which Casella also conducted the premiere of his *Venice* Ballet Suite). After that there was more business with Diaghilev, for Monteux again conducted the Paris season of the Ballets Russes. On 26 May 1914 Diaghilev presented, at the Paris Opéra, the world premiere of Stravinsky's short opera *Le rossignol* (The Nightingale), based on Hans Christian Andersen's story "The Emperor and the Nightingale." Diaghilev had produced opera in Paris prior to his ballet seasons, and this event marked his return to that medium. The work, begun in 1907, had originally been intended for the Free Theatre of Moscow. However, by the time Stravinsky finally completed it, having composed his three celebrated ballet scores in the interim, the theater had disbanded. Alexandre Benois designed the sets and costumes for *Le rossignol*, and the choreography was by Boris Romanov.

On 29 May 1914 Stravinsky wrote to Monteux:

> As I left the theatre after the second performance of The Nightingale, I felt the desire to thank you warmly for your interpretation of my work. You and the orchestra of the Opéra truly surpassed yourselves in the so-rapid study of this score, which I have had the pleasure to present to the public on the stage of the Académie Nationale de Musique. Your intelligent

devotion to the limits of the possible has truly touched me, and in asking you to convey my profound thanks to the valiant players, I assure you of my most sympathetic and devoted feelings. (Craft 1984, 60–61)

In the summer Monteux was back in Dieppe, where his concerts, thanks to his newfound celebrity, were extremely well attended. At the time no one realized that this would be his last season there, and that it would be the end of the Casino concerts for the foreseeable future. In June the Austrian Archduke Franz Ferdinand and his wife had been assassinated in Sarajevo. On 28 July Austria declared war against Serbia; on 1 August Germany declared war against Russia and two days later against France. By the end of August, World War I was under way. Monteux's regiment, the Territorials, was activated, and he was ordered to join them on bivouac at Melun. At age thirty-nine, the conductor of *Petrushka*, *Daphnis et Chloé*, and *The Rite of Spring* was again a *poilu* (enlisted man) second class!

After Melun, the Territorials were sent to Soissons, then Verdun, and finally to the trenches in the Argonne, where Monteux spent some months in what he called "filth and boredom." To provide relief from the terrible conditions, Monteux's colonel asked him to form a small band from whatever musicians might be available in the company. Battered old instruments were secured from Paris and Dieppe, and daily rehearsals began. The group was composed mostly of amateurs who had at least some minimal idea of how to play their instruments. According to Monteux, "As therapy, this was an excellent idea. As music, it was simply awful noise!"

Monteux recalled that one morning the company's sentry approached him and reported that he had had a conversation with his German counterpart the night before. The French and German soldiers often spoke to each other and even called a truce when either needed to draw water from the fountain in the village square. The sentry said that his opposite number had heard the band rehearsing a march and thought it was *très jolie, mais pas ensemble!* ("very pretty, but not together!"). Monteux's later comment was, "I am sure that sentry became a critic, because he was right. It was not ensemble, but it definitely was not jolie either."

After twenty-six months on the front lines, Monteux was relieved of duty in surprising and unusual fashion when his commanding officer informed him that he had been ordered by the War Office to report to Paris immediately. It seems that Diaghilev was organizing a Ballets Russes tour to the United States and had requested the French government to release Monteux from active duty so he could go on the tour as the principal conductor. It is difficult to imagine how even the charming Diaghilev could have accomplished this feat of bureaucratic legerdemain, but he was greatly aided by the fact that the French minister of culture at the time was none other than Monteux's former schoolmate at the Paris Conservatory, Alfred Cortot. Additionally, the government wished to promote French culture abroad, and Monteux was considered an emissary of French music. For as long as he remained a French citizen, the government, as a matter of record and of pride, kept track of his foreign engagements and the French repertoire he conducted.

While Monteux was naturally overjoyed at this unexpected development, there was still the matter of crossing a U-boat-filled ocean to be considered. The danger of the crossing caused much concern among his family, especially his mother. Before that, however, he had to trudge thirty miles on foot from where his regiment was stationed to a village where he was to be provided with motor transport. In doing so, he became the object of a certain amount of ridicule as he passed local peasants and companies of soldiers, a violin case in one hand, music under one arm, a rifle in the other, a large knapsack on his back: "Eh bien," he heard someone remark, "that's a queer way to fight a war" (D. Monteux 1965, 95–97).

Monteux made his voyage to America on the *Rochambeau*, which left Bordeaux under cover of darkness, lights dimmed and engine muffled. The not-too-comfortable trip lasted eight days, with arrival in New York City in late September 1916. Otto Kahn, chairman of the Metropolitan Opera board, met the boat, along with many reporters who were understandably more interested in the pretty ballerinas than in the conductor. Monteux went immediately to the home of a friend, the French flutist Georges Barrère.

Throughout his career, Pierre Monteux was generally perceived as a mild-mannered, good-natured person. Yet he could at times provoke controversy. Of course, that of *The Rite of Spring* was not of his making. However, after all the trouble others had taken to release him from the army, after the long and hazardous voyage to New York, as Romola Nijinsky put it, "Monteux suddenly discovered that he was French" (Nijinsky 1934, 343).

The opening night of the Ballets Russes' New York season at the Manhattan Opera House, rather than the Metropolitan, was to feature the first performance of a new ballet choreographed by Nijinsky to Richard Strauss's *Till Eulenspiegel's Merry Pranks*. Monteux, however, refused to conduct it. He told the press, "I'm a French soldier, and cannot conduct the works of Strauss, who signed the manifesto against France. While I am grateful to be here, I cannot forget that my regiment is fighting the Prussians." When it was pointed out that Robert Schumann's *Carnaval* was also on the program and that he had not refused to conduct this work by a German composer, Monteux responded, "But he is dead. Strauss is alive. A living Boche. No, never will I conduct his music." Also included was *Mephisto Waltz* by Liszt, a Hungarian whose country was on the side of Germany, but, of course, Liszt was dead, too.

The newspapers naturally gave a good deal of space to this story. Pride of place goes to the *New York Herald*, which carried an unsigned commentary on 29 September 1916 under the headline "Poilu Conductor Bars Strauss Work at Metropolitan [*sic*]." The writer quoted Monteux and continued:

His reasons . . . are patriotic—he is French, Strauss is German. M. Monteux's refusal is comprehensible, though more convincing artistic reasons could have been found. He might, for instance, have said that he does not like Strauss's music. And he would have found many of his way of thinking. Or he might have said that Strauss's music is bad. Here again he would not have been alone in his opinion; there are people who hold that Strauss's music is not music at all. Or, again, he could have said that he does not understand Strauss's music; and the majority of musicians would have cried: "Same here!" But to refuse to conduct Strauss's music because Strauss is a German, and to conduct Liszt's music because Liszt, though a Hungarian, is dead, is somewhat inconsequential. And it is decidedly indefensible from the artistic standpoint. Richard Strauss is undoubtedly the greatest figure in German music since Wagner. He has added, to a degree unsurpassed, indeed unequaled by any of his predecessors, to the harmonic fabric of musical composition and to the resources of the orchestra. His art is more than modern. It is in sound what Cubism is in painting—bewildering, stimulating, exasperating, hypnotizing. His trifles are big; his big works are monumental. It is a pity that M. Monteux missed a good opportunity to let the world know what he thinks of Strauss's music. No one cares particularly what he thinks of Strauss's nationality.

Monteux remained adamant, so Diaghilev and Otto Kahn had no choice but to engage another conductor, Anselm Goetz, for the sole purpose of conducting *Till Eulenspiegel*. After a week's postponement (to allow Nijinsky to recover from a sprained foot), it had a successful premiere in New York on 16 October. Monteux watched from a box and joined in the applause. Goetz conducted *Till* only in New York and Boston, however; the remaining performances were led by the orchestra's piccolo player. The orchestration, in any case, had been reduced to accommodate the freelance orchestra of fifty-five musicians, with many parts missing. Nijinsky was apparently not concerned by this, according to Monteux; for him the music was secondary to the choreography.

After New York, the Diaghilev tour extended from 30 October 1916 to 17 February 1917, traveling to Providence, New Haven, Brooklyn, Boston, Worcester, Hartford, Bridgeport, Atlantic City, Baltimore, Washington, Philadelphia, Richmond, Columbia, Atlanta, New Orleans, Houston, Austin, Dallas, Fort Worth, Tulsa, Wichita, Kansas City, Des Moines, Omaha, Denver, Salt Lake City, Los Angeles, San Francisco, San Jose, Oakland, Sacramento, Portland, Vancouver, Seattle, Tacoma, Spokane, Fargo, Duluth, Saint Paul, Minneapolis, Milwaukee, Chicago, Indianapolis, Cincinnati, Columbus, Dayton, Toledo, Cleveland, Buffalo, Toronto, Syracuse, Rochester, and Albany, in that order.

A prophetic review appeared in the *Boston Herald* during the ballet's visit to that city. Karl Muck was then conductor of the Boston Symphony and had performed *Scheherazade* the same week the Ballets Russes presented its production. Of this programmatic duplication, the venerable Philip Hale wrote that Muck and the Boston Symphony had played *Scheherazade* to perfection, but Monteux and the ballet orchestra had reveled in the score's sensuousness, its color and exuberance, every note fairly breathing with the exoticism of the Orient. He then urged his readers to buy a ticket for the ballet performance. It is entirely possible that, two years later, when the Boston Symphony's trustees were searching for a new conductor, they remembered this review.

Returning to New York after the conclusion of the tour, Monteux met with Otto Kahn, who, while initially angry over the *Till Eulenspiegel* episode, was nevertheless greatly impressed with Monteux's conducting and musicianship. Kahn in turn introduced Monteux to the general manager of the Metropolitan Opera, Giulio Gatti-Casazza (1868–1940), who had been responsible for bringing Toscanini to the Met. Gatti offered Monteux a three-year contract to conduct the French repertoire, beginning with the 1917–18 season, but Monteux was still technically a *poilu* in the French army. Having already received an extension of his leave of absence, he cabled Alfred Cortot with the news of his offer from the Met and of his wish to remain in the United States if his services were not otherwise needed. Cortot cabled back, "ACCEPT," and Monteux was officially demobilized by the French consulate in New York.

Although the Met season would not begin until the fall, Monteux was not kept idle, for Kahn was in the process of organizing a series of popularly priced concerts for the summer months. With an orchestra of eighty-five musicians called the Civic Orchestral Society (drawn largely from the ranks of the Metropolitan Opera), Monteux conducted a five-week season beginning on 20 June and consisting of Wednesday and Sunday evening concerts. These were held in a rather unlikely venue, the St. Nicholas Rink. As its name implies, this was a roller-skating rink (also used for boxing matches) located at 69 West Sixty-sixth Street in Manhattan. The structure no longer exists; the site is now occupied by the headquarters of the American Broadcasting Company, across Broadway from Lincoln Center.

This was actually the second season of the Civic Concerts, which had been given the year before in Madison Square Garden (the original one) under the direction of Walter Henry Rothwell. In terms of acoustics, the Rink was found to be markedly inferior to the Garden, a situation aggravated by the intrusion through open windows of noises from the street. According to Herbert F. Peyser, reviewing the opening concert in the 30 June issue of the magazine *Musical America*, Monteux was not the equal of his predecessor, nor was program-making his strong suit. Peyser felt that if Monteux planned to make the concerts largely a showcase for French music, much better works could have been selected than the mediocre scores of Lalo and Franck performed on the first program or those of Charpentier and Chabrier on the second.

Though popular in nature, with lighter works such as Emmanuel Chabrier's *España* and the "Procession of Bacchus" from Léo Delibes's *Sylvia* being programmed as well as movements of symphonies and concertos, the concerts did not neglect serious fare, for there were complete performances of Beethoven's Symphonies Nos. 3, 5, and 7, and the Prelude and "Liebestod" from Wagner's *Tris-*

tan und Isolde, among many other works. (The first season had, in fact, not included complete symphonies and concertos at all, for fear of alienating audiences expecting light summer fare.) Each program featured a guest soloist, usually a singer, such as Claudia Muzio, Léon Rothier, and Maggie Teyte in operatic excerpts. As it was wartime, the second half of each program opened with the guest soloist singing a patriotic number, such as "The Star-Spangled Banner," "The Battle Hymn of the Republic," or, in the case of Rothier, "La Marseillaise." There were a few instrumental soloists as well: the French pianist Robert Lortat appeared twice, performing respectively Saint-Saëns's Concerto No. 4 and Grieg's Concerto in A minor. Taking a cue from the Boston Pops (which had been founded in 1885), light refreshments were served.

The inclusion of the national songs, in which the audience would join, actually turned a portion of each program into a patriotic rally, for they would be preceded by a formation of soldiers, sailors, and Marines, along with a display of flags. Following the song, a guest speaker would exhort the audience to do its bit for the war effort, including joining up if at all feasible, taking up nursing, and so on, all accompanied by much cheering and applause. Rothier was an especially great hit with "La Marseillaise"; the crowd sprang to its feet with a shout as soon as he was spotted making his entrance from the rear of the stage carrying a large French flag. After his performance there was a further standing ovation, again with much cheering and shouting.

Writing in the 7 July issue of *Musical America,* Alfred Human had some fun with the recruiting aspect of the concerts. Why not have Monteux wear his service uniform?

Then, the baton might be a sword or a christened bayonet. Souvenirs of the battlefield should be exhibited at the entrance, guarded by a select lot of militiamen or soldiers of the Allies. A few German prisoners of war would lend a pleasant color to the scene and might draw many music lovers to the civic event. Of course, all persons seeking admission must show their blue registration cards. A certain dignity could be added to the patriotic event by having a series of patriotic tableaux, with "Art and War," "Refusing to Conduct Strauss," "From the Concert Hall to the Recruiting Office," and similar absorbing subjects. Under no circumstances should the recruiting officer be permitted to speak over one hour. If the music lovers insist, however, the symphony of the evening should be eliminated and the recruiting speech prolonged in proportion. At the end of the address the promoters of the community art movement will pass around application blanks for the army and navy, while the orchestra plays some appropriate work of a rising French composer.

As for Monteux, *The New York Times* of 12 July 1917 stated, concerning his performances of *Scheherazade,* Saint-Saëns's *Le rouet d'Omphale,* and excerpts from Berlioz's *Romeo and Juliet*, that Monteux had brought the orchestra to a high degree of perfection, and expressed regret that the concerts would not continue beyond the next three that were announced. Peyser, on the other hand, in the edition of 21 July, missed the sweep and the poetry called for by Rimsky-Korsakov's colorful score, the performance of which lacked precision. He did find grace in the Saint-Saëns piece but could have done without the Berlioz entirely. Commenting in the same article on the concert of 15 July, Peyser praised a few portions of Beethoven's Fifth Symphony, "but of the first movement Mr. Monteux has little notion. A more placid, ineffectual publication of its puissant stress and combative fury could scarcely be imagined." (Those who heard Monteux conduct Beethoven's Fifth in later years know that the first movement under his direction was anything but placid. However, what it was like in 1917 I am in no position to say.)

Curiously, given Peyser's antipathy to much of the French repertoire performed by Monteux in the series, he did have kind words to say about d'Indy's *Istar Variations*, a work that has since all but vanished from the repertoire. He felt, however, that it did not belong in the series, for it was too intellectual in content to be appreciated by the audience. Peyser's final dig at Monteux, at least for the moment, occurred in *Musical America*'s issue of 28 July. Concluding his review of the final program of the series on 22 July, he commented that Monteux's reading of the "Eroica" Symphony was on the unexalted level of that of his other Beethoven performances. There was indeed much sentiment for extending the season, as hoped for in *The New York Times*, but in the end the directors decided not to raise additional funds at that time.

Germaine accompanied her husband on his trip to America for the Diaghilev season and tour and remained with him during the summer concerts, the Metropolitan Opera engagements, and several years beyond. Their three-year-old daughter, Denise, however, stayed in Europe with an aunt. It seems strange that the little girl would be left behind when a great war was raging, but her parents feared the polio epidemic then rampant. She would join them once the Met season had begun.

CHAPTER 5

The Met

Monteux's debut at the Metropolitan Opera took place on 17 November 1917. The opera was Gounod's *Faust*, with a cast that included Geraldine Farrar as Marguerite, Giovanni Martinelli as Faust, and Léon Rothier as Mephistopheles. Other repertory works he conducted that season, when, because of the war, no German opera was given, were Bizet's *Carmen*, Jules Massenet's *Thaïs*, and Saint-Saëns's *Samson et Dalila*. In addition to these, there was the world premiere of *The Dance in Place Congo*, a one-act ballet by the American Henry F. Gilbert (1868–1928), as well as the American premieres of *Le coq d'or* by Rimsky-Korsakov and *Marouf* by Henri Rabaud (1873–1949).

Among the singers he worked with were Frances Alda, Pasquale Amato, Enrico Caruso, Giuseppe de Luca, Louise Homer, Margarete Matzenauer, and Clarence Whitehill. Monteux recalled that when he first rehearsed with Caruso, for *Samson et Dalila*, he was surprised to find the great tenor delivering his phrases quite neutrally and metrically, with very little interpretive insight. When Monteux spoke to him about this, Caruso replied that it was his custom, whenever he worked with a maestro for the first time, always to sing exactly in tempo until the conductor allowed him to do otherwise. Monteux, who did allow him to do so, also remembered Caruso as being extremely punctual, even early, for rehearsals, and entirely untemperamental, as opposed to Farrar, who was often late, usually left early, and always had charmingly expressed justifications for doing so.

Bearing in mind that the *Faust* cast included Farrar, Martinelli, and Rothier, and that Caruso was at the height of his career, a portion of the unsigned 18 November review in *The New York Times* is remarkably similar to the type of criticism one often reads or hears today:

> The performance was an interesting one in many ways; it was not such a performance in the matter of singing of pure vocal beauty and vocal technique as they used to give at the Metropolitan Opera House in the good old days when the art of singing was in a better state than it is now.

It was noted that Monteux conducted skillfully and authoritatively, demonstrating great knowledge of the score and control of the orchestra, a clearly rhythmic beat, and a fine dramatic sense.

The estimable W. J. Henderson of the *New York Sun* found Monteux's conducting to be excellent, all the beauties of the music emerging without the singers being dominated by the orchestra. Writing in the 24 November issue of *Musical America*, Herbert Peyser, while acknowledging that Monteux had made a more favorable impression than in the Civic Orchestra concerts, found his conducting to be definitely lacking in distinction and devoid of personality, elegance, elasticity, and subtle musical feelings. Peyser lamented that the love music emerged woodenly under Monteux's baton, while elsewhere his tempi were torpid and elongated. When the performance was not drowsily monotonous, it was crass and raucous, readers were told, and even the ballet music failed to display the delicacy expected of a Frenchman.

While some musicians claim that they never read reviews, in fact most do, especially when beginning their careers, and Monteux was beginning his in the United States. He was pleased with his reviews from the New York newspapers but distressed to read Peyser's unfavorable comments, as was Otto Kahn. The latter, however, was in a position to do something about it. He took out a fairly sizable ad in *Musical America* that promoted Monteux with a photo and excerpts from the favorable reviews he had received in the various New York papers.

Kahn's ploy may have been responsible for a lengthy interview with Monteux by the magazine's editor, John C. Freund, in the 1 December issue of the magazine. Under the heading "At Luncheon with Pierre Monteux," the conductor stated frankly, "I think I have not been justly criticized in *Musical America*." After detailing his time spent in the trenches in France, the *Till Eulenspiegel* episode with the Ballets Russes, and the problems in forming and rehearsing the Civic Orchestra at ten days' notice, he continued, "I am here, as I understand it, to conduct French opera. What does that mean? Surely it means that I shall, to the best of my ability, give French opera in the French style, with the French atmosphere, and as it is done in Paris."

Freund suggested that the critics and the public, who were used to the virility and vitality of Toscanini, Giorgio Polacco, Alfred Hertz, and Artur Bodanzky, would perhaps find the conducting of a Frenchman a bit pallid in comparison. To this Monteux retorted:

Just as I would not expect the Italians and Germans to conduct Italian and German music in the French style, so it is not right to expect a French conductor to conduct French opera in the Italian or German style. Each has its style. Each has its defined character. . . . I trust that in the course of time many of those who now criticize me will come round to my point of view, for, to tell you the truth, French opera, while it has often been given in this country, has not always been given in the French style. Many of the artists have not given the correct interpretation. They were Italians or Germans or Spaniards or Americans who sang it, maybe well, who gave their view. But it was not the French view.

Monteux said that at first he had been a bit concerned as to how the Met orchestra would react to him, because so many of the players were German; but he had received "the finest treatment, great courtesy from the members," which he had appreciated very much. He spoke warmly about the other conductors at the Met and about the great singers with whom he had the pleasure to collaborate.

Returning to the subject of his wartime experiences, he said, "Do you know that in the twenty-five months that I was in the *premier ligne*, that is the first line of trenches, I did not touch a cigarette or a glass of wine?" The editor pointed out that this was not too much of a hardship for Monteux, for he neither smoked nor drank, beyond a mild cocktail before a meal.

Then the subject of the Civic Orchestra concerts came up again. "Do you know," Monteux said, "that the orchestra got up a document which they all signed, not only expressing their confidence in me but expressing their disapproval of what had appeared in *Musical America* with regard to my conducting, especially as to the manner in which I followed the singers?" When Freund offered to print the document, Monteux replied, "Oh, no! The matter is passed. Let it go. Simply I carry it next to my heart as a consolation to me that the musicians are with me, even if the critics are sometimes not." (In fact, throughout Monteux's career, orchestral musicians respected him, venerated him, loved him.)

Freund concluded that Monteux would win out when audiences and critics began to understand him and his point of view and what he represented in music, and to realize that he did not try to emulate Italian or German conductors, that he had a place of distinction in music as a conductor, and that he represented a special taste and method. Freund was confident that in due time even those who did not agree with Monteux, or who had different tastes, would at least acknowledge his musical capacity and personal sincerity.

As to national styles of conducting, the French style generally involves a lightness of touch and clarity of textures, with a resultant transparency of sound, qualities for which Monteux was often praised in later life. The Italians also produce this lightness and clarity, but generally with a bit more warmth, while the Germans tend to favor a heavier, less detailed sonority. Occasionally one finds a combination of styles, as with Charles Munch (1891–1969). Born in Strasbourg, a city that has been at different times part of Germany and France, Munch had much of his early training in Germany, so he managed to combine the characteristics of both the French and the Germans.

In the 23 November performance of *Samson et Dalila*, the next day's *New York Times* deemed Caruso to be at his best, while it was felt that the role of Dalila, here undertaken by Julia Claussen in her Met debut, had been sung more beautifully in the past by others, and had also been acted more charmingly. Again

Monteux had conducted very skillfully, the reviewer noted, bringing out the opera's best effects. Peyser did not review this performance, but the *Musical America* review of 1 December, contradicting the *Times*, found Claussen to have a voluptuous contralto voice, dark and vibrant. She was a stately seductress, said the review, who thrilled her listeners with the emotional and impassioned character of her singing. Monteux, the review concluded, conducted tastefully and with great care, bringing out many effective nuances.

According to the 30 November *New York Times*, Geraldine Farrar, starring in the previous evening's *Carmen*, delivered a more polished and intensified interpretation than when she last performed it at the Met. Martinelli, on the other hand, was found by the *Times* critic to be a merely creditable Don José; his singing of the Flower Song failed to enhance Bizet's music, though it did earn him a good round of applause. Monteux's conducting was again found to be excellent, full of spirit and dramatic power, and produced highly polished orchestral playing. Again, Peyser did not review the performance, and on 8 December his deputy thought that Monteux's tempi were not what New Yorkers were used to and that there were moments when singers and orchestra were not together. While his interpretation was not as spirited, deliberate, and broad as Toscanini's or Polacco's, wrote the critic, the intermezzi were excellent, and Monteux took a bow with the principals after the second duet. (Apparently in those days recognition of the conductor was not limited to some bows after the final curtain.)

Gatti-Casazza, the Met's general manager, was married to the soprano Frances Alda, who was to have the leading female role in Rabaud's *Marouf*. Upon learning that there was no aria for her in the entire opera, she protested in no uncertain terms. Monteux suggested Gatti write to the composer asking him to insert an aria. There was certainly historical precedent for a composer's accommodating a singer in this way—Mozart, for example, did it all the time—but Rabaud refused Gatti's request. Monteux himself then wrote to Rabaud, pointing out to him a phrase found in the score he thought might be developed into an aria. The composer agreed and wrote a short aria, averting further strife with Alda.

Marouf, or *The Cobbler of Cairo*, first given at the Met on 19 December 1917, is based on an Arabian tale from the *Thousand and One Nights*. Even with Giuseppe de Luca in the title role, the opera was found to be monotonous, its orientalisms ultimately tiring. In reviews, De Luca was thought to have done nothing better than this impersonation, Alda's singing had greater attributes than some of her offerings that season, and Rothier's excellent French diction was thrown into relief by its lack in the rest of the cast. Monteux, who is not mentioned in the *Times* review, had hoped that this opera, with its exotic setting, would be a critical and public success. It was not, and though it did return the following season, *Marouf* was soon dropped from the repertoire. Its ballet music has been recorded and is occasionally heard in concert today.

No such objections were voiced concerning the orientalisms of Jules Massenet's *Thaïs*, given on 5 January 1918, but this was a relatively familiar work. In reviews

Farrar was highly praised, though Monteux was mentioned in the *Times* only as sharing in the applause. In *Musical America* of 12 January, Monteux's conducting was pronounced admirable, with a true Gallic spirit that had been notably absent from Polacco's reading the year before. In general, Monteux's reviews were quite good, but they cannot in any way be considered raves, as would be the case years later.

Rimsky's delightfully exotic fairy-tale opera *Le coq d'or* (The Golden Cockerel), so regrettably absent in later years from non-Russian stages, was considered to be one of the finest productions of Gatti's entire tenure and sold out days in advance. In this work, a combination of opera and mime, each role is performed by an unseen singer, stationed either somewhere in the chorus or at some other obscure position, and by an onstage dancer. Maria Barrientos, Sophie Braslau, and Adamo Didur were the principal singers; Rosina Galli, Queenie Smith, and Adolph Bolm, their choreographic counterparts. Monteux was praised for his subtly nuanced conducting and took part in several of the fifteen concluding curtain calls. Peyser, in his glowing three-page review, said that Monteux conducted more spiritedly than ever before in his local career. A relatively short work, *Le coq d'or* was given as the second part of a double bill, preceded by Pietro Mascagni's *Cavalleria rusticana*, which Monteux did not conduct.

Gilbert's *The Dance in Place Congo* was part of an unusual triple bill first given on 23 March 1918. It was preceded by the world premiere of *Shanewis*, a short opera by Charles Wakefield Cadman (1881–1946) on an American Indian subject, and followed by *L'oracolo* by Franco Leoni (1864–1949), an opera set in San Francisco's Chinatown that the company had already given. Monteux conducted only the Gilbert work, a twenty-minute ballet set in New Orleans with much use of Creole themes and jazzy inflections. Critics found *Place Congo* a highly original piece of work, and it was the hit of the evening, though *Shanewis* received its share of praise as well.

In all, Monteux led thirty-nine performances in his first Met season, mostly in the opera house, but occasionally in Brooklyn and Philadelphia. For his second season, 1918–19, he was responsible for forty performances, mostly of the same repertoire, minus the Gilbert work but including the American premiere of *La reine Fiammette*, an opera composed in 1903 by the Frenchman Xavier Leroux. Its cast featured Farrar and Rothier, as well as Hipolito Lazaro and Adamo Didur. Also given were the first Met performances of Gounod's *Mireille*.

The season opened with *Samson et Dalila* on 11 November, the day the armistice ending World War I was signed. While on opening nights the musical performance is often overshadowed by the social trappings of the occasion, this was obviously a most special opening in which even the social trappings were secondary. The *Times* review on 12 November by James Gibbons Huneker reported on the patriotic fervor that gripped audience and performers alike. After the curtain closed at the end of Act I, it immediately opened again to reveal Caruso and the entire company framed by the flags of the Allied forces, after which Monteux signaled for the national anthem, sung by the audience and led by Caruso. This was followed by the anthems of England, France, and Italy. Before the final scene of the opera, Belgium's anthem was played. The combination of patriotic pageantry, social display, and Saint-Saëns's opera led Huneker to exclaim, "It was the most extraordinary night in the history of the Metropolitan Opera House."

The paper also noted that on the afternoon before the performance the Met's stage department had unearthed a dummy Siegfried, once used in Wagner's *Götterdämmerung* for the scene after the hero has been slain by Hagen, and outfitted it as Kaiser Wilhelm. Helmet on head, the effigy was hung on a gibbet and carried out to Thirty-ninth Street accompanied by approximately four hundred members of the company, including Gatti-Casazza, Frances Alda, and Monteux, who led the entire Met orchestra, minus the double basses, in a procession to Broadway and up to Forty-second Street, then returning to the Opera House. Various members stabbed at the "Kaiser" with stage swords while the orchestra played Charles Gounod's *Funeral March of a Marionette*. It was a scene worthy of a Fellini film.

Monteux related an amusing episode in his personal life at the time that would not be out of place in a Charlie Chaplin film. He lived uptown and thought it would be convenient to have a car to take him to and from the Opera House, as many of his colleagues did, rather than rely on public transportation. Accordingly, he bought a Ford touring car for $300. Always early for rehearsals, he would be the first to park his car behind the theater. Next would come Caruso in a handsome chauffeur-driven Pierce-Arrow, then usually Gatti-Casazza's equally impressive vehicle, followed by those of other high-ranking members of the company. In the presence of these luxurious behemoths Monteux's car "looked like an insignificant baby-carriage," and he was not unaware of the disdainful looks of chauffeurs as he cranked the Ford himself. One day, as he was driving along Eighth Avenue, there was a gasp from the engine, then a small explosion, after which the car stopped completely near the curb. Monteux got out, politely tipped his hat to it, and walked away, never to return for it (D. Monteux 1965, 108).

On 24 January 1919 the Met gave the American premiere of *La reine Fiammette* by an Italian-born French composer totally unknown today, Xavier Henri Napoléon Leroux (1863–1919). Huneker lavished great praise on the play by Catulle Mendès on which the opera is based—a drama with much sexual innuendo involving the church in the Renaissance, material that had been altered to suit the requirements of the American stage—but was unsparing in his denunciation of the mediocrity of the composer and his music. Huneker felt that the cast members had done as well as they could under the circumstances and that Monteux had conducted with authority. The unfortunate composer died later the same year.

The evening of 6 February 1919 offered one of the most unusual double bills in the history of the Metropolitan. It began conventionally enough with a performance of *La traviata* with Frieda Hempel, Charles Hackett, and Giuseppe de Luca. Today *La traviata* is not normally given as part of a double bill, as it is quite sufficient to fill an evening. But just as symphonic programs used to be longer, so apparently were operatic evenings. The second offering, however, was not an opera at all.

Gatti-Casazza had decided that it was time for the Metropolitan Opera ballet to present *Petrushka*, and so they did, as a pendant to *La traviata*. Gatti was playing it safe, apparently feeling that traditionalists who might be offended by the modernities and grotesqueries of *Petrushka* could safely leave once the opera was over. Those who stayed, and they were in the majority, "greatly enjoyed the new piece," according to Huneker's review the next day. The work was given not in the Diaghilev staging, but with choreography by Adolf Bolm, who danced the title role, and scenery and costumes by the Russian-born John Wegner. The roles of the Ballerina and the Moor were taken, respectively, by Rosina Galli and Giuseppe Bonfiglio. The presentation was judged a triumph for all concerned, especially Stravinsky. Of course, Monteux conducted, and no one dared criticize him in this of all pieces.

Gounod's charming opera *Mireille* is not programmed any more, but on 28 February 1919 it was performed for the first time at the Met, with Maria Barrientos in the title role. Unfortunately the work's charm was misplaced, according to Huneker (1 March), for Gounod barely hints at the Provençal earthiness of Gabriel Mistral's story. Clarence Whitehill, an outstanding American baritone, was judged the dominant figure in the cast, while Monteux directed with his usual skill and enthusiasm. *Mireille* was also the first part of a double bill, the evening again concluding with *Petrushka*.

Monteux was not to have a third Met season, at least not consecutively. He would return thirty-four years later.

CHAPTER 6

The Boston Symphony

A history of the Boston Symphony Orchestra should not be necessary at this point. Suffice it to say that it was founded in 1881 by Major Henry Lee Higginson, who was its sole financier until his retirement in April 1918. A Civil War veteran, as a young man he had for several years studied music in Vienna. Before the end of World War I, the musical direction of the Boston Symphony had been entirely Germanic, with such men as Georg Henschel, Wilhelm Gericke, Arthur Nikisch (a Hungarian, to be sure), Emil Paur, Karl Muck, and Max Fiedler occupying the podium, Gericke and Muck each in two nonconsecutive terms.

Whatever else he accomplished in Boston, including the orchestra's first acoustic recordings, the direction of Karl Muck (1859–1940) is today remembered primarily for two incidents during the height of World War I: his apparent refusal, through a misunderstanding, to conduct "The Star-Spangled Banner" before a concert in Providence in 1917, and his arrest and internment as an enemy alien in 1918, even though there was no public disclosure of the grounds for his arrest. Muck was sent to Fort Oglethorpe, Georgia, where one of his fellow internees was Ernst Kunwald, conductor of the Cincinnati Symphony. As the two men detested each other, Muck's imprisonment was an extraordinary instance of adding insult to injury. Muck, by the way, protested that he was not German, but Swiss. Though born in Darmstadt, Germany, he was eight years old when his father took out Swiss naturalization papers. When he reached maturity, Muck also took out Swiss papers and traveled on a Swiss passport.

Until then Higginson had steadfastly supported Muck, but the turmoil caused the Boston Symphony's only financier to sever his connection with the organization. The announcement was made in the 28 April edition of the various Boston papers, which reported that the affairs of the orchestra would be under the direction of a board of trustees chaired by Judge Frederick P. Cabot, and that the board had filed for incorporation.

Obviously, the time was ripe for French leadership in Boston. There was much speculation in the press, however, on the possibility of Sergei Rachmaninoff's becoming the new conductor. He had directed the orchestra in his tone poem *Isle of the Dead* in 1908 and had made a great impression on the musicians, the audience, and the critics, both for his musicianship and for his personal magnetism. Also mentioned as a leading contender was none other than Arturo Toscanini, although there were concerns that his already legendary temper might prove unsuitable for Boston.

A third candidate was Sir Henry J. Wood, founder of London's Promenade Concerts. He was actually offered the position, and some newspapers in Boston and New York reported from London that he was to become the new conductor of the Boston Symphony. Others stated that he had been offered the job but had not decided whether to accept. In the end, he did not.

As the 1918–19 season approached, though no conductor had yet been selected, a new concertmaster was appointed, the twenty-six-year-old American violinist Fredric Fradkin ("Symphony Gets American Boy" was the headline in the 30 August *Boston Post*). His playing was already familiar to those Bostonians who had attended the performances of the Ballets Russes in 1916, for he had been the concertmaster of that ensemble's orchestra under Pierre Monteux's direction and had distinguished himself in many solo passages, including those in *Scheherazade*.

Still with no permanent conductor in sight, the trustees engaged Monteux to conduct the concerts in October, since his contract with the Metropolitan Opera, which would begin its season in November, precluded a longer tour of duty. On arriving in Boston, Monteux was quoted in the 24 September editions of all the Boston newspapers as saying that he would not play the music of Wagner, Richard Strauss, or any living German. "I will not play Wagner because of his attitude toward France in the war of '70–'71. Moreover, looked at from another point of view, much of the best music that Wagner wrote—*The Ring* and *Die Meistersinger*—is in glorification of German ideals as are found in the *kultur* of today." As for Strauss, besides the *Till Eulenspiegel* incident with the Ballets Russes, Monteux recounted a story about his preparation of Strauss's ballet *Joseph* for its Paris premiere in May 1914, two months before the beginning of the war. "Strauss's attitude toward France, French art, French music and French musicians was even then unbearable. He was arrogant and insulting and, even without war, I was almost persuaded to give up playing his music; but, in view of what followed, Strauss became impossible for me." On the other hand, he would continue to play the German and Austrian classics, whose composers (such as Beethoven and Mozart) were in no way responsible for the war. Their music had become the property of the world, and it was a vital and necessary part of the repertoire of musicians.

> If I can win the war by giving up sugar, I will give up sugar gladly; I will give up gasoline; I will go on short rations of bread; in fact, as a Frenchman, I will do anything to help win the struggle; and if anyone can convince me that the end will be brought nearer by giving up the great classics of German music, I am willing to give them up. So far, however, I cannot see

how the silencing of the music of these masters can do the least to help win the war, and it is my purpose, as it is the purpose, I am sure, of all French conductors, to give the great classics due place on concert programmes.

Monteux found a thoroughly demoralized orchestra awaiting him, partly because of the Muck episode and partly because at least two dozen of its German musicians had been forced to resign because they, too, were thought to be enemy aliens. The task fell to Monteux of auditioning and engaging at very short notice relatively inexperienced American musicians and whomever could be obtained from France, and then, along with the remaining members, welding them into a cohesive ensemble. To make matters worse, the season's opening was delayed two weeks because of the notorious influenza pandemic of 1918.

Meanwhile, even before Monteux's delayed first concerts, the trustees and the newly appointed orchestra manager, William H. Brennan, announced that they had engaged for the 1918–19 season the Parisian composer-conductor Henri Rabaud, whose opera *Marouf* had only recently been given at the Metropolitan Opera with Monteux conducting. Rabaud was to take over after the completion of Monteux's engagement.

Olin Downes, writing in the 13 October *Boston Post* of Monteux's first rehearsals with the orchestra, stated that "no conductor since the time of Wilhelm Gericke, the man who gave the Boston Orchestra its reputation, has rehearsed so meticulously, so scrupulously and with so fine an ear for tonal results," and that "very few orchestra leaders have such an ear." Much was made of the fact that Monteux "has restored to their original forms many orchestral works with which Dr. Muck felt free to tamper. Mr. Monteux believes in allowing the composer, and the composer only, to be responsible for his own greatnesses and shortcomings. In his opinion the duty of the conductor is solely that of the reverent and enthusiastic interpreter." Downes also noted that Muck had lived first in a fancy hotel and later in an elegant house on Hemenway Street, whereas Monteux lived in a more modest hotel for a week or so and then moved to a pleasant suburban apartment.

Finally, on Friday afternoon, 25 October 1918, Pierre Monteux conducted his first concert with the Boston Symphony Orchestra:

> Franck: Symphony in D minor
> Schumann: Overture to *Manfred*
> Dukas: *La péri* (first performance in Boston)
> Debussy: *Ibéria*

The Boston Symphony normally gave weekly pairs of concerts, Friday afternoon and Saturday evening, so to begin the season on a Friday afternoon was business as usual. Today the orchestra's season consists of various concert series on other days of the week, but Friday-Saturday still remains the core series.

The program was of a type frequently encountered at the time: a substantial symphony in the first half with shorter works after intermission. Often an overture would close a concert. In addition, of the four works programmed, only one was German. The critics, who had greeted warmly the news of Monteux's temporary appointment, were equally laudatory of the opening program. The headline in the 26 October *Boston Record* proclaimed "Ovation for Symphony at First Concert—Monteux in Brilliant Performance." The critic J. V. Clark proceeded to write in complimentary fashion about Monteux's readings of the Franck, Dukas, and Debussy works, though he found the playing of Schumann's overture to be rather heavy-handed. For Downes in the *Post*, Monteux "had not conducted two minutes before it was apparent that he had made of the Boston Symphony Orchestra a finer instrument than it has been for many seasons." He felt that "Mr. Monteux's interpretation of Franck's symphony surpassed in eloquence, in mastery of line and mood, in sympathy with the genius of the composer, that of his predecessor." Downes also stated that "the American musical public should awaken to the fact . . . that conductors are not exclusively manufactured in Germany." Monteux was, in fact, the first French conductor ever to direct the Boston Symphony in any capacity. (One cannot help but wonder if the various disparagements Downes and others made of Muck in reviews were colored by the two episodes mentioned earlier or were made purely on musical grounds.)

For the season's second week, the soprano Florence Easton was the soloist in arias from Mozart's *Marriage of Figaro* and Charpentier's *Louise*, and Monteux offered Beethoven's Seventh Symphony, Loeffler's *La bonne chanson*, Franck's *Les Éolides*, and the Boston premiere of the first suite from Ravel's *Daphnis et Chloé*. Writing in the 2 November *Boston Herald*, Philip Hale spoke of "an engrossing performance of the symphony, a musical and poetic performance that should have disabused any person laboring under the delusion that only a German can fitly interpret the music of Beethoven."

Of special interest is the work by Charles Martin Loeffler (1861–1935), an Alsatian-born composer and violinist who, after a childhood spent in Russia, Hungary, and Switzerland and studies in Berlin and Paris, immigrated to the United States in 1881 to settle in Boston. The following year he became the assistant concertmaster of the Boston Symphony, a post he held until 1903, after which he concentrated on composition. Though Loeffler's music later fell out of fashion, he was frequently performed in his time, and his piece *A Pagan Poem* is still occasionally programmed today.

Following the first two weeks of concerts, the Boston Symphony embarked on one of its periodic tours of the northeast, of which its appearances in New York City were always high points. The concert in Carnegie Hall on 7 November occurred amid much patriotic fervor, as the end of the war was imminent. Accordingly, the program was preceded by renditions of "The Star-Spangled Banner," "God Save the King," "La Marseillaise," and Italy's "Garibaldi Hymn." The actual program began with the Franck symphony, which is probably why the Belgian national anthem was not played.

In contrast to their Boston brethren, the New York critics, though appreciative of the orchestra's situation, were not very enthusiastic. "Boston Symphony's Playing Shows Need of Leadership to Restore Its Supremacy" ran the headline of Reginald de Koven's review in the 10 November *New York Herald*. De Koven (1859–1920), composer of the operetta *Robin Hood*, was writing of the orchestra's Saturday matinee concert; he thought the playing could only improve once Rabaud took charge. His colleague James Huneker of *The New York Times*, writing on 8 November of the first concert, had found the performance of the Franck symphony overblown, while W. J. Henderson in *The New York Sun* declared it to be "deficient in delicate shades of color, insistent in style, over-drawn in most respects and sadly opaque in the treatment of the instrumental parts."

Back in Boston, Olin Downes, who would remain a champion of Monteux throughout his life, took issue with the New York critics. Noting that "some people are hard to please," he continued:

> Are the gentlemen in New York still laboring under the mistake that conductors are born only in Germany? Or are ears and acoustics so different in different parts of the world that no scale of comparison can be instituted? Or did the Boston Symphony Orchestra, forgetful of its Puritan ideals, excited by the peace talk or the noise of the great city, suddenly go on a tear and escape the control of that admirable musician, Mr. Monteux? Or is it merely the custom, which gossip says is immemorial, for the critics of the one city to contradict the critics of the other city, whatever the occasion or the subject?

After his last New York concert Monteux returned immediately to his duties at the Metropolitan, conducting the opening night performance of *Samson et Dalila* on Armistice Day. (Presumably he was able to direct rehearsals for it while in New York with the Boston Symphony.) He little dreamed he would be returning to Boston within a year. Rabaud decided not to continue in his post but to return to Paris to head the conservatory there, and after the usual search, the orchestra's trustees once again turned to Monteux. This time they proposed a more permanent arrangement.

With the gracious assistance of Gatti-Casazza, who released him from the third year of his Met contract, Monteux made his first appearance as music director (though that term was not yet in use) of the Boston Symphony Orchestra on 10 October 1919, in a program that included Beethoven's Second Symphony, Franck's *Le chasseur maudit*, Debussy's *Prélude à l'après-midi d'un faune*, and the first Boston performance of Isaac Albéniz's Catalonia Folk Suite No. 1, a work that, in contrast to Monteux's two Boston premieres of the previous season, has since languished in obscurity.

In the 11 October *Boston Evening Transcript*, H. T. Parker wrote:

> As for Mr. Monteux, he may be a conductor of this, that or the other rank in our American liking for degrees, but unmistakably he is interesting. His modesty, his subordination of himself to the task in hand, stand clear. . . . A finely sensitive ear, hand and imagination surely ordered the performance of Debussy's prelude, discerning and maintaining the delicate formal out-line, missing no play of tonal tint and half-tint, summoning and sustaining the sensuous impulse, the vaporous atmosphere, the half-sportive, half-melancholy fancy of the music—and all this loveliness in flowing fusion.

Writing in the *Boston Herald* of the same date, Philip Hale felt that he was really hearing Franck's symphonic poem for the first time, even though the BSO had played it three times previously. On those earlier occasions the work's super-natural element had seemed tame and timid, with little suggestion of its demoni-acal character. It took an imaginative and dramatic conductor such as Monteux to elicit the score's horrific effects so overwhelmingly. These include the ominous horn calls at the beginning, the awesome tuba passage in the central section, and the wild galloping rhythm as the accursed hunter rides to his doom. Hale also thought the Second to be the least interesting and least characteristic of Beetho-ven's symphonies, though Monteux's performance of it was vital and beautiful. No one liked Albéniz's suite, and all the critics agreed that the Boston Symphony was in good shape.

Although two French pieces did appear on his first program, any expectation that Monteux's seasons would place heavy emphasis on French repertoire would soon be thwarted. Certainly French music appeared, but no more of it than of any other national school. Monteux's programming throughout his career was decid-edly cosmopolitan, a statement that cannot be made concerning many German conductors, whose repertoire tends to be dominated by their own native music. In fact, in later years as a guest conductor, Monteux was continually irritated by requests that he conduct primarily French music—this of a conductor whose favorite composer was Brahms.

In mid-November 1919 Major Higginson died, and in tribute to him the pro-gram for the concerts of 21 and 22 November was altered so as to include three of his favorite pieces: Schubert's "Unfinished" Symphony, Brahms's Piano Con-certo No. 2 (with Felix Fox as soloist), and Beethoven's Fifth Symphony. Louis C. Elson of the *Boston Advertiser* commented on 22 November concerning the Brahms concerto, "It is a work which may have appealed to Major Higginson, who was a trained musician, but it certainly can never be an appeal to the general public; it was too abstruse for that." Noting that the pianist did not play from memory, he remarked, "It is certainly better that the music, rather than the per-former, should be upon the rack." (Hopes that some if not all of Higginson's vast fortune would be left to the Boston Symphony were shattered with the announce-ment that all he had bequeathed to the orchestra was his music library.)

On 23 November 1919 the *Boston Post* published newly revealed letters "written to a girl" by Karl Muck while on tour in 1916 with the Boston Symphony. In the letter of 28 January 1916, written just after he had conducted in Pittsburgh, he raged:

> Of course Pittsburg [*sic*] is indeed the main center for the manufacture of American neutrality murdering instruments. . . . When, yesterday, I got onto the stage in Pittsburg in the sold-out house of Carnegie Hall, and saw the thousands sitting before me who through the murder of my people have earned and still earn millions, everything became red before my eyes. It required my full strength not to shriek out loud, but enough, there is a reckoning justice coming in the world history, that is my only comfort.

A letter postmarked 3 April 1916 informed his friend:

> This whole country is ruled by a crowd of bums who are tainted with English money, and my only hope is that the American people will finally wake up again and hang the few dozen bums to the highest tree which grows in the country. . . . My conscience is quite clear, and when the bums shall venture against me they will repent it bitterly—that I can assure you.

If Bostonians required proof that their former conductor had been an enemy alien, here it was. In spite of the feelings Muck expressed, though, there is no proof that he actively worked or plotted against the United States.

The Boston premiere of Debussy's *Jeux* was given on 2 January 1920. Under the headline "Tennis as Played by Symphony," Olin Downes began his 3 January review in the *Post* wondering whether the newspaper's sports editor should have attended and reported on the concert. He noted that, as Monteux did not conduct with a tennis racquet, he would take up his accustomed pen. Downes found the score "forced, unoriginal, without very much organic quality and about as far-fetched as the artificial and sophisticated scenario of the ballet for which it was written." Philip Hale, writing in the *Globe*, found the music to be greatly in need of the stage effects and dancers.

The 23 and 24 January 1920 editions of the various Boston newspapers carried the announcement that Pierre Monteux's contract had been renewed for another two years. The *Post* remarked that his inspired leadership had produced an almost unprecedented success.

On 29 January 1920 the Boston Symphony under Monteux's direction performed its very first Young People's Concert. Beethoven's *Egmont* Overture, Schubert's "Unfinished" Symphony, and a suite from Delibes's ballet *Sylvia* made up the bill of fare. All the major critics attended and reviewed the concert, not so much from the standpoint of performance, which was judged worthy of the regular subscription concerts, but from that of the behavior (exemplary) and response (enthusiastic) of the audience. There were some questions as to whether the program was a bit too serious for young listeners—whether there should have been a Strauss waltz or Meyerbeer march to lighten the program (Delibes was apparently not light enough)—but on the whole the event was deemed a rousing success.

If Monteux ultimately acquired a reputation as an orchestra builder, having already had the experience of reorganizing the orchestra prior to Rabaud's arrival, events in Boston during his first season certainly laid further groundwork for this perception. In February 1920 many of the orchestra's musicians requested an increase in salary from the board of trustees, which was denied on the grounds that the board would be unable to raise the additional funds required. Because the local chapter of the American Federation of Musicians supported the orchestra members, thirty of them applied for union membership.

All the other major American orchestras were by that time members of the federation, but the Boston Symphony had long been a holdout. Major Higginson, not wishing to be in the position of dealing with what he considered dictatorial outside sources, had opposed unionization from the very beginning. It was *his* orchestra, and he would build it and do with it as *he* wished. He had no patience with union regulations involving hiring, firing, and lengths of contracts. Among the orchestra members seeking union membership was the concertmaster, Fredric Fradkin.

At the concert of Friday afternoon, 5 March 1920, as Monteux motioned the orchestra to rise to accept the applause after Berlioz's *Symphonie fantastique*, Fradkin remained seated. Today the refusal of the concertmaster to rise is looked upon as a tribute to the conductor, as the orchestra remains seated, but in that situation it was thought to be an act of insubordination, especially as Fradkin was the only person onstage not standing. That evening the trustees fired him.

The sudden dismissal of the concertmaster, particularly one who had been an active proponent of unionization, caused great consternation among the musicians, forty-seven of whom voted not to play the Saturday evening concert. In the end, eleven of those changed their mind, and an orchestra of fifty-six assembled for the performance. As the *Symphonie fantastique* was not feasible with such reduced forces, Monteux led a hastily rearranged program including Mozart's *Magic Flute* Overture and Beethoven's Fourth Symphony, among other works.

The next week five more members returned to the orchestra. However, that meant there were still thirty-one absentees, twenty from the violin and viola sections. Only two principal chairs were vacant, those of concertmaster and first trumpet. The very model of a patient conductor—an oxymoron in those days (and possibly today as well)—Monteux set out with great equanimity to audition any and all available musicians, including some from theater and restaurant ensembles in Boston and New York. Many of them had never played symphonic music. Meanwhile, he had to continue conducting the orchestra's season.

With many sectional rehearsals, by season's end the strings had achieved a commendable level of respectability, so that performances of Handel's Concerto Grosso in D major, Op. 6, No. 5, were thought to be exemplary by both public and press. To demonstrate the full orchestra's capabilities, the *Symphonie fantastique* was repeated on the final concerts. By that time the personnel, which had stood at ninety-six before the strike and had decreased to sixty-one following it, had reached eighty-eight musicians.

During the summer months it was still necessary to make improvements, for not all the musicians who had been hired as a stopgap measure were retained. Before the beginning of the 1920–21 season, seventeen new musicians were engaged, including a new concertmaster. Monteux had gone to Paris for the summer, where he advertised for the concertmaster position. A twenty-eight-year-old Pole, born in Warsaw but trained in Russia, arrived from Finland, where he had been performing. After he had played five minutes of his audition, Monteux stopped him and said, "You are the new concertmaster of the Boston Symphony Orchestra" (D. Monteux 1965, 115). His name was Richard Burgin (1892–1981), and he was to be the orchestra's highly respected concertmaster from 1920 to 1962 and eventually its associate conductor.

Any fears that may have arisen concerning the quality of the orchestra owing to the events of the previous season were laid to rest with the opening of the 1920–21 season. Leading a program consisting of Beethoven's Eighth Symphony; the Belgian Guillaume Lekeu's *Fantasia on Two Folk Tunes of Anjou*; Franck's Prelude, Chorale, and Fugue in the orchestration by Pierné (the latter two works in their Boston premieres); and Franz Liszt's symphonic poem *Tasso*, Monteux achieved highly praised results. In the *Boston Post* of 9 October, Olin Downes wrote that the newly reconstituted orchestra achieved results even more remarkable than had the crippled orchestra that closed the previous season, with brilliant performances, especially by the strings. Most important, and a true test of an orchestra's quality, was the *pianissimo* playing, full of delicacy and tonal beauty.

Fred J. McIsaac of the *Boston American* thought that the orchestra produced beautiful sounds and that no other American orchestra could yet approach it. He also wrote, though, that he had never enjoyed Monteux's Beethoven interpretations and this time was no exception. He felt that Monteux invested Beethoven's music with passion and fire at the expense of its sweetness, elegance, and grace. (Perhaps McIsaac was confusing Beethoven with Mozart.)

Philip Hale, in a preliminary article in the 7 October *Herald*, demonstrated his abilities as a statistician by informing his readers that Beethoven's Eighth Symphony had begun the season only once in thirty years. He then proceeded to enumerate how many times Beethoven symphonies were on the opening program (nineteen), which one was the favorite (No. 5), which next (No. 3), and which after that (No. 7), though he failed to mention how many times each was played.

Until late in life a champion of new music, Monteux led a large assortment of world, American, and Boston premieres during his five seasons, as well as many works new to the Boston Symphony itself even if they were not premieres. None of the works given their world premieres during that time have survived in the repertoire, with the possible exception of *The Pleasure Dome of Kubla Khan* by

Charles Tomlinson Griffes (28 November 1919). This work does occupy a place on the fringe and has at least been recorded several times (once by the Boston Symphony).

As far as I am aware, at the time of this writing no recordings exist of, for example, the two symphonies of Frederick Converse, Seth Bingham's Passacaglia, or Edward Burlingame Hill's *Waltzes for Orchestra*. Only a few years ago did the first recording appear of Vincent d'Indy's Symphony No. 3 ("Sinfonia brevis de bello Gallico"), a work commemorating the Allied victory over Germany in World War I. While the work was generally well received after its premiere on 24 October 1919, the consensus was that it was not as strong as its symphonic predecessors. Though he was a champion of d'Indy, Monteux never played it again.

Of works given their American premieres, the most significant are:

Bliss: *A Color Symphony* (28 December 1923)
Debussy: Fantaisie for Piano and Orchestra; Alfred Cortot, piano (16 April
    1920)
Falla: Three Dances from *The Three-Cornered Hat* (30 December 1921)
Honegger: *L'Horace victorieux* (24 November 1922)
Milhaud: *Protée* (Symphonic Suite No. 2) (22 April 1921)
Ravel: *Le tombeau de Couperin* (19 November 1920)
R. Strauss: Suite from *Le bourgeois gentilhomme* (11 February 1921)
Szymanowski: Symphony No. 2 (20 January 1922)
Turina: *Danzas fantásticas* (28 December 1923)

While world and U.S. premieres are prestigious, the most important work a conductor can do is introduce to his city significant music that has already been heard elsewhere, for only in this way does the repertoire grow. Monteux's work in this regard far overshadows anything else he did in the way of premieres. Pride of place belongs to the Boston premiere of *The Rite of Spring* on 25 January 1924. Why Monteux waited almost five years to present this of all works is not known. Perhaps he did not feel that his orchestra or his audience was ready for it any sooner.

Monteux was not known as a champion of Mahler's works, yet 23 November 1923 saw the introduction to Boston of that composer's First Symphony, the only numbered Mahler symphony Monteux is known to have conducted. (He later programmed *Das Lied von der Erde* [The Song of the Earth], which is both a song cycle and a symphony. While Mahler designated *Das Lied* a "Symphony for a Tenor and an Alto [or Baritone] and Orchestra," it is not truly a symphony in the traditional classical sense. Its six movements are vocal settings of *The Chinese Flute* by Hans Bethges, which is a collection of texts derived from ancient Chinese poetry. Of course, if a composer calls his work a symphony, then we must accept it as such.) Other major works first heard in Boston under Monteux's direction include:

Bloch: *Schelomo*; Jean Bedetti, cello (13 April 1923)

Debussy: *Jeux* (2 January 1920)

Falla: *Nights in the Gardens of Spain*; Heinrich Gebhard, piano (28 March 1924)

Holst: *The Planets* (26 January 1923)

Ravel: *Valses nobles et sentimentales* (11 March 1921)

Ravel: *La valse* (13 January 1922)

Respighi: *The Fountains of Rome* (12 November 1920)

Saint-Saëns: *Carnival of the Animals* (3 November 1922)

Scriabin: Symphony No. 3, "Divine Poem" (24 February 1924)

Vaughan Williams: *Fantasia on a Theme of Thomas Tallis* (27 October 1922)

Vaughan Williams: *A London Symphony* (18 February 1921)

As for Boston Symphony premieres, Stravinsky's *Firebird* and *Petrushka* Suites, Schoenberg's *Verklärte Nacht* (Transfigured Night), Bach's Suite No. 4, Borodin's Polovtzian Dances, and Debussy's *La damoiselle élue* are representative of an impressive list.

Of the many guest soloists who performed with the orchestra during Monteux's tenure—and they included such artists as Wilhelm Backhaus (in Sergei Rachmaninoff's Second Piano Concerto, a work not normally associated with him), Pablo Casals, Alfred Cortot, Josef Hofmann, Fritz Kreisler, John McCormack, Benno Moiseiwitsch, Sergei Rachmaninoff, Arthur Rubinstein, Albert Spalding, and Jacques Thibaud—none attracted greater attention than the tenor Roland Hayes, who on 16 November 1923 became the first African American to appear as a soloist with the Boston Symphony. He sang arias from Mozart's *Così fan tutte* and Berlioz's *L'enfance du Christ*, as well as two spirituals, "Go Down, Moses" and "By-and-By." Writing in the *Boston Post* the next day, just before he moved to New York, Olin Downes spoke of Hayes's "astonishing fineness of nuance and style" and found him to be "an extremely thoughtful and sensitive interpreter." The chairman of the orchestra's board of trustees, Judge Frederick P. Cabot, had recommended Hayes to Monteux, who heard him sing at an afternoon tea at one of Boston's many fine homes. Said Monteux, "I was simply enchanted with Mr. Hayes' voice, his erudition in matters pertaining to music and his charming manners. I was so enchanted by that lovely recital that I said, 'He must sing with the orchestra in Symphony Hall. He is an American, and I want him'" (D. Monteux 1965, 116–17). William Brennan, manager of the Boston Symphony, resisted, fearing that such a concert would fill the hall with Negroes, a situation then not devoutly to be wished. Monteux countered that this would not be so, as the concerts were completely subscribed by white Bostonians. Brennan then suggested a special concert for Roland Hayes, whereupon Monteux replied, "Then the hall would be full of Negroes." In the end Monteux prevailed, and Hayes remained grateful to him for the rest of his life.

In sharp contrast to today's orchestral scene, where many music directors conduct less than half the season, if that, it is worth noting that in five years of twenty-four-week seasons, plus visits to New York, Providence, and other cities, Monteux had a total of three weeks off. Occasionally a composer conducted one or two of his pieces on a program otherwise led by Monteux, but only three men appeared as guest conductors for entire concerts. On 9 and 10 December 1921 Vincent d'Indy led a mixed program that included the Boston premiere of his *Poème des rivages*, on 30 and 31 March 1923 Bruno Walter appeared in a program on which Artur Schnabel performed Beethoven's Piano Concerto No. 4, and on 7 and 8 March 1924 the Finn Georg Schnéevoigt conducted Sibelius's Second Symphony, among other works. Walter was, in fact, the first ever BSO guest conductor who was not a composer. (He had written some lieder and other pieces as a young man but had long since become a full-time conductor.)

Germaine Monteux accompanied her husband on the voyage to America (as mentioned earlier, their daughter, Denise, joined them later). While in Boston the family lived in an apartment in the suburb of Brookline, at 31 Dwight Street. Summers would be spent in Maine, in the coastal town of Northport. Even at that time Monteux greatly enjoyed being in Maine, little dreaming that it would one day become his home state. On 15 October 1920 Germaine gave birth to a son, Claude. When Claude was two years old he developed a lung infection, and Germaine decided to take the children to the south of France, which she felt would provide a good climate for the improvement of Claude's health. During her and the children's absence, Monteux wrote often to his wife, and she to him, he begging her to return, she refusing because of Claude. After a time Monteux's letters became less and less imploring, even to the point of encouraging Germaine and the children to remain in France, at least for the time being. There was an important reason for Monteux's change of heart.

He had met Doris Hodgkins.

CHAPTER 7

Doris and Pierre

The village of Hancock, Maine, so small that it could just as easily be called a hamlet, can be found on U.S. Route 1 eight miles north of Ellsworth and across Frenchman's Bay from Bar Harbor, which can conveniently be reached only by driving down to Ellsworth and then connecting with Route 3. In earlier times a ferry connected Hancock Point with Bar Harbor. In Frenchman's Bay there are many islands, the largest of which is Mount Desert Island, on which Bar Harbor nestles, with Salisbury Cove its close neighbor. Since the mid-1880s the entire bay area has been a summer resort haven.

Growing up in Salisbury Cove in the late 1880s were young Eugene Hodgkins and Bethia (called Bertha) Emery, who were married in the Cove's Baptist Community Church when Bertha was nineteen and Gene twenty. In quick succession they became the parents of three baby girls: Doris in 1894, Hilda in 1895, and Charlotte in 1897. Gene's first job after marriage was at a stable in Bar Harbor, where he was hired to drive summer visitors around the island. He soon began to join the other stablemen in what was called "a daily bracer" and quickly became an alcoholic. In the hope that a change of scenery might cure Gene's addiction, Bertha decided that the family would move to Hancock, where Gene's parents then lived. This did not produce the desired result, so on they went to Bangor, where Bertha worked in a department store and Gene worked at odd jobs, such as house painting and barbering. By then the marriage was seriously deteriorating, and another move was made, this time to Newburyport, Massachusetts. As they were growing up, the three girls spent each summer and the Christmas holidays with their grandparents in Hancock.

In Newburyport Doris and Hilda were known as "those talented Hodgkins kids." Hilda was learning to play the piano and organ, and Doris was singing. Together they often performed at church socials and other community events, even as young as five and six, respectively. Hilda, in fact, had quickly developed the ability to transpose into other keys at the keyboard and also to improvise.

In 1905 Gene and Bertha divorced. Bertha moved to Boston with the girls, while Gene continued to do odd jobs in odd places. Bertha, who demonstrated a

73

talent for business, eventually became the treasurer for a wholesale nut firm and also married the boss, John W. Leavitt. Their marriage would endure happily for forty years.

As the girls grew older, Hilda began playing the piano at various vaudeville and movie houses in the Boston area, as well as in Bar Harbor in the summer. There she met Meyer Davis, who was just beginning to establish himself as the leader of society orchestras. After an off-again-on-again courtship, Hilda and Meyer married in 1917. Meyer Davis eventually became the dean of society orchestra leaders, and many groups under his direction played for presidential inaugurations, White House functions, debutante balls, and the like. Hilda's sister Charlotte would become the wife of David Michlin, the manager of Meyer's orchestras.

As for Doris, she attended the New England Conservatory of Music, where she studied voice, developing into a fine contralto. The principal alto in the Boston People's Choral Union, she also gave frequent recitals in Boston and elsewhere in New England, singing under the name Doris Gerald. An announcement for a Symphony Hall performance by the People's Choral Union on 8 January 1922 shows her listed as the contralto soloist in Handel's *Samson*. (There is no indication that "Gerald" had any family connection; it was apparently a name Doris chose of her own accord.) Meanwhile, she had married and divorced Edward Purslow, and by the time she met Pierre Monteux, she was the mother of two children, Donald and Nancy.

Attractive in an imperious sort of way, Doris had already come to Monteux's attention as a member of a chorus that sang with the BSO, and she succeeded in making an appointment to audition for him at some point in 1922, after Germaine had left for France. The audition was to take place in the conductor's room in Symphony Hall. If one is to believe the accounts of family members, which could only have originated with Doris and/or Pierre, a lot more than an audition occurred in that room, if, in fact, there actually was an audition. Their attraction to one another was instantaneous, and it was to deepen and remain vibrant for forty-two years.

At first Doris and Pierre were discreet about their relationship, but they became less so as it progressed. By the end of Monteux's Boston tenure they were living together, children and all. Germaine was aware of the situation but remained in France. When Monteux asked for a divorce, she refused.

In January 1922 the Boston Symphony's former conductor Arthur Nikisch died. At the concerts of 27 and 28 January Monteux conducted "Siegfried's Funeral Music" from Wagner's *Götterdämmerung* as a memorial tribute to his model conductor, still considered one of the greatest of all time.

On 29 January 1922 *The New York Times* carried an article under the headline "Monteux or Newcomer?" It was pointed out that Monteux's contract with the Boston Symphony would expire at the end of the 1921–22 season. Would it be renewed? A companion article by the critic Richard Aldrich speculated negatively. He did not say that Monteux should not be re-engaged, but he did express reservations about him and the orchestra:

The public support of the orchestra in New York, which fell off greatly during the troublous times of the war, has increased considerably, though it is hardly back to what it was when every seat in Carnegie Hall was taken, and there was a long waiting list. Nor has Mr. Monteux gained quite so high an opinion in the estimation of New York music lovers as he apparently has in Boston. He is respected as a capable, intelligent and vigorous conductor of wide sympathies; but he has not proved an inspiration to many, nor has he satisfied fastidious demands. While the playing of the orchestra has improved under his direction, it has not reached the perfection that was once such a joy that it seemed—as it was—too good to be true forever.

The 7 February editions of the Boston papers carried the announcement that the trustees of the Boston Symphony had reappointed Monteux for another two years. They mentioned that there was greater interest than ever before in symphonic concerts in Boston; that in addition to the twenty-four weekend concert pairs at Symphony Hall, a series of five Monday concerts had been added, as well as a series of Young People's Concerts; and that the orchestra was playing more and more in surrounding communities such as Lynn, Brockton, Lawrence, Lowell, Haverhill, and Fall River. Colleges and universities were becoming increasingly eager to hear the orchestra under Monteux's direction, and concerts had been given at Harvard, Yale, Cornell, Smith, Middlebury, and the University of Vermont. Only the *Boston American*'s story included the following sentence: "At that time [1924] by mutual understanding Mr. Monteux will complete his term as conductor and a newcomer will be his successor."

On 11 February Downes reported in the *Post* that Monteux had been given an ovation when he made his entrance, with players and audience rising to applaud him in approval of the trustees' decision to engage him for two more seasons. According to Downes, no abler conductor was available, and it was doubtful that a more popular one could possibly be found. No conductor since Max Fiedler's time had so favorably impressed the orchestra or its public. Monteux followed this enthusiastic welcome with a brilliant interpretation of Schumann's "Spring" Symphony.

In November 1922 the Boston Symphony made a successful tour to Canada—successful musically, that is, with performances in Toronto, Montreal, and other cities in the East. The only unsuccessful aspect of the tour occurred on the return trip to Boston, as the *American* of 16 November reported; an article over which the banner headline shouted "Symphony Orchestra Train Raided for Liquor" (remember this was the era of Prohibition) began:

The Boston Symphony Orchestra, an institution almost sacred to worshipers of music, is minus one hundred and eighty-seven bottles of wines and liquors, seized by U.S. customs officers.

Customs officials and federal agents of the United States and Canada, by an apparently concerted plan, raided the special train of the orchestra as it was crossing the border from Canada, held it up long enough to tie up traffic on the railroad, threatened the arrest of the whole train, and wound up by haling two members of the orchestra before the United States commissioner at Buffalo. . . . The cleanup of wet goods, which the inspectors ferreted out, even from the instrument cases, on brake rods under the cars and other desperate hiding places, brought forth the most sour chord the Symphony has ever intoned.

Whether Monteux was involved in this incident is not known.

During the 1922–23 season, shortly after Monteux's re-engagement, the Boston Symphony's board of trustees took note of a charismatic Russian conductor active in Paris and London named Serge Koussevitzky (1874–1951). In meetings with Koussevitzky, his interest in coming to Boston was made evident. No one knows whether it was he who actively sought the post or the trustees who pursued him—probably a combination of both. In any case, Monteux was still under contract, with one year remaining, when the announcement was made on 10 September 1923 that Koussevitzky would become conductor of the Boston Symphony Orchestra, effective with the 1924–25 season.

Cabot, attempting to mollify Monteux, explained to him that it was the orchestra's policy to change conductors every five years. To some extent this was true, for Henschel had served from 1881 to 1884, Gericke from 1884 to 1889, Nikisch from 1889 to 1893, Paur from 1893 to 1898, Gericke again from 1898 to 1906, Muck from 1906 to 1908, Max Fiedler from 1908 to 1912, and Muck again from 1912 to 1918—not all exactly five years, but close enough. The Koussevitzky appointment, announced more than a year in advance, made Monteux a lame-duck conductor for his final season, which began on 12 and 13 October 1923 with the following program:

Beethoven: Symphony No. 7 in A major
Brahms: *Variations on a Theme of Haydn*
Dukas: *La péri*
R. Strauss: Dance of the Seven Veils from *Salome*

Writing in the *Globe* of 13 October, Philip Hale reported on the unusually warm and prolonged welcome Monteux received upon his entrance, and described the concert as one of the most brilliant in the orchestra's history—not since Arthur Nikisch first appeared on the stage of the old Music Hall had there been such a concert. Hale further declared that he had not heard a finer interpretation of Beethoven's Seventh Symphony in many years.

The long-awaited Boston premiere of *The Rite of Spring* was given on 25 January 1924. On 31 January Monteux and the orchestra gave the New York premiere in Carnegie Hall. The work had received its American premiere by Leopold Stokowski and the Philadelphia Orchestra on 3 March 1922 and that orchestra also had a New York concert series, so it seems odd that Stokowski, known for his adventurous programming, did not seize the opportunity to present *The Rite* in New York. Nonetheless, that honor appropriately fell to Monteux.

On 27 January, W. J. Henderson of the *Sun* took Monteux to task for his programming. He felt that a new work, especially one of the complexity of *The Consecration of Spring* (the English title used at the time), should be placed first on the program so that the audience could hear it with fresh ears. Instead, Monteux planned to close the program with it, preceding it with Mozart's "Jupiter" Symphony and the Sibelius Violin Concerto with the concertmaster, Richard Burgin, as soloist. Henderson went on to say that Monteux's theory of audience psychology was shared by most other conductors, who feel that a novelty should be placed late in a program so as to keep listeners in their seats. Or perhaps Monteux felt that if *The Rite* were played first no one would wish to remain for the refreshment of a Mozart symphony. Whatever the reason, he, Henderson, could not excuse a poorly made program. (Henderson had the support of august company for his views: when the "Eroica" Symphony was new, Beethoven declared that it should ideally be heard at or near the beginning of a program, when the listeners' minds and ears were fresh.)

In his *New York Times* review of 1 February, Olin Downes, who had left Boston the year before, proclaimed the occasion a great success, in spite of a few hisses after the first part. He wrote of the long and loud ovation, which seemed to be sincere, the audience recalling Monteux repeatedly. Downes also found Stravinsky's masterpiece to be "a work of unprecedented energy, definiteness, and power. No orchestra that we have heard throws off such heat, such sonorities, such galvanizing, rhythmical force as this orchestra of Stravinsky."

In the *New York Herald*, Lawrence Gilman concluded his laudatory review:

> What Stravinsky has made of this conception (of spring) is one of the marvelous things of art, and we fancy it will remain so—a thing of gigantic strength, of terrifying intensity, of overwhelming imaginative veracity. Stravinsky may transcend it, may outgrow it, may disown it; but it will remain a lonely and incomparable achievement, an authentic masterpiece.

After praising the achievement of Monteux and the orchestra, Downes, Gilman, and others made fleeting reference to the other works on the program—Mozart's "Jupiter" Symphony and Sibelius's Violin Concerto—but in Gilman's words, "these things hardly counted. It was Stravinsky's night." Henderson was less appreciative, calling Stravinsky "a cave man of music."

Philip Hale of *The Boston Globe* had written on 26 January, "Nothing else in Mr. Monteux's conductorship has been so worthy of unstinted praise as this performance of *Le Sacre*, which will be remembered for years to come as a musical landmark." He noted that "Mr. Monteux was recalled again and again, even after he had bade the orchestra share the applause with him. Finally the players began applauding him, because this music is inhumanly difficult to conduct and he had given a thrilling performance."

Meanwhile, the *Boston Herald* described the piece as "spring fever in a zoo." On 9 February 1924, it published a piece of doggerel inspired by Stravinsky's groundbreaking work:

> The Rite of Spring
>
> Who wrote this fiendish *Rite of Spring*,
> What right had he to write the thing,
> Against our hapless ears to fling
> Its crash, clash, cling, clang, bing, bang, bing?
> And then to call it *Rite of Spring*,
> The season when on joyous wing
> The birds melodious carols sing
> and harmony's in everything!
> He who could write *The Rite of Spring*,
> If I be right, by right should swing!

No book on Stravinsky and his music has included this "critique."

Monteux conducted a stirring concert on 10 March 1924, but it was not with the Boston Symphony. For the first time in the history of that organization, its conductor appeared as a guest conductor of another orchestra in the same city, the People's Symphony, which was what might be termed today a civic, or community, orchestra. Monteux needed the permission of the BSO's trustees in order to accept this invitation, permission that was willingly granted.

The concert, an all-French program in the St. James Theatre, was sold out, with many turned away. The seemingly ubiquitous Franck Symphony in D minor led off the program, which continued with Debussy's *Prélude à l'après-midi d'un faune* and works of Saint-Saëns and Chabrier. In the *Globe* of 11 March, Philip Hale wrote that, accustomed as he was to hearing both Monteux and the People's Symphony, but not together, the combination offered further proof of Monteux's skill and taste as a trainer of orchestras, of which he already had much experience in his twice rebuilding the Boston Symphony. With only three rehearsals he was able to make the People's Symphony play better than it has ever played before, and in a difficult program.

We can see from the above that Monteux, besides having the ability to weld professional orchestras into superior instruments, could also accomplish the betterment of lesser orchestras under his direction, and in a fairly short time. This special talent of his was not lost on others, even if they did not always subscribe to the idea of Monteux as one of the greats. Many years later, when I was a conducting student at the Juilliard School of Music, where such students worked with an ensemble of decidedly less than stellar ability called the "second orchestra," our teacher, Jean Morel (1903–1975), not an unqualified admirer of Monteux, wondered aloud one day as to how many of the great maestros, such as Herbert von Karajan, Fritz Reiner, or George Szell, would be able to achieve acceptable results with that orchestra. He concluded that "probably only Monteux could get something."

In early March 1924 Germaine Monteux returned to Boston from France so as to be with her husband at the close of his final season. (Where Doris Hodgkins was during this time is not known.) Unfortunately, Germaine's visit was abruptly terminated by the sudden death of her mother. She sailed back to France on 22 March.

Pierre Monteux's final concerts as conductor of the Boston Symphony Orchestra took place on 2 and 3 May 1924. The program was:

> Beethoven: Symphony No. 5 in C minor
> Carpenter: Suite: *Adventures in a Perambulator*
> Debussy: *Prélude à l'après-midi d'un faune*
> Wagner: Overture to *Tannhäuser*

As can be seen, Monteux had made his peace with Wagner (as he had with Richard Strauss).

On the afternoon of the Saturday evening concert, a reception in Symphony Hall was given for Monteux by the trustees to which the subscribers to the various concert series and the members of the orchestra had been invited. Judge Cabot presented Monteux with a large book containing a letter of appreciation signed by five thousand subscribers. It had been available for signatures for some time at Symphony Hall.

After the performance of Beethoven's Fifth on Saturday evening, Monteux was presented with a large loving cup, the gift of the members of the orchestra. Standing, cheering ovations after the Beethoven and Wagner works attested to the audience's affection and admiration for their departing conductor.

Worth quoting are Monteux's remarks, made in 1963:

> It is the custom here in the United States to make an intensive *réclame* for the forthcoming conductor in the last year of the incumbent. Perhaps this is necessary, but I do not think the trustees of orchestras realize how very embarrassing and grievous, not to say vexatious, this policy (when carried out in the efficient manner of American managers) can be to a sensitive musician. In my case, I felt deeply my last year in Boston as a sort of interim between the known and the unknown. I was told by Judge Frederick P. Cabot, in a charming speech made at a reception in Symphony Hall just

before the season's end, "This is not goodbye; you will come back to your orchestra many times." I left Boston in the month of May 1924 and did not return for twenty-six years! Strangely enough, the five-year policy existed no longer. (D. Monteux 1965, 115–16)

In a Sunday *New York Times* article on 30 March, prior to Monteux's last New York visit with the Boston Symphony (which included the local premiere of *The Rite of Spring*), Olin Downes wrote of how Monteux, with patience and courage, had developed the orchestra from a disorganized and incomplete entity into the brilliant ensemble it had become, now ranking among the greatest symphony orchestras in the world. Downes admired Monteux not only for his technical abilities, but also for his breadth of programming and for how he often revealed new facets of compositions that his distinguished predecessors had failed to notice. He praised the conductor for his admirable ability as a musician and leader and for the modesty and self-effacement with which he carried out his duties, and remarked that Serge Koussevitzky should consider himself fortunate in finding such an orchestra at his disposal.

A week later, in the 6 April *New York Herald*, Laurence Gilman wrote that he would remember Monteux more for the quality of his interpretations than for his modest podium demeanor. He would also remember his sensitivity and intelligence as a musician and his feeling for style—under his direction Schubert did not sound like Richard Strauss, Wagner like Tchaikovsky, Handel like Mozart, or Debussy like Liszt. He would be grateful for his skill, craftsmanship, and indefatigable mastery of the orchestra. Finally, Gilman said he would remember Monteux's modesty and gentleness, his lack of pettiness, and his rare artistry.

The dean of Boston's music critics at the time was the venerable H. T. Parker of the *Boston Evening Transcript*. In the 1 May 1924 edition of the paper, prior to Monteux's final week of concerts, he wrote a lengthy and eulogistic tribute to the conductor (reprinted in the Boston Symphony's program book for the concerts of 6, 7, and 8 March 1975, in observance of the centennial of Monteux's birth). In it Parker summarized Monteux's tenure, praising him for having raised the orchestra out of the depths to which it had sunk at the time of his arrival and of the ensuing union difficulties.

Parker especially extolled Monteux for his programming, which widened and revitalized the orchestra's repertoire. In particular, he liked the fact that Monteux did not repeat the classics until they became routine for conductor, orchestra, and audience, and he also appreciated that he presented music that had been neglected but that deserved a place in a long season of concerts. Parker concluded that Monteux had always placed the music above himself and paid tribute to his saving of the orchestra, his renewal of its powers and prestige, and his maintaining of its standards.

For the rest of his career, critics would write about Monteux's selflessness in the service of music. While one can argue the validity of the Boston Symphony's "five-year policy" concerning its conductors, another possible factor must be taken into consideration concerning the non-renewal of Monteux's contract, apart from whatever machinations Koussevitzky may have engaged in. The term "proper Bostonians" comes to mind. For two years Monteux had been separated, geographically if not otherwise, from his wife, and had been having a relationship with another woman. It is doubtful that the good citizens of Boston who supported the orchestra looked kindly upon this sort of behavior from their conductor.

For his part, Monteux was quoted in the papers as saying that he would never return to the United States.

CHAPTER 8

Amsterdam

After leaving Boston, Monteux not surprisingly returned to Paris, though he was not happy to do so; for him the prospect of conducting French orchestras was not a pleasant one. In any case, they all had their own permanent conductors, so the possibility of his being offered a position with one was extremely slim. Meanwhile he spent time visiting his parents and the other members of his large family, though the pleasure of this reunion was greatly marred by the death of his father soon after his return.

At the same time, Monteux was receiving offers to conduct concerts in London, Manchester, Liverpool, Stockholm, Oslo, and Bergen, all cities where he would be a welcome guest but unlikely to obtain a permanent position because, again, all these orchestras had their own regular conductors. He was thus understandably concerned about his future prospects for employment.

While sitting in a taxi one day in the middle of a traffic jam on the Champs-Élysées, he "heard a familiar voice shouting, 'Monteux, Monteux, wait, wait, I must speak with you.' It was Diaghilev." Diaghilev climbed into the taxi and, after the usual hugging and kissing, told Monteux that he was just the person he wanted to see.

Diaghilev was planning another season in Paris that June, presenting French and Russian ballets; he said André Messager would conduct the French works and Monteux "must conduct the Russian ballets."

Monteux explained to Diaghilev that at the moment ballet was the furthest thing from his thoughts, and that he was very tired from his recent Boston season and looking forward to a vacation in Dieppe. Diaghilev, however, was at his most charming and persuasive and would not take no for an answer. So it was that a week later, Monteux found himself in the pit of the Théâtre des Champs-Élysées rehearsing the orchestra.

Of great interest this season was Stravinsky's *Les noces*, even though it had already been performed the previous year. It is a ballet with a Russian peasant wedding as its theme, scored not for orchestra but for the unusual combination of four pianos, percussion, chorus, and four vocal soloists. The music is quite primitive in its atmosphere and forcefulness and is often cited as a major influence on Carl Orff's *Carmina Burana* and *Catulli Carmina*. The premier of *Les noces* in Paris in 1923, with choreography by Bronislava Nijinska (Vaslav Nijinsky's sister), had been a great success. Monteux was greatly impressed with Nijinska's work; she "employed iconic gestures and primitive movement in her choreography which nobly suited the music."

Stravinsky was scheduled to conduct the opening performance in 1924, with Monteux to take over all the others. Attending the first rehearsal and following the score, Monteux observed that the singers, both chorus and soloists, rarely made their entrances on time; the entire ensemble, in fact, was rather shaky. Though the performance was very successful with the Parisian audience, Monteux afterward went to Diaghilev and asked him when he could have a rehearsal of *Les noces*. Diaghilev responded with a yell, "Rehearsal, what? Mais, mon cher Monteux, the composer just conducted it!"

Monteux replied calmly, "The composer can do what he wants with his work but I have to play what is written. It will cost nearly nothing, there is no orchestra" (D. Monteux 1965, 130–32).

Diaghilev seemed pleased with this last remark and, after mentally calculating the cost, agreed that Monteux could have his rehearsal. In it he was able to painstakingly rectify errors, including having the soloists relearn their parts. In the end Monteux's performances went very well, but he had to admit that they were not as successful as Stravinsky's own. After the Diaghilev season he spent the summer in Dieppe (no more Casino concerts), returning to Paris in the fall.

Monteux's insistence on following the score exactly as written was a general hallmark of his performances. Of the great conductors, perhaps only Otto Klemperer was comparable in this regard. Toscanini, for all his vaunted faithfulness to the score, often departed from it in the form of copious orchestral revisions. And yet, as we shall see in a later chapter, Monteux could also stray from this principle when it suited him.

In September 1924 Monteux was contacted by Samuel Bottenheim, secretary of the Concertgebouw Orchestra of Amsterdam. He asked if it would be possible for Monteux to come there immediately, as Willem Mengelberg (1871–1951), the orchestra's great Dutch conductor, was ill. Mengelberg had been in his position since 1895, when he was only twenty-four, and had developed the Concertgebouw into one of the world's finest orchestras.

Monteux accepted and made his first appearance at the Concertgebouw (which is the name of the concert hall as well as the orchestra—the word means "concert hall" or "concert building") on 9 October 1924, conducting the following program:

Weber: Overture to *Euryanthe*
Saint-Saëns: Cello Concerto No. 1 in A minor; Gerard Hekking, cello
Debussy: Two Nocturnes
Brahms: Symphony No. 4 in E minor

Monteux's presence in Holland aroused the interest of the critics, who wrote that the logical thing for him to do would be to conduct the Dutch premiere of *The Rite of Spring*. The artistic director of the orchestra, Rudolf Mengelberg (Willem's distant cousin—their great-great-great-great-great-grandfathers were brothers—and a respected Dutch composer), and its business manager, Paul Cronheim, concurred. They immediately asked Monteux to conduct this work with the Concertgebouw Orchestra.

Monteux felt that he could not refuse. Willem Mengelberg himself came to the first rehearsal and asked Monteux if he could speak to the orchestra before it began. Monteux agreed. As he finished his remarks, Mengelberg came to Monteux, put his arm on his shoulder, and led the orchestra in a cheer for their French visitor. Only later did Monteux learn that Mengelberg, who had spoken in Dutch, had told the orchestra "in no uncertain terms that they all owed a debt of gratitude to Monteux for bringing this colossal work for the first time to Holland, and that if he, Mengelberg, had studied it for weeks and months himself, he would never have been able to conduct it!"

Years later Monteux recalled:

My, what work that was! This work which was part of me seemed to have endless difficulties for the Dutch musicians. We persevered, and on the 12th of October played *Le Sacre* for the subscribers' Thursday night concert. We really played it, too; the heavy, rich strings of the orchestra suited the work admirably and I was truly thrilled by the sound. I have often regretted we have no recording of that eventful thirty-six minutes in the life of the orchestra. (D. Monteux 1965, 136–37)

(Monteux expanded the work's timing a bit. In his several recordings it lasts between thirty-one and thirty-three minutes.)

The success of *The Rite* prompted Willem Mengelberg to invite Monteux to share the season with him. In addition to his duties in Amsterdam, since 1921 Mengelberg had been spending a great deal of time, four and five months a year, as principal conductor of the New York Philharmonic Orchestra, and he needed someone on whom he could rely to conduct the Concertgebouw Orchestra during his absences.

It is likely that Mengelberg had heard some of Monteux's Boston Symphony concerts in New York and perhaps even met him there. Similarly, it is possible that Monteux had heard some of Mengelberg's concerts. In any case, the two men knew and respected each other, and Mengelberg felt that Monteux was just the man to collaborate with him in Amsterdam. (Actually, as principal violist of the Colonne Orchestra, Monteux had played under Mengelberg's direction when the latter, as guest conductor, had directed Richard Strauss's *Ein Heldenleben*. It is doubtful, however, that the two spoke to each other at that time, beyond normal rehearsal exchanges.) In a gesture of great generosity, Monteux was not treated as a guest conductor, but was given the title of co-conductor of the Concertgebouw Orchestra. This arrangement was to work very well for ten years, during which time he never received a contract or letter of agreement; the engagement was based solely upon mutual trust.

On the face of it, Monteux and Mengelberg were an odd couple, the former extremely straightforward in his performances, highly respectful of the composer's markings, of playing what is written, and the latter extremely personal and willful in his interpretations, often to the point of gross exaggeration.

In matters of repertoire Mengelberg gave Monteux first choice, knowing full well that he was unlikely to select symphonies of Mahler, which had become house specialties at the Concertgebouw (as had Bach's *Saint Matthew Passion* and works of various Dutch composers). Nor was Mengelberg particularly interested in conducting Debussy or Stravinsky. Beethoven, Brahms, and others they had in common, but these could be amicably divided. Mengelberg even gave Monteux first choice of the works of Richard Strauss, another Mengelberg favorite.

Not only did Mengelberg defer to Monteux in programming, but he allowed him to make any changes in personnel he deemed necessary. He was well aware of Monteux's ability as an orchestra builder, as evidenced by his Boston experience, and had complete confidence in his judgment.

Doris Hodgkins accompanied Pierre to Amsterdam, and though the two were not yet married, there was never a question of her not being accepted by the Dutch. In fact, Mrs. Mengelberg became quite fond of Doris. Since she could not introduce her to guests at parties and receptions as "Mrs. Monteux" and was reluctant to refer to her as Pierre Monteux's "companion," according to Nancie Monteux, she delighted in presenting her as "our Doris."

Monteux's personal life briefly became an issue early in his time with the Concertgebouw Orchestra. On 16 June 1925 he wrote to Rudolf Mengelberg stating that he had received a letter from Bottenheim to which his dignity forbade him to reply, and that between himself and Mengelberg he wished to dispute certain allegations contained in that letter.

He states that he never swore to Bottenheim that everything was arranged for an amicable divorce between Germaine Monteux and himself. What he did say was that Mme. Monteux could not do otherwise than agree to a divorce, and as soon as it was pronounced he would marry Miss Gerald, as he referred to Doris.

He further notes, with much surprise, that Bottenheim seemed to think that he, Monteux, had written a letter in which he refused to provide for his children, which he considered to be "a monstrous lie." Not only had he written that he would always pay their expenses, but furthermore he had left for the children and their mother a liquid sum of 125,000 francs. This was more than he earned in a year and seemed to him sufficient to provide for a woman and two children in Paris for at least two years.

As for his having left his family to live entirely with the woman he would marry, it seemed to him more honorable and more moral to live thusly than to do otherwise, with two households. He had made the decision to leave his family for important reasons that were too private to be divulged.

He continues that the truth rests in what he has just said. He will marry Miss Gerald as soon as Mme. Monteux agrees to a divorce, and furthermore, she cannot do otherwise than what he asks. In conclusion, he is sorry for burdening his friend with his private affairs, but after such a letter he cannot speak or write to Bottenheim.

Monteux's monthly payments for child support were equivalent to $150 (in 1925 dollars). On 17 February 1926 Paul Cronheim received a letter, dated the previous day, from Pierre Krettly of Krettly and Saphores in Paris, makers of *décolletage de précision*. (In this case, *décolletage* did not refer to low-cut dresses, but to detachable adornments for automobiles, such as hood ornaments.) Signed by Krettly, the letter states that as of the fifteenth, Monteux's payment had not been received. During the time in question Monteux was away from Holland conducting concerts in Moscow, Leningrad, Oslo, and Berlin, and Krettly wants to know if his brother-in-law had left instructions to effectuate the payment. (Krettly was married at the time to Germaine's sister, Simone.)

A second letter, dated 8 March, thanks Cronheim for his reply—in which he stated that he had nothing to do with this matter—and Krettly expresses the hope that the situation will be resolved so as to avoid grave results.

Eventually, Germaine Monteux herself wrote to Cronheim on 14 April 1926, asking if he would reveal to her the financial arrangements between her husband and the Concertgebouw Orchestra, as well as the length of his contract. In a reply dated 30 April, Cronheim informed her that the contracts of their conductors were absolutely confidential, and that consequently he could not give her the terms.   One must assume that Monteux made up the missing payment and continued to provide child support, for no further documentation exists on this matter, at least in the archives of the Concertgebouw Orchestra.

It is interesting to note that Germaine Monteux signed her name in a similar fashion to her husband, with a flourish on the final "x" consisting of a straight line descending to the left at approximately a 15-degree angle and extending more than halfway under the first name. (Actually, almost all the Monteuxs signed their name in this way, though Germaine was not, of course, née Monteux.)

The Concertgebouw gave every indication of becoming a long-term engagement, but for only about four months a year. Doris and Pierre therefore decided to live in the area of Brussels, convenient to Amsterdam and to the rest of Europe as well. They settled at first in a house in the suburb of Petite Espinette, later in the town of La Hulpe. Germaine remained adamant in refusing to grant Pierre a divorce. Apparently she preferred to remain and be known as Mme. Pierre Monteux. Denise and Claude continued to live with their mother while Donald and Nancy lived with Doris and Pierre, though there were occasional visits back and forth.

Over a ten-year period in Amsterdam Monteux conducted a vast repertoire, both standard and modern, with the leading soloists of the day as guest artists, as well as with solo appearances by members of the orchestra, such as the concert-master (Alexander Schmuller, and later Louis Zimmermann). Included on Monteux's programs were works by composers with whom he was not normally associated, at least in his later years. For example, on 11 December 1927 he conducted the Violin Concerto by Carl Nielsen, a work seldom heard even today, with Emil Telmányi as soloist, and on 15 December of that year he conducted the Netherlands premiere of the same composer's Symphony No. 5. The first Concertgebouw performance of Leos Janácek's Sinfonietta was given on 25 October 1928, while on 8 November Béla Bartók was the soloist in the Concertgebouw premiere of his First Piano Concerto. Three weeks later, on 29 November, Paul Hindemith appeared as viola soloist in his Kammermusik No. 5.

Dutch composers were not neglected by Monteux; in fact, he seems to have made a point of playing as much of their music as possible. Works by Hendrik Andriessen, Alfons Diepenbrock, Cornelis Dopper, Dirk Fock, Rudolf Mengelberg, Julius Röntgen, Robert de Roos, Leo Smit, Matthijs Vermeulen, and Johan Wagenaar appeared on his programs. He did not, however, continue to play their music once he had left Holland.

There was one Dutch composer, though, to whom Monteux was to remain faithful. After conducting works by some of the composers mentioned above, respectable but unexceptional music, he made inquiries to musicians and critics to determine whether there was a Dutch composer who was a bit more original and daring. Several people mentioned the name of Willem Pijper (1894–1947); but he was a bit strange and unsociable, they cautioned, even a little crazy. This description was all Monteux needed. His curiosity piqued, he wrote to Pijper three times without receiving a reply. There was then nothing to do but drive with Doris to Pijper's home unannounced and ring the bell.

Pierre and Doris were first confronted by the composer's formidable mother, who refused to let them in. Doris, not to be outdone in formidability, managed to create enough of a commotion to cause Pijper himself to come to the door. As Monteux recounted, "I will never forget his ascetic face, so thin and white, with burning eyes that seemed to pierce one's façade. There was no use in trying to placate Pijper with cajolery. He seemed to see right through you, and in his presence deceit was impossible. . . . He stared at us, and in an impatient voice asked us what we wanted." Monteux replied that he wanted to know Pijper and his music. After quite an extended pause, Pijper responded, "Oh you do, do you? Well, come on in, then" (D. Monteux 1965, 143–44).

Only in his early thirties, Pijper struck Monteux as already a very bitter man. He felt that his music had been unjustly neglected by the Concertgebouw Orchestra. His Second Symphony, a truly striking work, was to have been conducted by Mengelberg in 1922. However, in the end, Pijper conducted the premiere himself, with disastrous results as far as the generally conservative audience was concerned. Impressed by the older man's interest in his work, Pijper dedicated his Third Symphony to Monteux, who conducted the premiere on 28 October 1926 to a comparatively cordial reception. Monteux programmed the work often in Amsterdam and the other Dutch cities in which the orchestra had concert series (Rotterdam, The Hague, and Utrecht, among others) and continued to perform it for the rest of his life.

In notes for a talk she gave in San Francisco, Doris wrote of traveling with Pierre by train to Russia in November 1926. They were on their way to Leningrad, where Pierre was to conduct that city's Philharmonic Orchestra. The trip began in Brussels and continued across snow-covered Belgium, Germany, Poland, and Lithuania, and then to Tallin, Estonia, where they spent the night. Leaving the next morning on a trip that normally should have taken five or six hours, the Monteuxs were extremely discomfited by the time their rather decrepit train finally reached Leningrad seventeen hours later. After they had crossed the frontier, the train stopped in the middle of the night, whereupon at least seven Russian soldiers entered the Monteuxs' compartment, ordered them to get up, searched them thoroughly, ripped open the cushions of the car, tapped on the wall panels, inspected the baggage meticulously, and then decided that the only thing the Monteuxs could *not* take with them was all the music and scores Pierre had brought with him.

Doris became extremely agitated. Much of this music was in the form of manuscripts by Ravel, Milhaud, Stravinsky, and others. Unable to speak a work of Russian, she pointed to the music and began to sing something from *Prince Igor* and conduct it as best she could, pointing to Pierre and the music and delivering a quite vivid pantomime. The soldiers started laughing, went into the corridor for a whispered conference, returned, and allowed the Monteuxs and the music to proceed to Leningrad.

The concerts in Leningrad were given in the Salle des Noblesses, just across the street from the Monteuxs' hotel. Once a beautiful and elegant concert hall, it was now, even eight years after World War I, in a terrible state of decay. Concerts started at ten o'clock and usually lasted until about one in the morning. (Knowing some of the programs Monteux assembled at various stages of his career, one can well believe that.)

In the notes for her San Francisco talk, Doris wrote:

The public was very poorly clothed, but all of them were intent on the music to be heard, clothes in this instance being of no account. One of the most impressive sights I have ever seen was in the balcony up over the orchestra. Here stood at least one hundred and fifty little children, thin, white-faced little children, all lining the balcony railing the whole length of the orchestra, their bony elbows and frail hands holding up their tired little faces. Here they stood for three or four hours, barely moving, gazing down upon the conductor and listening with rapt attention to the music, with their heart and soul in their brilliant, fever-lit eyes. Never will I forget many of them, and Mr. Monteux has often said that it was the most impressive audience that he has ever played to.

When it came time to leave Leningrad, the entire orchestra came to the train station to see the Monteuxs off. Many brought gifts, having pooled their meager resources to buy candy and flowers. The tour continued into 1927 with concerts in Helsinki, Oslo, and Stockholm, and when the Monteuxs returned to Amsterdam, a Sunday afternoon concert was scheduled shortly after their arrival. As the concerts there were always well attended, the Monteuxs were a bit taken aback when shortly before the concert there were barely a hundred people in the hall. One of the directors of the Concertgebouw then entered the Artists Room dressed in sport clothes, a stocking cap in his hand. With a bit of a laugh he announced, "Mr. Monteux, don't expect much of an audience today . . . because when the canals are frozen, everyone in Holland goes skating, and as soon as the concert is finished, I am going too!"

While vacationing in Waldoboro, Maine, Monteux received on 23 April 1928 a telegram from A. Röell, president of the Concertgebouw Orchestra, informing him that, on the occasion of the orchestra's fortieth anniversary, Queen Juliana of the Netherlands had conferred upon him the country's highest honor: officer in the Order of Orange Nassau. On 24 April Monteux cabled back, "OVERWHELM-INGLY GRATEFUL FOR DECORATION MANY THANKS."

On 3 November 1929 Monteux and the Concertgebouw Orchestra presented an unusual group of guest soloists: members of the Paris-based Society for Ancient Music. They included the violinist Marius Casadesus, the violist Henri Casadesus, and the harpsichordist Regina Patorni-Casadesus. The society had acquired a reputation for discovering long-lost works by composers both great and obscure. In the former category were Mozart, whose early violin concerto the "Adelaide" was Marius's discovery; and Handel, whose Viola Concerto in B minor appeared in an edition edited by Henri. The latter category included various eighteenth-century Italian composers, three of whom were represented on the Concertgebouw program: Giovanni Lorenzitti by his *Symphonie vénitienne*, Giovanni Batista Borghi by his Concertino for Harpsichord and Ten Wind Instruments, and Bonifacio Asioli by his Concerto for Viola d'Amore.

Regardless of the merits of these compositions, or their performances, many years later Monteux was to inform his students that Marius Casadesus, after several drinks too many, had told him, also years later, that the brothers Casadesus had actually composed all that early music themselves. In fact, shortly before his death in 1981, Marius admitted publicly that he himself had written the "Adelaide" Concerto. One is reminded of Fritz Kreisler, who performed many pieces that were attributed to early composers only to confound an indignant musical community by confessing that he had written them himself. Today the Kreisler pieces are in the repertoire of most violinists. For many years conductors such as Serge Koussevitzky, Eugene Ormandy, Leonard Bernstein, and others performed a Concerto in D major by Carl Philipp Emanuel Bach in an orchestral arrangement by Maximilian Steinberg, the son-in-law of Rimsky-Korsakov, no less. Only if one reads the program notes carefully would one notice that the original was a chamber work that had been discovered and first performed by the Society for Ancient Music in Paris. As a result, no one plays this concerto any more, which is unfortunate, because it is a very attractive piece, no matter who wrote it.

Marius and Henri were the uncles of the great pianist Robert Casadesus (1899–1972), who performed often with Pierre Monteux. Robert, also a composer of merit, was an artist of great rectitude who never indulged in musical chicanery.

Another area of performance materialized for Monteux in Amsterdam as well. Paul Cronheim, in addition to being the orchestra's business manager, was also the director of the Wagner Society of Amsterdam, which presented staged performances not only of Wagner's operas, but of an internationally varied repertoire. Its original focus had been exclusively Wagnerian, but after World War I the need to be so restrictive became less evident.

On 10, 12, 14, and 16 November 1927 Pierre Monteux conducted the Concertgebouw Orchestra in the first performances in Amsterdam of Debussy's great opera *Pelléas et Mélisande*. At that time the venue for operatic presentations in Amsterdam was the Stadsschouwburg (Municipal Theater). The French government had originally proposed an ensemble of singers from the Opéra-Comique, where the work had received its world premiere in 1902, but Monteux had his own singers in mind, with whom he worked for several months. Among them were the two young artists who sang the title roles, Charles Panzéra as Pelléas and Yvonne Brothier as Mélisande, who were singing operatically for the first time before a paying audience. Amsterdam can thus take credit for starting them on their international careers. The role of Golaud was taken by Hector Dufranne.

Because the singers proposed by the French government had not been engaged, the French Ministry of Fine Arts, in high dudgeon, had originally forbidden the publisher, Durand, from renting the orchestral parts for *Pelléas* to the Wagner Society. It became necessary for the French ambassador in The Hague to intervene in order for the ban to be lifted. Later the French government, realizing it had made a tactical error, expressed its gratitude for what it considered an important event in the musical history of Amsterdam, as a result of which Pierre Monteux was inducted into the Légion d'Honneur. Membership in the Légion d'Honneur, signified by a little red lapel ribbon, is the highest honor that can be awarded a French citizen.

Monteux had become a great friend to the Cronheim family, to the point where the children called him "Uncle Pierre." So successful had the *Pelléas* performances been—and this undeniably great opera does not usually enjoy great acclaim from the general public—that Monteux was thought of as a spirit who brought good luck to the Wagner Society. This luck was embodied in the person of J. C. Bunge, a major supporter of the society, who, after the success of *Pelléas*, proclaimed that he was willing to spend an even greater amount of his assets in order to guarantee the society's continuity.

The following season Monteux led four performances of *Carmen*, on 15, 17, 19, and 21 November 1928. The title role was sung by Jane Bourgignon, with

René Lapelletrie as Don José and Yvonne Brothier as Micaela. While Wagner's music dramas continued to be performed by the eponymous society, they were conducted not by Monteux, but by the Germans Fritz Busch, Erich Kleiber, and Max von Schillings. Mozart's operas were conducted by Bruno Walter, and Richard Strauss's by Kleiber and by the composer. In certain ways, Monteux was still typecast as a conductor for French repertoire, at least where opera was concerned.

Other French works he conducted were Jacques Offenbach's *Les contes d'Hoffmann* on 11 and 12 June and 2 and 3 July 1932, and a double bill of Jean-Baptiste Lully's *Acis et Galatée* and Ravel's *L'heure espagnole* on 23 and 25 June 1933. The decor for the latter was designed by Vera Soudeïkine, who would soon become Mrs. Igor Stravinsky.

Monteux did, however, conduct three operas by non-French composers, though the first of these, Gluck's *Iphigénie en Tauride*, given on 20 and 22 November 1930, was, as its title implies, performed in French, with Germaine Lubin as Iphigénie and Martial Singher as Oreste. In addition, the world premiere of Willem Pijper's opera *Halewijn* was presented on 13 and 14 June 1933 in cooperation with the International Society for Contemporary Music. Most of Monteux's operatic performances were with the Concertgebouw Orchestra in the pit, but the Wagner Society actually employed several Dutch orchestras, as does the Netherlands Opera today, and for *Halewijn* it was the Utrecht City Orchestra.

For its 1932–33 season the Wagner Society made plans to produce Verdi's final masterpiece, *Falstaff*. One conductor alone was deemed the natural choice for this opera, and with Monteux's approval the society attempted to secure the services of Arturo Toscanini. Falstaff was to be sung by Mariano Stabile, an old friend of Toscanini's and a prime interpreter of the role. It was he who was to make the contact with Toscanini. The two met in the Oesterreichischer Hof in Salzburg, where the maestro was conducting that summer. The triple temptation of *Falstaff*, Stabile, and the Concertgebouw Orchestra was enough for Toscanini to seriously consider the offer. There was, however, one stumbling block—his intense dislike for Willem Mengelberg, which dated from the time they were both conducting the New York Philharmonic. Toscanini was then told that Mengelberg would be out of the country at the time of *Falstaff* and that Monteux would be conducting in Amsterdam, to which the maestro replied vehemently that in Monteux the group already had not only the best *Falstaff* conductor, but his dearest colleague; they did not need him. So it was that on 24 and 26 November 1932 Monteux conducted *Falstaff* with an all-Italian cast headed by Stabile.

For the first eight years of his association with the Concertgebouw Orchestra, Monteux had conducted from fifty to sixty concerts a season, effectively four months' work over several periods of time. These included performances in the orchestra's various subscription series in Amsterdam as well as appearances in Rotterdam, The Hague, Haarlem, and elsewhere in Holland. Meanwhile, with the arrival of Toscanini in New York in 1926, Willem Mengelberg began spending less and less time there. Toscanini's appointment as principal conductor of the New York Philharmonic in 1929 marked the end of Mengelberg's tenure with the orchestra.

As Mengelberg would no longer be making extended visits to New York, there was less need to have replacements for him in Amsterdam. Nevertheless, the arrangement with Monteux continued until plans were being made for the 1932–33 season, when he was offered approximately half as many concerts as previously. This schedule meant, of course, that his Dutch income would be halved as well. Whereas previously he had a guarantee of at least 20,000 florins for the season, now it would be only 10,000. Monteux, who was often asking for and receiving advances on his salary because of his financial obligation to Germaine and the children, and now to Doris and her children, requested that his minimum under the new schedule be 12,500 florins. However, because of the Great Depression, the Concertgebouw Orchestra itself was having financial difficulties that threatened its very existence, and thus refused Monteux's request—his minimum would be 10,000.

When it came time to plan the 1933–34 season, Monteux was offered only ten concerts at a fee of 400 florins each. These concerts broke down to seven in December and three in March. The Concertgebouw Orchestra's committee explained to him in a letter dated 2 June 1933 that the decision had been made to provide the public with a greater variety of conductors of different nationalities, as well as to provide opportunities for Dutch conductors.

The young Dutchman Eduard van Beinum (1900–1959) had been the orchestra's second conductor since 1930. Van Beinum, who was self-effacing to a degree virtually unheard of among conductors, was especially sensitive to the fact that Monteux's responsibilities were decreasing at the same time that his own were increasing. He feared Monteux would think he, van Beinum, was in some way responsible for this situation, which he was not. There is no evidence, however, that Monteux in any way blamed van Beinum.

Another factor governed the reduction of Monteux's concerts. It was not explained to him in the letter of 2 June but was revealed in the minutes of several of the orchestra's board meetings, especially that of 6 April 1933. What follows will seem strange to anyone who attended Monteux's rehearsals in later years, whether in San Francisco, New York, Boston, London, or anywhere else. Nevertheless, it was the opinion of several of the Concertgebouw Orchestra's members, as expressed in the minutes, that Monteux's rehearsals had become sloppy and inattentive to detail, that the orchestra as a result was not playing well for him, and that attendance at his concerts had declined.

It is true that Monteux's rehearsal methods, while firm and detailed, were generally easygoing and genial, and that this type of rehearsing was foreign to an orchestra accustomed to Mengelberg's martinet-like approach, in which every last detail was explained with great verbosity. But why, after eight years, was Monteux's way suddenly found to be "sloppy and inattentive"? With no direct aural evidence of what occurred at the rehearsals so long ago, one can only accept the statements in the minutes at face value.

Furthermore, these same minutes of 6 April reflect concern over Monteux's recommendation that the orchestra's string sections be reseated. Players had always been seated according to seniority. Monteux, however, had proposed auditions to determine seating, an idea never greeted favorably by musicians already established in their positions.

In the past Monteux had often recommended various artists to be engaged as soloists in his concerts and those of others—such young French musicians as the violinist Zino Francescatti and the pianists Robert Casadesus and François Lang. These recommendations were invariably greeted favorably. For the 1933–34 season he recommended only one soloist, the Hungarian-born pianist Lili Kraus. When the orchestra committee rejected her, he was incensed.

In a letter of 28 June 1933, Rudolf Mengelberg proposed a program for the concert of 21 December, for which he had engaged "your friend Enesco" as soloist. He suggested that the great Romanian violinist and composer-conductor perform a Mozart concerto and conduct one of his Romanian Rhapsodies.

Monteux was not pleased with this last suggestion, for on 1 July he replied:

21 December is my *only* concert in Series B, and it is not possible that a portion of my concert be conducted by another!! When I was part of the house [i.e., a member of the Concertgebouw "family"], it was entirely natural that I cede my place to a composer. But now that I am a *guest* engaged for a few concerts, that will no longer go. As for Lili Kraus, I insist *absolutely* on her for one of my concerts; she is the *only* artist I have asked of you. I have *promised* her that she will play with me, and since we have the date of 4 March free, I insist that she be my soloist on that date.

The reduction of his concerts and the rejection of his proposed soloist rankled Monteux, and he felt he was no longer appreciated by the Concertgebouw Orchestra. (In the preceding letter, and in many others, Monteux often underlined terms for emphasis, as shown in italic throughout this book.) Finally, in a letter to Roëll dated 5 March 1934, Monteux wrote:

I made my debut at the Concertgebouw in October 1924 and you have honored me by re-engaging me without interruption until now. I must tell you that I am very proud to have belonged, I, a foreigner, for 10 years to this institution at the side of my great colleague and friend Mengelberg; but everything must end and that is why I ask you to consider my concert of next Thursday 8 March, as my farewell concert. Naturally, in parting, I do not lose interest in the Concertgebouw and when you find yourself in difficulty, you can always count on me to the degree possible that I can be of service.

Even after he had ceased to work with the Concertgebouw Orchestra, Monteux returned to Amsterdam for the Wagner Society, conducting *Pelléas et Mélisande* again on 14 and 16 February 1935 and *Carmen* on 18 and 19 November 1936. The printed program for the *Pelléas* performances contained a statement written by Monteux in French concerning Debussy's orchestration:

> When one examines the work of Claude Debussy, one is struck by a considerable number of modifications of what is found in the original scores. Thus, in "The Nocturnes" the version used in concerts is totally different from the printed score. If the little pocket scores of "La Mer" have been corrected, it is not the same with the orchestral parts and the large score, which remain in the same form as they were originally conceived.
>
> The originality of this presentation of "Pelléas" is found in Debussy's personal score, a score brought to light since the death of the master, which conforms to the final wishes of the inspired composer.
>
> In fact, this orchestral score contains an extraordinary amount of modifications from the hand of Debussy himself, corrections in black pencil, blue pencil, in red ink, etc. . . . all of which have been transferred to our orchestral parts.
>
> In a way this presentation of "Pelléas," for musicians as well as musicologists, can appear a little as a first hearing.
>
> All these modifications can be considered as improvements to the orchestration.
>
> It is from this score that, on 14 and 16 February, I will have the immense pleasure of conducting the immortal work of Claude Debussy.

As for Monteux's willingness to be available to the orchestra in case of difficulty, another illness of Mengelberg brought him back for several concerts in October 1939. One of these, a French program on 12 October, included the Piano Concerto No. 4 by Saint-Saëns, with Robert Casadesus as soloist. The critics noted that Monteux conducted this work, which was not part of the orchestra's regular repertoire and even today not as familiar as the more popular Concerto No. 2, from memory.

Monteux would not return to Amsterdam and the Concertgebouw Orchestra until after World War II.

CHAPTER 9

Back to America

When he left the Boston Symphony, Pierre Monteux stated that he would never again conduct in the United States. But time has a way of healing wounds, and three years later, in 1927, he accepted an invitation to conduct summer outdoor concerts in the Hollywood Bowl and at New York's Lewisohn Stadium. At the Bowl he directed four concerts with the Los Angeles Philharmonic, beginning on 26 July. As might be expected, a significant amount of French music was programmed, including the Los Angeles premiere of Chausson's Symphony in B-flat major (only thirty-seven years after it was completed); as well as Rimsky-Korsakov's *Scheherazade*, which had become one of Monteux's calling cards; and works of Wagner and Strauss. Hal Davidson Crain, *Musical America*'s Los Angeles correspondent, was generous with his praise, though in the issue of 13 August he wrote that more poetry and color should have been present in *Scheherazade*.

At the time of Monteux's first engagement at Lewisohn Stadium and for many years thereafter, the concerts were held seven nights a week, a different program each night, with no days off for the musicians unless it rained. This schedule meant there could be only one rehearsal per concert. An interesting aspect of Monteux's programs, in light of the way the concerts evolved over the years, is that none featured a guest soloist; they were strictly all-orchestral concerts.

While they were popularly priced (during the 1940s, when I began attending, and into the 1950s, the cheapest seats cost twenty-five cents), the programs were not pops concerts, although some of the more popular classics would often be performed. For example, Monteux's first program, on 10 August 1927, included Berlioz's *Roman Carnival* Overture, Franck's Symphony in D minor, and, once again, *Scheherazade*. During the course of the week he performed, among other works, Schumann's Fourth Symphony, various Wagner selections, Ravel's *La valse*, Stravinsky's *Petrushka*, Felix Mendelssohn's Symphony No. 4 ("Italian"), and Brahms's Second Symphony. Two novelties for Stadium audiences (though *Petrushka* may have been one as well) were Enesco's Suite No. 1 and, undoubtedly because of Monteux's Concertgebouw association, the Dutch composer Cornelis Dopper's *Gothic Chaconne*.

Under the headline "Monteux Receives Ovation at Stadium," an uncredited review in *The New York Times* of 11 August mentioned that he had been greeted cordially by a large, delighted, and enthusiastic audience, and that the program had been a high spot in an uncommonly notable season of musical achievement. The performance of the *Roman Carnival* Overture was thought elegant and refined, sparkling and zestful. The unnamed critic appreciated the work's symmetry and proportion, such as audiences had come to expect from Monteux's past New York appearances, and observed that the beauty of the Franck symphony was enhanced by these qualities as well as an emotionally warm and imaginatively colorful delivery. He found Rimsky-Korsakov's showpiece exceptionally beautiful in Monteux's hands, the luminous tone of the strings a sheer delight. As for the great climax of the last movement's sea music, the critic could hardly imagine that passage more stirringly performed. Monteux, he said, inspired the orchestra to excel itself.

Here a comment may be in order from one who remembers the Stadium concerts of later years, when the inferior amplification system was often criticized in the press and elsewhere: without in any way wishing to minimize Monteux's accomplishment in this concert, I have difficulty imagining how a listener could perceive that the strings were playing with luminous tone or that a performance was notable for its imaginative color, when such qualities would as often as not reach the audience in rather distorted form. The Stadium concerts of 1927 must have either had a superior sound system to that of the 1950s or else, perhaps, none at all (doubtful, as the seating capacity was about 20,000). Of course, the critics would normally sit in the very front section, where one could hear a certain amount of the natural sound of the orchestra.

Petrushka on 12 August was cited in *The New York Times* as demonstrating Monteux's long acquaintance with this unique and subtle masterpiece, and the authority of his conducting was found to produce playing of great virtuosity. The critic remarked that the wit, humor, and pathos of the work were projected to the full, so that the listener hardly missed the stage action. This performance was of the complete score, except that Monteux played Stravinsky's rather abrupt concert ending rather than the original ballet ending. This was unusual for Monteux, who almost always ended with Petrushka's death scene, except when he played the shorter suite of excerpts. Perhaps the original ending was considered too subtle for an outdoor summer concert.

In spite of his success with the audience and the critics (as well as, one assumes, with the orchestra), Monteux was not to return to Lewisohn Stadium until 1946. There is no definitive reason for this long gap between appearances, though it is known that he disliked conducting there. He did, however, return to the United States less than a year later.

By 1928 Leopold Stokowski had been conducting the Philadelphia Orchestra for sixteen years, and in that time he had developed it into one of the world's greatest orchestras. His tenure, which was to last until 1936, was not without controversy, largely because of his championing the music of the day, but also because of his habit of lecturing audiences if he felt they were inattentive, and because of the general air of showmanship that surrounded his conducting and his persona.

After sixteen years Stokowski decided it was time for a sabbatical and accordingly took the 1927–28 season off. To replace him for twelve weeks in the second half of the season, he invited Pierre Monteux. As with Mengelberg and Monteux, the relationship between Stokowski and Monteux was a strange one. Stokowski was prone to extremely personal interpretations replete with reorchestrations and rewriting and had a batonless conducting style of great theatricality, with large sweeping gestures, at one time even accompanied by spotlights focused on his hands. Monteux was, well, Monteux—faithful to the score, with a straightforward conducting style that did not call attention to itself. Additionally, Stokowski stood over six feet tall, with copious blond hair and matinee-idol good looks, while Monteux was more than half a foot shorter and rotund. Indeed, this may have been a factor in Stokowski's inviting him, though at the time there really were no other conductors visually comparable to "Stokie." And, as with Mengelberg and Monteux, the two men genuinely liked and respected one another, and this was undoubtedly the prime factor leading to Monteux's engagement. (Stokowski had invited Fritz Reiner, then conductor of the Cincinnati Symphony Orchestra, for the first thirteen weeks of the season; Reiner was also on the short side—about five feet, six inches—and a bit plump.)

Monteux made his debut with the Philadelphia Orchestra in the concert pair of 3 and 4 February 1928 with the following program:

> Gluck: Overture to *Iphigenia in Aulis*
> Hindemith: Concerto for Orchestra
> Chabrier: *Bourrée fantasque*
> Beethoven: Symphony No. 7 in A major

In what was to be a recurring error throughout his career, the program page misspelled his name, in this case as "Montuex." (The most frequently encountered misspelling was "Monteaux," found in newspapers, magazines, in fact all sorts of publications for the rest of his life. The latter spelling would often result in the mispronunciation of his name as "Montoe." The family's pronunciation guide was that if one could count in French—*un, deux, trois*—then his name rhymed with *deux*.)

This program was presented in Carnegie Hall on 7 February, and Olin Downes's mostly laudatory review appeared in the *Times* the next day. "Mostly laudatory" because, while he had good things to say about most of the program and found Hindemith's concerto to be one of the wittiest and most incisive works of the contemporary German repertoire, with Monteux exhibiting his great knowledge of the orchestra and understanding of the score, the playing of the

Friday Afternoon
February 3

Saturday Evening
February 4

1928

The

PHILADELPHIA ORCHESTRA

LEOPOLD STOKOWSKI, CONDUCTOR

PIERRE MONTUEX, GUEST CONDUCTOR

PROGRAM

GLUCK · · · · · · · · · Overture, "Iphigenia in Aulis"

HINDEMITH · · · · · · · · · Concerto for Orchestra, Opus 38

    I. Mit Kraft, ohne Pathos und stets lebendig
    II. Sehr schnell
    III. Marsch für Holzbläser
    IV. Basso Ostinato

CHABRIER · · · · · · · · · Bourrée Fantasque

INTERMISSION

BEETHOVEN · · · · · · · · · Symphony No. 7, in A major

    I. Poco sostenuto. Vivace
    II. Allegretto
    III. Presto. Presto meno assai
    IV. Finale. Allegro con brio

The Steinway is the Official Piano of The Philadelphia Orchestra

If you must leave before the end of the concert please do so during
an intermission. The closing hour of this program will be approximately
4.00 P.M. on Friday and 10.00 P.M. on Saturday.

849

The autographed program page for Pierre Monteux's first concert with the
Philadelphia Orchestra. Note the misspelling of Monteux's name. Courtesy of
Nancie Monteux-Barendse

Beethoven symphony was not up to his usual standard. It was an energetic and muscular performance rather than a Dionysian one. It needed greater clarity and cleanness of attack.

During the first week of his engagement, Monteux was interviewed by Henry G. Hart of the *Philadelphia Record* (5 February), who asked him about his practice of conducting with the printed score before him, while others, such as Toscanini and Stokowski, conducted from memory. He replied:

> I feel that it is better to have the score, even though it is not referred to. Of course, I am, perhaps, old fashioned. Before I came to the Philadelphia Orchestra I was asked if I used a stand for the printed music, the music and a baton. I answered that, unlike others, who use any one or none of these things, I use them all. Showmanship has always seemed to me out of place at a symphony concert.

In later years, however, Monteux almost always conducted from memory and Stokowski always conducted with the score in front of him, even turning the pages.

While Monteux's programs for the twelve-week period contained a goodly amount of standard fare, they are also notable for presenting works that have almost, if not actually, vanished from today's concert repertoire. How often do we hear, for example, Franck's Suite from *Psyché*, Rimsky-Korsakov's *Sadko*, or Mily Balakirev's *Thamar*? He also presented, on 23 and 24 March, a sequence of miscellaneous short works of Beethoven, beginning with the Overture to *King Stephen*, continuing with the Dance of the Dervishes and the Turkish March from *The Ruins of Athens*, and concluding with two pieces from *Egmont*: "The Death of Clärchen" and the overture.

While some critics enjoyed hearing this miscellany, to Downes, writing in the *Times* of 4 April, they were, except for the *Egmont* Overture, extremely minor chips from Beethoven's workshop, of little or no musical interest. He went on to speak of defects that had crept into Monteux's programming, which he found all the more surprising considering that his last season of concerts with the Boston Symphony had displayed true originality and modernity.

On 17 and 18 February Monteux gave the American premiere of Willem Pijper's Symphony No. 3, which the Dutch composer had dedicated to Monteux. Downes's 22 February review following the New York premiere noted that Rudolf Mengelberg had described Pijper as one of the most gifted of the younger generation of Dutch composers. Downes hoped this was not true, for he found little to admire in the symphony, in spite of Monteux's brilliant and carefully prepared performance. He could not find a single significant idea in the whole symphony, which was a miscellany of various tricks then considered fashionable for a composer.

But of all the novelties presented by Monteux, none aroused more critical consternation than a rather innocuous work, *Music Hall Impressions*, by his one-time boss Gabriel Pierné. Upon hearing it in New York on 20 March, Downes wrote the next day, after commenting that Balakirev's *Thamar* had proven worthwhile in both music and performance, that Pierné's piece was not: it was devoid of any artistic value, banal and witless, apparently intended as a parody of jazz and circus music. He longed for a measure by W. C. Handy or George Gershwin rather than Pierné's flat effort, which he called "poor, senile music." However, Downes was not noted for a sense of humor, at least in his writings. It might be fun to hear Pierné's piece today, at least once.

While in Philadelphia Pierre and Doris stayed not in a hotel, but at the home of Doris's sister and brother-in-law, Hilda and Meyer Davis. Meyer was away at the time, as he had several orchestras playing in various Florida venues. Hilda and Doris, however, busied themselves hosting supper parties after each of the Saturday night concerts to which they invited the guest soloists and principal players of the orchestra. Among the former was the young Vladimir Horowitz, who had performed Rachmaninoff's Third Piano Concerto to great acclaim on 10 and 11 February. Hilda found him to be a great artist, but "disarmingly naive as a person" (Davis 1996, 43). Monteux left Hilda a wonderful memento of their visit: he not only autographed the program pages of each of his concerts for her, but carefully and clearly notated the principal theme of each of the compositions performed.

Meanwhile, Germaine had at last agreed to a divorce, and Pierre and Doris were now free to marry. They were united on 1 March in Elkton, Maryland, in a quiet ceremony conducted by C. M. Cope, a Baptist minister.

Besides getting married in the midst of his Philadelphia engagement, Monteux found time to participate in the American stage premiere of Stravinsky's acerbic *L'histoire du soldat* (The Soldier's Tale). This event took place under the aegis of the League of Composers on 25 March at New York's Jolson Theatre. Stravinsky wrote *L'histoire* in 1918 while living in Switzerland. With a text by C. F. Ramuz, it was designed as a touring piece for three actors, a narrator, and an instrumental ensemble of seven players. (These modest requirements were the result of the ravages of war, which precluded anything resembling prewar extravagances.) Today the suite from *L'histoire* is heard more frequently than the complete work.

For this performance Monteux conducted the chamber ensemble (from the New York Philharmonic). In spite of the small forces employed, the piece even today usually needs a conductor because of the work's rhythmic complexity. In those days it demanded one. Downes, writing in *The New York Times* on 26 March, felt that the work benefited from the visual element, for, when heard on its own several years before, the score had failed to ignite. He then compared the New York staging (unfavorably) with a performance he had attended the previous summer in London.

The Stravinsky was followed on the program by Manuel de Falla's *El retablo de Maese Pedro* (Master Peter's Puppet Show), a retelling of the Don Quixote story by means of singers and puppets, again with a chamber ensemble. This Downes found delightful. Falla's beautiful and inspired score, he said, benefited from having been preceded by Stravinsky's bare and bitter music. On the whole, wrote Downes, it was a brilliant evening, a triumph for the League of Composers.

One of the few major controversies in Monteux's career accompanied and followed his program in Philadelphia on 13 and 14 April. At the request of the orchestra's manager, Arthur Judson, Monteux had programmed *The Rite of Spring.* (In later years, though, when he was the manager of the New York Philharmonic, Judson would discourage conductors from playing too much modern music, especially on the Sunday afternoon broadcasts. For a time he was, in fact, manager of both orchestras simultaneously.) *The Rite* had been given its American premiere on 3 March 1922 by the Philadelphia Orchestra under Stokowski's direction. One might think its audience would have been somewhat familiar with the work, although there was no recording of it yet. In any case, after six years it probably felt like a new piece, and the Friday afternoon audience, composed largely of society women, did not react too favorably. No riot ensued, to be sure. However, there was a mass exodus not only between the two parts—so many left that the pause had to be extended to clear the aisles before the orchestra began again—but during the playing of the music as well, with much banging of seats and stomping up the aisles. The local critics were surprised at this response in light of the many modern works Stokowski had performed during the previous six years. One critic, as quoted in *The New York Times* of 14 April, stated that *The Rite* sounded mild and moderate compared with some of the works by Edgard Varèse that Stokowski had introduced. Nevertheless, he observed, the work seemed even more starkly original than at its only previous presentation in Philadelphia.

Following the Philadelphia performances, Monteux and the orchestra presented *The Rite* in New York on 17 April. In the *Times* of 18 April Downes found the performance sensationally brilliant, a triumph for Monteux, who understood the piece better than any other conductor. The audience remained to cheer and applaud for a long time. It was thought that Stravinsky's strange piece would probably not sound so impressive until Monteux played it again.

Although Monteux was generally well received by the Philadelphia critics, the response of the audiences there was rather tepid. During his final week in Philadelphia Monteux gave an interview to Philip Klein of the *Philadelphia Jewish Times* in which, obviously inspired by the behavior of the Friday afternoon audience the week before, he delivered himself of a few choice remarks that were picked up by the wire services and printed in other newspapers:

> Philadelphia has excellent musicians, but I cannot say as much for the so-called "music lovers." . . . Philadelphians want a slim conductor who pays a great deal of attention to his tailor. Perhaps that is the reason why my popularity here was sort of half-hearted. I overheard two women discussing me. They uttered not a word about the music or the composer. I was the sole topic of conversation. They agreed it was "shameful a conductor was so short and stout." Philadelphia audiences think they know something

about music, but they know nothing. They talk of teas and dresses and parties while the concert is going on. What do they care if the orchestra is playing them wonderful music? It is fashionable to go to the concert—so they go. They are fools. Philadelphians and, in fact, all Americans want to be bluffed. They have watched their conductors gyrate upon the dais before the orchestra for many years, and unless they can be kept entertained by the actions of the leader, they are disappointed.

He added that America was suffering from "the prima donna malady" and that audiences "disregarded everything but their beloved stars. This is what you Americans call 'bunk'." Additionally, he thought Philadelphia "the dirtiest city I have ever seen. Its streets are unkempt, its buildings unwashed."

No sooner did these remarks appear in print than Fritz Reiner, who was to follow Monteux and close the orchestra's season, leapt to the Philadelphians' defense. He was quoted in all the Philadelphia papers: "Monteux is a fool—talking bunk—and what I think of him is unprintable. . . . Philadelphia is the music centre of America. . . . [Walking out] is the inalienable right of the person who pays to hear the music. . . . People in Philadelphia know more about music than in any other city" (Hart 1994, 47).

Reiner was also quoted in several newspapers on 24 and 25 April as saying:

It's ridiculous. I know Philadelphia audiences. I do not think that M. Monteux knows them. If you have the ability, people will go to hear you. If you have not the ability, they will discover it. No publicity in the world can make a conductor a success forever.

Audiences are educated to comparative criticism. They seek the attitude of the director. If he is a mediocre man, with no personality, he may present a flawless performance, but he is not great. He has not the personality, the fire, the vigor, the delicacy.

As for the way audience members had walked out on *The Rite of Spring*, he added, "The first time I heard Stravinsky's 'Sacre' I was exhausted by close attention. How does M. Monteux know that the ladies were not exhausted?"

In his biography of Reiner, Philip Hart mentions that Reiner's remarks led many musically knowledgeable citizens in Philadelphia to begin to speak of him as Stokowski's possible successor. (Illness, in the form of neuritis, was the rumored reason for his sabbatical.) However, Stokowski remained for another eight years, and his successor was not Reiner, but Eugene Ormandy.

Monteux's comments about audiences preferring a slim, well-tailored conductor were quite naturally interpreted by many as a disparagement of Stokowski, an impression that he hastened to correct. In a letter to several Philadelphia newspapers and to *The New York Times*, not printed as such in the latter but appearing in an article on 25 April, he wrote:

Contrary to the headlines in many of the papers that my assertion that Americans prefer tall, well tailored conductors was said as a "well directed shot" at my friend Leopold Stokowski, I had absolutely no conductor in mind. In fact, I was thinking at the time of many conductors who have been decided successes here in America. I am convinced that the average concert goer attends the concerts to watch the conductor, be it Mr. Stokowski or any other artist.

They are so intent on seeing that they lose the charm and the emotion of the music; they forget the composer, the composition and the hard work of the orchestra in their adulation of the conductor who, after all, should be only the medium to interpret the composition.

Yes, I still insist that Americans, even Philadelphians, in spite of the wonderful ovation they gave me Saturday night, prefer to see a tall, slim conductor as, let us say, "gentlemen prefer blondes."

The newspapers and fair citizens of a great city did not take Monteux's comments lying down. A veritable hurricane of protest ensued in the form of editorial comment and letters to the editor. There was also, however, a mild breeze in support of Monteux, who had been criticized not only for his comments on Philadelphia audiences, but also for those on well-tailored conductors, and even for his remark about gentlemen's preferences. The bulk of the Friday afternoon audience, in any case, consisted not of gentlemen but of ladies. As for slim, well-tailored conductors, mention was made of other successful conductors, such as Mengelberg and Frederick Stock in Chicago, who were stocky (no pun intended) and not exactly fashion plates. On the other hand, Stokowski achieved his results not because he was tall, slim, and well tailored, but because he was a great conductor. Nor was it Toscanini's and Koussevitzky's waistlines and evening clothes that galvanized audiences. Monteux was considered to be a very capable though uneven conductor, certainly not yet a great one, and his remarks were judged petty and small minded. However, some letter writers felt that Reiner had been unprofessional in his criticism of a colleague.

Some writers disagreed with Monteux about Philadelphia's level of musical sophistication, or lack thereof, which was thought to be no better or worse than that of most American cities, and he was given credit for not waiting until he was safely back in Europe to deliver his screed but for "telling it like it is" while he was still there. But Lawrence Gilman, who had written so warmly of Monteux at the end of his Boston tenure, wrote in the *New York Herald Tribune* of 29 April 1928 that Monteux's difficulties in Philadelphia probably stemmed from the fact that he was not a conductor of genius, and that he was unfortunate enough to be replacing a conductor who was.

Not quoted by the wire services were some comments by Monteux in the *Jewish Times* about "the Jew in music," no doubt delivered because of the source of the original interview:

The Jew is the backbone of art. There is not one of the arts in which the Jew does not predominate. We are directly responsible for art. Were it not for our people, the artistic accomplishments of the world would almost face into oblivion. There would be no orchestras. Theatres would be unheard of. Art galleries would never be frequented. Perhaps it is because the Jew responds to the arts with such emotion. At any rate, we stand supreme as the cultural leaders of the world. George Gershwin is the "king of jazz" and Ernest Bloch's compositions bid fair to stand before all other modern musical writings.

Monteux did have one final week of concerts in Philadelphia after the Stravinsky performances, fortunately just before the interview in the *Jewish Times* appeared. For his final program he chose the Brahms First Symphony and *Scheherazade*, in that order. The critics noted that he conducted without a score for the first time since his visit began. Samuel L. Laciar, of the *Public Ledger*, on 21 April wrote that the orchestra had never played better under any conductor that season. In the green room after the concert, the members of the orchestra presented Monteux with a beautiful leather briefcase as a sign of their appreciation of his musicianship and their high personal regard for him.

The engagement with the Philadelphia Orchestra at an end, the Monteuxs set sail for Europe, Pierre again vowing never to return professionally to the United States. Having already married in Maryland, they decided that a European union would be appropriate, and on 6 September 1928 Doris and Pierre were wed a second time in a private ceremony in Brussels.

CHAPTER 10

The OSP

One of the great patronesses of French music was the Princess Edmonde de Polignac, who commissioned works from, among many others, Saint-Saëns, Gabriel Fauré, and Francis Poulenc, and hosted salons in her palatial Paris home. She was actually an American named Winnaretta Singer, of the Singer sewing-machine family, and hence was already quite wealthy when she married the prince. One of her colleagues in these activities was Gabrielle (Coco) Chanel, the famed fashion designer. The two women wielded great influence in Parisian artistic and financial circles and in 1928 were successful in organizing the funding for yet another symphony orchestra in the French capital—the Orchestre Symphonique de Paris.

A triumvirate of musicians active in Paris—the pianist Alfred Cortot and the conductors Louis Fourestier (1892–1976) and Swiss-born Ernest Ansermet (1883–1969)—spearheaded the idea for what became the OSP. Although Ansermet was active in Switzerland, having founded L'Orchestre de la Suisse Romande in Geneva in 1918, his interests were definitely Francophile, and he appeared often in Paris. He also had succeeded Monteux as conductor of Diaghilev's Ballets Russes.

It was the expressed mission of the OSP to present programs of lesser-known or misunderstood works of the great composers, as well as contemporary music, interspersed with standard repertoire, and in the best working conditions for the orchestra's eighty-four musicians. These included paying the players a salary sufficient to enable them to have the OSP as their primary activity. For years the orchestral scene in Paris had been a laughingstock in the rest of the musical world because of its infamous "deputy system." Under this system, a musician would contract to play a specific concert, but if he obtained better-paying engagements on any of the rehearsal dates, he could send a substitute to replace him at the rehearsals.

The practice had become so rampant that a famous story arose from this confusing situation, which was guaranteed to produce unpredictable performances. A long-suffering conductor had become especially distressed at the wholesale deputizing occurring in his orchestra, with new faces every day seemingly in every seat. One player in the second violin section, however, had faithfully attended every rehearsal. At the final rehearsal, when all were present, the conductor scolded his musicians for their cavalier attitude toward attending rehearsals. He then turned to the second violins and said, "I want to compliment and thank M. Leroux, the only member who has been present at every rehearsal." To which Leroux replied, "Thank you, maestro, but I will not be at the concert."

While the ranks of the OSP included some seasoned professionals, the majority of its members were prizewinning young professionals fresh out of the conservatory. Its concerts were to be given in the Salle Pleyel, which had opened in 1927. Pierre Monteux had originally been asked to conduct the group's first concerts, but his obligations in Amsterdam and Philadelphia in 1928 prevented his accepting. Meanwhile a fire in the Salle Pleyel delayed the orchestra's debut. It had to give its concerts in the Théâtre des Champs-Élysées until the end of December 1929, when the original venue was restored.

In the spring of 1929 Monteux accepted an invitation from his old friend Cortot to become the OSP's artistic director and principal conductor. This effectively removed Ansermet from the picture except for an occasional concert, not without understandable protestations on his part. (Fourestier was at the beginning of his career and thus accepted whatever he was offered. From 1946 to 1948 he was a principal conductor of French repertoire at the Metropolitan Opera, and from 1945 to 1963 he was professor of conducting at the Paris Conservatory.) For four years, then, Monteux was occupied with two major positions, as co-conductor of the Concertgebouw Orchestra and as artistic director and principal conductor of the OSP. That spring he conducted eight concerts that were billed as a Série de Printemps, beginning on 12 April with the following program:

> Weber: Overture to *Euryanthe*
> Brahms: Symphony No. 2 in D major
> Fauré: Ballade for Piano and Orchestra; Alfred Cortot, piano
> d'Indy: *Symphony on a French Mountain Air*; Alfred Cortot, piano
> Dukas: *The Sorcerer's Apprentice*

Monteux's series concluded on 31 May with an all-Stravinsky program consisting of the Suite from *The Firebird*, the complete *Petrushka*, and *The Rite of Spring*, a natural grouping for a concert but also a formidable one, which accounts for its being so rarely encountered. During its first season, 1928–29, the OSP performed sixty-three concerts under a variety of conductors, each preceded by at least six rehearsals.

Monteux's first program appears a bit contrary to the OSP's mission. But, he announced, it was important for a new orchestra such as this to have a grounding in the classic standard repertoire. Modern works would, of course, be presented, but not in such a way as to overshadow the classics, which were beneficial for the orchestra to play and were enjoyed by the public. Scanning the OSP's personnel list, one notices, amidst the cellos, the name of Boris Blinder, who would before long become the principal cellist of the San Francisco Symphony under Monteux's direction.

Later programs in the series of 1929 included the Paris premiere of Pijper's Third Symphony; the first performance of Francis Poulenc's *Concert champêtre*, with Wanda Landowska, who commissioned it, as harpsichord soloist; the first performance of Prokofiev's Third Symphony; and the Paris premiere of Leos Janácek's *Sinfonietta*. On 3 November 1929 Willem Mengelberg appeared as a guest conductor directing Richard Strauss's *Ein Heldenleben*, a work dedicated to Mengelberg and of which he was a prime interpreter. The following year he led a Beethoven festival. Interviewed in the 8 February 1930 issue of *Musical America*, Mengelberg remarked that he had not realized Monteux could develop a new orchestra into such a fine body of players in such a short time. He was greatly impressed to find, on arrival, such a carefully drilled orchestra, and such a thoroughly musical one. Monteux had created an ensemble upon which "any skilled conductor might play . . . as he would upon a first rate instrument." He further mentioned that each time he returns to the Concertgebouw Orchestra after Monteux has been in charge, he finds "no loss of excellence in the playing."

Monteux was greatly shaken by the news of Diaghilev's death on 19 August 1929. In later years, when Doris asked him why he had wept upon hearing of it (which he had done in private, alone), he replied:

> I wept for many reasons. Sergei Diaghilev was indubitably one of the first truly great personalities I had ever met. He was more to me than my Director. I respected his culture, his impeccable taste in all things, his continued awareness of talent in others and the fact that he dared! So few people dare. Then, too, he was kind to me and most thoughtful. He gave me my great chance and saw that it was not missed by lack of rehearsals. I owed him loyalty then, and still do. I loved him. (D. Monteux 1965, 90)

With the OSP Monteux gave an all-Prokofiev program on 18 December 1930, in which the composer was soloist in his Piano Concerto No. 2. Also included were the *Scythian Suite* and the first performance of the Fourth Symphony. The program of 29 March 1931 was devoted to Ravel's music, with the composer conducting *Le tombeau de Couperin* and *Boléro*, Monteux the complete *Daphnis et Chloé*.

While Monteux was not noted for performing the works of Alban Berg, or indeed of any members of the Second Viennese School, except for Schoenberg's *Verklärte Nacht*, he did conduct, on 29 March 1931, the Paris premiere of three fragments from Alban Berg's *Wozzeck* with the soprano Alice Bruhn. Stravinsky was a frequent visitor, conducting programs of his own music, and Monteux's old friends the Casadesus family appeared several times performing their latest newly discovered "ancient" music, one of which was a "Mozart" Concert Rondo for harpsichord, quartet of viols, and orchestra. The program carried the statement, "This work was published in the Breitkopf edition arranged for piano, and is given here in its original form."

It is interesting to note that all the programs contained the following admonition: "The public is respectfully requested to refrain from applause between the movements of a symphony." In later years Monteux would have a few words to say on that subject.

It was with the OSP that Monteux made his very first recordings, beginning with *The Rite of Spring* in May 1929. For some reason the group was identified on the labels and in the album simply as Grand Orchestre Symphonique. Considering the caliber of the orchestra as evidenced by later recordings, that of *The Rite* is really not very good. The timpani are very weak, the winds in general quite recessed. The recording favors the strings, which diminishes the piece's impact. Rhythms are often rushed, especially in the concluding "Danse sacrale," parts of which are frankly a mess. An exactly contemporaneous recording conducted by Stravinsky himself, with the Orchestre des Concerts Straram (another addition to the Parisian orchestral scene), is equally lacking in impact and precision. Of course, even in 1929, sixteen years after its premiere, *The Rite* still presented formidable difficulties for orchestras, and the OSP, a new ensemble, was inexperienced with the piece, as was the Straram Orchestra. These were the first two recordings of Stravinsky's masterpiece. (A recording made the following year by Leopold Stokowski and the Philadelphia Orchestra is notable for its precision and impact, but as they had given the American premiere in 1922 and had performed it again during the interim, the work was by that time fairly familiar to them. Besides, that was a well-established ensemble.)

The OSP's later recordings under Monteux (and under its own name), such as Ravel's *La valse* in 1930, give a greater indication of the group's abilities. This is especially true of Berlioz's *Symphonie fantastique*. Made in 1931, this recording was the first to reveal the OSP as the highly disciplined orchestra it was. To this day it is considered one of the greatest recorded performances of the work, and it remained Monteux's favorite of his several versions. Among its many attributes is the fact that the horns do not have the famous "wobble" so characteristic of horn playing of that period and even later in France.

A recording that was not made by the OSP was the source of another controversy in which Monteux was involved, though this one did not play itself out in the columns of newspapers. During 1928 and 1929 Stravinsky had composed his Capriccio for Piano and Orchestra, a score written with himself in mind as the soloist. He played the premiere on 6 December 1929 with the OSP conducted by Ansermet. Meanwhile, Stravinsky had become irritated when the French Gramophone Company, for whom Monteux had recorded *The Rite*, issued a press release making the following points:

1. That the interpretation of *Sacre* created by M. Monteux in his memorable premiere of 1913 has been approved and sanctioned by the composer.
2. That without the perseverance of M. Monteux, who repeated the *Sacre* in concert in 1914, the work would perhaps be forgotten today.
3. That the interpretation of M. Monteux is now considered as a classic, the only model on which all conductors base their performances. (Craft 1984, 65; Walsh 1999, 482)

Stravinsky had just made his own recording of *The Rite* for French Columbia, and he was not about to have someone else's recording, even Monteux's, trumpeted as the definitive version. Thus, in December 1929 he issued his own statement as part of an ad for his recording that appeared in the OSP's program book for the premiere of the Capriccio:

I am happy to state that the *Sacre du Printemps* just recorded under my direction for Columbia is a masterpiece of phonographic realization. To be specific, the dynamic element (which is the play of relationships, not the intensity of the sound), as well as the timbre of the *Sacre*, is conveyed by these new records in a way that could not be more evident. The result is a model of recording that renders a true service to all those who would like to learn the performance tradition of my work. (Craft 1984, 65)

Notice that Stravinsky's statement refers to the recording, not his conducting, of the work. Later, in a letter to Jean Bérard, Columbia's Paris director, he displayed his true colors and feelings concerning Monteux at that time:

If this poor Jew can find no other way of maintaining his prestige as an avant-garde musician with his admirers, I certainly shan't be the one to amuse myself by exposing this profiteer's intrigues. . . . This man of limited horizons, vain and small-spirited, something one often finds among orchestral musicians, was by a whim of fate the first to conduct *Petrushka* and *The Rite of Spring* at the Ballets Russes, since when he had dubbed himself the "creator" of *Petrushka* and the "creator" of *The Rite*. (Walsh 1999, 488)

The controversy did not stop there. Monteux was invited to conduct an all-Stravinsky concert in Brussels in the 1930–31 season, with the composer as soloist in the Capriccio. In a letter to Stravinsky dated 3 February 1930 Monteux stated that he had declined this engagement "since you are no longer satisfied with my interpretations." Stravinsky's reply of 4 March expressed astonishment at Monteux's statement. "Who told you that I am no longer satisfied with your performances of my works?" He continued, "I am sending a letter to the Brussels

Société Philharmonique accepting their offer to play my Capriccio under your direction and expressing my hope that you will reconsider your decision."

In a postscript Stravinsky added that he had learned that this concert on 13 December 1930 would now be conducted by Ansermet. "Since I saw Ansermet some days ago and told him of my desire to have you conduct this concert, . . . he was delighted and declared himself in complete agreement."

On 31 March Monteux replied, explaining why he assumed that Stravinsky no longer had confidence in his performances:

> First, you no longer entrust me with first performances of your works. Second, last spring, when I gave a festival of your music, you did not attend, telling me that you could not be in Paris; but I believe that you did not want to be seen at this concert. Third, the publicity pertaining to your recording of the *Sacre* says frankly that you do not approve of my "interpretations" of your works. These are the factors that led to my refusal of the Brussels concert.

Additional correspondence between the two refers to misunderstandings and the hope that these can be put behind them. But there was one more contretemps to come. Columbia Records was making arrangements for Stravinsky to record his Capriccio with the OSP conducted by Ansermet, not Monteux. To this development Monteux quite naturally took offense, since the OSP was now his orchestra, not Ansermet's, even though the latter had been involved in its creation. On 17 April Monteux wrote to Stravinsky:

> There is no such thing as recording an orchestra with a conductor other than its own. I still don't see a record from the Concertgebouw without Mengelberg, from the Concerts Colonne without Pierné, from the Concerts Pasdeloup without [Rhené] Baton!! etc., etc. You must understand that [being obliged to take] Ansermet is disagreeable to me; he is making a recording with the OSP without me."

Monteux then declared that he would be "prepared to allow you to have my orchestra for this recording on condition that the name of the orchestra is not mentioned."

To this letter Stravinsky replied on 19 April:

> Concerning the question of recording, I must tell you that I never had any intention of putting the name of the orchestra on the records; your proposal is therefore irrelevant. Neither in the case of *Petrushka*, nor in those of *Firebird* and *Sacre*, which I recorded with the Orchestre Straram, did the question of mentioning or not mentioning the name of the orchestra arise. As for Ansermet, ever since the premiere of the Capriccio, I have been

proposing to him to record the piece with me, and I do not think that I committed a blunder in asking him, and not you, to conduct the orchestral accompaniment. After all, he created the orchestra of which you are today the conductor, and he continues again this year to work with this orchestra: he can hardly be considered an outsider to the OSP. (Craft 1984, 66–70)

In the end, Stravinsky and Anserment recorded the Capriccio with the Straram Orchestra.

An important activity for the OSP was touring. In the spring of 1930 a tour of Belgium and Holland included, on 14 April, a concert in Amsterdam's Concertgebouw. As Monteux was still co-conductor of the Concertgebouw Orchestra, great interest naturally attached to his appearance with his "other" orchestra. In a program of Berlioz, Franck, Debussy, and Ravel, composers whose works he frequently conducted in Amsterdam, the two orchestras and Monteux's direction of them were compared, and the critics, not surprisingly, found them to be entirely different.

The differences of culture and mentality between the French and the Dutch were dispassionately remarked upon, as was the fact that Monteux had put his own personal stamp on the OSP, just as the Concertgebouw Orchestra, no matter who conducted it, was indisputably Mengelberg's ensemble. Suppleness, grace, and elegance were the principal characteristics found in the French group; the woodwinds were especially singled out for their delicate colorations. While not perfect, the brass were nevertheless not overbearing. The strings, though, were felt to be a bit weak, except for the double basses. The consensus was that, considering that the orchestra had been in existence only a year and a half, Monteux had obtained truly remarkable results, and one critic remarked (perhaps snidely) that he had never achieved such results with the Concertgebouw Orchestra. Present at the concert was Mengelberg himself, who responded with extremely vociferous support.

As 1930 progressed economic conditions in Europe worsened, the result of the Great Depression in which the world had become engulfed. The effect on the OSP was devastating, for two of the banks that had helped fund the orchestra since its inception failed, and other benefactors were unable to maintain their support either at its original level or at all. Robert Lyon, chief administrator of the orchestra, who was responsible for coordinating the fund-raising efforts, reached the conclusion that it was no longer possible for the OSP to continue paying the high salaries to which the musicians and conductors had become accustomed, so he worked with Monteux and the orchestra members to make the group truly cooperative. That is, an association was formed along the lines of that of the Colonne and Lamoureux Orchestras whereby each member was a shareholder, and at the end of a given period such money as had been acquired through concerts or recordings would be equally divided. Monteux often declined his share and even contributed money out of his own pocket to help keep the orchestra afloat. As a result of this new format, the orchestra now became known as Les Artistes Associés de l'Orchestre Symphonique de Paris.

It was now necessary, when engaging soloists and conductors, to persuade them to accept reduced fees. Such guest artists as Béla Bartók, Alfred Cortot, Arthur Rubinstein, and Jacques Thibaud, and guest conductors Alfredo Casella, Otto Klemperer, Dimitri Mitropoulos, and Paul Paray, among others, acquiesced. However, Monteux had a different experience with Rachmaninoff.

The great Russian composer-pianist had already been engaged at his normal fee, "exorbitant for Paris," but it was thought by the orchestra committee that a Sunday concert in the Salle Pleyel would attract the White Russians living in Paris and the Americans as well, especially as Rachmaninoff had not appeared in that city for many years. A full house was anticipated, but to everyone's desperation, only half a house materialized. The orchestra could not afford to pay Rachmaninoff his fee. Monteux wrote to him personally, explaining the orchestra's plight— that at the end of the year the musicians could not hope to make more than three thousand francs ("small, nearly valueless pre-war francs"). "I asked him as a gesture toward these French musicians to forfeit a part of his fee, calling his attention to the fact that after expenses were paid, there would be absolutely nothing left." Rachmaninoff's reply was "very, very polite, full of compliments for myself and the orchestra, but—alas, the master could not help us in our predicament; to do so would be contrary to his business rule, and after all there is a contract, n'est-ce pas?" (D. Monteux 1965, 159).

Monteux had a guest engagement of some significance during the summer of 1931. He made another trip to the United States, primarily for two weeks of concerts at the Hollywood Bowl. Afterward he journeyed a few hundred miles north for a single concert, on 25 August, with the San Francisco Symphony Orchestra in the city's Civic Auditorium. Here he led a program of French music, with works of Chabrier, Franck, and Rabaud preparing the way for a performance of Saint-Saëns's Third Symphony. He enjoyed a great success in both cities, and this time there was no talk of not returning to the United States.

In the fall of 1931 the OSP toured Germany and on 19 November became the first French orchestra to perform in Berlin since 1914, presenting the following program:

> Berlioz: *Symphonie fantastique*
> Franck: *Symphonic Variations*; François Lang, piano
> Debussy: *La mer*
> Ravel: *Rapsodie espagnole*

The newspaper reviews spoke of the great discipline of the orchestra and the extreme finesse of its tonal colorations. Critics felt that those German conductors who attended received a lesson in how to interpret French music. According to Monteux:

> When the symphony came to its dramatic end, the public rushed forward to the stage, crying, "Vive l'amitié, long live our friendship!" Hands were stretched toward us, many wept and waved handkerchiefs. This demonstration went on for seventeen minutes!
>
> We were profoundly impressed by this mass emotion for our music and felt that our tour had been more than a success. We could not believe there could be a war between our two countries ever again. Alas, just four months after this poignant episode, Adolf Hitler came into power and this same Berlin public with the same mass hysteria cried, "Vive Hitler, vive der Fuehrer!" and waved handkerchiefs and wept as they cheered. It was he who led their Fantastic Symphony to its bitter end. (D. Monteux 1965, 161)

(Monteux was a bit off in his recollection of dates: Hitler did not come to power until 1933.)

Monteux liked to tell of the concert at which the OSP presented the great Russian-born violinist Nathan Milstein (1903–1992) in his Paris debut. Milstein had asked to play the Glazunov concerto, so Monteux changed the announced program to one of all Russian music, ending with Tchaikovsky's "Pathétique" Symphony instead of Schubert's "Great" C major Symphony. After the first movement of the Tchaikovsky there was some commotion in the hall, after which a stentorian voice shouted from the second balcony, "Monsieur Monteux, Maître, you should be ashamed to play that dirty music when you promised us the divine music of Franz Schubert!" Later that week "we received a superb article from a leading critic praising our unplayed Schubert" (D. Monteux 1965, 162).

Because of the depression, it became necessary for the OSP to expand its activities so as to gain greater employment for the members. In 1932, principally to provide the orchestra with something to do in the summer months, Monteux began his conducting classes in Paris; twenty-three students were in the first one. The lessons were held twice weekly, with some of the OSP players participating. At the end of the session the orchestra members were to select one pupil to receive a prize: a diploma and a public concert the following season with the entire orchestra in the Salle Pleyel. So rigorous was Monteux's instruction, and so demanding were the musicians, that no student was chosen for the first three years.

The first to win the prize was Charles Bruck, who conducted his debut concert on 29 November 1936 with a program of Haydn's "Clock" Symphony, Ravel's *Le tombeau de Couperin*, and Stravinsky's *Petrushka*, along with vocal works sung by the Spanish mezzo-soprano Conchita Velásquez. Bruck went on to become the chief conductor of the French National Radio Orchestra in Strasbourg and of the Philharmonic Orchestra of French Radio and Television in Paris, eventually taking on another post of interest (of which more later).

In 1936 the school moved, without the orchestra, to Monteux's summer home in the village of Les Baux (so named because of the presence of bauxite in the area) in Provence. The French composer Marcel Landowski (1915–2000), a pupil there, described Monteux's teaching:

> His teaching methods were unpretentious. The student arrived at Monteux's with scores in hand. Every student had to be able to sing the various parts pretty much by heart, in the absence of orchestra or even piano. Monteux followed attentively, and he readily interrupted when a point of difficulty arose for conductor or instrumentalist. He prepared the musical terrain note for note.
>
> His instruction began with memory exercises, as a step to thorough knowledge of the score. A second run-through would then analyze its structures and scrutinize its layout. As his sacred maxim went: "One must have the score in one's head, not one's head in the score." [This remark has frequently been attributed to both Gustav Mahler and Richard Strauss. It is apparently one of those sayings the exact origin of which remains unknown.]
>
> This method encouraged a critical approach to works and discouraged any ambition for showy effects (such as "here come the trombones"). We students were ready to face an orchestra only after having worked out each nuance of the score, and not until we were able to reconstitute its structure mentally. Monteux had an extraordinary musical memory. Each of his directions took the totality of the score into account, and each, however small, had a purpose. He was at ease with the present because he had the wisdom and the humility to explore the past. (Landowski 1994)

When possible, four-hand piano arrangements of symphonies and other orchestral works were used for the conducting classes, and Monteux's sister-in-law Hilda Davis was often one of the pianists. She has left behind a description of a typical session in 1938:

> The students in conducting were two Americans, a young Dutch boy of thirteen with an amazing talent, and a Romanian. . . . As two of the conductors played piano, I often had a chance to look on, taking notes on Mr. Monteux's remarks, which were always amazing in his knowledge of the scores; sometimes funny because of his charming French way of speaking English and because of his love of American slang. But all in all the classes were most serious, sometimes almost tense. Two of the students conducted Brahms, the Dutch boy Mozart, and one American started with "Nuages" by Debussy but at the end of one hour was persuaded to "try something more simple" by Monteux. Naturally we occasionally made mistakes, in fact we were encouraged to make them as the conductor was supposed to

know the notes of every instrument we were imitating. (H. Davis, private papers)

Some of Monteux's remarks, with Hilda's editorial comments, follow:

"Well gentlemen. Who will start this morning? Tally? All right. You know it is more difficult to conduct here than with an orchestra because in an orchestra in mistakes of syncopation or wrong notes, one man would correct himself. Here the four hands take all parts. One must stop often to correct errors therefore learning the score better."

"What happened there? Yes, they have an imitation. But something terrible happened. They played together."

"Here you must have an absolute *pianissimo* to hear the horns."

"Tell him what he did. [The student doesn't know.] Well, he didn't play the syncopation."

"If they don't feel your beat then it makes a windmill and is of no use. [Student: "He doesn't follow me."] Well then, follow him. Sometimes, in an orchestra, that happens. Then you make the orchestra play with him then pick up the tempo later. Don't double your body just conduct with your hands."

"The trumpets and horns—*bum, bum, bum*. Make them sound."

"Attack it. You must do it with your head, or sing with them or anyway you can, but try to exteriorize. You have a whole orchestra, not just these two."

[Student starts the last *forte*] "Well, why! Tell them why! Tell them that they played wrong notes! Don't waste time. An orchestra is expensive. Make them work exactly like they were your players. Don't be kind to them."

"Give them a signal. At that interval they do not have time with their lips and bows. Make them give a pause."

"The real bass is F. You must hear it. Now stop! Correct all the wrong notes that they played.[The student doesn't know.] Well, he played a D-flat in the scale; it's not in the score."

"Your beat isn't decisive enough. Beat a little larger with your wrist. The timpani must see too."

"If you conduct with your whole body, it drags, and from the back it looks like you were conducting with your posterior. Give a real crescendo. Don't wiggle your fingers. It looks like you tickle a dog."

"You're going back? Did you tell him why? Don't stop the orchestra without explaining to them. If you stop for yourself don't let them know. They'll lose respect for you."

"Make the second part realize that's a bassoon part. He mustn't play it too loud. Now [impatiently] don't play it rotten any longer."

[Dazed expression on conductor's face] "Well, they didn't play the right notes."

"I didn't hear that tweet, tweet, twa, twa!"

"Your wrist is too stiff! It drags all the time [claps it in tempo]."

"Give them a sock in the puss. When the *forte* comes, give it, with your appearance. Don't have it look all the same."

"What was wrong there? [another dazed look]. I'll tell you! Nothing! Well, come on. Don't waste the orchestra's time."

"If you let him continue the wrong notes, you'll get it in your ear."

"C does not exist in that phrase. When the basses hold the note so long, you must give them the next change."

"There's no ritard but a little heavy. If you play that fast, it's vulgar."

"Conduct! Force them to play with you!" [The baton broke and flew across the room. We laughed but the conductor sank into a chair, exhausted.] (H. Davis, private papers)

Meanwhile, Monteux's daughter Nancie (as she now spelled her name) had begun to establish herself as a dancer, and on 8 November 1936 she performed as soloist with Monteux and the OSP. This, her European debut, was an unusual event, for symphony orchestras rarely engage dancers as guest soloists. On this occasion the program opened with Bach's Suite No. 2 in B minor, in which Nancie danced the Rondo, Menuet, and Badinerie movements. Later she appeared in the Ballet Music from Schubert's *Rosamunde*, Debussy's *Danses: sacrée et profane*, the March from Prokofiev's *Love for Three Oranges*, and the second of Chabrier's *Trois valses romantiques*. (Pierre had officially adopted Doris's children; Nancie took the name of Monteux, while Donald retained the name Purslow.)

Besides his work with the OSP and the Concertgebouw Orchestra, Monteux had attained a busy life as a guest conductor. The year 1932 saw him fulfilling engagements in Vienna, Brussels, Manchester, Liverpool, Florence, Barcelona, Valencia, Madrid, Bilbao, Lyon, Geneva, Strasbourg, and, in May 1933, Berlin. In the 25 January 1933 edition of *Petit Parisien*, René Jaubert referred to Monteux as "the Phileas Fogg of music."

There was concern in Amsterdam among the members of the Concertgebouw Orchestra and the Wagner Society, and in France among the members of the OSP and others, when, on 20 May 1933, Monteux conducted a concert in Berlin with that city's Philharmonic Orchestra. Coming so soon after Adolf Hitler and his National Socialist Party had assumed power in Germany, this engagement was severely criticized in both France and the Netherlands. It was thought that Monteux was replacing the Jewish Bruno Walter on that occasion. Monteux's defense was that he was not replacing Walter—he and Walter were *co-religionnaires*, and if this allegation were true, he would have been a traitor to his colleagues and to his religion. He had been engaged in November 1932, before the current government had come to power, and he was not replacing anyone. The invitation had come directly from the Berlin Philharmonic as a result of the OSP's success in Berlin the year before. Monteux asked the composer Florent Schmitt (1870–1958) to help exonerate him from an accusation that was odious to him. Schmitt, whose sympathies would ultimately lean more toward Germany than France, did so in a letter to various French newspapers, stating that Monteux had not been mistaken, that the whole affair was part of the puny ransoms of celebrity, and that Monteux's worth as a great conductor would not be damaged as a result. One cannot help but feel, however, that once Hitler came to power, Toscanini would have canceled such an engagement (as he did on a number of occasions.)

On 30 December 1933 Monteux was in Milan conducting the Orchestra della Società Antiche Italiana Concerti Orchestrali (Ancient Society of Italian Orchestral Concerts) under the auspices of the Federazione Provinciale Fascista Milanese (Milanese Provincial Fascist Federation), another aberration in his career, and another concert that Toscanini would surely have canceled.

Although Monteux was a frequent visitor to London in his last years, on 15 March 1934 he made what was then a rare appearance in the British capital conducting Sir Thomas Beecham's London Philharmonic Orchestra, formed just two years before. For this event his old Paris Conservatory classmate, the violinist Jacques Thibaud, was the soloist in Lalo's *Symphonie espagnole*; the all-French program concluded with the Second Suite from *Daphnis et Chloé*.

As for the OSP, the orchestra continued performing and recording until 1939, when the still-uncertain economic situation in Europe and the exigencies attendant to the beginning of World War II caused it to cease operations entirely.

INTERLUDE

Les Baux

Doris Monteux wrote in a private journal of traveling with Pierre in February 1929 to the south of France to visit the town of Monteux, whence the Monteux family originated. Pierre and Doris had a vague idea that if Monteux turned out to be a charming old Provençal town they might buy a home there. Doris thought it would look very chic and impressive to have engraved visiting cards announcing "M et Mme Pierre Monteux de Monteux."

First the Monteuxs visited beautiful Avignon. From there they drove to Monteux, only to have their hopes dashed. There really was not much to see there—the ruins where Pope Clement V had been imprisoned, a fireworks factory, some narrow filthy streets, and one small hotel. Seated at a table for lunch in the hotel and surrounded by factory workers, Pierre mentioned that his own name was Monteux. An old man seated opposite asked him if he was any relation to "Caddy" Monteux of Entraigues. "I should say so," replied Pierre; "that is my father." The old man then began a recitation on the young years of Gustave Monteux, his intensely romantic nature, his poetry in praise of rosy breasts and limpid eyes, and his great attraction to and fondness for beautiful women, none of which was news to Pierre or Doris.

Returning to Avignon, the Monteuxs proceeded to St. Remy, a village noted for Greek and Roman ruins and known as the garden center of France. After a few days there they were attracted by a description in the Michelin Guide of "Les Baux, historic feudal city, thirteenth-century castle, view of 100 kilometers," and so forth. In striking contrast to Monteux, this they found to be a place of dramatic ruins and ageless beauty. When they had finished sightseeing they repaired to the single hotel at the gate of the town, for it was time for their usual cup of chocolate and brioche.

Doris and Pierre were met at the door of the Hôtellerie de la Reine Jeanne by Madame Dumas, owner of the hotel, a charming woman who spoke excellent English. Having decided to spend the night there, the Monteuxs were shown the only room in the hotel with a bath. As they were enjoying their chocolate and brioche in the hotel's dining area, Doris noticed a child knitting by the stove in the

118

corner. The girl reminded her of an American Indian princess she had seen in pictures, with her dark eyes, ivory skin, and two long thick braids of black hair. Doris felt an immediate fascination, even love and sympathy, for her. Madame Dumas then presented her thirteen-year-old daughter Marianne Rose to Doris, explaining that everyone called her Mano.

So enchanted were the Monteuxs with Les Baux, the small hotel, and the Dumas family, which included an elderly grandmother, that they spent three weeks there. (Pierre apparently had no engagements at the time.) The grandmother and Mano accompanied them on various sightseeing excursions in the area. When it was time to leave, while saying their good-byes, Mano burst into tears and clung to Doris, who told her she would write to her every day, adding laughingly, "And what is more, *ma cherie*, you will be Donald's wife, I will see to it." Doris loved being a matchmaker (and could at times be an un-matchmaker as well). In this case she was successful, for several years later, her prediction came true. Donald and Mano would eventually open their own restaurant in the town, she doing the cooking, he tending to the nonculinary details.

Doris and Pierre returned to Les Baux each year until the outbreak of World War II. At first they stayed in the hotel, but later they bought a house there—the house where Pierre presided over his summer conducting classes.

CHAPTER 11

Arrival in San Francisco

In the United States the music directorship for which Pierre Monteux is best known is that of the San Francisco Symphony Orchestra, an organization that had experienced several periods of instability prior to his arrival. The year 1881, in which the Boston Symphony was also founded, saw the beginning of orchestral life in San Francisco with the formation of the San Francisco Philharmonic Society. This orchestra, along with a few others, led a sporadic existence until the great San Francisco earthquake and fire of 1906, which effectively put an end to most of the city's cultural life (not to mention most of the city itself).

It was not until 1911 that San Franciscans felt sufficiently recovered to welcome another orchestra, the San Francisco Symphony, which played its first concert on 8 December of that year. The American composer and conductor Henry Hadley was its first director, the only American to hold that post until Michael Tilson Thomas more than eighty years later. Hadley remained with the orchestra until 1915 and was succeeded by the German Alfred Hertz, whose tenure lasted until 1930. Under Hertz the orchestra made quite a few recordings for RCA, beginning in 1925, mostly of short pieces requiring a single 78-rpm disc, but also including Beethoven's *Leonore* Overture No. 3, Liszt's *Les préludes*, and excerpts from Wagner's *Parsifal*.

Like the rest of the country, the San Francisco Symphony went through a difficult period during the depression years, especially the early ones. From 1931 to 1934 the conductorship was shared by the Englishman Basil Cameron and the Russian Issay Dobrowen. As financial support for the orchestra waned, it became necessary to cancel the 1934–35 season entirely.

Enter a remarkable woman, Leonora Wood Armsby. A native New Yorker, Mrs. Armsby had grown up in a music-loving family and learned to play the piano by ear. However, in middle age she decided to study music more seriously, both aural training and reading and writing music. She composed a collection of simple children's pieces that was adopted by various settlement music schools in New York City, most notably the Greenwich School, for which she soon began to do charitable work. After a short time, in 1920 she was appointed treasurer of the school.

120

Her fund-raising activities brought her into contact with members of New York society, and soon she found herself on the board of directors of the Schola Cantorum, one of New York's major choral groups, which often performed with the New York Philharmonic. Meanwhile, at various social and musical functions (teas, musicales, and the like), she had the opportunity to mingle with and meet such figures as Stravinsky, Léon Bakst, José Iturbi, and Olin Downes, already the chief music critic of *The New York Times*. It was at one of these events that Mrs. Armsby first heard the name of Pierre Monteux.

After a short period of further musical study in Paris, she returned to New York in 1926 and almost immediately traveled west to her family's summer home in Burlingame, California, a suburb of San Francisco. There she became involved in plans to present the San Francisco Symphony Orchestra in a series of ten Sunday afternoon concerts in an outdoor theater in an area called Woodland. So great was her enthusiasm for this project that she became not only its president, but officially a Californian who visited New York, rather than the opposite.

Over a ten-year period the Woodland Theatre in Burlingame was able to secure the services of such conductors as Albert Coates, Ossip Gabrilowitsch, Eugene Goossens, Henry Hadley, Alfred Hertz, Bernardino Molinari, Artur Rodzinski, Nikolai Sokoloff, Frederick Stock, and Bruno Walter, among others. A photo in Mrs. Armsby's book, *We Shall Have Music*, shows the composer Ernest Bloch conducting a concert.

The decision by the Musical Association, the parent body of the San Francisco Symphony, to cancel its 1934–35 season for lack of funds created much consternation in the city, and various ideas for reviving the orchestra were discussed. The most unprecedented idea was the one actually adopted. With the cooperation of the city administration and Local 6 of the American Federation of Musicians, a special election was held in May 1935 in which the citizenry of San Francisco voted for an *ad valorem* tax of one-half cent per $100 in property valuation for the benefit of the orchestra.

To safeguard the use of these funds, estimated to be $40,000, the city government created an arts commission that would purchase concerts from the Musical Association and present them to the public at popular prices. Thus began the San Francisco Symphony's Municipal Concerts series in the Civic Auditorium, a ten-thousand-seat structure not at all well suited for symphony concerts.

Leonora Armsby's success with the Woodland concerts led to her invitation to become managing director of the reorganized Musical Association, a post she accepted somewhat reluctantly. Her first responsibility was to choose a conductor. While the term "music director" was not then in general use, that was what was wanted—someone who would be in charge of every musical aspect of the operation, auditioning musicians, training the orchestra, planning programs, selecting guest conductors and soloists, and, of course, conducting the bulk of the concerts. Of various conductors who might be available, one name stood out to Mrs. Armsby: that of Pierre Monteux. She was aware of his having premiered major works of Stravinsky and Ravel, of his rebuilding efforts in Boston, and of his work with the Orchestre Symphonique de Paris. Olin Downes had once told her, "There is a man over in Boston every bit as gifted as Toscanini, only he has a larger waistline!" (Armsby 1960, 38).

Monteux had made his first appearance with the San Francisco Symphony on 25 August 1931 at the Civic Auditorium under the auspices of the San Francisco Summer Symphony Association. A letter from the violinist Mischa Elman praised Monteux's work and expressed the opinion that he would be just the right man for San Francisco, of which Elman's wife, Helen, was, coincidentally, a native.

In the summer of 1935 Monteux was conducting again at the Hollywood Bowl. At the urging of the Musical Association, Mrs. Armsby traveled to Los Angeles to meet with him. She had no idea whether he would actually be interested in coming to San Francisco. Impressed by "the dignity, the modesty, the self-effacement of this great musician" (Armsby 1960, 39), she proceeded to outline for him the problems of the struggling orchestra, both musical and financial, capping it all off with the fact that they had only $12,000 in their treasury, though there was the prospect of more through the recent tax. It was also hoped that signing Monteux would increase interest in the orchestra and bring in further revenue.

What Mrs. Armsby may not have realized was that Monteux, world famous as he already was, did not at the time have a permanent position, was not wealthy, and frankly could have used the additional income, little though it may have been at first. After a day to think about it and discuss it with Doris, Monteux accepted the invitation, although not with great enthusiasm. He was concerned about relinquishing his work with the Orchestre Symphonique de Paris (even though he was making very little, if any, money from it) and other possible European engagements and giving up both the school for conductors and his home in France, all for a proposition that looked a bit risky to him. Nor was Doris enthusiastic. She "had the feeling that once out west, with the vast waters of the Pacific Ocean staring me in the face, I would be completely estranged from my world, which was the east coast of the United States and the old Europe which I loved so deeply. I felt no affinity for the west at that time" (D. Monteux 1965, 179–80).

In fact, the Monteuxs chose not to live year-round in San Francisco, odd as that may seem to those who know the city and its legendary beauty and charm. They were in residence for the length of the symphony season, which was never more than between four and five months a year, but they did not actually have a home there. Initially they lived in the Cathedral Apartments, but for most of Pierre's seventeen seasons with the symphony they occupied a suite in the Fairmont Hotel. Though it is less so in today's era of jet travel, being "a part of the community" was important in those days for a conductor of a symphony orchestra. Perhaps the Monteuxs felt that year-round residence would make them too much a part of the community—that there should still be a certain amount of distance between the maestro and his musicians and audience. Conversely, there was also some fascination, even glamour, to a community in the idea of their conductor's coming in from, say, Europe or New York just before the start of a season and immediately leaving at the end. But during the symphony season, the Monteuxs were, for all intents and purposes, a part of the community.

Before beginning his work in San Francisco, Monteux conducted the first four weeks of the Los Angeles Philharmonic's 1935–36 season. Otto Klemperer was then that orchestra's principal conductor but was fulfilling a ten-week engagement with the New York Philharmonic. Monteux's opening-week program consisted of Bach's Third Orchestral Suite, Schumann's *Manfred* Overture, Debussy's Three Nocturnes, and the Third Symphony of Saint-Saëns, otherwise known as the Organ Symphony. While this last work has since become quite popular, it was something of a rarity on concert programs in those days. Unfortunately, it is the only one of the great late-nineteenth-century French symphonies (including those of César Franck, Ernest Chausson, and Vincent d'Indy) of which no Monteux recording exists.

Of the Los Angeles programs, which included four subscription pairs, four separate Saturday night programs, a Young People's Concert, and several out-of-town dates, two are of special interest, for different reasons. The season's first Young People's Concert, on the morning of 7 December, was in the nature of a family affair, for Doris Monteux was the commentator and Nancie appeared as a dancer, performing to two of the dance movements of the Bach Third Suite, the ballet music from Schubert's *Rosamunde*, and the Brahms Hungarian Dance No. 5. According to the *Los Angeles Herald and Express* of 8 December, Madame Monteux was a very capable and engaging lecturer and Nancie a most graceful dancer, her sense of rhythm much like her father's.

That evening the actor Fritz Leiber participated in a program of music inspired by Shakespeare, reciting lines from *Coriolanus*, *Romeo and Juliet*, and *Hamlet*, in between the orchestra's performance of works by Beethoven, German, Honegger, Berlioz, Tchaikovsky, and Nicolai. (It was perhaps stretching things a bit to include Beethoven's *Coriolan* Overture, which is based not on Shakespeare but on a play by Heinrich von Collin.) Monteux was to offer a similar program in San Francisco.

Also of interest is a program that did not take place. During his Los Angeles visit, Monteux became acquainted with the work of the African American tap dancer Bill "Bojangles" Robinson, well known through his many motion picture appearances. So impressed was Monteux with Robinson's artistry and agility that he proposed an appearance for him with the Los Angeles Philharmonic if a suitable date could be found—otherwise he would perform in San Francisco. As quoted in the *Pasadena Post* of 8 December 1935, Monteux said of Robinson, "He expresses as much beauty with his feet as a singer does with his voice. I am happy to be the one to introduce him as a classical artist."

The prospect of Robinson's tap dancing to the great works of the masters brought a great deal of apprehension to the traditionalists among Los Angeles music lovers, but Isabel Morse Jones praised the idea in the *Los Angeles Times* of

15 December 1935. Her article emphasized the importance of rhythm in music and went on to say that a few years earlier, Maud Allan had managed to dance aimlessly to Tchaikovsky's "Pathétique" Symphony with no attention whatsoever to the work's rhythm, and that the public accepted it because it was thought to be highbrow art. She continued that Monteux believed rhythm was an important factor in American life and was impressed with the possibility of experimentation involving music and dance. Besides, Jones wrote, Robinson's sense of humor was something everyone could appreciate, and that combination of humor and rhythm was something the Philharmonic could use a little more of. She further felt that such a program could be beneficial in bringing about a better relationship between the Philharmonic and the general public. As might be expected, however, a suitable date could not be found for this program.

Monteux concluded his Los Angeles engagement with a special Saturday night concert on 28 December, for which the great soprano Maria Jeritza, a favorite of Richard Strauss's, was guest soloist. Considerable interest was attached to Jeritza's appearance, especially for the Hollywood crowd, for the glamorous soprano had recently married the film executive Winfield Sheehan. Although she did not sing anything by Strauss, she was hailed for her performance of an aria from Tchaikovsky's *Joan of Arc*, an arrangement of Fritz Kreisler's *Liebesleid*, and an aria from Franz Lehár's *Paganini*, not to mention her encore of Brünnhilde's battle cry from *Die Walküre*. For his part, Monteux's interpretations of Strauss's *Don Juan* and Ravel's *La valse* were also highly praised.

While Monteux was in Los Angeles, the city of San Francisco was abuzz with preparations for his arrival. Not one day went by without some sort of article heralding his coming in one or another of the many city and area newspapers. "San Francisco Plans for Splendid Year of Musical Achievements," "Brilliant Symphony Season Anticipated," "Sales Record Set by S. F. Symphony," "Pierre Monteux Arrives Monday," "Monteux Assuming New Post in S. F. Next Week," "Symphony Leader Here Today," "Monteux Conducts First Rehearsal"—these were just a few of the headlines announcing the rebirth of symphonic musical life in San Francisco.

Leonora Wood Armsby was correct in feeling that the engagement of Monteux would result in increased funding for the orchestra. Many members of the Musical Association's board of directors became regular visitors to the chamber of commerce, various civic clubs, and any other place where they felt money could be raised, with the result that, as Mrs. Armsby put it, "dozens of generous spirits ... opened their hearts to the liberation of music" (Armsby 1960, 52).

Meanwhile, Pierre Monteux's much-anticipated first rehearsal was held the morning of 31 December 1935 in the War Memorial Opera House. This imposing structure, seating 3252 and dedicated to the heroes of World War I, had been completed in 1932 as a home for both the symphony and the opera company. As quoted in the *San Francisco Chronicle* of 1 January 1936, Monteux somewhat cautiously declared:

Of course, a first rehearsal is merely an introduction and there is little to be said. After all we are musicians, all of us, and had no difficulty understanding each other. This first rehearsal, though, carries out the preconceived impression that I would have a particularly intelligent and musicianly body of players.

He later told his wife more frankly that

> it was necessary to make many additions as the orchestra had been severely diminished by the exodus of many musicians to the studios of Hollywood where work was steady and the pay excellent. Unhappily, I found that there were very few truly first-class musicians of symphony caliber to choose from in the Bay region. (D. Monteux 1965, 180)

At that time and throughout his tenure, the Musicians Union insisted that only local musicians be employed by the symphony, unless absolutely no one was available for a given position.

The week before the opening concert, a small contretemps arose over this very issue of union musicians. As there was still an opening for principal oboe, Monteux wanted to engage a player from New York, while the Musicians Union lobbied in favor of promoting the second oboist, Julius Shanis, to principal. The New York oboist duly arrived, and for two days Monteux listened to both him and Shanis during rehearsals. Finally he decided that Shanis should get the job. "2nd Oboe First!—Monteux Admits Mistake" was the headline in the 9 January *San Francisco Examiner*. Monteux commented that "the way to correct a mistake is to correct it."

Curiously, Mrs. Armsby misremembers the date, year, and program of the opening concert, giving it as 10 December 1935, when Monteux was still in Los Angeles (an error repeated in Jean-Philippe Mousnier's book). It was actually on Friday afternoon, 10 January 1936, that Pierre Monteux led the newly reconstituted San Francisco Symphony Orchestra in the following program:

> Bach-Respighi: Passacaglia and Fugue in C minor
> Beethoven: Symphony No. 7 in A major
> Debussy: Three Nocturnes (with women of the Municipal Chorus)
> Strauss: *Till Eulenspiegel's Merry Pranks*

Respighi's Bach transcription, unfashionable today, was a special favorite of Monteux's, and he programmed it as the opening work on several important occasions. (Respighi had made the transcription just a few years before at the behest of Arturo Toscanini, who wanted his own version to counter his rival Leopold Stokowski's transcription of the same work.)

The previous Sunday's edition of the *San Francisco Chronicle* contained the critic Alfred Frankenstein's notes for the program. His 11 January review of the

opening concert began, "There is a symphony orchestra again in San Francisco."
Monteux was hailed as

> one of the world's most authoritative and imaginative symphonic con-
> ductors, [who] does not bat an eye no matter how vast the wave of sound
> or how spicy the excitement of the music. He conducts Bach and Beethoven
> and Debussy, bringing out their essence. He does not conduct Pierre
> Monteux. Not a gesture or movement was addressed to the galleries. . . .
> Eulenspiegel was played yesterday afternoon as if it were being given its
> world premiere. . . . The San Francisco Symphony is a first rate ensemble,
> which means an aggregation of splendid artists.

For Alexander Fried in the *Examiner*, "At one stride, the orchestra stands in
the highest estate of its 24 years' career. . . . Its balance and its lyric articulation are
as fine as only a master leader, a master ear and a master taste can make them."
All the area newspapers were unanimous in declaring the event a triumph for
orchestra and conductor.

Writing in *The San Francisco News* of 13 January, the music editor, Marjorie
Fisher, exclaimed:

> Believe it or not, it is fun to go to the symphony concerts now. . . .
> Symphony-going, thanks to Pierre Monteux, now seems destined to become
> San Francisco's favorite sport. . . . [On Saturday night] auditors stamped
> and shouted their approval. They don't do that unless they're having a right
> good time. Such spontaneous enthusiasm is contagious.

Monteux's first season consisted of ten Friday afternoon–Saturday night subscription pairs, ten Municipal Concerts, several Young People's Concerts, and
concerts on the campus of the University of California, Berkeley, and in other
surrounding cities.

On the heels of the opening Friday-Saturday pair, the orchestra gave its first
Municipal Concert on Tuesday, 14 January. While this series was designed to be
popular in nature, there was no condescension in the programming, for Joseph
Szigeti was the guest soloist in the Brahms Violin Concerto. Weber's Overture to
Euryanthe, Richard Strauss's *Don Juan*, Wagner's Prelude to *Lohengrin*, and
Dukas's *The Sorcerer's Apprentice* completed the program.

Guest soloists for the subscription concerts included the pianists Josef Lhévinne
and José Iturbi and the violinists Jascha Heifetz, Bronislav Huberman, Sylvia
Lent, and Mischa Elman, while the municipal series brought, among others, the
pianist Alexander Brailowsky, the violinists Albert Spalding and Isaac Stern, and
the cellist Emanuel Feuermann. The sixteen-year-old Stern's performance of the
Saint-Saëns Third Violin Concerto on 18 February marked that local boy's debut
with the orchestra.

Also appearing as soloists in the subscription series were the orchestra's concertmaster, Naoum Blinder, and Willem Van den Burg, its newly appointed principal cellist. Together they performed the Brahms Double Concerto. The Russian-born Blinder, teacher of Isaac Stern and many others, had been concertmaster prior to the arrival of Monteux, who pronounced him "superb . . . one of the finest leaders I have ever encountered" (D. Monteux 1965, 180). The Dutch-born Van den Burg, until the year before principal cellist of the Philadelphia Orchestra, moved to San Francisco for the same position but also with the attraction of the associate conductorship. (Cellists often become conductors—witness Toscanini, Pablo Casals, John Barbirolli, Alfred Wallenstein, and others.) He had performed as soloist with Monteux in both Philadelphia and Amsterdam, and it was he who conducted Isaac Stern's debut performance.

Monteux had conducted in Los Angeles, so as a reciprocal gesture to Otto Klemperer, he asked the German maestro to appear as a guest conductor in San Francisco during Monteux's first season, though it would be for only one week. Klemperer led an all-Beethoven program of the *Egmont* Overture and the Third and Fifth Symphonies. He was hailed by Alfred Metzger in the 15 February *Chronicle* as, along with Wilhelm Furtwängler, Walter, and Toscanini, one of the world's greatest conductors. (Monteux apparently had not yet reached that status, though his training of the orchestra was praised.)

Appearing in the municipal series was the orchestra's former conductor, Alfred Hertz, who directed an all-Wagner program with Lotte Lehmann as soloist. Hertz had gone from San Francisco to Houston, where he was in the process of building up the orchestra. In the *Chronicle* on 25 February he voiced great praise for Monteux, claiming that he had produced phenomenal results with the San Francisco Symphony. The all-Wagner program prompted a letter to the editor of the *San Francisco News* from one B. Blumenthal protesting that the performance of such music would certainly have satisfied Hitler in keeping German culture before the public. He pointed out that Wagner disliked the Jews, and the legends and themes of his operas formed the basis for the Nazi's beliefs. The greatest disgrace, the letter writer continued, was that Pierre Monteux refused to conduct a Wagner program and that a Jew (i.e., Hertz) did. There is no indication, however, that Monteux refused to conduct the Wagner concert. It was simply a matter of Hertz's being engaged and then choosing to do a Wagner program.

A major event in the municipal series was the first complete San Francisco performance of Berlioz's *Damnation of Faust*, with Monteux conducting. This "dramatic legend," as the composer designated it, is even today rarely encountered in its entirety on concert programs, though the orchestral excerpts are often given. For this premiere Monteux availed himself of the services of the Municipal Chorus, prepared by Hans Leschke, and the soloists Joy McArden, mezzo-soprano; Felix Knight, tenor; Perry Askam, baritone; and Douglas Beattie, bass. (Knight often appeared in Hollywood musicals, usually operettas.)

Monteux's programming for his first season contained very little outside the standard repertoire. As with the Orchestre Symphonique de Paris, he felt the orchestra should initially have a thorough grounding in the classics before the introduction of new works, which would come once the orchestra was well organized. Still, three new works received their first performances. Monteux conducted a Theme and Variations by the orchestra's principal bassoonist, Adolph Weiss, and a Chinese Rhapsody by Max Donner, while none other than Meredith Willson, future composer of *The Music Man* and *The Unsinkable Molly Brown*, conducted his own First Symphony, subtitled "A Symphony for San Francisco."

Marjorie M. Fisher summed up the season as follows in the *San Francisco News* of 25 April 1936:

> If every candidate for an elective office fulfilled his platform pledges as completely and wholeheartedly as Pierre Monteux has done as conductor of the San Francisco Symphony, the world would be a better place.
>
> About eight months ago, when Mr. Monteux accepted the local appointment, he said he would give San Francisco beautiful music played by a beautiful orchestra. Yesterday he completed his first term as conductor (except for tonight's repetition of the same program) with his initial promise more than well fulfilled. Since last January Mr. Monteux has magically wrought order and harmony out of chaos and discord, won the affection as well as the respect of the players under his baton, and the admiration and appreciation of a constantly increasing audience on the basis of sheer merit. The San Francisco Symphony Orchestra stands today as one of the truly fine symphonic instruments in the country. . . . The season ends with a balanced budget for the first time in history.

Following the conclusion of his first season, Monteux's contract was renewed for three years.

Pierre and his first wife, Victoria Barrière. Courtesy of Claude Monteux, Paris

Pierre and Doris, Nancie and Donald, with Pierre's mother, c. 1930.

Pierre Monteux and Willem Pijper in Les Baux, 1938.

Monteux with Charles Bruck.

Pierre Monteux at the time of his conductorship of the Boston Symphony (1919–24). Photo by Photo Incorporated, courtesy of the Boston Symphony Orchestra Archives

Guest violist with the San Francisco String Quartet. Photo by Mason Weymouth

Pierre Monteux and the San Francisco Symphony Orchestra in the War Memorial Opera House. Morton Photo

Santa Pierre, San Francisco, 1943.

Pierre, Doris, and Fifi on tour with the San Francisco Symphony, 1947.

Monteux in San Francisco. Photo by Roy Flamm

Pierre and Doris Monteux arriving at Pierre's retirement reception, San Francisco, 1952.

Monteux with a Paris classmate, violinist Jacques Thibaud. Photo by J. Rosenthal

Monteux with Maurice Chevalier. Photo by Cutler

Monteux, Serge Koussevitzky, and Charles Munch in "friendly" conversation. Photo by John Brook

Welcome to Tanglewood, 1952. Charles Munch greets Monteux with BSO manager Thomas D. Perry looking on.

Monteux and Charles Munch (in cap) on tour with the Boston Symphony, 1952. A friendly railroad employee makes three. Courtesy of the Boston Symphony Orchestra Archives

Monteux at Tanglewood, 1952. The concertmaster is Richard Burgin. Photo by Will Plouffe, courtesy of the Boston Symphony Orchestra Archives

The most famous Monteux photograph, 1953. Photo by Karsh of Ottawa,
courtesy of Woodfin Camp & Associates

Pierre with Ginia Davis, c. 1955.
Courtesy of Ginia Davis Wexler

Pierre cutting his eightieth-birthday cake, April 1955, with the assistance of Doris. Charles Munch looks on. Courtesy of the Boston Symphony Orchestra Archives

Monteux and Joseph Barone in Hancock, c. 1955.

Pierre with Doris during an intermission in Hancock, c. 1955.

Raising of the flag on the new flagpole in Hancock, 1955. Doris's father, Eugene Hodgkins, does the honors.

Getting ready for a Maine winter.

The fire chief of Hancock, Maine.

A rare photo of Monteux
conducting the orchestra
at L'École Monteux.
Photo by, and courtesy of,
Adrian Sunshine

The 1956 class and performers of L'École Monteux. Flanking Monteux are Joseph
Barone (l.) and Ladislas Helfenbein (r.). The author is to Barone's immediate right.
Author's collection

The Monteuxs and David Zinman arriving in Vienna, 1963. Photo by Foto Vinek

With Jean Madeira after a performance of *Carmen*, c. 1960.

Rehearsing the London Symphony Orchestra, 1960.

The author with Pierre Monteux at L'École Monteux, 1961. Author's collection

A favorite pastime, 1960. Photo by Hall

Nancie Monteux-Barendse, 2000.

Monteux with viola case in Hancock, 1951. Photo by George Z. Gaska, a pupil of Monteux's at L'École Monteux. Courtesy of Henry Barendse

CHAPTER 12

San Francisco and NBC

In the early years of Monteux's tenure the symphony season did not begin until early January because most of the orchestra played in the fall for the San Francisco Opera, which occupied the same hall and whose season did not end until late December. Gradually the opening of the orchestra's season advanced by a few weeks.

The year 1937 marked the San Francisco Symphony Orchestra's silver jubilee. Beethoven's Fifth Symphony was the major work on the opening program on 8 and 9 January; the second concert pair a week later brought George Gershwin as guest artist, who performed his Concerto in F under Monteux's direction and conducted the San Francisco premiere of "Catfish Row," his own suite from *Porgy and Bess*.

Gershwin is known to have been displeased with many performances of his music by symphony orchestras and symphonic conductors; he felt that classically trained musicians lacked feeling for and understanding of the jazz element in his music. Monteux was different, though. As the pianist Oscar Levant, one of Gershwin's closest friends and ardent champions, wrote in *A Smattering of Ignorance*:

During his final visit to California he [Gershwin] found an extremely sympathetic interpreter in Pierre Monteux, of the San Francisco Orchestra. Gershwin was thoroughly impressed with Monteux's excelling technical skill as a conductor, his exceptional rhythmic sensitivity and his amazing grasp—for a conductor of traditional background and alien nationality—of the spirit of Gershwin's music. (Levant 1940, 192–93)

It is tempting to attribute Monteux's feeling for Gershwin's music, as well as his great rhythmic sense, to his early involvement with light music at the Folies Bergères, as he himself acknowledged, and to his conducting of ballet. But he would not have been a great ballet conductor had he not already possessed that sense, and while the Folies Bergères may have honed it, undoubtedly the basic feeling was already there to begin with.

129

Monteux had an opportunity to return to ballet conducting and display his mastery of it when, from 28 to 31 January, the orchestra was in the pit of the opera house for an engagement of the recently reconstituted Ballets Russes, now known as the Ballet Russe de Monte Carlo. Diaghilev had died in 1929, and the troupe was now under the direction of Colonel W. de Basil. Monteux led performances of the *Symphonie fantastique, Le spectre de la rose, Petrushka, L'après-midi d'un faune,* and the Polovtzian Dances, while other repertoire was conducted by Antal Doráti and Efrem Kurtz, both of whom went on to have distinguished symphonic careers in the United States and Europe. Monteux's conducting of the Berlioz score contradicts his negative stance on conducting choreographed performances of works not intended for the ballet. Perhaps he felt that the symphony's graphic and hallucinatory images justified visual representation.

Other composers who appeared in San Francisco that season were the Polish-born Alexandre Tansman, who was the soloist in the local premiere of his Concertino for Piano and Orchestra and conducted the American premiere of his Aria and Alla Polacca on 22 and 23 January; and the American Ernest Schelling, who conducted his most celebrated work, *A Victory Ball,* on 9 and 10 April. Schelling was also the soloist in the Schumann Piano Concerto. Other works that were premiered in San Francisco were Isadore Freed's *Jeux de timbres* and the *Bret Harte Overture* by Philip James.

On 19 and 20 March the young Isaac Stern played the Brahms Violin Concerto, his first appearance with Monteux on the podium, and the first of many they would give together over the years. In what would become almost an annual event, the season closed on 23 and 24 April with Beethoven's Ninth Symphony, with the Municipal Chorus and the soloists Lina Kroph, Myrtle Leonard, Roy Russell, and Douglas Beattie. Stravinsky's *Symphony of Psalms* opened the program. Critical consensus was that the orchestra continued to improve.

While Monteux may have agreed with the critics, he felt that still further improvement was in order. At the end of the season he announced that all the string players, except for the first stand in each section, would have to play an audition before the start of the next season. Whether there was dead wood to be cut out remained to be seen, but he felt that a number of the musicians had allowed their playing to deteriorate, the result of playing in a large string section in which they were not exposed and could thus get by.

These auditions led to quite a bit of reseating in the string sections, not to everyone's satisfaction. One member who was relegated to the last stand of the second violins was particularly outraged at his demotion and actually threatened Monteux with physical violence of the "let's step outside and settle this" variety. After the personnel manager had assuaged his feelings, the player took his seat, but before Monteux could begin the rehearsal he came forward and offered his resignation, which Monteux accepted. The player soon began writing to Doris Monteux, perhaps venting his frustrations on her. The two kept up a fairly lively correspondence, after which the player returned to the orchestra for one year. He finally left to go to Hollywood.

In 1936 Arturo Toscanini retired from his position as principal conductor of the Philharmonic-Symphony Society of New York. With considerable fanfare, he conducted his American farewell concert with the Philharmonic in Carnegie Hall on 29 April of that year, with Jascha Heifetz the soloist in the Beethoven Violin Concerto. Toscanini's intention was to return to Italy, work as a guest conductor in Europe (Vienna, Salzburg, the BBC, and so on), and live a life free of the exigencies of regularly directing a major symphony orchestra. He had reckoned without David Sarnoff, president of the Radio Corporation of America (RCA), which controlled the National Broadcasting Company (NBC); Sarnoff envisioned just such an orchestra, but one whose primary function would be radio broadcasting. Sarnoff had sent his emissary, Samuel Chotzinoff (Heifetz's brother-in-law), whom Toscanini already knew, to Europe to interest him in becoming the principal conductor of the soon-to-be-formed NBC Symphony Orchestra. After much negotiation (having to do not with money but with the manner in which the orchestra was to be constituted), he finally accepted. He thus began, at age seventy, a seventeen-year Indian summer of activity in which he made most of his celebrated recordings. Already an American household name because of his Philharmonic Sunday afternoon broadcasts, he would now become a cultural icon. His presence would be felt even more strongly later, with the advent of television.

It was planned that Toscanini would conduct his first NBC concert on Saturday, Christmas day, 1937, from ten to eleven-thirty in the evening Eastern Standard Time—a rather odd time to hold the weekly broadcasts, which were to originate in Radio City's Studio 8-H before a studio audience of over a thousand people. But this was not to be the orchestra's debut, for it was felt that several weeks of "warm-up" concerts were necessary to get the ensemble in shape for the maestro's arrival.

Artur Rodzinski (1892–1958), then conductor of the Cleveland Orchestra, had been selected to audition and engage the members of the orchestra, which was to consist of staff musicians already employed by NBC and about sixty others to form an ensemble of ninety-two players. Many outstanding musicians left their positions in existing orchestras for the opportunity of playing with Toscanini. He already knew Rodzinski, liked him personally, and was enthusiastic about him professionally. Rodzinski also had the task of training the orchestra into a cohesive unit with about a month of rehearsals.

There are differing accounts of what happened next. Doris Monteux quotes her husband as having been told that NBC was concerned because the orchestra was not playing well together, a dubious claim since Rodzinski was, if nothing else, an excellent orchestra builder (D. Monteux 1965, 189). Harvey Sachs, in his admirable biography *Toscanini*, states that the paranoid Rodzinski was afraid that Toscanini would not be satisfied with the musicians he had chosen (Sachs 1978, 263). Now it was too late to make personnel changes, and those players with whom Rodzinski was displeased were not treated well by him during rehearsals, causing considerable tension within the orchestra and the NBC administration.

The official version as announced by NBC was that the date for the orchestra's first concert conflicted with the opening of the Cleveland Orchestra's season, which Rodzinski was contractually obligated to conduct. Surely this conflict of dates was known in advance, and perhaps Rodzinski could even have made some arrangement with Cleveland so that he would have been available for the prestigious NBC engagement. In any case, Pierre Monteux, still at his home in Les Baux, where he was preparing for his third San Francisco season, received a phone call from Fred Bates of NBC, who invited him, at Toscanini's request, to conduct the orchestra's first concerts. Toscanini and Monteux, through various concerts and transatlantic voyages, also knew and highly respected each other. (Remember that Toscanini had said that Monteux was his dearest colleague.)

Monteux was at first reluctant to accept the offer, as both he and Doris disliked New York City. He decided to ask an extremely large fee, much beyond the normal American concert fees, in the belief that NBC would then rescind the offer. To his surprise, his proposed fee was accepted, and he subsequently learned that NBC would have doubled it if necessary.

Arriving in New York, he found a first-class orchestra awaiting him, but one that lacked cohesion and balance among its sections. By now a highly experienced orchestral trainer, Monteux was able to rectify the problems in time for the first concert on 13 November 1937, when he conducted the NBC Symphony Orchestra in the following program:

> Bach-Respighi: Passacaglia and Fugue in C minor
> Mozart: Symphony No. 35 in D major ("Haffner")
> Franck: "Psyché et Eros" from *Psyché*
> Debussy: *Ibéria*
> Strauss: *Till Eulenspiegel's Merry Pranks*

While the bulk of the reviews naturally concentrated on the excellent quality of the new orchestra and on the sound of the concert as heard both over the air and in the studio, Monteux did come in for his share of praise. In *The New York Times* of 14 November, Olin Downes wrote that the concert not only had introduced a new symphony orchestra of very high rank but also had displayed Pierre Monteux at the height of his powers. The orchestra's admirable cooperation confirmed his international reputation, wrote Downes, and made everyone realize that it had been too long since he had last been heard in New York. Downes went on to say that Monteux was remarkable in his control of the orchestra as well as in his musical imagination and the freedom with which he utilized his authority.

Lawrence Gilman, in the 14 November *New York Herald Tribune*, wrote of Monteux's persuading the orchestra's string section to play deftly and beautifully in Mozart's delicious symphony. However, Oscar Thompson of the *New York Evening Sun* (15 November) felt that the Mozart plodded and was without sparkle and lightness, though his colleagues listening to the broadcast in an adjoining room felt exactly the opposite. Thompson thought the performance of *Ibéria* one of the finest in many years, though not of the greatest tonal beauty. Heard on the radio, *Till Eulenspiegel* was radiant and vital, separating it from all that had preceded it. Almost all accounts I have read, including those of Harvey Sachs and Doris Monteux (but not that of Mortimer H. Frank in his *Arturo Toscanini: The NBC Years*), state that Monteux conducted the NBC Symphony's first two concerts. Actually, however, he conducted the first three, on 13, 20, and 27 November. The program of 20 November was a potpourri of shorter compositions, concluding with Ravel's *Daphnis et Chloé* Suite No. 2, while that of 27 November featured César Franck's Symphony in D minor and Stravinsky's *Firebird* Suite.

As the Monteuxs were packing on Sunday morning, 28 November, in preparation for leaving for San Francisco that evening, they were visited by the personnel manager of the NBC Symphony, H. Leopold Spitalny, who, on behalf of the orchestra, asked if Monteux would lead them in a rehearsal of Debussy's *La mer* that very morning. The work was scheduled for one of Toscanini's early programs, and the musicians were fearful of incurring his wrath if they were not well prepared in one of the basic scores of the maestro's repertoire. (He programmed it quite often because he himself was never satisfied with his performances of it.) Monteux agreed, and after a three-hour rehearsal it was evident that the orchestra had learned *La mer* quite well.

Following Monteux's departure, Rodzinski conducted the next three NBC broadcasts, after which Toscanini began his tenure with a series of eleven. Subsequently other guest conductors took over, including Rodzinski and Monteux, who returned for two concerts on 30 April and 7 May 1938. His last program consisted of Chausson's Symphony in B-flat major and works by four American composers active at the time but rarely heard from since: John Powell, Emerson Whithorne, Jon Cowley, and Hilda Davis—Monteux's sister-in-law. Hilda was no amateur. Not only had she had early training as a pianist and organist, but she was especially known for her improvisational skills and had also studied composition with Isadore Freed in New York. Monteux programmed her tone poem *The Last Knight* in its very first performance. It had been inspired by a quotation from G. K. Chesterton's *Lepanto*, which deals with the 1571 victory of Don Juan of Austria over the Turks. Monteux later presented the work in San Francisco, and Eugene Ormandy conducted it with the Philadelphia Orchestra. Unfortunately, the *Times* review was not very favorable, the critic (G. G.) finding it difficult to discern the form of the work at first hearing. A test pressing of the NBC performance reveals it to be an atmospheric, impressionistic piece, sensitive to orchestral colors and building to a great climax.

Monteux obviously enjoyed successful appearances during the NBC Symphony's first season, so it is curious that he was not invited back for quite some time, whereas Walter, Stokowski, Ansermet, and others appeared in several consecutive seasons. Whether the situation had to do with Monteux's schedule, his dislike of New York, a decision of Toscanini's (doubtful, for he and Monteux were genuinely good colleagues), or one of NBC's (perhaps Monteux's high fee played a part) is not known. The fact is that Monteux did not return until much later.

CHAPTER 13

Established in San Francisco

Because of the success of Monteux's first two seasons in San Francisco, the 1937–38 season was increased to twelve subscription pairs, beginning a month earlier than usual, on 10 and 11 December, with the program Mrs. Armsby had erroneously given for Monteux's first concert two years before:

> Beethoven: Overture to *Egmont*
> Franck-Pierné: Prelude, Chorale, and Fugue
> Ravel: *Daphnis et Chloé* Suite No. 2
> Brahms: Symphony No. 1 in C minor

While César Franck was known as a great organist and often achieved organ-like sonorities in his orchestral works, the Prelude, Chorale, and Fugue is one of his few works for solo piano. Pierné, who studied organ with Franck, made his orchestral transcription in 1903. It has never entered the repertoire in the manner of other, more-celebrated orchestral arrangements of piano originals, most notably the Mussorgsky-Ravel *Pictures at an Exhibition*, but it was occasionally performed by Monteux, as well as by Dimitri Mitropoulos, who programmed it with the New York Philharmonic in 1951 and 1953.

Maurice Ravel had died on 28 December 1937, and in his memory the third pair of concerts, 7 and 8 January, included a performance of Beethoven's Three Equali for four trombones. While one might have thought one of Ravel's own works appropriate for the occasion, such as the *Pavane pour une infante défunte*, *equali* is an eighteenth-century designation for a funeral quartet of instruments of the same kind, often trombones, as well as the music written for such a quartet. Two of Beethoven's Three Equali, which date from 1812, had in fact been played at his own funeral in 1827.

Instrumental soloists for the season included the pianists Josef Hofmann, Arthur Rubinstein (in the municipal concerts series), Artur Schnabel (unusually, in both the subscription and the municipal series), and the teenage virtuoso Ruth Slencynska, while the violinists were Mischa Elman, Grisha Goluboff, Jascha Hei-

135

fetz, and the French player Yvonne Astruc, who presented the San Francisco premiere of the Violin Concerto by Germaine Tailleferre (1892–1983). One of the early-twentieth-century group of French composers known as Les Six (the others were Georges Auric, Louis Durey, Arthur Honegger, Darius Milhaud, and Francis Poulenc), Tailleferre achieved distinction as one of the few woman composers active at a time when it was still difficult for women to achieve success in the creative arts. Today quite a few women composers have risen to prominence, as witness the careers of Sofia Gubaidulina, Kaija Saariaho, Augusta Read Thomas, Joan Tower, and Ellen Taaffe Zwilich, among others.

The Hollywood actor Brian Aherne appeared on a program of Shakespeare-inspired music similar to the one Monteux had given in Los Angeles three years earlier, and the soprano Lotte Lehmann was the soloist in an all-Wagner program in the Municipal series. Monteux conducted, and this time no letter of protest appeared in the newspapers. Beethoven's Ninth Symphony was given in the same series. It was preceded on the more-than-generous program by his *Leonore* Overture No. 3 and "Emperor" Concerto, with Schnabel as soloist.

As he had done the year before, Monteux participated in the season of the Ballet Russe de Monte Carlo, leading performances of the *Symphonie fantastique, L'après-midi d'un faune, Le spectre de la rose,* and, surprisingly (if not astonishingly, considering his convictions in the matter), the Brahms Symphony No. 4. This last was the music for a ballet choreographed by Leonid Massine, called *Choreartium.* Monteux's change of heart may have had to do with the fact that the symphony's finale is a chaconne, a dance form that originated in the seventeenth century, if not earlier. The other movements, however, are certainly not dances (though perhaps the boisterous Scherzo would qualify).

Works that received their world premieres during the season were *Evocations* by Ernest Bloch and *Thus Spake the Deepest Stone* by Edward Schneider. San Francisco premieres included, in addition to the Tailleferre Violin Concerto, *Fandango* by Emerson Whithorne and Two Dances from the *Crazy House* Suite by Jon Cowley, which Monteux had conducted with the NBC Symphony Orchestra the previous year. The inclusion of the Cowley and Whithorne works demonstrates Monteux's interest in representing San Francisco and California composers on his programs, something he continued to do for the rest of his tenure.

In February 1938 Monteux received from the French Minister of National Education a document, dated the fourth of that month, informing him that he had been promoted to the rank of Officer in the Legion of Honor.

The opening program for the 1939 season, on 6 and 7 January, is another illustration of the longer orchestral programs of the past:

Berlioz: *Roman Carnival* Overture
Mozart: Piano Concerto No. 22 in E-flat major; José Iturbi, soloist
Mussorgsky-Ravel: *Pictures at an Exhibition*
Brahms: Symphony No. 2 in D major

If either the Mussorgsky-Ravel or the Brahms works were omitted, this would be a perfectly normal program today. Even for its time it was unusually long. One might suspect that the program book was in error, but the various newspaper critics all confirmed the program and reviewed it favorably, and no one complained of its length.

Among the guest soloists, interest attaches to Monteux's discovery from his Boston days, the tenor Roland Hayes, who, on 17 and 18 March, sang music by J. S. Bach, Baldassare Galuppi, Jean-Philippe Rameau, and Berlioz, as well as a group of spirituals. Other instrumental soloists, besides Iturbi, were the pianists Alexander Brailowsky, Robert Casadesus, and E. Robert Schmitz; the duo pianists Pierre Luboshutz and Genia Nemenoff; and the violinists Sylvia Lent (of San Francisco), Nathan Milstein, and the orchestra's concertmaster, Naoum Blinder.

From the guest standpoint, the highlight of the season was the appearance, as both soloist and conductor, of the composer Paul Hindemith. On 24 and 25 February he gave the San Francisco premieres of two of his major works, the viola concerto entitled *Der Schwanendreher* (The Swan Turner), in which he played the solo part with Monteux conducting, and the Concert Music for Strings and Brass, which he conducted. Other local premieres were Milhaud's *Suite provençale*, Davis's *The Last Knight*, and Horace Johnson's *Imagery*, with Willem Van den Burg on the podium.

The Municipal Concerts presented, as the season's only non-composer guest conductor, Leopold Stokowski in his debut with the orchestra. Though of drastically opposing musical viewpoints, he and Monteux liked and respected one another, as confirmed by the latter's extensive Philadelphia engagement in 1928. On 17 February in the Opera House Stokowski gave a program of some of his specialties, including the Brahms First Symphony and his own arrangements of Bach's "Little" Fugue in G minor and Mussorgsky's *Night on Bald Mountain*, the latter arrangement a world premiere. Usually the Mussorgsky work was (and still is) performed in the orchestration of Rimsky-Korsakov, which is, in fact, a recomposition. Stokowski would have none of that and, as he was often wont to do, had rearranged and recomposed the piece in his own inimitable fashion. (Since then Mussorgsky's original score has resurfaced and been recorded several times and has proven to be an effective work of great originality.)

As reported in several of the area newspapers the next day, Stokowski broke precedent (for San Francisco) by addressing the audience, declaring that the San Francisco Symphony "is an orchestra of marvelous sensitivity, and I congratulate my colleague, M. Monteux, upon its excellence and for its musicianship."

In the *Chronicle*, Alfred Frankenstein ended his rave review, "The morning press could not remain for the performance of Debussy's 'Afternoon of a Faun' and Wagner's 'Fire Music,' and rarely has this penalty for the possession of a punched ticket seemed so insupportably severe." (The "punched ticket" refers to the critic's complimentary ticket, which in earlier times had a hole punched into it.)

An unusual program in the Municipal series was that of 29 March 1939, when Monteux conducted a rare performance of Schumann's complete music for Byron's *Manfred*. Even today, apart from the great overture, this music is almost never heard. Besides vocal soloists and chorus, the work calls for a large speaking cast headed by the role of Manfred himself, which was taken on this occasion by the noted actor Basil Rathbone, known to an early generation of moviegoers as Sherlock Holmes. As *Manfred* was apparently considered insufficient for a full concert, the evening ended with another rarity: *The Rio Grande*, by the English composer-conductor Constant Lambert (1905–1951), set to a poem by Sacheverell Sitwell. Scored for chorus, orchestra, and solo piano, played in this performance by Douglas Thompson, the work is notable for its jazzy rhythms, at the time of its composition (1929) still infrequently encountered in concert music. (The "Grande" of the title is pronounced in the English manner, "grand"—"By the Rio Grande, they dance no sarabande.")

The 8 September 1939 edition of the *New York Herald Tribune* carried a brief dispatch, dated the previous day, reporting that the State Department had begun a search in France for Pierre Monteux and his niece Virginia (Ginia) Davis, who were thought to be missing. As the war in Europe was already under way, there was much concern on the part of Ginia's parents, Hilda and Meyer Davis, as to the whereabouts of their daughter and, of course, of the Monteuxs. Ginia had left for Europe the previous month to study voice and had since cabled home requesting money, but at that time it was impossible to wire funds. Since then nothing had been heard from her. Monteux was supposedly in Les Baux giving what would prove to be the last of his conducting classes there. San Francisco had heard nothing from him either.

Eventually everyone surfaced, though not before Ginia was arrested for failure to have an identity card. She was thought to be a spy, but finally was released through the intervention of Secretary of State Cordell Hull (Meyer Davis did have connections, after all).

A signal event took place in 1939, one with so little fanfare that perhaps "event" is too strong a word for it. Eight fraternity men from the University of California at Berkeley pooled their resources and bought a box for the Saturday evening concert series. Soon students from Stanford University, Mills College, and other institutions followed suit, purchasing boxes as well as season tickets in other sections of the opera house. Campus forums were organized to discuss the music that would be performed. Members of the orchestra and even Monteux himself came to the meetings to talk about the programs and answer questions. So was born the San Francisco Symphony Forum, the student affiliate of the Musical Association of San Francisco, through which students throughout the Bay area are able to purchase seats for the regular symphony concerts.

The orchestra began its 1939–40 season on 8 and 9 December with a program featuring the Second Symphony of Sibelius, the first symphony by that composer Monteux had conducted in San Francisco. On 9 December Frankenstein, who felt that other conductors had provided more majestic interpretations of the finale, nevertheless proclaimed it the greatest performance of the work he had ever heard; Monteux brought out the score's grimness, gruffness, and passion, its blazing eloquence and huge sonority.

Among the soloists, Sergei Rachmaninoff performed his own Second Piano Concerto, Jascha Heifetz presented violin concertos by Bruch (No. 1) and Prokofiev (No. 2)—the latter work in its San Francisco premiere—and Josef Hofmann was heard in the Schumann Piano Concerto. There were two guest conductors, each a composer. On 15 and 16 December Igor Stravinsky directed his *Jeu de cartes* (The Card Game) and Suite from *Petrushka*, as well as the San Francisco premiere of the Second Symphony of Tchaikovsky. Known as the "Little Russian" Symphony, this work had long been a favorite of Stravinsky's, one that he liked to program in company with his own music. The other guest conductor was the Mexican Carlos Chávez, who led his *Sinfonía di Antígona* and *Sinfonía india*, along with works by Haydn, Debussy, and Falla.

Stokowski again appeared on the Municipal Concerts series, this time with his arrangements of Bach's Passacaglia and Fugue in C minor, Debussy's *Clair de lune*, and Mussorgsky's *Pictures*. From Monteux's standpoint, the highlight of his season was the 1 March presentation, also in the Municipal Series, of the Verdi Requiem. The performance, with the Municipal Chorus and a quartet of local soloists, moved Frankenstein to comment in the 2 March *Chronicle*:

> In the last analysis what one carried away was the memory of two great masters, Verdi who wrote the music, and Monteux who brought it to life. It was one of Monteux's most inspired presentations, and one that makes triply regrettable the infrequency of choral concerts in our schedule of events. It is a minor detail, perhaps, but it is worth mentioning that a conductor whose reputation is supposed to rest on his work in opera, concert and ballet directed one of the major choral works of the repertoire from memory.

There were no world premieres this time, but quite a few pieces new to San Francisco, in addition to the "Little Russian" Symphony and Prokofiev Violin Concerto, all conducted by Monteux: Copland's *El salón México*, Weinberger's *Under the Spreading Chestnut Tree*, Bloch's Two Symphonic Interludes from *Macbeth*, Milhaud's *The Creation of the World*, Pijper's Third Symphony, and Daniel Gregory Mason's *Suite after English Folk Songs*. There was one American premiere, Nikolai Berezowsky's Toccata, Variations, and Finale for String Quartet and Orchestra, with the participation of the Coolidge Quartet, in which the Russian-born Berezowsky (1900–1953) played second violin. It should be noted that the local premieres were, for the most part, of works of greater substance than in previous seasons. In his laudatory *Chronicle* review of 27 January, of the concert with Heifetz as soloist, Frankenstein concluded with some remarks unrelated to the concert:

A pair of recent letters in the Safety Valve [a column in the paper] call for a moment's attention. Mr. Monteux has apparently been quoted to the effect that performing a certain work by a local composer would establish a precedent for playing such compositions at the Symphony concerts, the implication being that the performance of locally created scores is undesirable. Anyone who has spent five minutes in Monteux's study knows that his attitude is consistently friendly to local musicians, and that he is constantly engaged in reading their scores. In the past two seasons he has presented three works of Bay Region composers, Albert Elkus' "Impressions of a Greek Tragedy," William Denny's concertino and Edward Schneider's "Thus Spake the Deepest Stone." This is not many, but there is opposition to modern music at the concerts, and these three works represent at least a decent percentage of attention to the local composer. Of the facts, merits or demerits of the present controversy I know nothing, but I shall attempt to examine them at a later time. I do know, however, that generalizations unfavorable to Monteux on the grounds cited are entirely unfair to him, and completely misrepresent his point of view.

As they had done the previous year, Monteux and the orchestra began the 1940–41 season with a symphony by Sibelius, this time the Fifth (not a regular work in Monteux's repertoire), played in honor of the composer's seventy-fifth birthday. Frankenstein, writing in the *Chronicle* of 7 December, found the performance magnificent, while noting that the Third Symphony is Sibelius's best (a view few would hold today or would have held even then, regardless of the work's likability). After intermission came the Brahms Second Symphony—nothing unusual there, except, as noted by Frankenstein,

> if you go tonight and follow the outline of the Brahms in the program book, please observe that the exposition in the first movement will be repeated. This is not accounted for in the book because it is almost never done. The first ending with which the repeat is prepared almost sounded like a false entrance yesterday, so rarely is it used.

It should be noted that the author of the orchestra's program notes was Frankenstein himself. He was not the only critic to be involved in such a conflict of interest. At that time, and even later, critics in New York and Philadelphia, and perhaps elsewhere, also wrote their respective orchestra's program notes. Did their fee for doing so influence the reviews they wrote? Only they could answer that question.

War was now raging in Europe, and Monteux was understandably concerned about the safety of his family in France. In October 1940 he had written to the American Embassy in Paris requesting information as to their welfare. A reply on 28 November from Tyler Thompson, Third Secretary of the Embassy, informed Monteux that his sister Marguerite, Madame Bloc, was well, as was his son, Jean

Paul. Marguerite was still living in her Paris apartment, but her son, grandson, and daughter-in-law were all in Nantes. Pierre's brother Henri was also in good health, and Marguerite said that everything was in order in Pierre's apartment, which was being looked after by the concierge.

One of the highlights of the 1940–41 season was the appearance of Sergei Rachmaninoff on two subscription pairs, performing his First Piano Concerto and *Rhapsody on a Theme of Paganini* on 7 and 8 February and his Third Piano Concerto on 14 and 15 February. (He had already played the Second Concerto the year before.) On the first pair Monteux also conducted the composer's Second Symphony. A broadcast recording of the symphony's second and third movements (played in reverse order!—all that was played of it on the broadcast) reveals Monteux to have been an extremely sympathetic Rachmaninoff interpreter, even though many years later he told some of his students that he thought the Second Symphony was "horrible music." He is thus perhaps the sole exception among the great musicians who claim that they cannot perform a work, and certainly cannot perform it convincingly, unless they truly believe in it. No doubt Monteux performed the Second Symphony on this occasion because of the presence of the composer, about whose concertos he did not feel the same.

The San Francisco premieres of this season were of William Schuman's *American Festival Overture*, Barber's *Music for a Scene from Shelley*, the Third Symphony of Roy Harris, the First Symphony of Darius Milhaud, conducted by the composer, Harl McDonald's *San Juan Capistrano*, and *A Color Symphony* by Arthur Bliss, also conducted by the composer. Sometimes conductors allow a composer to lead his own composition because they do not wish to take the time and trouble to learn the work themselves. Such was not the case with Monteux. But if a composer was an able conductor and one whose presence would lend stature to the season, Monteux was more than willing to cede the podium to him.

Two Englishmen occupied the podium as guests, Sir Thomas Beecham for the subscription concerts of 3 and 4 January, and John Barbirolli (not yet knighted) for a Municipal Concert on 14 December. Beecham offered one of his typically unconventional programs, including Mozart's "Paris" Symphony (No. 31) and the Seventh Symphony of Sibelius, as well as works by Handel, Frederick Delius, and Bizet. Barbirolli, then in his penultimate season as conductor of the New York Philharmonic, programmed one of his specialties, Elgar's *Enigma Variations*.

Among Monteux's repertoire that season were two works of Richard Strauss that he rarely programmed; in fact, these were probably the last performances he gave of *Thus spake Zarathustra* and the *Symphonia domestica*. The other tone poems he played quite often. Of the soloists, there was considerable interest in the appearance of the great soprano Kirsten Flagstad, who triumphed on 8 February in an all-Wagner program culminating in what amounted to her signature piece, the Immolation Scene from *Götterdämmerung*. This concert was conducted not by Monteux, but by Flagstad's longtime collaborator, Edwin McArthur.

The season of 1941–42 marked the San Francisco Symphony's thirtieth anniversary. Celebrations were inaugurated with a gala pops concert on the evening of 2 December 1941. Held in the Civic Auditorium with an audience of ten thousand present, the event was quite informal; the auditorium was decorated to resemble a Viennese beer garden flanked by California greenery, and the program was suitably, though not entirely, light in nature. There were, of course, the requisite speeches, the highlight of which was one by Monteux himself, the first time he had spoken in public in San Francisco. In his heavily French-flavored English, occasionally groping for a word, he spoke appreciatively of the many kind words that had been addressed to him and the orchestra, and ended with an eloquent tribute to his predecessor, Alfred Hertz, whom illness had prevented from attending. Many telegrams arrived from dignitaries, musical and otherwise, of which the most attention was bestowed on one addressed to Mrs. Armsby, in which the writer spoke of her great devotion to the San Francisco Symphony and expressed his most sincere and hearty congratulations on the important occasion of the orchestra's thirtieth anniversary. He then congratulated her on her astute management of the organization. With his wife, Carla, he sent her his most affectionate greetings. It was signed, "Arturo Toscanini."

On the musical program Brian Aherne narrated Prokofiev's *Peter and the Wolf*, the Katherine Dunham dance troupe performed (according to the *San Francisco Call Bulletin*) "with the typical abandon of the Negro race," and Monteux conducted Johann Strauss's *On the Beautiful Blue Danube* and Ravel's *La valse*, though this last was not exactly a pops piece. The regular season opened on 5 and 6 December with works of Bach, Mozart (the "Jupiter" Symphony, commemorating the 150th anniversary of Mozart's death), William Walton, and Beethoven (the "Eroica" Symphony). Monteux, who had made his reputation with Russian and French music, was found by Frankenstein to be equally great as a conductor of Beethoven.

The next day, Sunday, 7 December 1941, the Japanese attacked Pearl Harbor.

Like everyone else, the San Francisco Symphony suffered the effects of World War II. Many of its members were drafted into the armed services, creating openings in the ensemble that had to be filled hastily. Initially, there was also concern by the symphony management and board as to whether evening concerts should be discontinued, for fear of air raids. In the end, there was no disruption of the orchestra's normal schedule, for San Francisco's mayor, Angelo Joseph Rossi, had decreed that they continue and even installed a blackout system and air raid wardens throughout the opera house. While Mrs. Armsby and many others were apprehensive about the size of the audience that would materialize for the first concert after Pearl Harbor Day, fears of a probable decline in attendance proved unfounded, for there was a full house as usual.

That particular program, on 14 and 15 December, featured the San Francisco premiere of the Fifth Symphony by Shostakovich, another work not normally associated with Monteux; he was to play two other Shostakovich symphonies in the coming seasons. On 16 December the great bass-baritone Paul Robeson appeared in the Municipal series performing works of Mussorgsky and, appropriately for the time, *Ballad for Americans*, by Earl Robinson. Monteux's interest in the music of local composers extended even to members of the orchestra, for on the same program the violist Emanuel Leplin conducted the first performance of his own Prelude and Dance.

As part of the war effort, the symphony began to expand its activities, playing at service clubs and military hospitals. Additionally, buses and ambulances brought service men and women, healthy and wounded, to the opera house, where they were guests of the symphony. Such activities naturally increased the orchestra's popularity. Mrs. Armsby received many letters from service personnel once they had left the area. One contained a money order for $10, which accompanied the following letter:

I was once an usher in the War Memorial Opera house. I received great pleasure and instruction from my afternoons listening to your orchestra, and often I said to myself—"I wish I might give some money to this fine orchestra which has done so much for me." At last I can add my little gift to those that others are making. I send this ten dollars which is the money I earned by a recent jump from a parachute into Sicily. I hope it will help some. (Armsby 1960, 74)

Among the venues where the orchestra played for service personnel was Treasure Island, situated in the bay between San Francisco and Oakland. There Monteux and the orchestra performed on 3 February and 9 April 1942, with José Iturbi and Maxim Schapiro respectively as piano soloists. In December of that year the orchestra gave a Christmas concert at the army base theater. Monteux conducted dressed as Santa Claus and then distributed gifts to the service personnel. Among the performers at the concert were a juggler called Truzzi and a group of acrobats from the Folies Bergères. No doubt Monteux felt quite at home with them.

A great friend of the Monteuxs was Fleet Admiral Chester W. Nimitz. He and his wife were frequent attendees at symphony concerts. Once war against Japan was declared, he spent much of his time in the Pacific, though he often had to be flown back to San Francisco for a conference. Even with the war raging, the admiral tried to schedule these appointments at a time when he could hear a concert.

On 9 and 10 January 1942 Stravinsky conducted the San Francisco premiere of his Symphony in C, and later in the season Monteux gave the local premiere of Walter Piston's entertaining ballet suite *The Incredible Flutist*. The other premieres that season were not of works that have remained in the repertoire, with the possible exception of Milhaud's *Four Ronsard Songs*, which guest conductor André Kostelanetz led on 8 April with his wife at the time, the soprano Lily Pons, as soloist. The other guest conductor was the American Charles O'Connell, who appeared on 6 and 7 March. He was the chief producer for RCA, which had just begun recording the San Francisco Symphony (see the chapter "Recordings and Broadcasts") and harbored conducting aspirations that Monteux was apparently pleased to satisfy. His program also contained a San Francisco premiere: that of the Australian Arthur Benjamin's *Overture to an Italian Comedy*, an attractive work that enjoyed a vogue for a time and has unfortunately disappeared.

Monteux's repertoire that year again contained further works not normally associated with him, first and foremost scenes from Mussorgsky's *Boris Godunov*, performed in the Municipal series on 11 March with the Russian-born bass Alexander Kipnis as the featured artist. Unfortunately, Kipnis was singing under the handicap of a cold, but Frankenstein (12 March) found the San Francisco Symphony to be in top form, the Municipal Chorus giving its finest of recent performances and Monteux conducting a performance of great re-creative genius. Frankenstein lamented the fact that San Franciscans, in having Monteux as a symphony conductor, were only experiencing one portion of what he had to offer. Another work not associated with Monteux was the rarely heard (even today) Third Symphony of Sibelius, played on 16 and 17 January (perhaps to please Frankenstein). Another seldom-heard work (again even today) with which he *was* associated was the Second Symphony of Vincent d'Indy, performed on 20 and 21 February. Monteux and the orchestra would soon make the first recording of this piece.

A frequent soloist with the orchestra over the years was the Russian-born pianist Maxim Schapiro. A resident of the Bay area, he usually appeared in works that were not, at least then, part of the standard repertoire. For example, on 28 and 29 March 1942 he performed Szymanowski's *Symphonie concertante* (also known as Symphony No. 4), and on 26 and 27 February 1943 he gave the San Francisco premieres of Ravel's Concerto for the Left Hand and Heitor Villa-Lobos's fantasy *Momoprecoce*. Schapiro's name is most strongly associated with Monteux's as the pianist in the first recording of d'Indy's *Symphony on a French Mountain Air*.

In 1942, 2 March was a special day in the life of Pierre Monteux, for on that date he ceased to be a citizen of France and became a citizen of the United States. In a naturalization ceremony at City Hall, Monteux, at the invitation of Judge Elmer E. Robinson, stood upon the witness stand and led the thirty members of the class, the court attachés, and spectators in reciting the pledge of allegiance to the flag of the United States. A more-than-special evening of chamber music took place in Veterans' Auditorium on 17 March 1942, a benefit for the San Francisco chapter of the American Red Cross Blood Procurement Center. Billed as "An Evening of Quartet Music," the program consisted of quartets by Beethoven, Fauré, and Brahms played by the violinist Naoum Blinder, the cellist Boris Blinder (Naoum's brother), and the pianist Maxim Schapiro. The violist was none other than Pierre Monteux. The advance publicity stated that "the concert will mark Monteux's first musical appearance in San Francisco off the conductor's stand." It recounted his early experience as a violist and went on to say that he would play the same viola he had had since 1896, when he was graduated from the Paris Conservatory.

After the orchestra had concluded its final Friday matinee concert of the season and the audience had departed, Monteux reassembled the musicians on the stage and informed them of the death of their former conductor, Alfred Hertz, who had passed away earlier that day. Monteux spoke warmly of Hertz, of what he had done for the orchestra and for the community, and of the great debt that he, Monteux, owed his predecessor, who had established the finest symphonic traditions in San Francisco. Afterward the orchestra members rose for a moment of silence. The following evening, before the scheduled program, the Funeral March from Beethoven's "Eroica" Symphony was played in tribute to Hertz. That program included the Suite from Richard Strauss's *Le bourgeois gentilhomme*, of which Monteux had given the American premiere with the Boston Symphony in 1921, and the First Symphony of Brahms, two works that would also have been at home under the baton of Alfred Hertz.

On 23 April Monteux and the orchestra performed a charity concert for the benefit of the French War Relief Fund. A letter of thanks to Monteux from the president of the organization, dated 2 May, informs him that the concert had produced $511 for the fund, which would be divided equally among Free French Relief, French Milk Fund Quakers, and Packages for Prisoners. Even acknowledging that $511 was worth more in 1942 than it is today, it seems a rather paltry sum.

The most significant San Francisco premiere of the 1942–43 season was given not by Monteux, but by Stokowski, who conducted the Seventh Symphony by Shostakovich on 8 January 1943. Called the "Leningrad" Symphony, this evening-length work is the first of the composer's wartime symphonies, for which there was much vying among conductors in the United States as to who would be honored with the American premiere. In the end the broadcast premiere (and first actual American performance) was awarded to Toscanini, who performed it with the NBC Symphony on 19 July 1942, while the concert premiere was given by Koussevitzky at Tanglewood, though not with the Boston Symphony. Wartime restrictions on travel, including gas rationing, prevented the BSO from performing at Tanglewood that summer, so the work was performed by the Berkshire Music Center Orchestra, the student ensemble at Tanglewood.

Stokowski had been in the running for the premiere, as Monteux had not, and even tried to persuade Toscanini to cede the work to him (Stokowski and Toscanini shared the NBC Symphony from 1942 to 1944) on the grounds that he would be a more convincing interpreter of the score than Toscanini because of his Slavic ancestry. Having lost this contest, Stokowski nevertheless performed the work for a time whenever he could, including on a concert with the NBC Symphony later in 1942.

Two major American works received their San Francisco premieres under Monteux's direction during that season, Barber's Violin Concerto on 15 and 16

January 1943, with the American virtuoso Albert Spalding as soloist, and the Third Symphony by William Schuman the following week, 22 and 23 January. Schuman's Third had won the New York Music Critics Award as the best new work of the 1941–42 season. In presenting it in San Francisco, Monteux was following his usual practice of giving his audience the most significant of the newer works. It was one of a handful of major American scores he continued to conduct for the rest of his career. On this occasion it was presented as part of a pan-American program that also included works by the Mexican Carlos Chávez, the Brazilian Heitor Villa-Lobos, and the Chilean Domingo Santa Cruz. The soloist was the Chilean pianist Claudio Arrau, who was making his California debut in a decidedly foreign work in this context, Robert Schumann's Concerto in A minor.

Commenting on William Schuman's symphony, Frankenstein (23 January) found it "the most powerful American symphony yet presented here" after the Third Symphony of Schuman's teacher, Roy Harris. "It will, in all probability, take its place in the future repertoire as one of the greatest musical contributions this country has yet made." Frankenstein was correct in his assessment, though not quite in his prediction. While the Third has proven to be the most frequently performed of Schuman's symphonies, even among musicians more people do not know it than do.

Other works presented in local premieres were the Fifth Symphony by the Polish-born Alexandre Tansman, which the composer conducted, and José Iturbi's Fantasy for Piano and Orchestra, also conducted by its composer, with his sister Amparo as soloist. Iturbi, who was himself a frequent piano soloist in San Francisco, was guest conductor for the entire concert on 5 and 6 February. He was then quite a popular personality through his several appearances in Hollywood films and was also conductor of the Rochester Philharmonic Orchestra. (He once said, concerning his films, that he could never be accused of being a poor actor because he always appeared as himself.)

The *San Francisco Chronicle* ran a lengthy article by Alfred Frankenstein on 14 March 1943 under the headline "The Symphony Has Modernism Trouble." A greater-than-usual number of complaints about "too much modern music" had prompted Monteux to cancel a performance of "the first American orchestral score by the most distinguished composer now residing in the Bay Region." (One assumes he means Darius Milhaud, who was teaching at Mills College.) Frankenstein went on to discuss the points raised in an editorial in *The Daily Californian*, the student newspaper of the University of California, Berkeley, which was severely critical of Monteux's programming of contemporary music. One would have thought students would be more open minded on this issue than their more conservative elders, but this was apparently not the case. Both the student editorial and Frankenstein cited statistics concerning the percentage of modern music and the percentage of "the classics" appearing on the orchestra's programs. Frankenstein summed up:

A blanket condemnation of modern music implies as gross a lack of judgment as would a blanket oath of allegiance to everything written since 1900. And those who do issue such blanket protests are so lacking in powers of discrimination that one wonders what the "classics" can mean to them. It has been my observation that this kind of cry for the "classics" does not mean what is says. A program of Bach, Beethoven and Brahms without soloist will not draw any better than a program of Bliss, Berg and Bartók; the "classics" these people demand are Tchaikovsky, Godard and such eminent old masters as Edward German and Victor Herbert. . . . Most Americans are tolerant, and there are some, even among the students of the University of California, who are inquisitive and informed about their own world. Unfortunately the intolerant are always more vociferous than the others, and if in this instance they have their way, the results may easily be disastrous.

On 2 and 3 April Monteux conducted an all-Beethoven program consisting of a string-orchestra version of the Grosse Fuge, and the Fifth and Seventh Symphonies. In memory of Rachmaninoff, who had died on 28 March 1943, "The Death of Clärchen" from *Egmont* was also given.

Monteux was always alert to young talent, and if it was local, so much the better—hence the debut of Isaac Stern several years before. On 16 and 17 April another San Francisco native, a fifteen-year-old pianist named Leon Fleisher, made his debut with a performance, to great acclaim, of Liszt's Concerto No. 2.

The following season, 1943–44, brought a change in format. There were only eight subscription pairs, but there were eight other single-subscription concerts, making a total of sixteen different programs. The popular André Kostelanetz was a guest conductor for two of the single concerts, on 27 November and 4 December. His programs included several local premieres: Dmitri Kabalevsky's Overture to *Colas Breugnon*, Nikolai Miaskovsky's Symphony No. 21, Aaron Copland's *A Lincoln Portrait* with Richard Hale as narrator, and the Symphonic Picture of Gershwin's *Porgy and Bess*, arranged by Robert Russell Bennett. Kostelanetz also gave the American premiere of the tone poem *Frontiers* by Paul Creston (1906–1985).

For his part, Monteux conducted the world premiere of Milhaud's *Opus Americanum* No. 2 (the composer's first orchestral work composed in the United States, postponed from the previous season because of the "modernism trouble"). He also led the San Francisco premieres of Gilbert's *Dance in Place Congo*, which he had premiered at the Metropolitan Opera in 1918; Morton Gould's *Spirituals for Orchestra*; Stravinsky's Capriccio for Piano and Orchestra (the cause of so much acrimony between Monteux and Stravinsky in 1930), with Jesús María Sanromá as soloist; David Diamond's *Psalms*; Isadore Freed's *Pastorales*; and the dynamic and combative Fourth Symphony by Ralph Vaughan Williams. Freed (1900–1960) had been born in Russia but immigrated to the United States while still a child. He had studied in Philadelphia and in Paris (where he was a pupil of d'Indy) and was on the faculty of the Hartt College of Music in Hartford, Connecticut, from 1944 until his death. At some point he became a good friend of Monteux's, who conducted his music frequently.

In writing about the Gilbert and Gould works, given on 18 February, Alfred Frankenstein found the former to be the finest early score on American folk themes, a harbinger of similar works by Copland and Chávez, and thought Monteux's revival of it among the most important events of the season. Morton Gould was able to polish his craft by writing and arranging for radio, and while Frankenstein did not think his *Spirituals* possessed the originality of Gilbert's music, he nevertheless appreciated the piece's bright and clever orchestration.

Gould was then thirty years old. In later years he recalled, in a conversation I had with him, that he had spoken to Monteux rather apologetically about the fact that his piece had been written for a radio performance. "That's all right," replied Monteux. "When I was young I played in a house of prostitution." There is no evidence that he actually did. We know that he played at the Folies Bergères, which is risqué but not quite the same thing. Could Gould have misremembered or embellished the story? Possibly. Could it have been a joke on Monteux's part? Also possible. Could Monteux have played in a house of prostitution? Equally possible.

To commemorate the centennial of Rimsky-Korsakov's birth, Monteux performed, on 18 March, the March from *The Tale of the Tsar Saltan*, the tone poem *Sadko* (almost never played any longer), and the *Russian Easter* Overture. On 21 and 22 January Leon Fleisher returned to play the First Piano Concerto of Brahms. The week before, in an unusual presentation for a symphony concert, Monteux had as guests the Spanish dancer known as La Argentinita and her ensemble, who performed to various Spanish works, authentic or otherwise, by Enrique Granados, Bizet, Isaac Albéniz, Tomás Bretón, and Falla.

The 1944–45 season reverted to the standard twelve pairs of subscription concerts, on the first of which, 1 and 2 December, Monteux conducted what appear to have been his first ever performances of Elgar's *Enigma Variations*. In later years in England it was thought that this quintessential English masterpiece was a new addition to Monteux's repertoire, but his mastery of it goes back at least to 1944.

As the season began Monteux received the tragic news that his favorite brother, Henri, who had established himself in France as an actor, had perished in a Nazi concentration camp. In Henri's memory he conducted a work he had refused to play during World War I, Richard Strauss's *Death and Transfiguration*. He told Mrs. Armsby, "It shall be my message and my prayer for my brother" (Armsby 1960, 79). This particular Strauss work has been denigrated by many critics as the least worthy of the composer's tone poems. They feel that as the deceased person's soul ascends to heaven, the music descends into bathos. Perhaps their opinion was influenced by Mengelberg's last Concertgebouw recording of the work, in which the closing pages are milked for all they are worth, with sickening string glissandos. But it was probably Monteux's favorite of them all, for many of the performances he gave of the score, like the single recording he made of it, were shattering. Perhaps it was the thought of his brother that made it so. While Monteux obviously was greatly affected by Henri's death, he was not one to openly display his emotions; outwardly he could appear quite stoic.

On the same program with the Strauss, 21 and 23 December 1944, Monteux conducted the San Francisco premiere of the Violin Concerto by the Russian-born Louis Gruenberg (1884–1964). Jascha Heifetz, who had commissioned the work, was the soloist, as he was for the RCA-Victor recording that ensued.

A greater-than-usual number of works new to San Francisco were presented that season under Monteux's baton, of which the most significant were the Sixth Symphony of Shostakovich, the Suite from *The Plow That Broke the Plains* by Virgil Thomson, *Folk Rhythms of Today* by Roy Harris, *Protée* (Symphonic Suite No. 2) by Milhaud, and, unusually for Monteux, Schoenberg's Chamber Symphony No. 2. Additionally, Carlos Chávez as guest conductor led the local premieres of his Sarabande for String Orchestra and Concerto for Four Horns and Orchestra. Other atypical repertoire for Monteux, though obviously not a premiere, was heard at the concerts of 29 and 31 March 1945, when the program was devoted to scenes from Wagner's *Parsifal*. The soloists were the soprano Dusolina Giannini, the tenor Frederick Jagel, and the bass Douglas Beattie. Also heard was the San Francisco Municipal Chorus, of which Hans Leschke was the longtime director.

Efrem Kurtz was a guest conductor on 12 and 13 January, and there was a most unusual such guest for the concerts of 23 and 24 February, a fourteen-year-old conductor named Lorin Maazel. Monteux had heard this wunderkind conduct in Philadelphia at the Robin Hood Dell the previous summer and had been impressed enough to invite the young man to share a program with him in San Francisco, where he conducted Schubert's *Rosamunde* Overture and Mendelssohn's "Italian" Symphony. (Maazel had, in 1939, conducted the New York Philharmonic at the New York World's Fair at the age of nine.) On the same program, with Monteux conducting, Naoum Blinder performed Ernest Bloch's Violin Concerto.

A highlight of the season was a Brahms Festival, 13, 15, and 17 March, the concerts not part of the subscription series. The programs included all four of the symphonies; the Violin Concerto, played by Erica Morini; the Piano Concerto No. 2, with Artur Schnabel as soloist; the *Song of Destiny*, with the Municipal Chorus; the two overtures, the *Academic Festival* and the *Tragic*; and a group of five songs orchestrated by Alfred Hertz, in which the soprano Dusolina Giannini was the soloist.

In 1939 Monteux had conducted the first San Francisco performance of *The Rite of Spring*. Now he felt it was time to do it again, and performed it on 9 and 10 March 1945, after which the orchestra recorded the work for RCA Victor.

The season ended on a note of tragedy, not for Monteux personally but for the country at large. President Franklin D. Roosevelt died on 12 April 1945, and many orchestras that normally played Thursday evening concerts canceled their performance on that date. Since the San Francisco concert pair began on a Friday afternoon, the concert of 13 April was not canceled. Instead, Monteux and the orchestra began their program with the Funeral March from Beethoven's "Eroica" Symphony, during which the audience stood silently throughout its fifteen-minute length.

CHAPTER 14

Recordings and Broadcasts

After Monteux had been in San Francisco five years and the orchestra had amply demonstrated its worth, a contract was signed with RCA Victor to begin recording the symphony. The first recordings were made under unusual circumstances, at least for the time. Even though the orchestra had previously made records for RCA under Alfred Hertz's direction, the technical equipment in the San Francisco area was now deemed inadequate. The best equipment and facilities were in Los Angeles, but rather than transport the orchestra four hundred miles south or bring the equipment up to San Francisco, it was decided that the recordings would be made over a telephone line, the orchestra playing on the stage of the War Memorial Opera House, the recording machines running in Los Angeles. But the telephone line would only be available after midnight, which is when the first sessions took place on 21 and 22 April 1941.

The first works to be recorded were Ravel's *La valse*; the "Bridal Procession" from Rimsky-Korsakov's *Le coq d'or*; d'Indy's *Symphony on a French Mountain Air*, with Maxim Schapiro as piano soloist; and Franck's Symphony in D minor and his *Pièce héroïque* in the orchestration by Charles O'Connell, who was, perhaps not coincidentally, the RCA producer for the recordings. It is entirely possible that Monteux was giving O'Connell a sort of birthday present, for the recording of the Franck *Pièce* was made on O'Connell's birthday.

La valse was, of course, an old standby with Monteux, even though he once told his students that he thought the piece was poorly orchestrated. He had already recorded it with the Orchestre Symphonique de Paris in 1930, but the San Francisco version is a great advance both orchestrally and technically, in spite of the unusual recording method. This performance has more thrust and greater lilt and is ultimately more exciting than the earlier recording. It does contain, however, one brief but obvious flaw. As recounted in David Schneider's *The San Francisco Symphony*, the orchestra's principal trumpet, Benjamin Klatzkin, did not play on the recording because he was refused the additional overscale pay he had requested. In his stead was Charles Bubb, who played very well—except that he cracked on the final note of a short but tricky solo passage. Several takes were

151

made of this particular 78-rpm side, but Monteux's preference overall was for the one with the mistake, so that is the one that was issued (Schneider 1983, 35–36). Certain recordings, not necessarily from San Francisco, have acquired an endearingly legendary status because of such bloopers. The San Francisco *La valse* is one of them, notwithstanding the excellence of the recording in other respects. Some time later, when Klatzkin had returned to the orchestra and *La valse* was again scheduled, in the first rehearsal he made the same mistake, prompting Monteux to remark, "Oh, you want to sound just like the record." (Bubb would eventually become the orchestra's principal trumpet.)

In general, Monteux did not like making records, at least in the 78-rpm era, when works had to be chopped up into approximately four- to four-and-a-half-minute chunks. His thinking was that a recording should demonstrate the quality of an orchestra's playing, and if there was an error, so be it. If mistakes were made in performances, they could also be made in recordings. If a mistake had to be corrected for its own sake, then that was not a true picture of the orchestra's performance. He did not, of course, reckon with the effect such an error would have on the listener with repeated playing. And yet, most of Monteux's recordings, with or without mistakes, whether on 78s, LP, or CD, whether spliced together or not, give the impression of being actual performances rather than recordings.

In 1942 the orchestra made a recording that became an instant classic, one that was never out of the RCA Victor catalog on either 78s or LP and is now available on CD—Rimsky-Korsakov's *Scheherazade*. In spite of the dull recorded sound, which obscures some details, and the acidic-sounding oboe, it is a performance of great excitement and forward momentum. Monteux is not as languorous as some of his colleagues in the lovely third movement, "The Young Prince and the Young Princess." Here he directs a graceful 6/8 in two beats per measure, a faster tempo than normally heard when the piece is conducted "in six." It is possible that Monteux's tempo was influenced by his many performances of the score with the Ballets Russes, where the brisker tempo may have been the norm. His tempos for actual ballet scores by Ravel, Stravinsky, and others always reflected the tempos to which the music could be danced. (Of course, the movement is marked Andantino quasi allegretto, not a very slow tempo.)

Contributing to the recording's success was the elegant and masterly playing of the orchestra's legendary concertmaster, Naoum Blinder, in the many solo violin passages. Also not to be forgotten is the album cover, one of the most celebrated examples of that art form. Depicted was a sultan seated on a phonograph record, in the air as if on a magic carpet.

A complete listing of Monteux's recordings can be found in the discography. This chapter will deal with only a few of the more significant ones from San Francisco. Bearing in mind Monteux's philosophy of recording, one can definitely say that the ensemble transcended its limitations under his direction and produced a distinctive sonority that could not be confused with that of any other orchestra. As heard on records, this was a bright and open sound that had an appealing sweetness to the strings and woodwinds (except for the first oboe in the early days) and an arresting bite to the brass. Playing an integral role in this sonority were the acoustics of the War Memorial Opera House.

Probably the most celebrated of the San Francisco recordings are the two versions of Berlioz's *Symphonie fantastique*, dating from 1945 and 1950 respectively. This is the most frequently recorded work in Monteux's discography—five official versions in all (the others are from Paris, Vienna, and Hamburg). Monteux was one of a very few conductors who played the work on its own terms, in the full spirit of its title. Under so many well-meaning but uninspired interpreters it might as well be called Symphony No. 1 in C major, Op. 14. Monteux was able to preserve order and proportion while still projecting the fantastic element excitingly (in spite of the fact that the closing few measures of the 1950 recording are a bit of a scramble).

The fantastic aspects of Monteux's interpretation include a great flexibility of tempo, especially in the "Scene in the Fields" (for "fantastic" can also refer to fantasy); the menacing quality of the muted horns at the beginning of the "March to the Scaffold," and, later in the same movement, the emphasis of the bass trombone's lowest notes to produce a quite grotesque sonority; and in the finale, the "Dream of a Witches' Sabbath," the stressing of isolated muted horn notes to produce a particularly nasty sound. Monteux was very alert to the work's strange orchestral colors, either specified or implied.

There are also two San Francisco recordings of the Franck Symphony in D minor (1941 and 1950) and the Brahms Second Symphony (1945 and 1951). In the case of the former, the first recording became so popular that the master discs deteriorated to the point of uselessness, necessitating a new recording. Monteux's superb reading was to be surpassed in 1961 by his one and only recording with the Chicago Symphony.

Considering Monteux's love for Brahms and the great feeling and insight he brought to that composer's music, it is ironic that instead of creating a single set of the four symphonies, he recorded the Second Symphony four times (the others in Vienna and London). Both of the San Francisco recordings of this work are remarkably lithe and fleet, with none of the turgidity often encountered even in this, the most amiable and radiant of the composer's works. The 1945 version was complete on four well-filled 78-rpm discs, when all other recordings of the work required five discs. (The recording of the Brahms Second reissued on CD in RCA's 1994 Pierre Monteux Edition, while identified as the 1951 recording, is actually that of 1945.)

Not to be overlooked is the 1950 recording of Chausson's Symphony in B-flat, by the early twenty-first century considered a thoroughly unfashionable work (so unfashionable, in fact, that when the New York Philharmonic performed it in 2000 it was the first time that organization had programmed it in thirty-six years). The work is, admittedly, an acquired taste, but once acquired an unforgettable one, and Monteux's is an especially glowing and noble account. In this regard, his

1942 recording of d'Indy's Second Symphony, also in B-flat, is of interest, principally because it was the work's premiere on disc, and it would not receive another recording for fifty years. There are those who regard it as the finest of the symphonies in the late-romantic French tradition, though to some it lacks the thematic distinction of any of the others. The d'Indy Second Symphony was recorded on 2 March 1942, the day Monteux became an American citizen.

Of the three Beethoven symphonies (Nos. 2, 4, and 8) recorded by Monteux in San Francisco, the Eighth (1950) is particularly outstanding, extremely unbuttoned and ebullient. Stravinsky admired it. Perhaps the most remarkable recording of all is that of *The Rite of Spring* made in 1945, a stupendous performance in which the still-second-tier orchestra truly outdoes itself. Also worthy of mention are the three Debussy *Images* (1951), transparently clear, and Strauss's *Ein Heldenleben* (1947), again with Naoum Blinder in the solo violin passages (and for some reason not released by RCA until 1994). Monteux made two further recordings on his return to the orchestra in 1960.

Mention should also be made of Monteux's two recorded collaborations with the violinist Yehudi Menuhin, a native San Franciscan who performed often with Monteux throughout both their careers. While the recording of Bruch's Concerto No. 1 is not technically of the highest quality, it reveals a superior performance and interpretation, as does that of Lalo's *Symphonie espagnole*, unissued until 1995. Two recordings were also made with Jascha Heifetz. One is the first, and so far the only, version of the concerto by the Russian-born American composer Louis Gruenberg, a work composed especially for Heifetz, and the other is Chausson's *Poème*, released only in 2001. Oddly, except for d'Indy's *Symphony on a French Mountain Air*, Monteux made no San Francisco recordings with a piano soloist.

In the autumn 2000 issue of the magazine *International Classical Record Collector* (now *Classic Record Collector*), Pierre Paquin wrote of RCA's butchery of many recordings by Monteux and other conductors on their roster, such as Koussevitzky, Charles Munch, and Toscanini. In 1943 the company began employing a device designed to compress the dynamic range of the recordings, eliminating the need for the engineer to monitor the recording levels. The result was that loud passages were automatically reduced in volume and soft passages boosted, producing an all-purpose sound quality that drastically compromised the effectiveness of the recorded performances, most of which were musically of the very highest quality. This unfortunate situation lasted for seven years.

In January 1941 the San Francisco Symphony and the Los Angeles Philharmonic began a series of alternating Sunday evening broadcasts that were heard on the West Coast only, under the sponsorship of Standard Oil of California. Called *The Standard Hour*, the sixty-minute program was performed by the "Standard Symphony Orchestra," an alias used for whichever ensemble was heard. Pierre Monteux conducted in San Francisco, Alfred Wallenstein in Los Angeles, and most of the programs featured a well-known soloist, either vocal or instrumental.

The early San Francisco broadcasts originated in a tightly cramped studio in NBC's downtown headquarters, but soon the War Memorial Opera House became the site, complete with "studio" audience. The sponsor modestly did not include commercials but did make one stipulation: no musical selection was to exceed twenty minutes in length, give or take a few minutes.

Such a policy meant that the programs included many overtures, tone poems, and light pieces, but some of the shorter symphonies of the repertoire were not excluded, such as Haydn's No. 88, Mozart's "Haffner," and even Mendelssohn's "Italian" and Schumann's Fourth. With longer symphonies and concertos, selected movements would be performed. For example, on 16 February 1947 Monteux presented the first two movements of Beethoven's Fifth Symphony and on 10 December 1950 the rest of it. Many of the lighter works would never appear on the subscription series, pieces such as Chabrier's *España* and John Philip Sousa's *Stars and Stripes Forever*.

Standard Oil made an exception to its twenty-minute rule on 7 April 1946, when it allowed a complete performance of the Franck symphony. It is possible that this gesture was meant as a slightly belated birthday tribute to Monteux—the actual date had been three days before. In any case, it was his seventy-first birthday, not the round-numbered event that is normally celebrated with special fanfare.

A ten-CD compilation of performances from the *Standard Hour* series was released in 1997 by Music and Arts Programs of America. This set is valuable for its inclusion of many works Monteux did not otherwise record commercially. Beethoven's *Leonore* Overture No. 3 (of which he did make a commercial recording that was never issued) is a truly great interpretation, rhythmically alert, warmly expressive, and very exciting, especially in the coda. Mozart's "Haffner" Symphony is particularly fine, spirited in the Allegro movements, elegant in the Andante, with good string sound. Monteux occasionally indulges in ritards common at the time but unfashionable today. The finale, which follows Mozart's wish that it be "played as fast as possible," has especially playful touches; Monteux is having fun with a piece that demands it.

Several Mozart overtures (including *Don Giovanni*, *The Magic Flute*, and *The Abduction from the Seraglio*) make one regret not having heard Monteux conduct the operas. Haydn's Symphony No. 88 is straightforwardly presented, the Minuet unlumbering for once, the jovial finale pushed along a bit, demonstrating the well-placed confidence Monteux had in his musicians.

Other high points of the set include a Richard Strauss collection with an impassioned and sensitive *Don Juan*; a furious *Death and Transfiguration*, its one true climax magnificently realized; and a *Till Eulenspiegel* that is capricious in the best sense of the word. In the numerous Wagner selections, the slow pieces, such as the excerpts from *Parsifal* and *Tristan und Isolde*, are not stretched to the breaking point, as they so often are these days, but allowed to flow naturally. And the buoyant *Meistersinger* Prelude reminds the listener that this is, after all, the introduction to a comic opera.

The marvelous rendition of Dukas's *The Sorcerer's Apprentice* is a graphic portrayal of Goethe's amusingly terrifying tale—no Mickey Mouse here. There is also much Berlioz, Rimsky-Korsakov, Franck, and Mendelssohn, as well as a smattering of Brahms, Borodin, Glazunov, Liszt, Rachmaninoff, and Tchaikovsky, among others.

What is disturbing and disappointing, however, is the number of cuts in works where one does not normally expect them, perhaps because of broadcast demands. Rimsky-Korsakov's *Russian Easter* Overture and the suite from Strauss's *Der Rosenkavalier* each have about five minutes missing; the latter omits the music of the duet before the final waltz. The "Forest Murmurs" from Wagner's *Siegfried* and "Siegfried's Rhine Journey" from his *Götterdämmerung*, the Polovtsian Dances from Borodin's *Prince Igor*, and several other works are presented in truncated form. Worse, and surprisingly for Monteux, the cuts are often awkward and arbitrary. Nevertheless, the level of the orchestral playing is extremely high, with few mistakes, and those minor. The set documents the work of a master conductor and his musicians operating at a consistently high level in performances never intended for posterity.

CHAPTER 15

The Philharmonic and a Return
to Philadelphia and Amsterdam

Many symphony orchestras throughout the world carry the designation "Philharmonic." Of course, there is no difference between a symphony orchestra and a philharmonic orchestra. Some orchestras, such as those of Philadelphia and Cleveland, dispense with an adjective entirely. Occasionally, just to confuse the issue, one finds a philharmonic-symphony orchestra. Such was the case for many years in New York City. The New York Philharmonic, founded in 1842, and the New York Symphony, founded in 1878, consolidated in 1928 to form the grandly named Philharmonic-Symphony Society of New York. Even at that, especially once the Sunday afternoon radio broadcasts began in 1930, everyone referred to the organization simply as the Philharmonic. The existence of such orchestras as the Berlin Philharmonic, the London Philharmonic, the Vienna Philharmonic, and the Los Angeles Philharmonic notwithstanding, when one says, at least in New York, "the Philharmonic," it is that city's orchestra that one is talking about. In 1957 the name was officially shortened to the New York Philharmonic (though it is still the Philharmonic-Symphony Society that maintains and operates it).

Pierre Monteux's first appearances with the Philharmonic took place at the Stadium Concerts in the summer of 1927. His first Philharmonic appearances in Carnegie Hall were also summer concerts, on 6 and 13 June 1943. At that time the orchestra began a summer Sunday afternoon radio series under the sponsorship of the United States Rubber Company. The series lasted through 1945, though the regular winter series continued to be broadcast as well. Monteux's programs included such standard fare as, once again, the Franck symphony and the Tchaikovsky Fourth Symphony, as well as the Schumann Piano Concerto, with Artur Schnabel as soloist. In 2002 Music and Arts released a long-awaited off-the-air recording of the Schumann concerto. This marvelous performance is a valuable document, for neither Schnabel nor Monteux ever recorded that concerto otherwise.

In 1943 Artur Rodzinski began his relatively brief tenure as musical director of the Philharmonic. For the 1944–45 season he invited Monteux to be guest conductor for two weeks in celebration of his seventieth birthday.

157

Today when a major symphony orchestra performs three or four concerts a week, the same program is repeated for each of the week's concerts. In the 1940s this was not necessarily the case. At that time the Philharmonic's season consisted of twenty-eight subscription weeks of Thursday-Friday pairs and Sunday matinees (the Fridays were also matinees). Additionally, in fourteen to sixteen of those weeks there would be a Saturday night concert. Often the Saturday program was completely different from the others, and the Sunday program partially different. The ninety-minute broadcast time on Sunday also affected the programming, which had to be reshuffled as a result, and often an extra piece was played after the broadcast.

Monteux's two weeks of Philharmonic concerts show the great variety of music orchestras in those days played in a single week and throughout a season, which produced more interesting and varied seasons than is often the case today. Again, programs tended to be longer then than they are now.

Here, then, are Monteux's Philharmonic programs for two weeks in the fall of 1944:

2 and 3 November
Beethoven: *Leonore* Overture No. 3
Brahms: Symphony No. 3 in F major
Debussy: *Images*
Respighi: *The Pines of Rome*

4 and 5 November
Beethoven: Overture to *The Creatures of Prometheus*
Brahms: Piano Concerto No. 1 in D minor; Leon Fleisher, soloist
William Grant Still: *Old California* (New York premiere)
Debussy: Two Nocturnes
Strauss: *Don Juan*

9 and 10 November
Weber: *Jubilee* Overture
Beethoven: Symphony No. 1 in C major
Milhaud: *Protée* (Symphonic Suite No. 2)
Franck-O'Connell: *Pièce héroïque*
Hindemith: Symphony, *Mathis der Maler*

11 and 12 November
Berlioz: Overture to *Benvenuto Cellini*
Sibelius: Violin Concerto in D minor; Michael Rosenker, soloist
Prokofieff-Byrns: *Suite diabolique* (New York premiere)
Ravel: *Rapsodie espagnole*
Wagner: Prelude and "Liebestod" from *Tristan und Isolde*

William Grant Still (1895–1978) was the first African American composer to achieve international recognition. Monteux's 5 November performance of the symphonic poem *Old California* is included in the Philharmonic's CD set of historic broadcast performances of American music. The *Suite diabolique* was an orchestration by the conductor Harold Byrns of several piano pieces by Prokofiev, opening with the *Suggestion diabolique*.

The Philharmonic normally had four rehearsals for its Thursday-Friday program and an additional rehearsal (or perhaps two) for its Saturday and/or Sunday program. Even allowing for the fact that Monteux may have consolidated rehearsals so as to cover all the week's repertoire, no single work could have received a lot of rehearsal. One might think rather slapdash performances would be the result. And yet, here is the esteemed Virgil Thomson writing in the 12 November 1944 *Herald Tribune*, in a Sunday article summing up Monteux's visit, quite possibly the most celebrated and perceptive appreciation of Monteux's work to have appeared in print:

Pierre Monteux's two-week visit as guest conductor of the Philharmonic-Symphony Orchestra has led music lovers of all schools (the critical press included) to two conclusions: namely, that this conductor has drawn from our orchestra more beautiful sounds and more beautiful mixtures of sounds than any other conductor has done in many years, and that his readings of Brahms are highly refreshing.

It has been a long time, a very long time, since our Philharmonic sounded like an orchestra.

Thomson goes on to describe the inconsistency of the orchestra's playing over the years, and how such conductors as Toscanini and Rodzinski had produced fine results without any particularly distinctive quality of sound. He continues:

It has remained for Pierre Monteux to achieve what many of us thought was hopeless. He has made the Philharmonic play with beauty of tone, many kinds of it, and with perfect balance and blending—to sound, in short, like an orchestra, a first-class orchestra requiring no apology. And he has also played music as familiar as that of Brahms and Beethoven (not to speak of Debussy) with not only a wonderful beauty of sound but a far from usual eloquence as well. His is the way a real orchestra should sound, the way the first-class orchestras of the world all do sound. And this is the way many musicians have long wished the music of Johannes Brahms could be made to sound.

It should be mentioned here that Brahms was far from being one of Thomson's favorite composers.

Thomson then compares Monteux's Brahms performances with those of the late Frederick Stock with the Chicago Symphony. He finds that

> Mr. Monteux is less expert than Dr. Stock was at preserving a poetical and rhythmic unity throughout, but he is more expert than anybody at lifting the velvet pall that is accustomed in our concerts to lie over the Brahms instrumentation and allowing everything, middle voices too, to shine forth with translucency. His strings never obscure the woodwinds. His trumpets and trombones never blast away the strings. His horns, when force is indicated, play very loud; but their loudness is bright, not heavy; it is a flash of light rather than a ton of bricks.

Although he finds some fault with Monteux's occasionally allowing the slower passages in Brahms and Debussy to go dead, the animation disappearing, the sounds not blending, Thomson observes that such moments are never long and concludes:

> Listening lately to Pierre Monteux conduct Brahms and Debussy on the same program brought to mind how much the music of these two composers is alike, or at least demands like treatment. The secret of their rhythm is very much the same secret. And non-violation of their rhythm is essential and preliminary to producing among their orchestral sounds luminosity. That and the use of transparent, or nonweighty, orchestral tone. By what occult methods Mr. Monteux produces in our Philharmonic-Symphony Orchestra a real community of rhythmic articulation, not to mention the delights of delicate balance and blending that proceed from this, I cannot even guess. The guest conductors who have failed where he has succeeded would like to know too, I imagine. (Thomson 1981, 258–60)

Of interest are the two soloists who performed on Monteux's weekend concerts. The programs of 4 and 5 November marked the New York debut of the sixteen-year-old San Franciscan Leon Fleisher in a work with which he was to become especially well associated, Brahms's First Concerto. He had already appeared with Monteux in San Francisco the season before, and it was through Monteux's intervention that Fleisher had begun his studies with Artur Schnabel. Today, when all sorts of historic broadcast performances are turning up on various labels, pirated and otherwise, it is curious that, at the time of this writing, Fleisher's national radio debut remains in limbo.

The Russian-born Michael Rosenker (c. 1900–1996), who played the Sibelius Violin Concerto on 11 and 12 November, was the Philharmonic's associate concertmaster, then in his second season with the orchestra. Rosenker recalled that

Monteux had said that he had never conducted the Sibelius concerto before, apparently forgetting that he had performed it with Richard Burgin in 1924. Rosenker also remembered that in the finale's syncopated second theme, at each accented afterbeat, Monteux executed an uncharacteristic swivel of his substantial torso.

For whatever reason, Monteux did not again conduct the Philharmonic in its winter season for eleven years. He did not like New York, but this cannot be the reason for his absence, for he was soon to begin annual appearances at the Stadium Concerts.

Back in 1928, after the controversial conclusion of his engagement in Philadelphia, Monteux had announced, for the second time, that he would never return professionally to the United States. We know, of course, that he soon changed his mind. Had he vowed never to return to Philadelphia, there would have been greater reason to take him at his word, not to mention that Philadelphians would have been happy for him to keep it.

Perhaps sixteen years, though, is long enough for such feelings to cool. In any case, Eugene Ormandy, Stokowski's successor in Philadelphia, was probably not even aware of what had occurred in 1928. He invited Monteux for a two-week engagement in January 1945, which Monteux accepted. In reading the Philadelphia press coverage of that engagement, one finds relatively little reference to the earlier incident. All had been forgiven or forgotten.

Monteux's first concerts were on 5, 6, and 8 January in the Academy of Music, the program as follows:

> Bach-Respighi: Passacaglia and Fugue in C minor
> Mozart: Symphony No. 35 in D major ("Haffner")
> Ravel: *Daphnis et Chloé* Suite No. 1
> Prokofiev: *Romeo and Juliet* Suite No. 1
> Stravinsky: Suite from *The Firebird*

Though many of Monteux's earlier concerts in Philadelphia had been received rather coolly, if not unfavorably, the response to those of 1945 was unmistakably enthusiastic, though there was some question as to the effectiveness of having three ballet suites on one program. Linton Martin of *The Philadelphia Inquirer*, who had not been particularly kind to Monteux in 1928, wrote on 6 January that Monteux had sustained interest throughout the concert, impressively demonstrating his superb musicianship. He noted that the orchestra sounded magnificent under his direction, playing with a full and robust tone and the greatest sensitivity and flexibility, all of which was a pleasure to hear.

New to the Philadelphia critical fraternity was Edwin H. Schloss of the *Record*, who did not mind all the ballet music. He found *Romeo and Juliet* to be highly engaging music and the performance of the *Daphnis* suite exquisite, leading him to wonder why the First Suite should have been neglected over the more familiar

Second Suite. Schloss also pointed out that Monteux had played the original 1910 version of the *Firebird* Suite (which includes two numbers omitted from the 1919 version, later restored in that of 1945) and the last two movements of the 1919 suite.

The same program was played in New York at Carnegie Hall on 9 January. Virgil Thomson wrote the next day in the *Herald Tribune* that "Pierre Monteux and the Philadelphia Orchestra gave us double pleasure last night in Carnegie Hall, the second from being able to play modern orchestral music with clarity and delicacy and all sonorous loveliness, the first from really knowing how it goes." Later he thanked both the Philharmonic and the Philadelphia managements for having brought Monteux to New York, for he had the courage and the knowledge to play correctly, and in no small dosage, the great orchestral music of our century. Thomson had actually not enjoyed the Prokofiev work, finding it thin both in texture and substance and lacking in interest as concert music, though he was "glad to have had the privilege of being a bit bored by it once."

For his second week in Philadelphia, 12 and 13 January, Monteux brought Isaac Stern with him as soloist in the Beethoven Violin Concerto. It was the twenty-four-year-old violinist's debut at the Academy of Music, though he had played at the Dell the previous summer, and in the same concerto. Stern was praised for not playing the Beethoven as a virtuoso display piece, for interpreting the music introspectively as poetry rather than drama. For his part, Monteux offered Beethoven's *Egmont* Overture, the Philadelphia premiere of Paul Creston's *Pastorale and Tarantella*, and Elgar's *Enigma Variations*.

Creston was a composer of whose music Monteux was quite fond, and he would soon add the young man's Second Symphony to his repertoire. The *Pastorale and Tarantella* was thought to be agreeable, not terribly original in content, but rhythmically exuberant, a frequent criticism of the composer's music. Not much was written about the Elgar performance other than that Monteux had succeeded in minimizing the work's intrinsic dryness and academicism (not something one reads about the piece today).

The critics felt that Monteux had made an excellent impression on his visit. Schloss concluded, writing on 13 January, that his "gifts of musicianship and taste seem to grow the more one hears him. Not that the San Francisco conductor has not been a full-grown artist of the baton for many decades. We just don't hear him often enough to take him for granted." They would hear him again very soon.

Shortly before the close of the 1944–45 season Monteux received a telegram, dated 3 April 1945, from Olin Downes complimenting him on his tenth anniversary in San Francisco and of the fine work he had done in conducting and building the orchestra. He went on to say that if New Yorkers needed any proof of his great musicianship, they received it with his brilliant concerts with the Philharmonic. He felt that not only had Monteux achieved much with the San Francisco

Symphony, but he had made important contributions to the musical history of America in the past twenty-five years.

On 18 July 1945 Pierre Monteux wrote the following letter to the members of the Concertgebouw Orchestra:

My dear friends,

During these five terrible years, I have not ceased thinking of you, and if I did not write sooner it is because it was not possible for you to receive my letters.

I hope with all my heart that the Orchestra has not suffered too much from the German atrocities and that it remains well within you to continue and even to augment your efforts towards an ideal of art in which music is the most beautiful expression.

As to what concerns me, you doubtlessly know that for ten years I have conducted the San Francisco Symphony. I am very busy with this orchestra that I have rebuilt and which is now one of the best in the United States. But I hope soon to have the occasion and the pleasure of traveling to Europe and to have the joy of seeing you again and giving some concerts with you. My ten years of association with you have been among the happiest of my life and these ten years remain engraved in my memories.

I send you my very best wishes for a brilliant resumption of your concerts and for a season full of success and hope for the future.

Your old and very devoted friend,
Pierre Monteux

When Monteux speaks of the "resumption of your concerts," he is referring to the fact that during the Nazi occupation of Holland the orchestra had undergone severe hardships and, while it did perform, was unable to present a consistent series of concerts. Its chief conductor, Willem Mengelberg, was branded a Nazi collaborator and never conducted the orchestra again after World War II, having been forbidden by the Dutch government to appear in public for a period of six years. This situation resulted in Eduard van Beinum's promotion to the top position. (Mengelberg died in 1951, just before the ban was lifted. There has since been some question as to the validity of the charges against him.)

Rudolf Mengelberg, however, was still in charge of the managerial side of the orchestra, and he responded to Monteux's letter in the friendliest terms. Nevertheless, it was not until 1948 that Monteux returned to Europe and to Amsterdam, although even then there was some doubt whether the engagement would actually take place. Mengelberg had offered Monteux two concerts in Amsterdam and several in surrounding cities. On 18 February 1948 Monteux cabled Mengelberg: PREFER NOT UNDERTAKE SO LONG VOYAGE FOR ONLY TWO REGULAR CONCERTS AMSTERDAM WHICH IS MY GREATEST INTEREST. Mengelberg cabled back that he was offering three concerts in Amsterdam and four in other cities. This satisfied Monteux, who triumphantly conducted the Concertgebouw Orchestra on 20 May in a program of some of his favorites:

Weber: Overture to *Euryanthe*
Brahms: Violin Concerto in D major; Yehudi Menuhin, soloist
Berlioz: *Symphonie fantastique*

The favorites included, of course, the soloist. Monteux enjoyed having good soloists on his programs, for he appreciated the great depth of the concerto literature. If the soloist was someone with whom he was especially in sympathy, such as Menuhin, so much the better.

Besides the 20 May concert, the engagement included two Jubilee Concerts in Amsterdam on 25 and 27 May in celebration of the Concertgebouw Orchestra's sixtieth anniversary. For these Monteux programmed, among other works, Ravel's complete *Daphnis et Chloé* and Pijper's Third Symphony. A few weeks later, on 18 and 20 June, he and the orchestra participated in the Holland Festival, which since the war has become an annual event, a prestigious festival encompassing all the arts. Brahms's First Symphony, of which Monteux was a supreme interpreter, figured in these programs, as well as Liszt's Piano Concerto No. 1, with the young American Julius Katchen as soloist. On 21 June, also as part of the Holland Festival, Monteux conducted an opera and ballet evening in the State Theatre, an all-Ravel program of the *Valses nobles et sentimentales* and *L'heure espagnole*, the latter with the Dutch singers Lidy van der Veen, Theo Baylé, Gerard Groot, Jan Voogt, and Frans Vroons.

Monteux returned for concerts in Amsterdam in 1949 and 1950. In 1949 he also gave performances with the Netherlands Opera (successor to the Wagner Society) of Massenet's *Manon* and Gluck's *Orfeo ed Euridice*. Marjorie M. Fisher of the *San Francisco News* was in Amsterdam and reported to her readers on the *Orfeo* performance of 5 July, its opening night, which Queen Juliana had attended. The role of Orfeo was taken by the great English contralto Kathleen Ferrier (1912–1953), who was particularly associated with it. Fisher, who had expected a dull evening, left with the knowledge that *Orfeo* could be a truly wonderful theater piece, especially as performed by Ferrier and conducted by Monteux.

Apparently Rudolf Mengelberg had suggested that for one of his concerts Monteux program the Franck symphony, perhaps the most often requested of all works associated with him. In a letter dated 1 March 1949 Monteux responded, "I will tell you frankly that I am tired to death of the César Franck Symphony." In this instance the Chausson symphony was substituted, followed by the complete *Petrushka*. Nonetheless, "tired to death" though he may have been of it, the Franck symphony would continue to be a central work in his repertoire. Later in the same letter to Mengelberg, Monteux stated, "Frankly, my dear friend, I hate going to Holland and conducting things I conducted year in and year out. Here in San Francisco you would be surprised how little of the French and Russian repertoire I conduct." This remark is itself surprising, for an examination of his San Francisco programs reveals a fairly substantial representation of that very repertoire, especially in the immediate postwar years. But Monteux was beginning to tire of certain works he had performed throughout his life.

CHAPTER 16

Coast to Coast

So pleased were the Philadelphians with Monteux's visit that he was immediately re-engaged as the first guest conductor for the 1945–46 season, though only for one week. (In those days, before jet travel, seasons were not planned years in advance.) For this concert pair, on 26 and 17 October, he programmed Brahms's *Academic Festival Overture*, Beethoven's Fourth Symphony, the first two of Debussy's Nocturnes, the world premiere of Bloch's *Suite symphonique*, and Strauss's *Till Eulenspiegel*. It was an extremely generous bill of fare. One is struck by how many times in his career Monteux constructed a program of five works, at a time when three or four were the norm. Of course, some pieces are shorter than others, but taken as a totality a Monteux concert amounted to a rather full evening, especially considering that the more pieces there are on the program, the more time is taken up by applause and by the shifting around of the players between pieces.

Commenting in the *Evening Bulletin* of 27 October, Max de Schauensee referred to Monteux as "one of the really great conductors of our time." He did find the program a bit long but rewarding nevertheless. All the critics hailed Bloch's suite as a masterful work of great originality. It is interesting to note that while de Schauensee found Monteux's reading of Debussy's Nocturnes an authentic interpretation, Schloss in the *Record* thought it disappointing, lacking the full potential of the score's enchantment; and while de Schauensee and Schloss praised the Beethoven performance, Linton Martin of the *Inquirer* found it phlegmatic.

If this was considered a long program, what of the performance in New York's Carnegie Hall on 30 October? The Debussy Nocturnes were dropped, and in their stead the great African American soprano Dorothy Maynor sang arias from Mozart's Mass in C minor and *The Marriage of Figaro*, as well as "Asie" from Ravel's *Shéhérazade*, all of which she had performed earlier in Philadelphia with Ormandy conducting.

Virgil Thomson had taken the night off, at least from Carnegie Hall. He was replaced by Jerome D. Bohm, who, in his *Herald Tribune* review of 31 October, summed up what many have felt about Monteux, at least during his maturity.

This writer has remarked before that perhaps the chief attribute of Mr. Monteux's interpretive art is its profound humanity. Mr. Monteux's unfailing ability to make the orchestra sing at all times, his concern that the melodic contours of the music in hand shall always be as beautifully realized as possible, are reflections of the man's innate warmth and inwardness.

There were differing opinions about Maynor's performance. Some found her Ravel to have been sung with great sensitivity and feeling for color, the diction itself clear and colorful; others mentioned faulty enunciation of the unimaginatively delivered French text. For Bohm, it was Monteux who provided the essential Ravel. It should also be mentioned that the New York critics were less enthusiastic about Bloch's suite than their Philadelphia brethren. The only reference to the program's length came from Edward O'Gorman of the *New York Post*. Commenting on the equilibrium of Monteux's performances, the rightness of them, he wrote, "Mr. Monteux, with his gentle gestures, could go on in this vein until midnight, and he nearly did."

It was now time for Monteux to return to San Francisco to prepare for the opening of the season (now increased to fourteen subscription pairs), which began on 23 and 24 November with Sibelius's Second Symphony and Strauss's *Ein Heldenleben* as the major works. Among the works receiving their first San Francisco performances were Prokofiev's *Summer Day Suite*, Bloch's *Suite symphonique* (odd that he should not have chosen his own orchestra to give the world premiere of this work, but perhaps he felt it would attract greater attention in Philadelphia and New York), Copland's *Appalachian Spring*, William Bergsma's *Music on a Quiet Theme*, George Antheil's Symphony No. 4, Halsey Stevens's Symphony No. 1 (the composer conducting), and four pieces by Stravinsky. These last—*Scherzo à la Russe*, Symphony in Three Movements, *Scènes de ballet*, and the 1945 version of the *Firebird* Suite—were also conducted by the composer, who had become a fairly regular visitor to the Bay city.

One other local premiere deserves mention: Bartók's Piano Concerto No. 2, with the indefatigable Maxim Schapiro as soloist. In fact, Schapiro became, on 29 and 30 March 1946, the first person other than the composer to play this concerto in the United States. Vladimir Horowitz made a rare appearance on 30 November and 1 December when he was heard in one of his signature pieces, Rachmaninoff's Third Piano Concerto. The Municipal Concerts included the local debut of Leonard Bernstein, who on 13 February 1946 conducted Tchaikovsky's "Pathétique" Symphony and his own Dance Episodes from *On the Town*, plus the Grieg Piano Concerto with Jesús María Sanromá (1902–1984) as soloist. The Puerto Rican–born Sanromá was for many years the orchestral pianist of the Boston Symphony, which is how Bernstein first came to know him, and he also taught at the New England Conservatory of Music. Monteux closed the series, and the season, with Beethoven's Ninth Symphony as the conclusion of an all-Beethoven program in which the first half consisted of the *Coriolan* Overture and Joseph Szigeti playing the Violin Concerto. The audience that night got its money's worth.

Late in 1946 a tempest of sorts between Monteux and the San Francisco Art Commission, sponsor of the Municipal Concerts, blew up when Monteux announced that he would no longer conduct in the series. (These were the concerts the orchestra performed in the Civic Auditorium in return for the city's contributing a portion of its property tax revenue to the symphony.) According to the *Oakland Tribune* of 16 December 1946, the art commission had advertised its concert of 21 December with the names "Isaac Stern" (the soloist), "Municipal Chorus," and "San Francisco Symphony" in large type, with Monteux's name underneath in a smaller font. Monteux felt "belittled" by this listing, and was quoted as saying, "That in itself is not important, but it comes in a long train of circumstances that make it impossible for me to continue with the art commission." He added that under such circumstances he would not conduct the concert.

He went on to say that "never in the 12 years since I have been conductor of the San Francisco Symphony has the art commission sought my advice about anything. It never has paid any attention to my suggestions when they were made." He further stated that the art commission had ignored his recommendation for the choice of a local soloist after he had held auditions for that very purpose at the commission's request and added that he was "not prepared to take such treatment"—the whole affair was part of a "definite, planned program" to embarrass him.

Edward Keil, president of the San Francisco Art Commission, said that the advertising would be changed according to Monteux's wishes and explained that this was the first ad prepared by a new publicity agent who was apparently not aware of Monteux's standing as a musician. Monteux did conduct the concert but apparently then severed his relationship with the art commission, for subsequent Municipal Concerts were led by guest conductors, including Dimitri Mitropoulos, Artur Rodzinski, and Leopold Stokowski.

The 1946–47 season brought yet another increase in the subscription season; there were now sixteen subscription programs, each performed three times. The usual Friday afternoon–Saturday night pair was now preceded by a Thursday evening performance—the direct result of the activities of the San Francisco Forum. So great was the demand for tickets among area college students that the forum began sponsoring its own concert series, after which the Thursday series was known as "students night." Of the various premieres presented, the most important was the world premiere, on 9–11 January, of the Second Symphony of Roger Sessions (1896–1985), who at the time was on the faculty of the University of California at Berkeley. An important American composer, he later taught for many years at Princeton University and then at the Juilliard School of Music.

Sessions's style of writing was influenced by the expressionism of Arnold Schoenberg and Alban Berg. Though not yet twelve-tone, it was extremely complex, not the sort of music an audience can easily assimilate at one hearing (though the Second Symphony's perky little Scherzo does contain an eminently hummable tune). It is certainly not written in a style that can have appealed to Monteux. According to David Schneider, while Monteux respected Sessions as a musician, he did not understand his music, nor did he wish to (Schneider 1983, 72). During rehearsals he made unflattering remarks about the piece, delighting those musicians who hated modern music anyway. The score achieved a critical if not a popular success, though, again according to Schneider, when it was played on the Berkeley campus the students cheered and gave it a standing ovation. (Monteux never played the Second Symphony again, although he did continue to perform Sessions's Suite from *The Black Maskers*, which he had first played in Boston.)

Monteux continued to encourage those members of the orchestra who were composers. On 26–28 December Emanuel Leplin conducted the first performances of his *Comedy*, and on 13–15 January Monteux led the first performances of David Sheinfeld's *Adagio and Allegro*. An important American premiere was belatedly given on 27 and 28 February and 1 March: Olivier Messiaen's *L'ascension* (Four Symphonic Meditations), a work dating from 1933.

There was a second belated premiere, this time for San Francisco: Debussy's *Jeux*, of which Monteux had given the world premiere with the Ballets Russes back in 1913. Another local premiere of interest was given on 28–30 November: Richard Strauss's Parergon to the *Symphonia domestica*, a work for piano (left hand alone) and orchestra commissioned by Paul Wittgentstein, who played it on this occasion. (A parergon is a sort of appendix or appendage. The work is based on themes from the *Symphonia domestica*.) Wittgenstein had lost his right arm in World War I and had later commissioned a number of leading composers, including (besides Strauss) Ravel, Prokofiev, Benjamin Britten, and Erich Wolfgang Korngold. The most famous and greatest of the commissioned works is Ravel's Concerto for the Left Hand, first given in San Francisco by Maxim Schapiro in 1943 and also played by Wittgenstein at this engagement. (Wittgenstein never really liked the various works written for him and played very few. While he did play the Ravel piece, he had reservations about it as well.)

Also given their San Francisco premieres under Monteux's direction during 1946–47 were Isadore Freed's *Festival Overture*, Shostakovich's Ninth Symphony, the orchestral version of Milhaud's *Le bal martiniquais*, John Alden Carpenter's *The Seven Ages*, and, on 15–17 May, Prokofiev's Fifth Symphony. One other major premiere was given in the series, but by a visiting orchestra and conductor (the Los Angeles Philharmonic and Alfred Wallenstein).

RCA Victor had been recording Monteux and the San Francisco Symphony since 1941. The recordings had been distributed throughout the United States and in Europe and had sold very well and been critically well received. In addition, many photos of Monteux in San Francisco had appeared in national publications—Monteux walking the city's hills with the family poodle, Fifi, on a leash;

Monteux selecting a lobster at Fisherman's Wharf; Monteux (of course) in front of the orchestra. He and San Francisco had become a world-famous combination. It was only natural that for several years there was talk of providing people in other cities who had bought the recordings the opportunity of hearing the orchestra in person, an idea that RCA Victor and Charles O'Connell had done their best to foster. After much discussion and appropriate fund raising, a tour was planned that would take the orchestra across the United States and back again, an eight-week journey starting on 16 March in Visalia, California, and ending on 10 May 1947 in Sacramento—fifty-six concerts in fifty-three cities. As the orchestra played both matinee and evening concerts in Madison, Wisconsin, on 27 April, they actually performed on fifty-five of the fifty-six days in the eight weeks, which means they had a total of one day off during the entire tour. At least that day was in New York City. (Musicians' unions and orchestra committees did not have the power then that they do now. A one-month tour in the same year by the New York Philharmonic provided no day off. When the NBC Symphony Orchestra made its transcontinental tour in 1950, it performed only three or, at most, four times a week, for the tour had been planned in deference to Toscanini's age of eighty-three. In 1947 Monteux was a youthful seventy-two.)

While the orchestra played in all the major cities from coast to coast, many concerts were in smaller cities, such as Wichita Falls, Texas, and Davenport, Iowa. And how did the orchestra travel? With so many stops en route, the only feasible mode of transportation was by rail, but at least the orchestra had its own private train. Schneider describes the train as a mixed blessing.

> Private train sounds very glamorous, but on seeing our accommodations we were appalled. A closet-sized cubicle was to be the living quarters of *two* musicians. To store our gear and move around without doing ourselves bodily injury seemed impossible. Here we were embarking on this wonderfully exciting tour, condemned to spend half the time in a room smaller than a prison cell. (Schneider 1983, 67)

In a few cities the orchestra did stay in hotels, but most of the sleeping was done on the train.

Mrs. Armsby has written, concerning the stay in Los Angeles, where the orchestra played a pair of concerts:

> The Monteuxs, who always traveled with their French poodle, were refused permission to bring their pet to the downtown hotel. Our manager, Howard Skinner, already harassed by minor upsets in his plans, was now rushing from one hotel to the other, looking for a place which would admit the poodle. In a fortunate attitude, a hotel, far out in the suburbs, offered the Monteuxs a comfortable little cottage adjacent to their well-kept Inn. The hotel management liked dogs. They would gladly take "Fifi" as their

guest. All was again well with the Monteuxs and Pierre showed up at the first rehearsal in a jovial mood, with a flower glowing from his coat lapel. (Armsby 1960, 90)

For the Los Angeles concerts the orchestra had arranged an exchange with its Philharmonic Orchestra. While the San Francisco Symphony and Monteux played a pair of concerts in the Los Angeles subscription series, the Los Angeles Philharmonic under its conductor Alfred Wallenstein (1898–1983) appeared on a subscription pair in the San Francisco series. It was at these concerts that Wallenstein led the San Francisco premiere of Bartók's Concerto for Orchestra. The extremely capable but irascible Wallenstein was, in 1947, a great rarity: an American conductor of a major American orchestra. The situation has changed somewhat; today he would be merely a rarity.

To afford himself some relief as well as security, Monteux engaged one of his former pupils, James Sample, who had studied with him in France, as associate conductor (some of the programs list him as assistant conductor). In this capacity he occasionally led one of the works on a program, usually Strauss's *Don Juan*, in one or another of the smaller cities. He would soon become conductor of the Portland Symphony Orchestra in Oregon and later of Pennsylvania's Erie Philharmonic.

The orchestra performed an enormous repertoire on its tour, having played much, but not all, of it that season at home. Beethoven's Seventh, Brahms's First and Second, the Franck, the Tchaikovsky Fourth—these were just the symphonies in the repertoire, which also included a multitude of tone poems, suites, overtures, and other short pieces. Monteux also generously programmed works by the San Francisco composers William Denny, Emanuel Leplin, and David Sheinfeld, Leplin again conducting his *Comedy* on several occasions. (Monteux later told his students that so many cities had requested the Franck symphony "that I did not play that *symphonie* again for ten years!" He exaggerated a bit, for available programs show that he did play it again in San Francisco only three years later.) On two occasions, 1 April in Birmingham and 3 April in Atlanta, Isaac Stern played Mendelssohn's Violin Concerto, and on 20 April in Buffalo the pianist Leonard Pennario was heard in Saint-Saëns's Concerto No. 2 with Sample conducting; otherwise there were no soloists. Audience and critical response throughout the tour was overwhelmingly enthusiastic. An example is Mildred Norton's review in the *Los Angeles Daily News* of 21 March.

A "Daphnis and Chloe" that was buoyant, brightly colored and sweeping, but not heavy of line. Monteux brought the touch of a master to his unfoldment of the music's sensuous rhythms. . . . I do not think, however, that I have heard the German Brahms sing and soar more beautifully than as played by this deft and perceptive little French conductor.

A highlight of the tour was the concert in Washington, D.C., on 7 April. As might be expected, it was a most distinguished audience that filled Constitution Hall, including diplomats, members of Congress, and even President and Mrs. Harry S. Truman. The president was a great music lover, if a less than great pianist. Mrs. Armsby wrote of meeting him and being told, "All orchestras should travel and give to everyone a chance to hear what only a symphony orchestra can give." He continued, "By the way, I stopped back stage on my way in to speak to Mr. Monteux. I am a great admirer of his" (Armsby 1960, 96).

The excitement of Washington notwithstanding, the fact remains that no touring musicians, whether soloists, chamber music groups, or full symphony orchestras, feel they have arrived until they have performed successfully in New York at Carnegie Hall. The great day arrived for Monteux and his musicians on Friday, 11 April, when they appeared in the august auditorium offering the following program:

> Bach-Respighi: Passacaglia and Fugue in C minor
> Messiaen: *L'ascension* (first New York performance)
> Strauss: *Death and Transfiguration*
> Brahms: Symphony No. 1 in C minor

Many prominent San Franciscans made the trip to New York and some of the other East Coast cities, and the sold-out house included quite a few New York dignitaries and prominent musical figures, among them, according to Schneider, the conductors Efrem Kurtz, William Steinberg, and André Kostelanetz. "And seen standing and cheering in one of the boxes was a little Italian man, also well known as a conductor—Arturo Toscanini" (Schneider 1983, 68).

Mrs. Armsby writes:

> When the final note sounded, the little white haired man, who had divided the attention of the audience with Monteux, rushed from his box down to the stage. Here, he clasped the perspiring Monteux and placed a kiss fervently on each cheek. "I have heard many ovations for my orchestra and for myself," said Arturo Toscanini, "but I never heard anything like this!" (Armsby 1960, 93)

The next day Olin Downes wrote in *The New York Times* that Monteux "has made a symphonic body to be reckoned with nationally." After singling out several wind players, though not by name, for their beautiful solo playing, he continued:

> But more important than these . . . is the balance and blending of the choirs, which has been accomplished remarkably. . . . The summit of the

concert came with the magnificent reading of the Brahms symphony; a
reading which represented the thinking, feeling, doing of a great musician.
. . . From the orchestral standpoint this was a triumph of execution and
of responsive interpretation. The conception and its masterly realization
represented the achievement of one of the great Brahms interpreters of this
period.

References to "the balance and blending of the choirs" appeared frequently in
descriptions of Monteux's performances.

Virgil Thomson, writing in the *Herald Tribune*, lavished his usual praise on
Monteux but felt that the orchestra's strings were weak, not in sound but in transparency, their tone "live but scratchy." The woodwinds and brass he found to be
"of good quality," and Messiaen's piece was a "a convincing synthesis of musical
modernism with devotional piety."

When the tour was in its planning stage, Monteux had resisted the idea of
playing in Boston. Even after twenty-three years, he was still sensitive to the fact
that his contract had not been renewed there in favor of Koussevitzky, and that he
had not been invited to return to the Boston Symphony as a guest conductor; he
was afraid he would not be welcome there. The tour planners, however, had convinced him of the necessity of appearing in this major city, and he had agreed,
though with little enthusiasm.

He need not have worried. The concert in Symphony Hall on Sunday afternoon, 13 April, was a triumph. Mrs. Armsby reported, "As the music progressed,
any remaining bitterness was overcome and when the concert closed Monteux
was given a standing ovation. It was the best reward for his courage in returning
to this once hostile city" (Armsby 1960, 99). Cyrus Durgin of *The Boston Globe*
(14 April) wrote of the tremendous ovation, with stamping and cheering, for
Monteux and his players from normally cool Boston, and pronounced the visit a
complete success.

Koussevitzky attended the concert, and he and Monteux met at a dinner party
afterward. Though there was some awkwardness in their first few minutes together, before long a discussion of the world of music, including Koussevitzky's
enthusiasm over Tanglewood, brought about a cordial atmosphere, though he
still did not extend an invitation to Monteux.

Little known, however, is that Monteux, in spite of everything, had earlier
invited Koussevitzky to guest conduct in San Francisco. In 1943 Koussevitzky's
wife, Natalie, had died and Monteux wrote him a letter of sympathy in which he
tendered the invitation. Though Monteux's letter is not available, Koussevitzky,
in his letter dated 2 March of that year, thanked Monteux for his expression of
sympathy and stated that he would very much like to accept the friendly invitation, but feared that he could not as long as he was with the Boston Symphony
Orchestra—that his work in Boston absorbed his time and energy to the extent
that he benefited from a few weeks of rest and preparation for his future concerts.

One of the most difficult critics of that era was Chicago's Claudia Cassidy, then of the *Herald American*. Of the orchestra's visit to that city she stated, in the edition of 26 April, that it was one of the major pleasures of the season. Monteux was considered the great favorite among the guest conductors of the Chicago Symphony Orchestra's summer concerts at the Ravinia Festival. In Orchestra Hall he gave a distinguished concert of tremendous vitality.

Successful as the tour was from a musical and public relations standpoint, it was nevertheless a financial failure, in spite of sold-out houses. But such was the enthusiasm of the orchestra's board of governors, composed as it was of business leaders from throughout the Bay area, that the debt was quickly retired.

CHAPTER 17

Summertime

When it came to summer concerts, no conductor was busier than Pierre Monteux. From the 1940s on it was a rare summer indeed when he could not be found conducting at New York's Lewisohn Stadium, Philadelphia's Robin Hood Dell, and the Ravinia Festival in Highland Park, Illinois, not far from Chicago. During the 1950s Tanglewood in Massachusetts was added to this list, as was, a bit less frequently, the Hollywood Bowl, though he had performed there in earlier years. His regular engagements in these concert series made him the most beloved of all the participating conductors, with orchestras and audiences alike. In fact, a poll taken by Lewisohn Stadium, the results of which were published in the *Stadium Concerts Review*, the official program book of the series, pronounced Monteux the all-time favorite conductor of Stadium attendees.

The oldest of these summer series was the Stadium Concerts, founded in 1918. Located on the campus of the City College of New York (CCNY) between 136th and 138th Streets on Amsterdam Avenue, the Greco-Roman-style amphitheater known as Lewisohn Stadium, an athletic field during the school year, was for many years the site of popularly priced concerts by the New York Philharmonic. For as little as twenty-five cents one sat on the stone steps that extended in a semi-circle at the rear of the amphitheater, from one side to the other. For a little more one could sit a bit closer on wooden folding chairs, and for the top price, never very high, in the front section at tables. The total seating capacity was twenty thousand.

Many of the world's leading conductors and soloists performed at Lewisohn Stadium over the years, including, among the former, Leonard Bernstein, Dimitri Mitropoulos, and Fritz Reiner; and among the latter, Claudio Arrau, Jascha Heifetz, and Arthur Rubinstein. But while these conductors were at the Stadium only from time to time, Pierre Monteux alone among the great maestri appeared there regularly, year after year, from 1946 to 1961 (with the exception of 1957 and 1959), conducting anywhere from three to eight concerts per engagement.

The Stadium concerts were a highly popular cultural attraction in spite of several drawbacks. The most notable of these was the frequent sound of air-

175

planes flying directly overhead, usually during the quietest portions of the music (La Guardia airport was just a few miles away). Another distraction was street noises, such as fire engines, car horns, and police sirens. Even without those distractions, one still had to contend with the Stadium's less-than-state-of-the-art, not-exactly-hi-fi amplification system, whose effectiveness depended on how the wind was blowing. And, of course, there was the weather. Since the audience was not under cover, a sudden downpour in the middle of a concert would send people scurrying for shelter and most likely cause the rest of the program to be canceled. There was provision for two or three of the week's concerts to be postponed in case of rain, and audience members could have rain checks if it rained before intermission.

Ever since its inception the Stadium Concert series had been under the chairmanship of Mrs. Charles S. ("Minnie") Guggenheimer (1882–1965). Trained as a pianist, in her younger years she could play Chopin études and Liszt's transcription of the "Liebestod" from Wagner's *Tristan und Isolde*. To describe Minnie Guggenheimer as a colorful character would be an understatement. She almost always addressed the audience before the second half of a concert, ostensibly reading from notes but actually saying whatever popped into her head, in a way that would have made Mrs. Malaprop proud. "In all likelihood," according to her daughter Sophie's loving memoir, *Mother Is Minnie*, she was

> wearing the same heavy rubber-soled sport shoes and dowdy, five-year-old cotton dress she put on to walk the dog before breakfast, with a frumpy inverted flowerpot of a hat borrowed at the last minute from the cook— and, waving her right hand giddily in mid-air, chirp a cheery "Hello, everybody" to a motley mass that choruses its reciprocal "Hello, Minnie" in ecstatic unison. (Untermeyer and Williamson 1960, 16)

It was said that people attended the Stadium concerts as much to see and hear Minnie as for the actual concert.

Her purpose in delivering these speeches was to inform the audience of future concerts, to encourage them to support the Stadium by their attendance and by contributions, and occasionally to announce a change in the program. Some of her remarks follow, as gleaned from Sophie's book (Untermeyer and Williamson 1960, 16–20) as well as from my own remembrance:

> "Tell everybody you know to come to the Stadium. And tell everybody you don't know too, because unless we have people in the empty seats I'll simply go bust!"

> [Next week we will have] "one of the best-known names in the musical world, Ezio Pinza, *baass*. . . . Oh dear, that can't be right. A bass is a kind of fish!"

"We won't be able to have that thing by Smetana tonight, but I don't think it matters very much. Smetana is some kind of mustard or sour cream, isn't it?"

When Mayor Robert F. Wagner would arrive to make some opening-night remarks, Minnie inevitably introduced him as "Mayor Vahgner."

Summoning the Crown Prince of Sweden onstage, with a snap of her fingers, "Here, Prince, Prince!"

While three highly paid stars of the Metropolitan Opera were waiting in the wings, she told the audience, "If I get enough money, I'll be able to give you *better* artists in the future."

Minnie was tireless in working on behalf of the Stadium in fund-raising, publicity, engaging of artists, and even battling the airlines and the elements. She actually succeeded, at least for a time, in getting the airlines to reroute their flights so as not to pass over the Stadium during concerts. When it appeared that rain was imminent, she often promised the audience that it would not rain, and it did not. If rain started, she would promise that it would be over in a few minutes, and it was.

Minnie's favorite of all the conductors appearing at the Stadium was Pierre Monteux. According to Sophie,

Her own greatest pride in recent Stadium seasons has been not so much the occasional presentation of a box-office record-breaker from Hollywood as the annual re-engagement for many years of artistically unimpeachable Pierre Monteux. His are the only concerts Mother herself sits through to the very end. "They are what makes the darned thing worth while to me," she once said in a moment of rare seriousness. (Untermeyer and Williamson 1960, 122–23)

Monteux made his Lewisohn Stadium debut back in 1927, but nineteen years were to pass before he returned for a two-week engagement of eight concerts beginning on 15 July 1946. Whereas the earlier engagement did not include guest soloists, by this time soloists were an important feature of the concerts, which now numbered five per week. Mondays and Thursdays were reserved for the most celebrated soloists, with provisions for postponement in case of rain. The programs for Tuesdays and Wednesdays would either have a lesser-known soloist, often a young newcomer, or none at all, and would not be postponed in case of rain, though the soloist might be rescheduled for a later date. Saturdays were reserved for lighter programs, such as Rodgers and Hammerstein night (which, Minnie announced, would be personally conducted by Rodger Hammerstein). The Tuesday and/or Wednesday concerts were broadcast locally on radio station

WNYC, and one year (1953) WQXR broadcast the Thursday concerts. During
the 1950 season some of the Monday concerts were even televised locally.
Monteux returned with a fairly conventional program:

Brahms: *Academic Festival Overture*
Chausson: Symphony in B-flat major
Tchaikovsky: Violin Concerto in D major; Nathan Milstein, soloist

Five of Monteux's eight 1946 concerts included soloists; besides Milstein, they
were the pianists William Kapell and Abbey Simon, the violinist Mischa Elman,
and the soprano Lily Pons. While the programs offered fairly standard fare, with
only one rehearsal for each, Monteux did perform Copland's *Appalachian Spring*,
which had received its world premiere only the year before. One program contained a French group of Ibert's *Escales*, d'Indy's *Istar Variations* (not in the
orchestra's regular repertoire), and Ravel's *Daphnis et Chloé* Suite No. 2. Also
included on the various programs were Beethoven's Seventh and Eighth Symphonies, the Second and Third Symphonies of Brahms, Tchaikovsky's Fourth
Symphony, Mozart's "Haffner" Symphony, and the Franck Symphony in D
minor, as well as a suite from *Petrushka*, Milhaud's *Suite française*, a generous
helping of Wagner excerpts, Strauss's *Don Juan*, Debussy's *L'après-midi*, and a
work Monteux had premiered in Boston, Griffes's *Pleasure Dome of Kubla Khan*.
If one attended some of Monteux's Stadium rehearsals, one noted the extreme
efficiency with which he operated, in the standard symphonies touching on the
most problematic passages and trusting the musicians' familiarity with the works
to carry them through. This allowed time for rehearsing with the soloist or working in detail on a relatively unfamiliar work, such as *Appalachian Spring* or *Istar*.
But his efficiency did not preclude his lacing his remarks with humor when appropriate. What was especially notable was how, with a work one knew from his
recording, such as the Brahms Second or the Franck, he was able quickly to reproduce the sonority of that recording, with an absolute minimum of fuss or explanation. Monteux had one of the clearest baton techniques of any conductor and
was living proof of a master conductor's ability to transmit his wishes not merely
through gestures, but through mental telepathy.
Although the orchestra for the Stadium events was nominally the New York
Philharmonic, not all the members played the summer concerts, notably the section
principals. That meant there were quite a few substitutes in the ranks, some of
whom were not necessarily familiar with a particular conductor or with certain
works. I recall a 1955 performance of Berlioz's *Symphonie fantastique* conducted
by Efrem Kurtz. In addition to the requisite bells in the finale, Kurtz employed a
piano to play low octaves in unison with them. (The score indicates a piano as a
possible substitute for the bells.) After a few bars the pianist and the bell-playing
percussionist became out of sync with each other and remained a measure apart for
the rest of the passage, with Kurtz wildly gesticulating in their direction to no avail.

In 1955 the summer orchestra was officially designated the Stadium Symphony Orchestra. It had already made some recordings under that name and would continue to do so, including some notable releases conducted by Leopold Stokowski, who almost never appeared at the Stadium. When it became the Stadium Symphony, the orchestra was peopled by even more substitutes, but Monteux was still able to achieve his usual results.

The problem of noisy airplanes was exacerbated during a concert on 19 June 1947, which I attended. The first half had been especially disturbed by unusually loud and frequent flyovers. After the intermission, Monteux and the Russian-born pianist Simon Barere were about to begin Liszt's Concerto No. 1 when the audience could see, as the performers could not, the lights of a plane approaching from a distance. "Wait!" "Don't start!" "Airplane!" Shouts and cries from the audience reached pandemonium level before eventually subsiding and allowing the performance to begin. When the craft finally wended its way overhead, it proved to be a single-engine airplane, its sputtering engine barely audible.

Mischa Elman was an annual soloist at the Stadium, usually with Monteux conducting. He was known to be sensitive about the fact that Jascha Heifetz was considered the greatest violinist of his time. In fact, the aforementioned poll had named Heifetz as the audience's favorite violinist. On 9 July 1953 Elman was the soloist in an all-Beethoven program conducted by Monteux, one of the concerts WQXR was to broadcast. Listeners to the broadcast heard the *Egmont* Overture and Seventh Symphony live from the stadium. After the intermission the announcer informed everyone that Mischa Elman had refused permission for his performance to be broadcast (because he would not be receiving the special broadcast fee he had requested), and instead listeners would hear a recording of the Beethoven concerto—played by Jascha Heifetz.

On the morning of Monday, 27 June 1955, several of Monteux's pupils gathered at the Stadium to attend the rehearsal for his first appearance of the season, another all-Beethoven program with Elman as soloist. At ten o'clock the New York Philharmonic/Stadium Symphony Orchestra was assembled on stage and Elman was present and ready to begin; in fact, everyone was there except Pierre Monteux. After some delay, the information was circulated that he had conducted a concert of the Concertgebouw Orchestra in Amsterdam the day before and had been scheduled for a night flight to New York, but the flight had been delayed. His arrival was expected at any moment, however. So as not to waste the rehearsal time, Elman and the orchestra played through the concerto, conducted by one of the orchestra members, the cellist Mario Caiati.

At the concerto's conclusion a break was called, during which a somewhat weary and concerned Monteux arrived directly from the airport. What with the delay in beginning and the time taken to play the concerto, including Elman's own rather lengthy cadenza, not much time remained for further rehearsal, which was canceled. That night Monteux conducted the unrehearsed *Leonore* Overture No. 3 and Seventh Symphony, and the rehearsed (but not by him) Violin Concerto, all without a score in front of him. The performances gave no indication of what had occurred, or not occurred, that morning.

During my student years, in the summer of 1956, I had the privilege and the pleasure of driving Monteux to and from his Stadium rehearsals and concerts. On the morning of Thursday, 22 June, after the rehearsal of an all-Tchaikovsky program yet again with Mischa Elman as soloist, storm clouds began to gather, and it appeared that it might be necessary to postpone the concert to the next night. I naively asked Monteux if, should the concert be postponed, there would be another rehearsal the next morning, to which he replied, "No, once it is rehearsed, it is rehearsed for life." On one of these trips Monteux commented about how little respect there was for artists in this country. While the Boston Symphony provided a chauffeured car to take him to and from rehearsals, that was an exception; had I not offered to drive him, he would have ended up on the sidewalk looking for a taxi.

A pianist who appeared annually at the Stadium, if infrequently elsewhere, at least in New York, was Stell Andersen. Often her vehicle was the Grieg concerto, but on occasion she ventured further afield. In 1953, with Monteux conducting, she played Mozart's somewhat infrequently heard "Coronation" Concerto (No. 26) and gave the New York premiere of Milhaud's *Fantaisie pastorale*. She was apparently a friend of Milhaud's, as was Monteux, and on 25 June 1956 the two gave the world premiere of his Piano Concerto No. 5 on an all-French program.

The concerts at the Robin Hood Dell were inaugurated in 1930 and performed by the Philadelphia Orchestra under its alias, the Robin Hood Dell Orchestra. Under that name it made many recordings with conductors who for contractual reasons were unable to lead the Philadelphia Orchestra. The concerts were free because the city provided the financing, though one had to obtain tickets by means of ballots printed in the local newspapers. The site was named after the Robin Hood Tavern, an old colonial structure that stood nearby. Monteux began conducting there in the summer of 1941, and though he did not appear quite as regularly as at Lewisohn Stadium, he was nevertheless a fairly frequent visitor.

Monteux's programs at the Dell were similar to those at the Stadium, some with soloists, some without, and with similar repertoire. One difference was in the format of the programs with soloists. At the Stadium his soloists almost invariably appeared last on the program, so they could play encores without the orchestra. Apparently encores were not given at the Dell, because the soloists there often concluded the first half of a program. Though most conductors prefer that format, as they like to end their concerts in a blaze of glory, unencumbered by a soloist, Monteux was not among them. Available programs do not show Elman as a soloist at the Dell, but one does find Claudio Arrau, Yehudi Menuhin, and Isaac Stern collaborating with Monteux.

The Chicago Symphony Orchestra's Ravinia Festival began in 1936. The orchestra always performed not as the Ravinia Symphony Orchestra or some such designation, but under its own name. (The Ravinia Festival Orchestra is a separate entity from the CSO, which still plays most of the concerts.) Monteux's first concert at Ravinia, on 5 August 1941, had the expected all-French program consisting of the Franck symphony and *Daphnis et Chloé* Suite No. 2. He was to appear there every summer through 1961, with the exception of 1958; thus, his association with the Chicago Symphony, if only as a guest, proved to be his longest with any orchestra, including the San Francisco Symphony. He usually led four concerts each year, but occasionally six or eight. The concert schedule was Tuesday, Thursday, and Saturday evenings, and Sunday afternoon.

Of all these summer venues, Ravinia is the most scenically attractive and the most listener friendly, for the audience sits in a pavilion with a roof overhead; there is no need to make provisions for rained-out concerts. One sees from the Ravinia programs that Monteux performed a greater variety of music there than at the Stadium or the Dell. Perhaps because he was leading the actual Chicago Symphony and not a pseudonymous group with many substitutes, he felt comfortable in playing a wider repertoire. Also, Ravinia allowed for a bit more rehearsal time than did the other places.

Among the works Monteux conducted at Ravinia but not at the Stadium or the Dell were Beethoven's Symphony No. 4, Berlioz's *Harold in Italy*, Brahms's Symphony No. 4, Copland's Suite from *Billy the Kid*, Dukas's *La péri*, Haydn's Symphonies No. 85, 103, and 104, Hindemith's *Mathis der Maler* and *Nobilissima visione*, Mendelssohn's Symphony No. 3, Prokofiev's *Romeo and Juliet* Suite No. 1, Saint-Saëns's Symphony No. 3, Schumann's Symphonies Nos. 1 and 2, Scriabin's *Poem of Ecstasy*, Shostakovich's Symphonies Nos. 6 and 9, Sessions's Suite from *The Black Maskers*, and Strauss's *Don Quixote* (with Gregor Piatigorsky the cello soloist) and *Ein Heldenleben*, not to mention two concert performances of Gounod's *Faust* on 27 and 29 July 1954 and Beethoven's Ninth Symphony on 21 July 1955.

Most of the Ravinia programs did not have soloists, but when there was one—such as Zino Francescatti, Arthur Rubinstein, or Isaac Stern—he would be heard in two consecutive concerts, a different concerto for each. During the first half of the 1940s many of the Chicago Symphony's key players were in the service in World War II, and in the latter half the orchestra went through an unstable period of music directorship, which changed rather quickly. Some seasons were led entirely by guest conductors. The orchestra was thus not at its best at that time, but according to the music critic and annotator Richard Freed, "You would never know that at Ravinia" when Monteux conducted.

For fifty years the Chicago Symphony's principal trumpeter was Adolph (Bud) Herseth, who retired in 2001. Herseth has stated that Monteux was his favorite of all the conductors he played with, for many reasons—his profound knowledge of every score he conducted, the diversity of his repertoire, his very acute ear, his no-nonsense style of rehearsing, the great clarity of his beat, his unpretentiousness, his sense of humor, and the fact that he was "a strong and gentle ruler." He recalled an incident at a Ravinia rehearsal of Beethoven's Seventh Symphony. Anyone who has seen Herseth play knows that his face turns bright red in strenuous passages. Such was the case in the trio of the Seventh's Scherzo, where the trumpet must sustain a high A *fortissimo* over several measures. Observing Herseth's crimson visage, Monteux stopped the orchestra, pointed to his own face, and said, "Monsieur Herseth, you should put on some powder."

CHAPTER 18

Letters to Doris

Doris Monteux never accompanied her husband on his summer trips because she intensely disliked the heat in New York, Philadelphia, and Chicago. The Berkshires enjoyed a certain amount of cooler weather, and, of course, were not too far from Maine, where they now lived, so she would often go with him to Tanglewood. Her absence from the other venues provided the raison d'être for a remarkable series of letters between the two. If this correspondence is anything to go by, they could not bear to be separated from each other for even a day, much less a week or two, for the letters were written almost, if not actually, daily. Most of them are undated, beginning, for example, "Monday afternoon" or "Tuesday evening." However, the postmarks on the envelopes attest to the close proximity of their mailing. If a day went by without Pierre's receiving a letter from Doris, he would comment on this in his next letter.

Monteux's letters, in quite legible though not always impeccable English, are of interest on three levels: first, as a description of his work with various orchestras and soloists; second, in delineating his coping with the many mundane details involved with touring, such as train and plane schedules, hotels, and so on; and third, as expressions of his great love for Doris. While her letters obviously did not deal with the first of these factors, they describe the routine of her life back in Hancock, including preparations for the annual sessions of the conducting school and presenting concerts of chamber music, and are also manifestations of her equally great love for her husband.

On 10 August 1941 Pierre writes from Highland Park, site of the Chicago Symphony's Ravinia Festival:

The concert, last night, was another triumph! You have no idea of the success!! First, after Petrouchka, the whole orchestra and audience *standing* and they gave me an interminable fanfare!! Public shouting, pounding, whistling. I thought they would never finish. Then, at the end of Gotterdammerung they started again (no fanfare but applause etc.) with [Helen] Traubel. We came back at least 5 times. Then, I told her to go *alone*, that I would go *alone* too the next time. When I came alone, it was a thunder of applause, shouting, whistling, pounding, so much that I was embarrassed for her!! It was twice, three times much louder than when *she* came alone!!! Darling, I was really crying that you were not here. I have never had such a success *in my life*.

The "interminable fanfare" to which Monteux refers is what is known as a *Tusch*, a greeting played by the brass section as a conductor the orchestra especially loves and respects enters the stage or returns for a bow. Monteux received at least one *Tusch* each summer he appeared at Ravinia, from 1941 to 1961. The custom of the *Tusch* appears to have since disappeared from today's musical life.

From Philadelphia, undated, but before he began staying with Hilda and Meyer Davis:

This morning I had rehearsal with Heifetz, what a barbe! He rehearsed 2 encores!! So I had no time for the rest of the programme and I had to hurry everything else!! And tomorrow is the last rehearsal with Brian [Aherne] who wants to rehearse all his programme and Peter & the Wolf and the baritone for Friday. I will not be able to *touch* the 2nd of Brahms!! Really it is not fair for conductors, especially as many in the orchestra do not belong to the Philadelphia Orchestra and many 2nd men play first and the 2nd is from somewhere else!! It is not safe. Well, I will do my best, that is all.

The hotel is not efficient either. Yesterday I asked the head porter to get my reservation for Friday after the concert at 1:08 in the morning (which makes 1:08 Saturday morning). I gave him my railroad ticket. He came back saying everything will be taken care of and brought my ticket back. Well, this afternoon, they telephoned from the railroad station saying that they reserved a *seat* for *Sunday* morning 1:08!! I said what I wanted: a kind of *room*; all right, they telephoned again saying they have the room and for me to send a boy to get it. The boy came back with the room *and ticket*!! He had to go back and show that I have my ticket already!! So, everything the head porter did yesterday was wrong!! And also, yesterday the waiter left my table after my lunch, the whole day! And today, coming from my rehearsal, my room was not made. It is really a 2nd rate hotel.

In 1942 there was great excitement in the classical music world over Shostakovich's Seventh Symphony. The first of his great "war symphonies," it had already been performed in Russia, and several conductors in the United States were vying for the American premiere, with Toscanini (who was eventually awarded the radio premiere), Koussevitzky (who gave the concert premiere), and Stokowski among the most prominent. The newspapers and news magazines all ran stories of how the score and parts of the work had to be sent to America on microfilm by way of Tehran and Cairo.

While Monteux was never in the running for the American premiere, he was interested in presenting the piece in San Francisco. He wrote to Doris from Philadelphia on 19 July 1942, just after listening to Toscanini's broadcast:

> The symphony is just finished and I am disappointed. It is a long thing with endless repetitions which has for me no musical value. Very inferior to his 5th—not difficult at all and finishing with a great fortissimo. There is 110 men in the orchestra, much noise. One theme is played 9 times in succession with very little variety. Well, anyhow, that is *the* thing to play this year and I will learn it.

He was concerned, however, about the possibility that Mrs. Armsby and Howard Skinner, the San Francisco Symphony's business manager, might not want to incur the additional expense required for engaging the extra musicians needed for the Shostakovich Seventh, but remarks that this would be compensated for by the fact that there would be no soloist for the concert, as the ninety-minute work would take up the whole program. Additionally, he felt that Mrs. Armsby would never agree to pay the music rental fee for two performances: $250. Finally, he worried that she would probably want Stokowski to conduct the work. Of all these concerns, the only one that materialized was the last, for Stokowski did conduct the San Francisco premiere of the Shostakovich Seventh Symphony on 8 January 1943, the opening of the Municipal Concerts series (this meant the piece would have only one performance and therefore a lower rental fee). As Monteux really did not care for the piece, he was perhaps relieved at not having to bother learning it.

From Philadelphia, 23 July 1942:

> Well, when I come back to you, you will have a little less to do as I can always make the bed, get the wood and water and even make the breakfast. I will have to flâner [lounge about] less, because I will have pupils and scores to learn. I think I will buy Mathis der Maler records, that will help me. As for the 7th of Shostakovich, it will not be recorded on time for me to learn it. And the symphonies of [David] Diamond and William Schuman are not recorded. That will give me a lot of work!!

This is a surprising indication that Monteux did rely on recordings, when available, to help him learn unfamiliar works, especially when pressed for time. The same can undoubtedly be said about many other conductors, even when they are not pressed for time, and in some cases even with familiar pieces.

From Philadelphia, 26 July 1942:

> I played the Rachmaninoff by memory and I "épatéd" [astounded] the whole orchestra!! I don't know how many came to tell me how wonderful

I am! And some said they played this work with Stokowski everywhere and each time, some awful things happened. He could not be ensemble with Rachmaninoff, he had the score and twice it was near a catastrophe!! You have no idea, my darling, how these men hate Ormandy and how they wish I would come to Philadelphia for good. Even the most hard boiled come to me to say how they love to play with me!! Enough of that, or else my head will swell and I will never want to empty my pipi pail again!!

Whenever Monteux's engagement in a given city was about to end, or if there would be a free weekend between engagements, he always wanted to return to Hancock and Doris, even if only for a few days. Thus his letters frequently deal with his rather complex travel plans, often affected by odd train and plane schedules and by postponed concerts. Typical is this proposed schedule, which one hopes Doris was able to decipher, in an undated letter from Philadelphia:

There is a terrible thing about my reservations. Mr. Hocker [manager of the Dell] has 2, from Phila. to Boston one for Saturday one for Sunday at 12 noon, but there is nothing to be had for Monday, the 9th, which means that, if that week, we have to postpone two concerts, and have to play Saturday and Sunday I will not be able to leave Phila. before the Tuesday! I will have to stay here Monday without anything to do. That is *only* if we have *two* postponed concerts, because if we have only *one*, I will leave on Sunday the 8th. If we have none of them postponed I can start on Saturday and take the train in Boston at 9:30 P.M. arriving Ellsworth Sunday 6 A.M. Let's hope!! But, already this week, we had to postpone yesterday's concert, with [Paul] Robeson. We give it tonight, and the one we were supposed to give tonight will be played tomorrow (Saturday) (perhaps!! if it does not rain tonight).

In the same letter he writes about

the Tchaikovsky Piano Concerto that we rehearsed this morning with the winner of the contest who is simply wonderful. I even think it was unfair to have him in the contest because he is absolutely a very experienced and brilliant artist and he is not from Philadelphia, he is from Los Angeles. His name is Zadel Skolovsky. He is just as good if not better as [Jesús María] Sanromá. He puts in his pocket every one who played the Tchaikovsky with me anywhere. And the orchestra say that he is as good a violinist!

Monteux had conducted the Tchaikovsky Piano Concerto with Vladimir Horowitz and Arthur Rubinstein, among many others. Skolovsky went on to have a distinguished career performing with many major orchestras and teaching at Indiana University.

From Highland Park, 15 July 1943:

Even with the success that they make me, I don't want to come again. And there is something strange about here. I am the favorite of all the conductors and, not only they chose [Désiré] Defauw as their regular conductor but they give me one week and they give [George] Szell two, last year also, what does that mean? and what do they think *I* think about that? Oh! well, I don't care as I don't want to come back. But I think for San Francisco, it is a good thing that I was re-engaged twice and that I got every time such critics. Really, last night it was as a protestation against Defauw. You have no idea of such a clapping, pounding, whistling! I could not start the concert and they made me come again and again at the intermission and at the end.

From Highland Park, 16 July 1943:

I must tell you a folly I did!! You remember that I tried to buy a light coat for my rehearsals because I have only this linen one and after one rehearsal I had to give it to clean and press *outside*, and it did not come back yet. So, the tailor where I went did not find one to fit me (it is the same tailor where I bought the one I have). Yesterday, he telephoned that he had one *suit* come from Chicago exactly my size, 44 short stout, exactly sent for me!! So I let him come and try it on me. The coat was perfect, the pant, one inch too short. He fixed it, put some buttons for suspenders and . . . I took it. I had it this morning for rehearsal and it is *so* light, it is really a pleasure. The coat is lined in some sort of light silk. It is tan and especially made to be worn without vest. Darling, will you forgive me? It costs 35 dollars!! But, for here, Philadelphia and Hancock it is ideal. That is my folly.

From Philadelphia, 27 July 1943:

They really don't know Petrouchka, I mean, they played it often but they don't *know* it and I spent a lot of time on it this morning, though I play only 12 minutes of it, only the little suite. As for the Prokofieff [*Classical Symphony*], they know it pretty well, except that they were used to play the slow movement *exactly* twice too fast!!

While in Philadelphia Monteux would stay at the home of Hilda and Meyer Davis, so there was always news of family life there. From Philadelphia, 29 July 1943:

Well, the weather is not so sure today and I am afraid we will have a storm before the concert that will postpone it to tomorrow—then the Tuesday concert, my last, would be Wednesday—unless it rains again in which case my last concert would take place Saturday!! That would be a terrible bore because, really I have enough of here!! Now, every one of the children are here. At every meal one or another has a friend. Garry talks as loud as your stepfather and Margie tries to talk louder!! Meyer and Hilda argue before us all! Quelle tranquillité!! And naturally, I have to share the bathroom with those four!! I see how convenient is a bathroom for 5 persons!! Tonight, after the concert (if there is a concert) there is a big party here: Garry opens in his theatre and it is his 21st birthday! He has invited all the troup, about 20 people after the show!! I already told Hilda that I will stay only a few minutes and go to bed. I asked her what to give Garry and she and Meyer think the best is to give him money. That is good, it saves me to go buy something. I will give him 10 bucks.

These disagreeable aspects of family life aside, he often writes of the enjoyable time he spent playing chamber music in the basement, called the "dugout," with Meyer Davis on violin, him on viola, and visiting members of the orchestra. Sometimes Meyer and Hilda's son Emery would join in on clarinet for the Mozart Quintet.

From Philadelphia, 2 August 1943:

So we had the Menuhin concert last night at last and it went very well. I certainly had as much success as Yehudi and the orchestra made *me* a personal success. Oh! I forgot to tell you: Szell had his first rehearsal Friday and the orchestra *hates* him. They call him Hitler!! So, when I came on stage last night, *they* made me such a success I am sure Szell, who was there, must have been very surprised!!

From Highland Park, 6 August 1945:

[Leon Fleisher] was the soloist last night and Tuesday night with Bernstein conducting!! I went to the concert because I wanted to see him conduct. . . . He conducts like an epileptic, in the lyric passages he makes faces as he was going to come, conducts without baton, poses all the time, everything for the public, nothing for the men. In his music for ballet he really actually *dances* [underlined twice]. He is a show! And some musicians said to me that the audience looks at him and don't listen—oh, well. I don't think San Francisco could stand him. But he is a nice young man, we had dinner together with Leon and 4 friends of his (he insisted to have me for dinner).

Bernstein, of course, conducted in San Francisco the following year.
From Highland Park, 7 August 1945:

Yesterday, when I was at Ravinia I went to the library of the orchestra and asked for a few scores. I wanted to see especially if, in the first suite of Daphnis, the passage for chorus was in the woodwind parts—and it was not!! [Frederick] Stock played it once and made a horrible cut at that place. So I took the score and some music paper and since this morning after my breakfast I reconstituted the orchestration of Ravel and, of course, by memory. It took me until now. . . . Besides my work in Daphnis, I also arranged the score of Harold in Italy, as I did for [Ferenc] Molnar [the San Francisco Symphony's principal violist] so the viola can be heard. You see, I worked well.

From Highland Park, 11 August 1945:

This afternoon from 1 to 4 I rehearsed the Shostakovich 6, the Tableaux d'une exposition and Russlan + Ludmilla, also Tchaikovsky. And tomorrow morning I have my last rehearsal. If it is official that the war is finished, I must play, tomorrow or Sunday the anthems of the big five!! But only if it is official. As for now, everybody is excited but I am not. I wish it was really finished but I have an idea that it is going to be a long discussion. Shall we let their Emperor stay on or not. For me he is a War Criminal just like Hitler and they should surrender unconditionally. . . . I have to stop now because I must work on the Moussorgsky-Ravel—I have forgotten a few spots.

From New York, 16 July 1946:

No letter today!! I had two yesterday. I hope to receive one before my concert. This one will be short because I must review my scores, especially Escales [by Ibert]. That the orchestra does not know. They played it and recorded it, but that is the Philharmonic, and the orchestra of the Stadium is *far* from being the Philharmonic—not *one* [underlined twice] first chair man and many substitutes in the other parts—so I must be *so* [underlined twice] sure in Escales and in Istar [by d'Indy].

   The concert yesterday went very well and I had many compliments, people coming and saying they never heard the orchestra play so well, members of the orchestra thanking me for the wonderful experience and even *Chotzinoff* who came and said he received a cable from Maestro who wants me at N.B.C. in January!! I was so glad to be able to say that it was impossible!! And of course all the pupils very excited—I did not get the critics yet but I will try and get them. . . . Well, I must stop and study. I am worried for tonight. This morning, I never heard the solo flute in Daphnis so badly played! It is simply awful!! Of course, that I cannot help, but I have to be so sure of myself as I am not sure of them at all. . . . I wish I had not accepted this engagement—but I realize it is coming very handy.

From New York, 17 July 1946:

Paul Renzi [the San Francisco Symphony's principal flute] came to the concert and heard that awful flutist play Daphnis!! . . . [Today's] rehearsal was not very good, but I suppose the concert will go. There is so many men that don't belong to the Philharmonic, it is terrible. For instance *none* of the 4 horns belong to that orchestra. That makes the rehearsals so penible [painful, distressing] for me and I tell you, after two concerts and 3 rehearsals, I am very tired. . . .

Wanda Landowska came at my rehearsal this morning and bored me—but not too long!! She wants to play for me alone, next week, (I don't remember the name of) some old piece for clavecin.

From New York, 25 July 1946:

Just a word today. I had rehearsal this morning and my last concert tonight—Thank God!! And I must review all these cheap scores that Lily [Pons] sings tonight—one bar fast, one slow, one half bar "rit," one half bar "tempo," and "fermata"!! It is simply awful! I must say that was the way Elman played last night and 12,000 people gave him an ovation!! . . .

You remember that a Miss Jarmel wrote about the program of Lily Pons and I answered that, as she was going to sing 3 times instead of two, I simply took off the Suite Française [by Milhaud]. Then I wired the whole program. Well, the Suite Française *is* on the program which makes it 15 minutes too long!! That is the way they make things here—just a mess!! I don't want to come back again it is worse than the Dell!!

From Highland Park, 31 July 1947:

I am sorry they gave me ——— as soloist. She is going to spoil my program tonight. She just plays the *notes*, not any feeling and not any virtuosity!! I don't know how she got that engagement and why with me? . . . By the way, I asked about dogs in this hotel and they don't admit them!! They have a place for them, a dog house, but they cannot come in the hotel. What fools they are!!

From Highland Park, 1 August 1947:

The concert went well last night and was a great success—but, I have an impression that, now they are used to have me there, they certainly applaud, but it is no more as it was, they don't stamp their feet, they don't whistle, they don't shout, they simply clap, loud and long. Maybe the programs are not so exciting as I try to give them works that are rarely played—and they don't know them. They cannot make comparisons with what they know, played by other conductors and by me. Just the same, it was cold last night and it was a big crowd. ——— was all right, nothing more. . . . Did I tell you that I had to re-learn the Schubert Italian Overture? I did not remember even the first bar!! You will notice in Cassidy's article, she talks about the Overture in D—and I played the one in C!! There is two Overtures in Italian Style!! Well, that is good: she did not notice that the Overture was in C and the Schumann, following immediately, was also in C!! (a fault of me, making the program!)

(Monteux's feelings about the soloist, who happened to be from San Francisco, were echoed in Claudia Cassidy's review; she found her incompetent.)
From Highland Park, 2 August 1947:

Mr. Knight [manager of Ravinia] began to talk about Ravinia—*I am Ravinia*—without me it would no more be Ravinia and so forth and so forth. Then he said it is too bad that now, they own the whole park with so many buildings on it, etc. and they use it really only 28 times in the course of the year what would I think of a big summer school of music, they have all the teachers possible with the orchestra and musicians living in Chicago, and what would I think of being the head of the school, me teaching only conducting!!! I said, do you mean that I would come in Ravinia and teach in that heat instead of spending the summer in Maine where it is cool and where I have my home?? Well, he is thinking of it seriously, but not me. I told him that Rodzinski would be the man for that.

From Highland Park, 4 August 1947:

The concert went well and we had a big success with Petrouchka. I don't think, if I come back, that I should try to play things they don't know. Why take the trouble when even the critics don't care for what they don't know—for instance the Bal Martiniquais [by Milhaud], they seem to like it but I even did not come back *once* after it (just before the intermission). . . . I want to study my scores (Sheinfeld, Scriabine and Enigma) I hope the critics will not find those light music. For once that I made my programs alone, I have no luck!! And you found them wonderful, remember??

  Well, if I have worn out my welcome, better not come back. But you know what I will do? I will let them announce my 8th engagement and then let them know that *I* prefer not to come again.

Monteux continued to return to Ravinia repeatedly through 1961.
From Highland Park, 4 August 1948:

Well, I had my rehearsal and concert last night. They made me such a welcome I did not know if I could start the concert!! And it was like that the whole evening!! I don't have the critics as they are published now one day later, there is a sort of printer strike, so every article comes late. I hope Claudia [Cassidy] was satisfied with my programme? Of course she will not like the Couperin-Milhaud [Overture and Allegro]! That is not deep enough for her and anyway she will say that the orchestration is not in the style of Couperin—of course!! But the piece had a very big success just the same. I must say the orchestra is much better than it was, maybe Rodzinski is for something in that. . . .

Oh! I forgot to tell you: in last week's program, it was a big Victor advertisement with reference to me in big letters, then they gave a list of records—*not one of mine*!! I will try to find one of those programmes for you. [Fritz] Stiedry was the conductor. He played the 4th of Brahms Saturday evening and *again* on Sunday afternoon!!!! So, yesterday morning, I say to the orchestra at the rehearsal: Gentlemen, let us take the 4th of Brahms!! (as if I was mistaken for the 3rd that was on my programme) Did they laugh!!!

From New York, 20 July 1949:

The concert last night went very well and I had rehearsal this morning for tonight's concert-broadcast. It is said that even if it rains we must play, without public, for the broadcast!! My rehearsal this morning was very hard because I had a new harpist and I had to work hard for Alborada [Ravel's *Alborada del gracioso*]—I still don't know what will happen tonight with that man!! In places the harp plays alone!! Nothing else in the orchestra!! Well, if you hear it, you will know why it is no good!!

From the foregoing it is clear that Monteux did not care to conduct such summer concerts and that he did it largely for the money, which, after his manager's fee, hotel and transportation costs, and other expenses were deducted, really did not amount to a huge sum. He often comments on the cost of things, from the price of his hotel room to something as trivial as, for example, $1.25 for a sandwich, or the price of stamps when he discovers that a letter with airmail postage took longer to reach him than one with an ordinary stamp. Even at that time, when he was a beloved, often-engaged conductor, he was not a wealthy man by any means.

Monteux also lets Doris know precisely what he had for lunch or dinner each day, including that he had ice cream for dessert. Sometimes he is invited to dinner at the home of one of the board members or the manager of the organization he is conducting at the moment, which elicits from him the comment that he has saved the cost of a meal. He tells of his problems getting his laundry done, how long it takes, and what it costs. Invariably, after a concert and before going to bed, he has crackers and milk. The detailing of such minutiae can be interpreted as his seeking Doris's approval, for in the normal course of events, when she and Pierre were together, she took care of virtually everything for him, making it possible for him to devote his time to music without extraneous distractions. In these summer situations, he was rather lost without her.

The intense summer heat is always a topic, not only because of the difficulty of conducting in such circumstances, but also because of the difficulty he has sleeping, for his rooms are not air conditioned. He has fans blowing on him constantly and often sleeps in the nude but is still uncomfortable. Each letter also mentions the fact that he has worked on his scores. This is an important piece of information, for it shows that no matter how well Monteux knew his scores, conducting with great authority from memory, the *reason* he knew them so well is that he studied them continually.

It is also clear that, unlike some artists, Monteux read his reviews, though more out of curiosity than anything else. He had enough self-confidence not to be affected by them one way or the other. It was mainly for Doris's benefit that he referred to them and sent them to her.

Lines in two of the letters—"a fault of me, making the program!" and "For once that I made my programs alone, I have no luck!!"—appear to confirm a rumor that continually surfaced among Monteux's pupils and has been confirmed by family members: that Doris made out his programs for him. One would have thought Monteux capable of devising his own programs from his vast repertoire. But Doris was, of course, a trained and knowledgeable musician whose opinion Pierre valued and trusted. What is more likely, from the use of the word "alone," is that the two consulted with each other on the programs.

One of Monteux's longtime pupils was Gordon Peters, for many years principal percussionist of the Chicago Symphony Orchestra until his retirement in 2001. He told me of the concert at Ravinia on 15 July 1961, which proved to be Monteux's last appearance there. Originally Sibelius's First Symphony was programmed, but in the end the Second Symphony was substituted, after which Monteux remarked to Peters, "Don't tell Doris!"

As mentioned earlier, a good portion of each letter from one to the other is taken up with expressions of extreme love and devotion, often stated in the most intimate terms. After much deliberation, and despite the likelihood that a revelation of the Monteuxs' private feelings in such matters would increase the sales of this book, I have decided that they will remain private.

CHAPTER 19

Au revoir to San Francisco—
But Not Good-Bye

Although Pierre Monteux's reputation as a benevolent maestro remains secure, it is well to record here that he was not without his shortcomings in dealing with the musicians under his command. The benevolence was largely a characteristic of his later years when, no longer a music director, he did not have to concern himself with the administration of an orchestra.

In his history of the San Francisco Symphony, David Schneider pays tribute to Monteux's great musicianship and skills as an orchestral trainer. He does, however, point out some weak spots in his attitude to his musicians and to the city.

> He always acted like a visiting conductor, never becoming a part of the city's musical structure. He arrived in San Francisco the day before a season started and left the day after it ended. He lived in a hotel or in a hotel/ apartment. Monteux had nothing invested in the city or the orchestra. That we were out of work the major part of the year did not seem to disturb him in the least. . . . In Europe, orchestral musicians were generally in the lowest economic stratum, and he saw no reason that American musicians should fare any better. (Schneider 1983, 41–43)

In the same passage, Schneider recounts how Monteux " sabotaged" an opportunity for the musicians to earn some extra money. The arts commission was planning to present three concerts conducted by Sir Thomas Beecham. The plan, however, was to engage not the San Francisco Symphony, but an independently contracted orchestra for the series, one that would nevertheless include many of the symphony's members. When Monteux learned of this, he forbade the musicians to participate on the grounds that the concerts would be in direct competition with the regular symphony season and implied that anyone who did so would be in danger of not having his contract renewed.

For the making of recordings, the musicians voted that even if they played a work calling for a reduced orchestra, every member would benefit from it to some extent. Monteux's response was, "This will not take place. I have to wait for my

194

money until all expenses are paid, including your wages. If you want this rule to go into effect, I will take my recordings to another orchestra. The recording company wants me, not you." The musicians then voted to rescind their resolution. (Today no American orchestra can make a recording without all its members being paid, even if not everyone has participated in it. Record companies have gotten around this rule to some extent by issuing recordings played by the "Columbia Symphony Orchestra" or the "RCA Victor Symphony Orchestra" when the orchestra may have actually been made up of members of the Cleveland Orchestra or the New York Philharmonic.)

Schneider continues:

> It was true that our lot had improved because of the success that had come to the orchestra. But it was also true that Monteux was detached from musicians' problems, except when they touched his own life. The orchestra members felt that Monteux could have done much more to better the financial condition of the musicians. Our salaries had gone up from the starvation level when he arrived to poverty level when he left. There was a feeling of sadness in the orchestra that such a great man could have failings that clouded the ideal image we would have preferred. (Schneider 1983, 79–80)

Schneider tells of the appearance in San Francisco of the Israel Philharmonic Orchestra in late 1950. Serge Koussevitzky conducted, and it undoubtedly took a special effort on Monteux's part to attend the concert, what with the history between him and Koussevitzky. Nevertheless, attend he did, and Koussevitzky apparently went to great lengths to impress Monteux. The next day Monteux arrived at rehearsal "livid with rage and vindictiveness."

> "I was told," he said, "that strings cannot sound good in this building, as the hall is too dead. Last night I heard strings of another orchestra, and they sounded tremendously alive—brilliant. I've been watching you string players lately. Some of you can play and aren't trying. Some of you used to be able to play but can't anymore, and some of you never could play. I'm going to hear each one of you before the end of the season, and we'll see what happens." (Schneider 1983, 80–81)

This was a threat that the musicians would not accept, and a meeting was soon held at the Musicians Union hall. There a resolution was passed that such auditions would not be permitted, and in fact they were not held. However, Schneider states that the members of the orchestra committee and those who had spoken out at the meeting were fired at the end of the season. "Such a vindictive act," he observes, "did not become a man of Monteux's stature and certainly did not add to his popularity with the musicians" (Schneider 1983, 82).

To begin the 1947–48 season Monteux was re-engaged as a guest conductor of the Philadelphia Orchestra. As a tribute to his old friend Willem Pijper, who had died in 1947, he included on the program the Third Symphony, which Pijper had dedicated to Monteux. Pijper's Third is a symphony in one movement, with several subsections, lasting barely fifteen minutes, if that. While not without some banalities, it is a striking and often acerbic piece, scored for an extremely large orchestra. Monteux played it fairly often internationally, but today it seems to be the exclusive property of Dutch conductors.

In Philadelphia, on 24, 25, and 27 October 1947, Monteux programmed Pijper's Third with Beethoven's Seventh and Chausson's symphony; the concert was repeated in New York on 28 October. He had given the American premiere of the Pijper in Philadelphia in 1928. At that time it had been coolly, if not negatively, received, and its reception was not much better in 1947. Pijper's work had been thought of as an expression of its time and now was deemed rather faded in its pseudo-modernisms. In contrast, Chausson's symphony, never at the center of the standard repertoire, was revivified by Monteux's glorious performance. Beethoven's Seventh was the one undisputed masterpiece on the program. Irving Kolodin, writing in the *New York Sun* of 29 October, felt it was clear and poised in delivery, but also stolid and dry, and did not compare with Toscanini's NBC performance of the previous Saturday.

Monteux programmed the Pijper symphony for his opening San Francisco concerts on 13, 14, and 15 November. Works new to San Francisco that season included Morton Gould's perky *Minstrel Show*, Paul Creston's Poem for Harp and Orchestra, Lukas Foss's Ode for Orchestra, Hindemith's *Symphonia serena*, and Stravinsky's *Four Norwegian Moods* and Concerto in D for String Orchestra, both conducted by the composer. In addition, Monteux conducted repeat performances of two great American symphonies, the Third of Roy Harris and the Third of William Schuman. It is one thing to give first performances; to play works a second or third time demonstrates one's belief in them and also enables one's audience and critics to become familiar with them, to better appreciate them.

As we know, Monteux was not a frequent performer of the works of Mahler, so it is all the more striking that on 8, 9, and 10 April 1948 he gave his audiences the opportunity to hear what many feel is the composer's greatest work, *Das Lied von der Erde*, with the mezzo-soprano Jennie Tourel and the tenor Charles Kullman as soloists. In the *Examiner* of 10 April, Alexander Fried wrote that Monteux led the work "with extraordinary beauty and dramatic force, taste and lucidity." While a German might have evoked greater intensity and poignancy, "Monteux's performance was so fine that it had its own complete conviction."

In 1948 the Chicago Symphony Orchestra was seeking a new conductor. During the first fifty years of its existence it had had only two: its founder, Theodore Thomas, and Frederick Stock. The latter's death in 1942 led to the relatively brief appointment of the Belgian Désiré Defauw (1885–1960), who served from 1943 to 1947, and the even briefer tenure of Artur Rodzinski, who had quit the New

York Philharmonic in 1947 over a disagreement with the manager, Arthur Judson, and then led the Chicago Symphony for a single season, 1947–48. By 1948 Monteux was seventy-three years old, probably too old to be considered for the permanent post, but not too old to be engaged as a guest conductor for the first five weeks of the 1948–49 season. Even though he had been a regular visitor to the Ravinia Festival since 1941, these were his first concerts with the Chicago Symphony in Orchestra Hall.

While they featured the usual assortment of standard symphonies (Beethoven's Seventh, Brahms's Second, and Tchaikovsky's Fourth) and other works (*La mer, Till Eulenspiegel, Death and Transfiguration*), his programs also included three Chicago premieres: William Schuman's Third Symphony, Pijper's Third Symphony, and the Violin Concerto by Hindemith, with Ruth Posselt as soloist. Posselt was the wife of Richard Burgin and had established a career in her own right, especially as a performer of contemporary works.

Schuman's Third was part of a Schumann-Schuman program that included Robert Schumann's Overture to *Manfred* and Third Symphony (the "Rhenish") and Schuman's *American Festival Overture*. Monteux also treated his Chicago audiences to his interpretations of Ravel's complete *Daphnis et Chloé*, in which the Northwestern University Choir participated, and *The Rite of Spring*. A novelty was a work by the orchestra's principal oboist, Florian Mueller, *Five Symphonic Etudes Based on the American Folk Song "El-A-Noy"* (a folksy way of saying "Illinois").

On 17 November 1948, the evening before the opening of San Francisco's symphony season, Monteux once more appeared as a guest violist in a concert of chamber music. The occasion was the season-opening concert by the San Francisco String Quartet, which was composed of members of the orchestra. Monteux modestly took the second viola part in Mozart's Quintet in G minor and was quoted in the next day's *Examiner* as having said, upon accepting the engagement, "If I play a blue note, I'll frown at the other musicians, the way I do when I conduct. Then people won't know I was the one who made the mistake."

According to Alexander Fried, there was nothing to frown about. It was the first time Monteux had played the viola in a public concert in San Francisco. (His previous appearance had been at a private benefit.) Back on the podium, Monteux presided over an unusually interesting season that included many local premieres and one American premiere. For the latter, Darius Milhaud was guest conductor for an entire program culminating in his Third Symphony, a choral setting of the Te Deum. He also gave the San Francisco premieres of his Introduction and Funeral March and *Kentuckiana*, written for the Louisville Orchestra. In fact, Milhaud's entire program was of local premieres, with other works by Lalande, Chabrier, Satie, Rameau, and Roussel, whose Suite in F was given.

Probably the most unexpected of Monteux's local premieres was of Leonard Bernstein's "Jeremiah" Symphony, with Jennie Tourel as soloist in the final movement. Whatever he may have thought of Bernstein as a conductor, Monteux greatly admired him as a composer, spoke well of him in that regard, and greatly pleased Bernstein with his comments.

The other San Francisco premieres were of Stravinsky's Violin Concerto, with Tossy Spivakovsky as soloist; Britten's Piano Concerto, played by Jacques Abram; Morton Gould's Suite from *The Fall River Legend*; Bloch's *Voice in the Wilderness*, with the orchestra's principal cellist, Boris Blinder; George Antheil's Symphony No. 6; and David Diamond's Symphony No. 4. Additionally, the guest conductor William Steinberg presented Stravinsky's *Song of the Nightingale* and Bartók's Rhapsody for Piano and Orchestra. The soloist for the Bartók was Corinne Lacomblé, a Bay area resident and friend of the Monteux family who made a fine career as a soloist and chamber musician and often performed twentieth-century works.

Not a premiere but a decided novelty in the season was the presentation on 17, 18, and 19 February of Berlioz's complete dramatic symphony, *Romeo and Juliet*. The orchestral excerpts are often heard in concert, but opportunities to hear the complete work are rare. On this occasion, it was performed with the mezzo-soprano Nan Merriman, the tenor David Lloyd, the bass Stanley Noonan, and the University of California Chorus from Berkeley. In the *Examiner* of 19 February, Alexander Fried thought the Love Scene and the "Queen Mab" Scherzo to be the only sections worth "hauling back out of dusty oblivion" (but not, for some reason, "Feast at the Capulets"), though the performance itself was highly praised.

Monteux's interpretations of Beethoven's works were greatly valued by the San Francisco critics, who had often expressed in print the hope that the orchestra would present a Beethoven festival. Their wishes were answered after the close of the regular subscription season when, from 4 to 23 April, Monteux conducted seven programs, some in multiple performances, consisting of all the symphonies in numerical order, all the piano concertos (though not in order), the Violin Concerto, nine of the eleven overtures (only *Leonore* No. 3 and *Namensfeier* were omitted), and even *Wellington's Victory*, also known as the "Battle Symphony." The only non-Beethoven work on these programs was at the opening concert, 4 April, when the orchestra played and the audience sang "Happy Birthday" to Monteux for his seventy-fourth.

Claudio Arrau was the soloist in the First, Second, and Fourth Piano Concertos, Myra Hess in the Third, and Egon Petri in the Fifth, while Isaac Stern performed the Violin Concerto. Petri (1881–1962), a great German pianist of Dutch ancestry, rarely appeared in orchestral concerts, though he was often heard in America in recitals during the postwar period. At the time of the Beethoven festival he was teaching at Mills College in Oakland, where he would remain until 1957.

As might be expected, the festival was a great success with audiences and critics (a few orchestral bobbles excepted), with Hess and Stern singled out for special praise. Fried wondered in print (16 April) how Monteux was able to memorize *Leonore* No. 2 after a lifetime of conducting the more popular No. 3, as they are so similar in content yet unexpectedly different at points. Fried also felt that, in general,

> Monteux's performances have always been gripping and vital where the music had intent vigor, grandeur and quick pace. In slow movements, no matter how finely he has controlled them, he has been inclined to let the music settle back and get too static to keep up its best measure of interest and emotional value.

This criticism of Monteux would surface from time to time.

Finally, after the Beethoven cycle Dimitri Mitropoulos was guest conductor for a series of four Spring Festival concerts. One of them, on 7 May, featured Joseph Szigeti as soloist in the first San Francisco performance of Alban Berg's Violin Concerto.

In the fall of 1949, Richard Strauss died, and Monteux programmed his *Ein Heldenleben* in tribute on the season's opening concerts of 10, 11, and 12 November. The ill will Monteux had harbored toward the composer during World War I had long since been cast aside, and Monteux performed his works quite often. Even what appeared to be Strauss's less-than-perfect record during the Nazi period failed to dissuade Monteux. (In 1933, without consulting him, the Nazi regime appointed Strauss president of the Reichsmusikkammer, then removed him in 1935 because of his collaboration with the Jewish librettist Stefan Zweig, after which the Nazis tolerated Strauss, who appeared to tolerate them. Following World War II Strauss was officially cleared of any collaboration with the Nazi regime.)

In the *Examiner* of 12 November, Alexander Fried found Monteux and the orchestra to be in their very best form, and while many critics have found fault with this sprawling and most autobiographical of Strauss's tone poems, Fried thought it a masterpiece, with Naoum Blinder's solos particularly mentioned. At this time Monteux and the orchestra recorded *Ein Heldenleben* for RCA Victor. For some reason it was not released until RCA issued its Pierre Monteux Edition in 1994. Instead of bringing out the Monteux recording in 1950, RCA released a version by Sir Thomas Beecham and the Royal Philharmonic Orchestra. It is possible that Monteux did not approve his recording for release, though a hearing of it today gives no indication why.

On the same program with *Ein Heldenleben* Monteux gave the San Francisco premiere of Schoenberg's Theme and Variations, Op. 43b, a work not to be confused with the Variations for Orchestra, Op. 31. The latter is an extremely complex score, the composer's first orchestral work written in the twelve-tone system, with which Monteux had little sympathy. The new piece, however, had been written at the suggestion of Schoenberg's publisher for American student bands, then orchestrated by the composer. It is a tonal work of simpler textures, more ingratiating for audiences, yet still recognizably by Schoenberg.

Other San Francisco premieres during the 1949–50 season were of Virgil Thomson's Suite from *Louisiana Story*; Alan Hovhaness's Concerto for Flute and String Orchestra ("Elibris") with the principal player, Murray Graitzer, as soloist; *The Enormous Room*, by David Diamond; Manuel Rosenthal's *Jeanne d'Arc*, conducted by the composer; and, fourteen years after it was written, Bartók's Music for Strings, Percussion, and Celeste, under the direction of guest conductor Leonard Bernstein. Bruno Walter was also a guest conductor, offering Mozart's Symphony No. 40 and Beethoven's "Eroica" Symphony. Lili Kraus, whose rejection by the Concertgebouw Orchestra in 1934 had so angered Monteux and contributed to his resignation, was a soloist on 1, 2, and 3 December, playing Mozart's Piano Concerto No. 9 in E-flat major. Kraus would remain a favorite artist of Monteux's and would later make recordings with him. In the *Examiner* of 3 December, Alexander Fried spoke of her playing as "completely alive, sensitive and captivating." The same program also included not a San Francisco premiere, but Monteux's and the orchestra's first performance of Bartók's Concerto for Orchestra.

Besides the regular symphony concerts, the 1949–50 season offered a series of concerts for chamber orchestra called "Classic Interludes." On the first of these programs, 24 November 1949, Monteux conducted Bach's Brandenburg Concerto No. 5, for which the soloists were Naoum Blinder, Murray Graitzer, and Putnam Aldrich, a guest harpsichordist. At that time the niceties of baroque performance practice were not generally known by most musicians, except for specialists and musicologists.

In an article in the March 1971 issue of *Notes: Quarterly Journal of the Music Library Association*, Putnam Aldrich wrote that Monteux had guaranteed that they would be giving "an absolutely authentic performance." After all, he was conducting from the Bach-Gesellschaft edition. At a rehearsal with Blinder and Graitzer, Aldrich began realizing the figured bass of the opening tutti. Monteux interrupted, "What are these chords you are playing? Bach wrote no chords here!" Aldrich attempted to explain that the figures under the keyboard part represented chords, but Monteux would have none of that, saying, "If Bach wanted chords he would have written chords. This is to be an authentic performance. We shall play *only* what Bach wrote!" Monteux then said to the others, "You see, musicologists have always their noses in books and forget to look at what Bach wrote."

Aldrich admitted that the lack of chords in the opening tutti was not too serious,

> but in the second movement, scored for three solo instruments, the effect of the harpsichordist's playing one note at a time with the left hand only was nothing short of ludicrous. Even Monteux began to suspect that something was wrong. At the dress rehearsal he said to me in a whisper, "In this movement you may add a few discreet chords."

To the end of his life, Aldrich felt rage when he thought of what he considered to be Monteux's shocking display of ignorance, arrogance, and rudeness. (Even at that date, the principles of figured bass were quite well known among musicians. Perhaps this was not an aspect of music that was taught at the Paris Conservatory, though one would think that Monteux would have learned something about it in the normal course of events.)

Throughout his career, except at the very end, Pierre Monteux was in excellent health and never missed a concert because of illness. An exception to his perfect record almost occurred with the concert of 30 March 1950, when he was incommoded by an acute attack of indigestion. Uncharacteristically arriving at the opera house several minutes late, he entered the stage rather cautiously, with some effort scaled the podium, which had been heightened by an extra step, and proceeded to conduct, of all works, the Berlioz Requiem. Taking part were the tenor Carl Siegert and the 650 members of the combined Municipal Chorus, University of California Chorus, University of California Glee Club and Treble Clef Society, and San Francisco State College Chorus, not to mention the orchestra. Seldom performed at the time because of the huge forces required and the logistics involving four brass choirs and umpteen timpani, Berlioz's masterpiece never fails to achieve its desired effect, which is one more of quiet devotion than tonal bombast. So it did on this occasion, which, according to Alexander Fried (1 April) made local history.

Each spring for several years the Musical Association of San Francisco, parent body of the symphony, had been presenting a festive event called Tombola. The purpose was to raise money for the orchestra's contingency fund, which could be used for any emergency. The funds raised were necessary to offset the organization's lack of a large endowment fund.

On 4 April 1950 Pierre Monteux, who was enjoying excellent health and the high esteem of audiences, critics, and colleagues, turned seventy-five. In honor of this significant birthday, the 1950 event was named Tombola 75 and dedicated to Monteux, who along with Doris was the guest of honor. (In fact, the whole week of 10–17 April was designated "Tombola 75 Week" by Mayor Elmer E. Robinson.) Held in the Civic Auditorium on 17 April, it was both a concert and an entertainment, with food and drinks available. For the first part of the program Arthur Fiedler conducted the orchestra under a stylized Eiffel Tower that had been designed by the local artist Antonio Sotomayor, the musical bill of fare consisting of light and boisterous numbers from the French repertoire. After an intermission Meyer Davis appeared and led everyone in "Happy Birthday" and some dance music. He was followed by the Hollywood actor Frank Fay, who took over as master of ceremonies for the drawing of Tombola prizes, contributed by many San Francisco merchants. The evening concluded with a series of brief celebratory ballets performed by members of the San Francisco Ballet and various student groups. In the end, $45,000 was raised for the symphony.

In a letter dated 17 April 1950, Arthur A. Hauck, president of the University of Maine at Orono, informed Monteux that the trustees of the university had voted to award him the honorary degree of doctor of music. The letter mentioned that the people of Maine took great pride in his distinguished career and that the university would consider it a privilege to thus make him one of its alumni. Monteux gladly accepted this invitation, and at the commencement exercises on 18 June he officially became Dr. Monteux, although he would not allow anyone to call him that.

Though he had been involved in the first season of the NBC Symphony in 1937, conducting its opening concerts and others as well, he had not conducted the orchestra since then. In the summer of 1950 he conducted, besides his by now customary engagements at Lewisohn Stadium, Robin Hood Dell, and Ravinia, a single broadcast with NBC on 23 July. At that time the orchestra was playing a series of summer broadcasts under the sponsorship of the United States Steel Corporation, programs that were basically light in nature, each with a guest soloist, usually vocal. For this broadcast the soprano Dorothy Maynor was the guest, singing a pair of spirituals and "Lia's Air" from Debussy's *L'enfant prodigue*, and Monteux's orchestral contributions included Smetana's Overture to *The Bartered Bride*, Debussy's *Petite Suite*, and Liszt's Second Hungarian Rhapsody.

Monteux had also become a welcome and beloved visitor to Amsterdam and the Concertgebouw Orchestra, especially for concerts during the Holland Festival, held in the spring. In 1950, however, he was there in the fall as well, with concerts from 11 October to 6 November, an engagement similar in length to those of earlier years. During this time he performed a wide variety of works in the orchestra's several series in Amsterdam and other cities. There were many permutations and variations among the programs, but the major works included Beethoven's Fourth Symphony, Brahms's Second Symphony, Elgar's *Enigma Variations*, Mendelssohn's "Reformation" Symphony (No. 5), and Stravinsky's *Firebird* Suite, with the soloists Wilhelm Backhaus in Brahms's Piano Concerto No. 1, Robert Casadesus in Saint-Saëns's Piano Concerto No. 4, Edwin Fischer in Beethoven's "Emperor" Piano Concerto (No. 5), and Nathan Milstein in Brahms's Violin Concerto, a performance preserved on Tahra Records. Additionally, the orchestra's concertmaster, Jan Damen, played Sibelius's Violin Concerto (also on Tahra records), and the principal cellist, Tibor de Machula, was heard in Dvořák's Cello Concerto. The programs also contained two contemporary Dutch works, *Ballade* for Orchestra by Henk Badings, and the Organ Concerto by Hendrick Andriessen, with the composer as soloist.

The opening of San Francisco's 1950–51 season, on 23, 24, and 25 November, commemorated the centennial of the French pioneers in California with a French program featuring the principal violist, Ferenc Molnar, as soloist in Berlioz's *Harold in Italy*. Berlioz's overture *Le corsaire*, Ravel's *Le tombeau de Couperin*, and Debussy's *La mer* completed the program.

Igor Stravinsky returned as guest conductor on 14, 15, and 16 December presenting the San Francisco premiere of his ballet score *Orpheus*. Other works receiving their local premieres were Aaron Copland's Third Symphony; Paul Cres-

Pierre Monteux by A. Sotomayor

Caricature by Antonio Sotomayor, San Francisco, included in an exhibition
sponsored by the San Francisco Performing Arts Library and Museum in 1993.
Courtesy of Nancie Monteux-Barendse

ton's lyrical and jaunty Symphony No. 2, another American work that Monteux would continue to perform; Symphony No. 1 by the Oakland native William Bergsma; Symphony No. 2 for Brass by Isadore Freed, conducted by the composer; and Symphony No. 2 by the San Franciscan William Denny, also with the composer conducting. Receiving its American premiere was the Symphony No. 1 by the Dutch composer Jan Koetsier. We can see that Monteux did continue to perform works by the Dutch, but they were of fairly recent vintage, as opposed to those dating from his Amsterdam tenure, which he no longer programmed, except for Pijper.

Program highlights of the season included the appearance of Rudolf Serkin in all five Beethoven piano concertos in four concerts from 2 to 6 January and, on 30 and 31 March, Vincent d'Indy's *Wallenstein's Camp* and Symphony No. 2 in observance of the centennial of the composer's birth. Guest conductors were Bruno Walter, who gave Mahler's "Resurrection" Symphony, and Guido Cantelli, in his local debut, in a program of Haydn, Hindemith, and Tchaikovsky. Dimitri Mitroupoulos was the conductor for all the Municipal Concerts. He gave the local premiere of Ernst Krenek's *Symphonic Elegy* for String Orchestra and performed some of his specialties, such as Prokofiev's Third Piano Concerto (conducting from the keyboard) and two concert performances of Richard Strauss's *Elektra*.

During 1951–52 Monteux had a private conducting pupil, a young American soldier who was stationed at the nearby Presidio. He was André Previn, who at the age of twenty-two had already had considerable experience composing and arranging music for MGM in Hollywood. As Previn relates in his amusing book *No Minor Chords*, Monteux did not hold his commercial work against him; after all, he himself had played in the Folies Bergères:

His knowledge was incredible; it seemed to me there was absolutely nothing pertaining to music that he didn't know. . . . What he taught me, that year and after, is impossible to describe. Technically he was a walking textbook. As a human being he had strength and grace, and he imparted knowledge without impatience. (Previn 1991, 49–50)

Previn also felt that Monteux, in his own self-enclosed world of music, did not always seem aware of what was going on outside it. At the end of one lesson he informed Monteux that he would most likely soon be placed on overseas orders to Japan, to which Monteux responded:

Listen, my dear, you are making a mistake. Oh, I know that the orchestra in Tokyo is meant to be good, but believe me, I have heard them, and the winds and brass are very undernourished. Strings are all right, but you can do as well without traveling such a distance. (Previn 1991, 49–50)

Some years later Monteux gave Previn a very important lesson in just a few words. He attended a concert Previn was conducting with a provincial orchestra. Backstage after the concert he asked Previn, "In the last movement of the Haydn symphony, my dear, did you think the orchestra was playing well?" Running through the performance in his mind, and not really knowing what kind of answer Monteux was expecting, he hesitatingly replied, "Yes," to which Monteux rejoined, "So did I. Next time, don't interfere!"

Another gifted Monteux pupil was Anshel Brusilow, who at age sixteen was in the first small group of students to attend the conducting school in Maine. While obviously not yet the skilled conductor he would become, he was very talented at that early age and already a virtuoso on the violin. He quickly became a great favorite of the Monteuxs, who began guiding him in his career while he continued to study privately with Pierre in San Francisco. On 19, 20, and 21 April 1951 Brusilow was soloist with Monteux and the San Francisco Symphony, and on 25 July of the same year with Monteux at New York's Lewisohn Stadium.

The good relationship between Brusilow and the Monteuxs continued unabated until late in 1951, when they learned that he had fallen in love with a young woman and planned to marry her. This news was not greeted favorably by the Monteuxs, especially Doris, who felt it would be difficult for Brusilow to pursue a career if there were a wife and potential children to be concerned about, unless the spouse had a high enough social status to be able to help him—apparently not the case in this instance. Matters came to a head one afternoon when Brusilow visited the Monteuxs at the Fairmont Hotel. A fairly animated discussion took place in which Brusilow was asked to discontinue his romance, which he refused to do. Then he would receive no further help from the Monteuxs, he was told.

As related by Brusilow, once he left the hotel in quite an agitated state, he had the feeling that someone was following him. To make sure, he turned a corner and waited. Sure enough, along came an employee of the Fairmont Hotel. When Brusilow questioned him, he was told, "The Monteuxs gave me money to follow you, to see where you went." The exact purpose of this espionage is not known. Where did the Monteuxs think he would go? To see the girlfriend? To a burlesque house? Nobody knows.

While there was now a rift between Brusilow and the Monteuxs, there remained an already scheduled concert with the orchestra in the San Francisco suburb of Richmond. Meanwhile, Brusilow appeared as soloist in the Tchaikovsky concerto with the Boston Symphony Orchestra, conducted by Ernest Ansermet, in early January 1952. Returning for the Richmond engagement of 11 January, at which he was to play the Glazunov concerto, he received only a cold nod backstage from Monteux, who would not speak to him at all. The normal procedure for going onstage is that the soloist enters, followed by the conductor. But when the time came, Monteux, without saying a word, walked on stage first with Brusilow trailing behind him.

In his book David Schneider states that only a few hundred people attended the concert, which caused Monteux to remark sarcastically that Brusilow was really a drawing card for attendance (Schneider 1983, 73). This comment prompted Schneider, in turn, to observe that Monteux seemed oblivious to the fact that he himself had not been able to attract a large audience to the concert.

Anshel Brusilow was to become concertmaster of the Philadelphia Orchestra (a post he held from 1959 to 1966), then founder and music director of the Chamber Symphony of Philadelphia, much to the irritation of Eugene Ormandy, who disliked the competition. As of this writing, he still conducts, as he has for many years, the orchestra at North Texas State University in Denton, and is still married to Marilyn, his girlfriend in 1951.

For several years Monteux had considered resigning his post in San Francisco, for he felt there was a danger inherent in remaining too long in one post. He had, in fact, broached the idea to Mrs. Armsby as early as 1946, when he had been there ten years. Just as she had persuaded him to take the job in the first place, so she persuaded him to stay on a bit longer, with the United States tour as an added inducement. Finally, prior to the start of the 1951–52 season, Monteux announced that it would be his last in San Francisco. He had been receiving more and more offers of guest engagements with orchestras throughout the country and in Europe, and he wished to take advantage of some of them.

The first program of the season, 15 and 16 November 1951, had as guest soloist a seventeen-year-old San Francisco pianist, Samuel Lipman, who was heard in Beethoven's Concerto No. 3. For Alexander Fried in the *Examiner* of 17 November, Lipman's playing was "completely artistic and absorbing, warm and full of life." Sam Lipman became a regular attendee of Monteux's conducting school in Maine, never as a conductor but as a resident pianist in concerto and chamber music performances. He went on to give two very successful recitals in New York's Town Hall and performed at Lewisohn Stadium and the Aspen Music Festival but eventually gravitated toward writing and music criticism, becoming the critic for *Commentary* magazine and finally the publisher of *The New Criterion*. At his untimely death in 1994 he was regarded as one of America's finest writers and critics.

During his final season Monteux gave the San Francisco premieres of Peter Mennin's Fifth Symphony; the Third Symphony of Charles Ives; Ernest Bloch's *Concerto symphonique* for piano and orchestra, with Corinne Lacomblé as soloist; and the overture *Laughter, Yet Love* by the Chicago-based composer, pianist, and conductor Rudolph Ganz, who at the time was in charge of the San Francisco Symphony's Young People's Concerts. He had previously done the same for the New York Philharmonic. Another premiere was the first performance anywhere of the Symphony No. 2 by the Hawaiian-born composer Dai-Keong Lee.

On 29 January 1952 Monteux and the orchestra played a benefit concert for State of Israel Bonds. An audience of six thousand assembled in the Civic Auditorium for a program that included works by Ernest Bloch and Darius Milhaud.

Monteux soon received letters of thanks and appreciation from Benjamin H. Swig, the chairman of State of Israel Bonds, and Abba Eban, Israel's ambassador to the United States.

As the season drew to a close, the Municipal Chorus was kept busy, as was the University of California Chorus, in performances of Berlioz's *Damnation of Faust* on 20, 21, and 22 March, and in Monteux's farewell concerts on 10, 11, and 12 April. This program began with the "Good Friday Spell" from Wagner's *Parsifal*; continued with César Franck's Symphonic Variations, in which the piano soloist was Agnes Albert; and concluded with—what else?—Beethoven's Ninth Symphony, featuring the soloists Phyllis Moffet, Jean Bonacorsi, Caesar Curzi, and Donald Gramm. Agnes Albert, a San Franciscan, was a frequent performer in the Bay area as well as a financial supporter of the symphony.

In the *Examiner* of 12 April, Alexander Fried wrote that Monteux conducted the Ninth "with an especial great mastery, poetic feeling and final monumental thrill. . . . Rockbound strength, mystic hints and meditations and a lofty, exciting idealism characterized Thursday's whole performance." After an ovation lasting at least ten minutes, Monteux quieted the audience and said to them, "I do not say goodbye. I say au revoir."

The Musical Association and the orchestra gave a farewell party for Monteux at which the women of the orchestra performed a lively cancan, causing him to remark that it had taken him seventeen years to see what pretty legs they had. He then cut into a huge cake with the inscription "Au revoir, cher Maître." As a gift from the association he received a silver bowl and, as in Boston in 1924, an immense autograph book filled with the signatures of thousands of subscribers to the concerts. The orchestra musicians presented him with an engraved pair of binoculars, something he had apparently always wanted. At the party Monteux made a significant announcement: "My hair, it is not dyed."

A perception of Monteux that continually irritated him in his later years was the assertion that he dyed his hair, which appeared to be jet black, at least from a distance, while his moustache was unmistakably white. He denied this allegation in one interview after another and often challenged the interviewer to wash his hair to see whether it was truly black. What most people did not realize was that Monteux came by his black hair naturally, for his mother did not begin to turn gray until very late in life. And from up close one could easily see that his hair was flecked with gray.

In an article in the *Examiner* on Sunday, 6 April, Fried summed up Monteux's tenure, comparing the orchestra before he arrived with the one it became under his leadership. He referred to Monteux's "memory of music—in all its grand scope and tiny detail, in hundreds of scores"—as

absolutely incredible. Surely no musician in history has ever surpassed it. . . . In still another particular, he is all but unique. His technique of leadership—that is, his control of the meaningful baton, and his ear for interior orchestral sound—is the endless admiration of all musicians who play for him. . . .

Some of us think that he has at times overstressed French Impressionistic music, minor modern music and the like. Handel, Bach, and Haydn have not been his most frequent favorites; nor Germanic Bruckner, nor expressionistic Schoenberg. On the other hand, he has been invariably powerful in Beethoven, Wagner and Brahms. He's been supreme in Stravinsky, and also in such French romantics as Franck. He's been superfine in Schubert, and often in Mozart. He personally has recreated for us the genius of Berlioz, whom otherwise we should not know and love so well. It is going to be very, very hard to find a new conductor who will keep up Monteux's standards of mastery and will lead the San Francisco Symphony to still new, ambitious achievements.

It was.

The program book for Monteux's final concerts contained the following tribute:

To Pierre Monteux

A man who belongs to the world but who lives in the hearts
of San Franciscans

The first day you came to San Francisco you gave us hope. In the days that followed you translated the hope into promise. With the passing years, you have brought the promise to magnificent fulfillment in the greatness of our San Francisco Symphony Orchestra. Now you are moving on. The challenge to your art, you say, is elsewhere. You leave behind not only a great musical instrument but also an example, which will stay fresh always, of the sincere artist's approach to music. And you leave warm memories in the hearts of thousands. Go with our gratitude, and our blessing.

During the intermission of the final concert, Charles Kennedy, president of Local 6 of the American Federation of Musicians, presented Monteux with a life membership card, the first time the local union had ever bestowed such an honor on anyone. The engraving on the card read, "To a great man whose membership we shall always cherish, both as a musician and a humanitarian." Perhaps recalling the many times the union had thwarted him by insisting that only local musicians be employed, Monteux accepted the card without a word and put it in his pocket.

There was one final honor for Monteux before he left San Francisco. In a letter dated 18 April 1952, Monteux was informed by Henri Bonnet, the French ambassador to the United States, that in recognition of the contribution he had made to the dissemination of French music in the United States, he had been promoted to the rank of Commander of the Legion of Honor. The symbol of this honor is a small circular red lapel rosette, which Monteux always wore with pride.

CHAPTER 20

Return to Boston

$\mathbf{W}$hen Pierre Monteux left the Boston Symphony Orchestra in 1924, Judge Frederick P. Cabot, chairman of the board of trustees, had told him, "You will come back to *your* orchestra often." Then Koussevitzky took over the conductorship and enjoyed a tenure of twenty-five years, none of which included a guest appearance by Monteux. Some have claimed that "Koussy" rarely invited guest conductors, or that in his later years guests were limited to his favored Tanglewood pupils Leonard Bernstein, Eleazar de Carvalho, and Thor Johnson. Both suppositions are flawed.

During Koussevitzky's final six seasons alone the guest conductors included, besides those just mentioned, Ernest Ansermet, Sir Adrian Boult, Vladimir Golschmann, André Kostelanetz, Dimitri Mitropoulos, Charles Munch, Paul Paray, Fritz Reiner, George Szell, and Bruno Walter. Igor Stravinsky conducted a program of his own music, and the associate conductor, Richard Burgin, appeared several times each season. Of Pierre Monteux, though, there was not a sign. When I asked the retired BSO violinist Harry Ellis Dickson, who joined the orchestra in 1939, if he could account for Koussevitzky's exclusion of Monteux, he replied, "I can give you the reason in a single word—jealousy."

Koussevitzky was succeeded in 1949 by the Alsatian-born Charles Munch (1891–1968). During his first season Bernstein was the only guest conductor, with Burgin again on the podium for a few weeks. However, as plans were being made for the 1950–51 season, Munch felt it was time for the BSO to redress a grievous error and invited Monteux to conduct a week of concerts. Perhaps understandably, Monteux was reluctant to accept the invitation, for he was very sensitive to the fact that he had been ignored for twenty-five years. It took a letter from Henry B. Cabot, chairman of the trustees, to convince him that he was genuinely wanted in Boston, and to change his mind. (The Cabot family has a long history with the Boston Symphony.)

In an interview in *The Boston Globe* of 24 January 1951, Monteux was found, at age seventy-five, to be quick and amiable of spirit. "Do you want to ask me how I feel to be back with the Boston Symphony?" he inquired. "I will tell you. It feels

209

wonderful, but I think it is 10 years too late. But 10 years ago Mr. Munch was not here to invite me." A famous photograph taken during this visit shows Monteux, Koussevitzky, and Munch in an amicable pose, but assuredly there was no love lost between the first two.

On 26 January 1951, Pierre Monteux made his extremely belated return to the Boston Symphony conducting the following program:

> Wagner: Overture to *The Flying Dutchman*
> Beethoven: Symphony No. 4 in B-flat major
> Stravinsky: *The Rite of Spring*

By this time the phalanx of Boston critics had also changed; it now consisted of Cyrus Durgin in the *Globe*, Rudolph Elie in the *Herald*, Harold Rogers in the *Christian Science Monitor*, and Warren Storey Smith—the lone holdover—in the *Post*. "What a superb musician, what a master is this Pierre Monteux!" began Elie's review on 27 January. Referring to the conductor's "outrageously belated return to Boston," Elie said that Monteux "ranks with the very greatest conductors of our time" and that he was "not fully appreciated" by the general public because

> he can conduct an orchestra and make it sound gloriously without disturbing a lock of his shaggy mane. As it happens this sort of conducting went out of fashion with the button shoe. Whole generations have been reared on virtuoso conductors who combine the beauty of a collar model with the athletic prowess of a pole vaulter.

Elie further stated that "in the Fourth Symphony it was Beethoven who spoke," while *The Rite* was given "the ultimate, definitive performance, one of the most sensational performances of any music to be heard in my memory."

Durgin was no less effusive:

> I doubt that anyone can conduct *The Rite* so well as Mr. Monteux. He has the whole score in his head . . . and he makes it sound like music. . . . This performance was a long crescendo of tension released only by the final crisp chords at the end of each section . . . a triumph of the conducting art.

The reviews by Smith and Rogers were equally laudatory. Harry Ellis Dickson, who eventually became a conducting pupil of Monteux's, has recalled that in the 26 January performance of *The Rite*, Monteux, conducting from memory, beat one measure incorrectly during a complex passage, causing some momentary confusion among the musicians. At the repeat performance the next day, as that passage drew near, he held up his left hand and pointed at himself, smiling the while as if to say "My fault!" The orchestra loved him for it.

RCA Victor took advantage of Monteux's return to record the *The Rite* and produced the finest of Monteux's four versions of the piece, one that remains a classic to this day. Along with the composer's own renditions, it is surely the touchstone reading of this landmark of twentieth-century music. While other versions (Leonard Bernstein's, Igor Markevitch's, and Georg Solti's) may surpass it in terms of visceral energy or personalized interpretation, Monteux's remains the classic account in terms of projecting what is written in the score, so that all the disparate elements—savage, mysterious, sensuous, rhythmic, and lyrical—are presented in proper proportion. Everything unfolds naturally, as always in a Monteux performance, with no lack of excitement.

Monteux was not without his detractors, however. Prime among them was probably B. H. Haggin, music critic of *The Nation*. In a collection of his reviews and articles entitled *Music Observed*, he refers to

the story of the Monteux career as that of one of the giants to whom recognition has come belatedly, with its built-in estimate of Monteux as one of the giants. This one has been kept rolling for several years by one writer after another incapable of hearing Monteux's repeatedly demonstrated musical mediocrity, until it is now part of the body of accepted belief in terms of which most writing about music and musicians is done. (Haggin 1964, 127–128)

Haggin neglects, however, to point out the nature of this mediocrity. Later in the same volume Haggin speaks of

the idea . . . that since Monteux conducted the first performance of *Le Sacre du Printemps* his performance must be the definitive one, instead of the hard fact of Stravinsky's own recorded performance, which should enable anyone to hear that the work in Monteux's performance hasn't the power it should have. (Haggin 1964, 141)

Monteux's reputation as a firm but gentle and genial maestro suffered a severe setback during his rehearsals of *The Rite of Spring*. He was deeply dissatisfied with the playing of the timpanist, the long-serving Polish-born Roman Szulc, who was having difficulty with the work's many rhythmic intricacies and thus not playing forcefully enough. By all accounts Monteux was merciless in his many criticisms of Szulc, to the point where the player was completely devastated and demoralized. An attempt was made to secure the services of Saul Goodman, master timpanist of the New York Philharmonic, but to no avail. On the recording the timpani playing, while not overly prominent, as is often the case, is well balanced in the context of RCA's sound picture, and it is certainly accurate.

More important to Monteux than any of the enthusiastic Boston reviews was a letter he received from Charles Munch, dated 8 March 1951. In it Munch tells Monteux how much he admires him, that he is "the greatest example and most marvelous of masters." He asks permission to express to Monteux "my profound gratitude, to thank you from the bottom of my heart. Your week here was the great event of the season and has left an extraordinary memory." That extraordinary memory produced an extraordinary document; it is difficult to think of another music director of a major orchestra who would describe a colleague's concerts as "the great event of the season."

The success of this great event paved the way for invitations to Monteux for further visits, to the extent that he was to return in each subsequent season but one for the remainder of his life. He became what is known these days as a "principal guest conductor," though that term was not in use at the time.

In the fall of 1951 he returned for two weeks, 20 November to 2 December. The program for the second week's concert pair, on 30 November and 1 December, was an unusual combination of works by Wagner and Debussy:

Wagner: Prelude to *Parsifal*
Debussy: Excerpts from *The Martyrdom of St. Sebastian*
Wagner: "Siegfried's Rhine Journey" and "Funeral Music" from
    Götterdämmerung
Debussy: "Gigues," from *Images*
Debussy: *Jeux*
Wagner: Overture to *Tannhäuser*

The juxtaposition of composers is curious in that Debussy was in the forefront of a revolt against "Wagnerism" by French composers of the late nineteenth century. Yet the religious mysticism that imbues *Parsifal* is also very much present in *St. Sebastian*, which probably would not have been written in quite the same way without the example of its predecessor. The relationship between the other Wagner and Debussy pieces is more obscure, and it is likely that Monteux selected them for the purpose of contrast rather than to demonstrate similarities.

Actually Monteux conducted three programs during the two weeks, repeating *The Rite of Spring* on 2 December in a series outside the usual Friday-Saturday subscription pair, where it was preceded most attractively by Beethoven's "Pastoral" Symphony. The two works make a natural pairing, though one not often encountered, each with its own distinctive representation of the glorification of the earth. Its significance was not lost on Walt Disney, who included portions of both works in his classic film *Fantasia* (1940).

The Wagner-Debussy and Beethoven-Stravinsky programs were both played in New York, on 5 and 8 December respectively, marking the first time Monteux conducted the BSO in that city since 1924. Reviewing the former in the 1 January 1952 *Musical America*, Robert Sabin wrote, "Mr. Monteux was not invariably poetic or inspired, but he was always intelligent, tasteful, and completely in command. He is a marvelous antidote for the clenched-fist and tremulous-fingertip schools of conducting." The Beethoven-Stravinsky program was reviewed by the faithful Virgil Thomson in the 9 December *Herald Tribune*. Again he stressed the "lovely sounds, clean blends, straightforward metrics, impeccable balances. . . . [Monteux's] offerings to the spirit, to the mind and to the sensuous ear are so abundant that complete acceptance, complete absorption are the result for this listener." Sabin felt that Monteux humanized *The Rite* "by conducting it as he conducts Beethoven."

In the spring of 1952 the Boston Symphony set sail for Europe, where it would be performing for the first time. On 2 May, the last day at sea aboard the *S.S. Île-de-France*, twenty-nine members of the orchestra gave a little concert for the benefit of the Seamen's Fund. Monteux conducted, opening the program with Mozart's *Eine kleine Nachtmusik* and closing it with Haydn's Symphony No. 88. In between, Samuel Lipman played solo piano works of Bach and Bartók. The raison d'être for the tour, from 6 to 26 May, was to participate in a festival in Paris entitled "L'Oeuvre du XXème Siècle" (The Art of the Twentieth Century), under the aegis of the Congress for Cultural Freedom, of which the composer Nicolas Nabokov was president. In one of a number of acts of generosity toward his senior colleague, Charles Munch had invited Monteux to share the tour with him. Prior to making this trip the orchestra concluded its Boston season with programs of twentieth-century music that would be played in Paris: Monteux conducted Pijper's Third Symphony, Milhaud's Protée Suite, and the Third Symphony of William Schuman, one of two such American works in which he truly believed and which he programmed often in his last years. (The other was the Second Symphony of Paul Creston.)

The highlight of the tour for Monteux had to have been the performance, on 8 May in the Théâtre des Champs-Elysées, of *The Rite of Spring*, which climaxed a program that also included Vaughan Williams's *Fantasia on a Theme of Thomas Tallis*, the Milhaud suite, and the Schuman symphony. During the ovation that followed *The Rite*, Stravinsky, who had taken a bow in the audience, was pushed onto the stage by both Monteux and Munch, to even greater applause. According to Cyrus Durgin's report in the 17 May *Boston Globe* (the Boston critics had made the trip for this event), the seventy-year-old Stravinsky bowed once, kissed Monteux on both cheeks, and left the stage with tears streaming down his face. The July 1952 issue of *Musical America* reported that Monteux silenced the audience and addressed them: "Thirty-nine years ago I conducted the first performance of the Sacre; may I invite you to hear me do it again thirty-nine years hence!" Members of the BSO who had played *The Rite* under Koussevitzky, Bernstein, and others felt that this particular performance was the greatest in which they had participated. Two of them, the double bassist Henri Girard and the English horn player Louis Speyer, had actually played in the world premiere in 1913. Speyer felt that the choreography, the settings, and the costumes were as much responsible for the riot as the music.

The low point of the trip for Monteux was described by Samuel Lipman in the January 1984 issue of *Commentary*. Lipman, seventeen years old in 1952, had come under Monteux's wing in San Francisco and played Beethoven's Third Piano Concerto with him and the San Francisco Symphony on the opening concerts of the 1951–52 season. He accompanied the Monteuxs on the tour of Europe, not as a performer but for his own education. His description follows:

> On this trip I had a chance to contrast the worshipful way Monteux was treated in Holland when he conducted the Concertgebouw, and in London when he conducted the BBC Symphony, with the demeaning behavior displayed toward him by his own French musical world. At the end of May 1952, he conducted a French orchestra in a concert for the United Nations at the Palais de Chaillot in Paris. The program included Aaron Copland's *El Salón México*, an orchestral showpiece then still rhythmically problematical even for American orchestras. But what was chancy for American players seemed impossible for the French. The first rehearsal, in a hired room, was a disaster, an outcome not mitigated by the timeworn diversion of the orchestra string players who pushed a mute along the floor with their bows from one stand to the other until it had traversed the entire section— while the orchestra was playing or the conductor was talking. In Richard Strauss's *Rosenkavalier* Suite, the harpists missed their cue because they were openly filing their nails. The final insult to this grand old man of French music took place when he (with me carrying his brief case) turned up at the hall the morning of the concert a half-hour before the rehearsal and was told by the commissionnaire that he had no right to be there and should go away immediately.

The French ensemble in question was the Lamoureux Orchestra. The *Musical America* critic, composer Everett Helm, spoke of the orchestra as ordinarily not a top-rank group, but claimed that it had played beyond its capacity, giving most likely their best performance in recent years. The program had been a curious hodgepodge of works by Berlioz, Liszt, Sibelius, Copland, Pijper, Fauré, d'Indy, and Strauss, with *El salón México* indeed proving to be a bit too much for the orchestra, even under Monteux's ministrations. What Berlioz and Liszt were doing on a program of twentieth-century music is anyone's guess.

In a letter dated 21 June 1952, the directors of the festival, Nicolas Nabokov and Hervé Dugardin, after thanking Monteux for his participation, stated that the performance of *The Rite*, the masterpiece that he had created amid rioting and that had become a great classic of contemporary music, had been one of the most moving events of the festival. The concert at which he conducted a French orchestra was also not to be forgotten by the Parisian public and by the festival directors, who were very proud and happy for his success.

Upon his return to America, Monteux's summer concerts included his first appearances at Tanglewood, the summer home of the Boston Symphony in western Massachusetts, which he would visit annually for the rest of his life. In 1952

he led two concerts there: on 26 July a program featuring Schubert's Ninth and.
The Rite of Spring, and on 2 August an all-Wagner program of excerpts from
Die Walküre, Siegfried, and *Götterdämmerung*, with Margaret Harshaw the solo-
ist in the Immolation Scene.

In spite of his earlier objections to Wagner during wartime, Monteux loved his
music and gave convincing performances of it when he was allowed to do so.
French conductors are rarely asked to play Wagner, which for many years was
thought to be the exclusive property of German conductors (and one Italian—
Toscanini). Yet the French are able to bring a certain lightness of touch to Wagner that benefits the music.

After its 1952–53 season, the Boston Symphony embarked on a coast-to-coast
tour of the United States, for which Munch invited Monteux to share the conducting with him. Included on the tour were two concerts in San Francisco. When
he left that city in 1952, Monteux could hardly have dreamed that he would
return so soon. Again Munch demonstrated his great generosity by seeing to it
that Monteux conducted the opening night. Munch, who had been concertmaster
of the Gewandhaus Orchestra of Leipzig before beginning his conducting career
and had played under the direction of Wilhelm Furtwängler and other great conductors, was quoted in the papers as saying, "I have known two conductors who
were masters, Toscanini and Monteux." So it was that on the evening of 7 May
1953 Monteux once again stood on the podium of the War Memorial Opera
House, this time in front of the Boston Symphony Orchestra, which he directed in
a generous program:

> Beethoven: Symphony No. 2 in D major
> Creston: Symphony No. 2
> Stravinsky: Suite from *The Firebird*
> Strauss: Suite from *Der Rosenkavalier*

As expected, the entire audience rose in greeting as Monteux entered the stage.
Obviously it was a strange sight to see him on his regular podium, but with a different orchestra in front of him. Virtually the entire membership of the San Francisco Symphony was scattered throughout the audience, seeing Monteux from
the back for the first time. In the *Examiner* the next day, Alexander Fried wrote
of "passages of intimate performance that had the taste and balance of chamber
music" contrasted with "climaxes that were stupendous without being forced
and without losing the ultimate true heroic quality of reserve." Monteux had
come home triumphantly, but only fleetingly.

CHAPTER 21

The "Eroica"

The title of this chapter refers not to Beethoven's Third Symphony, but to Pierre Monteux's third wife. As Doris was no. 3 he referred to her as the "Eroica," and she was known to tell interviewers, "I am the 'Eroica.'" Of course, to people who knew Monteux during the last thirty or more years of his life, it was Doris who personified the designation Madame Monteux. But the chapter title could just as easily have been "Mum," for that is how she was known to the vast legion of Monteux pupils. In truth, she deserves a book of her own.

Doris was, of course, a formidable yet charming presence in San Francisco; she could not possibly have been otherwise. Often she could be found speaking at various events helping to promote music and the symphony, hosting or being a guest at society teas and coffees, and in general becoming as recognizable as her husband. Occasionally the imperious side of her personality would rear up.

At the symphony concerts she sat in Box One, the conductor's box, in the War Memorial Opera House. As this was the box closest to the stage on the first-violin side of the orchestra, she had an unobstructed aerial view of the proceedings, and she became irritated that the bright overhead lights emphasized the orchestra members' many perspiring bald pates, which glared unnecessarily in her direction. Accordingly, an edict went out from Doris that henceforth all the bald members were to wear toupees. Such an order would be unthinkable today, and even then it was thought to be something of a joke, but it was taken seriously enough to be obeyed for at least one concert. One of the reviewers wrote that while he thought he recognized certain musicians on stage, he could not be quite sure, for there was something different about them. Oh yes, they had grown hair since the last concert.

Conditions in Europe leading up to World War II made it impossible for the Monteuxs to continue returning there between seasons in San Francisco. No more going to Les Baux, no more conducting classes there. However, they chose not to spend the entire year in San Francisco and preferred to find some other location they could call home. While the Monteuxs considered several areas of the country, and even French-speaking Canada, it seemed most natural to Doris that they settle in her home state of Maine, and in her hometown of Hancock.

As has been mentioned, Hancock nestles across Frenchman's Bay from Bar Harbor, and it overlooks Taunton Bay as well. In 1940 Doris's father, Eugene Hodgkins, wrote to her about a small cabin and surrounding land on the Taunton River, on the west side of U.S. Route 1, which he thought would be an ideal spot for her and Pierre to spend the summer. The property was owned by Edith Joy, a Hancock native whom Doris remembered from earlier times (many of Monteux's students would remember her as Edie Towle) and who was happy to rent it to the Monteuxs for that summer. So enamored were Doris and Pierre of this lovely property that before the next year they prevailed upon Edith to sell it to them, the cabin and sixty-four acres. At first, plumbing fixtures were rather primitive (hence the earlier reference to the "pipi pail"), and bathing was done in the river. Eventually various amenities were added, and the building was expanded to include a fairly large room with a small stage at one end, an appropriate venue for chamber music rehearsals and performances and for the early conducting classes.

Also in 1941 the Monteuxs bought a second house, a much larger one on the other side of route 1 and closer to the center of Hancock, where there is an intersection and a road leading east to Hancock Point. (When one speaks of the village of Hancock, one should bear in mind that its native population is even now little more than five hundred, though it tends to swell in the summer with visitors and students.) As the Monteuxs spent portions of the fall and winter months in their larger house, when they were not in San Francisco, it came to be known as Winterhaven, while the spring and summer home was known simply as "the camp."

As can be imagined from its population, Hancock is a closely knit community where everyone knows everyone else. When the Monteuxs moved there, Doris, who had been away for many years, was not really well known to her neighbors. Nor was Pierre, in spite of his fame as a conductor: the good citizens of Hancock did not possess a musical sophistication that would have encompassed the world of symphonies and concertos. While they of course knew of San Francisco, that it had a symphony orchestra and that Pierre conducted it would have been news to most of them.

Doris did have relatives and old school friends in town, however, and between them and her irrepressible personality, soon the Monteuxs were strangers no longer. The townspeople took to them very quickly, especially to "the little Frenchman," who could often be seen walking about among them in his red lumberjack shirt and chatting with them, for Pierre Monteux was nothing if not approachable.

A couple of years after the United States entered World War II, as patriotic fervor was running very high, Doris came up with an idea that would involve the townspeople and that would also make them amenable and hospitable to the conducting school that had just begun. Her idea was what came to be known as the Hancock Pageant. In his book *The Sun Never Sets on Hancock Point* (actually two substantial volumes), Sanford (Sandy) Phippen, a Hancock native and the town historian, writes:

As a child, as far as I was concerned, the Hancock Pageant was one of the great fairy tales of Downeastern civilization, and practically every adult I knew had either participated in it, or been a spectator of it. Always there had been references to the good times had while putting on the pageant; and I had even seen pictures of my relatives and neighbors dressed up as Indians, Pilgrims, soldiers, foreigners, angels, spirits, statues, and southern belles; but what they were all doing in such get-ups, I could never, until now, clearly ascertain. (Phippen 2000, 370–71)

Phippen then quotes from *The Ellsworth American* of 7 July 1943, which reported on the first pageant, held three days earlier on the Fourth of July. The article describes the dedication of a service flag by the citizens of Hancock on a Sunday evening, followed by a program at the Union Congregational Church. This program, a pageant entitled "The Cavalcade of American History," was directed by Doris Monteux and performed by the members of the town's Pilgrim Guild, accompanied by a six-piece orchestra conducted by Pierre Monteux, no less. The music was of an American historical nature appropriate to the dramatic offering, and there were readings by the pastor, Reverend Thomas Roden, and by Doris.

As part of the performance, "Indians" entered through a church window, and in the distance the *Mayflower* could be seen approaching, the Pilgrims arriving to the reading of Felicia Herman's poem "The Breaking Waves." The Revolutionary period was then represented by the Spirit of '76, a *tableau vivant* of the famous painting depicting three marching Revolutionary War soldiers, one carrying an American flag, the other two playing fife and drum, after which Patrick Henry's famous speech ("Give me liberty or give me death!") was recited. The War for Independence was represented by a Revolutionary soldier saying good-bye to his mother. A rendering of "La Marseillaise," sung by Mary Gallison, paid tribute the role of France in our revolution.

Then came the Civil War, with a soldier, Andrew Partridge, in the company of two Southern belles, followed by the Gettysburg Address. Partridge's wife, Eleanor, represented World War I. "Flanders Field" was read, then "Last Flight" for World War II, followed by the assembling of the entire cast led by groups of soldiers and sailors. Mrs. Arthur Colwell represented the "Red Cross Mother," after which the eight points of the Atlantic Charter were read.

Phippen then describes the service flag, made by Eleanor Partridge and brought to the front of the church by two ushers. As the flag was unrolled, Reverend Roden read the names of the young men from the town who were in the service and then offered the prayer of dedication.

First Selectman Albert Colwell received the flag and placed it upon a staff, symbolizing the community's contribution to the war effort. Spruce trees and a portrait of George Washington decorated the altar of the church, where Betsy Ross, impersonated by Louise Hamlin, was shown at work on the Stars and Stripes.

Most of the costumes had been made by the ladies of Hancock, and others were ordered from Boston by the Monteuxs at their own expense. Admission was fifty cents for adults and twenty-five cents for children, with proceeds from the first pageant donated to the Red Cross and the County Community Chest.

After 1943 Doris Monteux added more scenes from American history, with additional dialogue and music, and the last pageant, in 1946, had seventy-two participants. The first pageant had been given one performance. So popular did these events become, however, that two were presented in 1944 and three in 1945, the last at Hammond Hall in Winter Harbor.

In its edition of 27 June 1945, *The Ellsworth American* reported on the participation in the pageant of Meyer Davis and Ted Leavitt, a nephew of Doris's. The *American* observed that it was a unique event to be able to see and hear a major conductor, a famous theatrical producer, and a leading American composer performing together. Pierre Monteux and Meyer Davis both played in the string section, which included musicians from the conducting school as well. (*The Ellsworth American* was rather confused here, for Ted Leavitt was not a composer, but an actor, and Meyer Davis was not a theatrical producer, though he did back some shows.)

In the 1945 and 1946 pageants, according to Phippen,

a number of women, dressed in native costumes of various countries, trooped around the church to stirring music, carrying flags of their respective lands. After the countries were arrayed on either side of the church, a speech was read, proclaiming the importance of the establishment of the United Nations; but after the speech was given in the 1946 pageant, a dramatically ominous note was sounded when a dancer, the wife of one of the Hancock musicians, did a dance representing omnipresent war, but which many townsfolk (some of them rather outraged at what they thought to be a sacrilegious display) felt symbolized the atom bomb, and afterwards referred to the dancer herself as such. (Phippen 1978, 372–73)

In an interview, Doris told Phippen that Monteux had traveled to New York City and researched the authentic period music used in many of the pageant scenes. She also told him that in rehearsals for the Pioneer Women scene, she had difficulty in getting "the shy Hancock ladies to speak the Whitman poetry loudly enough, and in frustration, had to raise her voice to tell them, 'You're heading westward, girls! It's Onward, ever Onward!'"

Researching his own book, Phippen interviewed many Hancock citizens about the pageant, almost all of whom remembered the several events joyfully. The lone exception was a summer resident who commented drily, "It was as good as any elementary school pageant in any city in the country." After 1946 the increasing demands of Pierre Monteux's summer conducting schedule brought an end to the Hancock Pageant.

While some local citizens may have disapproved of Hancock's newfound attention once the Monteuxs moved there, the Monteuxs put the sleepy little village on the map. The establishment of the school, with its influx of students and other visitors in the summer and the concerts it presented, added immeasurably to the local economy. Many of the students, even after they ceased to be students, bought land and homes in Hancock, usually for summer use but in some cases for year-round residence.

Once the Monteuxs had settled in Hancock and the conducting school had become established, Doris began to put her early vocal training and professional singing to good use by accepting voice pupils. She often said that her desire was to produce a great singer for the state of Maine. Whether or not she achieved this objective, several of her pupils deserve mention, beginning with her niece Ginia Davis, who often performed with Monteux in concerts and opera. Cynics might cite these appearances as examples of nepotism, but Monteux's musical integrity would not have permitted Ginia to sing with him had he not genuinely felt her to be talented. In fact, she became his favorite singer for Ravel's *Shéhérazade* and Debussy's *Mélisande*.

Another of Doris's pupils was the Maine native Freda Gray-Massé, a mezzo-soprano who performed with Monteux in Beethoven's Ninth Symphony in Boston and at Tanglewood. The Maineiac (as residents of Maine like to call themselves) native Nancy McKay also studied with Doris, as did Kathryna Blum, who later married Joseph Barone (pronounced Baroné), administrator of the conducting school. Doris was an effective teacher: all these singers were heard as soloists, at one time or another, in the school's Sunday concerts.

Doris could be very single-minded toward a pupil who she felt had the potential to make a professional career, and anything in the pupil's life that might hinder the establishment of a great career had to be dispensed with. In the case of Freda Gray-Massé, the unfortunate (to Doris) encumbrances were a husband and children. Doris was convinced that one could not hope to establish oneself professionally if one had a family to be concerned about. And if one did have a spouse, that spouse should be someone of status who could be of help. Doris went so far as to suggest, if not actually insist, that Freda divorce her husband and leave her children with him, in which case Doris would continue to teach her and help her in her career. Freda naturally refused, and that was the end of her relationship with the Monteuxs.

Religion played an important part in Doris's life. Entries in a diary she kept in 1956 mention that she prayed and read from the Bible each day. Raised as a Protestant, she thought enough about religion, and questioned it often enough, that in 1956, under the guidance of Father Daniel J. Honan of Ellsworth, she converted to Catholicism. So convinced was she in this matter that she persuaded Pierre to convert to Catholicism as well. One can only assume that he did so not out of any passionate conviction, but simply to please Doris. After all, his Jewishness was merely a circumstance of his birth; it was not something he observed in his daily life any more than Catholicism would be.

The conductor Max Rudolf told me of discussing religion with Monteux and mentioning that he himself was Jewish. To this Monteux replied, "Oh, my grandfather was Jewish." Rudolf thought it strange that he would refer to his grandfather in this way, rather than his father. What Monteux meant was that his grandfather actually practiced his religion, whereas his father did not. Rudolf further stated that as far as he knew, Monteux did not practice Judaism, nor did he himself. "After all," Rudolf added, "we are musicians—artists—we don't need religion."

After Doris's death on 13 March 1984, Samuel Lipman wrote a tribute to her in the May 1984 issue of his magazine *The New Criterion*. As a native San Franciscan Lipman had grown up during the Monteux era, performed as a piano soloist with Monteux and the San Francisco Symphony, attended the conducting school, and also traveled to Europe with the Monteuxs. He was therefore in a very good position to observe Pierre professionally and personally, as well as the role Doris played in both areas of the conductor's life.

After giving some details of her life, Lipman hits the proverbial nail on the head in describing her value to the world of music. "Her true genius lay in being a conductor's wife. In this very public role she was an exemplar of a vanishing species: the woman without whom a man would amount to very little." He then summarizes how Pierre and Doris met in Boston, went to Europe in 1924, and married in 1928. "Here she began her work of making him a major figure. She had absolute confidence in his brilliance, and he must always have felt secure in the boundless strength of her admiration."

Lipman then gives an example of Doris's "resolutely aggressive behavior": During the depression, when Monteux was conducting the Concertgebouw Orchestra and not getting paid on time, though he desperately needed the money, Doris locked him in his dressing room during intermission.

She stationed herself outside the door and demonstratively put the key in her bodice. She then called for the orchestra manager and told him that the concert would not resume until the check arrived. It soon did. She opened the door, and Monteux marched out to conduct the rest of the performance.

Lipman continues:

In San Francisco . . . Doris was a master at dealing with the several patronesses who ran the music scene there. She treated them as great ladies and they loved it. But she never made herself so familiar that they forgot the distance that must separate the artist from his supporters, and the art from its audience.

As Pierre Monteux grew more famous, it was increasingly his wife to whom dealings with managers and the press fell. And as he became more feeble in the years before his death in 1964, she devoted herself to making an environment, whether at home or on the road, where his strength could be conserved. She was always there to take some of the pressures off him, to do for him everything that he did not have to do himself. She protected without fail his time for study and reflection, and she screened with an often brutal hand the visitors who thought more of themselves than of her husband's musical work. Doris Monteux was not perfect. She was something of a spendthrift, and she could be both manipulative and shrewish. But she never took her eye off the ball: to make it possible for her husband —and, ultimately, for both of them together—to present great music in great performance.

In this regard, one can say that she was truly the "Eroica."

CHAPTER 22

L'École Monteux

The activity closest to Pierre Monteux's heart, though there were times when it seemed to him less so, was without doubt the school for conductors in Hancock, Maine. Originally called L'École Monteux, later the Domain School for Conductors, it still exists today as the Pierre Monteux School for Conductors and Orchestra Musicians. (The name of the Monteux estate is the Domaine du Grand Sapin [Domain of the Great Pine].)

The school had its origins in Paris in 1932, principally as a means of providing summer employment for the members of the Orchestre Symphonique de Paris. In the summer of 1942 a young conductor and teacher from the Philadelphia area, Joseph Barone, knowing that Monteux had settled in Hancock, drove up to meet with him. Barone was the director of a small music school, the Bryn Mawr Conservatory of Music, and the conductor of the New York Little Symphony, which presented concerts in New York's Times Hall, usually featuring young artists in debut performances. He intended to convince Monteux that he should resume his teaching; he, Barone, could provide him with several pupils at the outset and would also do all the administrative work.

Apparently Barone reawakened Monteux's desire to teach conducting. Doris Monteux was also in favor of the idea, which was actually the deciding factor, for she was often the decision maker in the family. As she was to say later, Monteux was not a composer, so he could not leave anything tangible to posterity. Having conducting pupils would be his way of passing on his knowledge, handing down his ideas and traditions to future generations of conductors, who would, in turn, do the same.

The first class in Hancock met in August 1943. It is characteristic of Monteux's unselfishness that, until his death at eighty-nine, he was willing to devote his attention to the training of conductors during the one month of the year when he could have enjoyed some rest and relaxation.

The first enrollees were just Joseph Barone's small group of students. They met in the Monteuxs' summer home, a kind of large cabin on the shore of Taunton Bay. There was no orchestra to work with, "merely" two teenage pianists named Leon Fleisher and Vera Franceschi, who played the scores four-handed at a single keyboard. Leon and Vera were both from San Francisco, where they had come to Monteux's attention.

As the school gradually grew in attendance, it became necessary to house it in larger quarters. In 1947 the Forest Studio was constructed, a rustic wooden building with a stage that could accommodate a 50-piece orchestra and seating for an audience of approximately 250 for the public concerts now being presented. The hall was built at Doris's instigation while Pierre was away for his summer concerts and presented to him as a surprise when he returned. It was expanded somewhat in 1950 to provide for a slightly larger orchestra and an audience of 400.

The pupils came from all over the country and from abroad, conductors young and old, inexperienced and experienced, students and professionals, at least fifty each year. I was among them from 1953 to 1958, and again in 1961, in the first category in each instance. For the most part, they were housed with the citizens of Hancock and surrounding towns, such as Hancock Point and Sullivan, and many established lasting friendships with their host families. Each year's session was for the entire month of August; no matter what day of the week on which the first of August fell, that was when the school started. Tuition was a paltry $100, room and board $150.

All students were expected to play an instrument, and together they made up the school's orchestra, in which their playing abilities were as varied as the categories of conductors. Because of the number of students, one could not expect to conduct more than four or five fifteen-to-twenty-minute sessions. During rehearsals, the students conducted in turn and Maître, as we called him, sat on the shallow stage, in the last row of woodwinds between the bassoons and the timpani, facing the conductor, his keen eyes watching every move that was made, his even keener ears listening carefully. He never had a score in front of him and made all his observations and corrections without reference to one. He knew intimately every detail of every score that was studied, knew every orchestral part from memory, and knew which instrument had failed to play in a complex chord or passage, unlike the helpless student, who *had* the score. "Something eez missing" was a refrain frequently heard while on the podium. (It was said that Monteux still knew from memory all the French solfège exercises he had studied at the Paris Conservatory. What he did not know from memory were the various rehearsal letters and numbers found in scores. When a student would ask, for example, "Should I start at letter C, Maître?" the reply would often be, "I don't know the letter; I am not Mitropoulos"—a reference to Dimitri Mitropoulos, whose legendary photographic memory did encompass such minutiae.)

Examples of the repertoire that was covered include the following:

1954: All-Beethoven—the complete symphonies and concertos plus selected overtures. (During the 1954 session, one of the newer students [myself] ventured to ask Barone if the following year could be devoted to French repertoire. His response was that Monteux was tired of being associated with French music and would never agree to such an idea.)

1955: All-French repertoire—symphonies of Berlioz, Franck, Chausson, Saint-Saëns, and d'Indy, plus works of Debussy, Ravel, and others.

1956: Mostly Brahms and Mozart—the complete Brahms orchestral works, including the two serenades, and several Mozart symphonies and concertos, plus, as an excursion, scenes from *La traviata* and *Carmen*.

1957: Varied repertoire, including the last three Tchaikovsky symphonies and several Haydn symphonies.

While such major twentieth-century works as Bartók's Concerto for Orchestra and Prokofiev's Fifth Symphony were studied, I do not recall, in seven years' attendance, the inclusion of *Petrushka* or *The Rite of Spring*—curious omissions except that they were considerably beyond the playing ability of the orchestra, and we simply did not have enough musicians for the latter. We did do the *Firebird* Suite. Concerning Stravinsky's three versions of the work, Monteux commented, "Each time he changed it, he made it worse." He never commented on the two different versions of *Petrushka*, though he always performed the original 1911 version. As a matter of fact, after Stravinsky made the 1947 revision, so he would be able to receive royalties, only Monteux and Ernest Ansermet were authorized by the composer to continue playing the original version.

Although Monteux had one of the clearest baton techniques of any conductor, one studied with him not so much to improve technical expertise, though that was certainly a factor, but for musical reasons—to gain access to his interpretive insights and his vast storehouse of knowledge. His philosophy was captured in the title of Doris's book, *It's All in the Music*; that is, all a conductor needed to know about performing a work could be found right there in the score. This did not preclude, however, the espousal of certain traditions, particularly in the French repertoire. For example, Monteux maintained that toward the end of the finale of the Franck Symphony in D minor (the world premiere of which he had attended in 1888), where the themes from the first movement are recalled, the restated themes should be played as much as possible in their original tempos, even though no such indication appears in the score. Also in the finale, when the second movement's theme returns for the last time, *fortissimo*, the missing upbeat should be inserted into the trumpet part. (When one student was having difficulty getting through the Franck symphony, Monteux, usually not one to promote his own recordings, asked in desperation, "Have you heard my record?" "No, Maître," came the timid reply. "Go and buy my record!" he shouted; then, in an aside, "I will get five cents.")

Some of the points Monteux would make in his lessons were: the development section in a Beethoven symphony should be played a fraction slower than the rest of the movement; the trio in a classical work should be somewhat slower than the minuet or scherzo proper; and all trills in Beethoven should end with a turn, whether so written or not, as espoused in Leopold Mozart's violin method, a work Beethoven knew and used as a reference. As with all respected teachers, the devoted students did as they were told at the time. Later, one could sift everything through one's own personality and mental processes and do as one felt or, if one was convinced, as one had learned from the teacher.

Concerning specific works, Monteux made the following point about the Funeral March in Beethoven's "Eroica" Symphony, a movement he felt was almost always played too slowly: it is a march representing the public funeral of a great personage. As such, it must be played with great dignity and avoidance of sentiment, for on such occasions the public does not shed tears, but stands in solemn witness to the proceedings. The final moments, where the theme is played in fragmented form, depict the departed's family alone. It is they who cry. (Monteux also felt that the dramatic trumpet calls in the middle of the movement depict nothing less than the Last Judgment.)

In the finale of Berlioz's *Symphonie fantastique*, the "Dream of a Witches' Sabbath," after the witches' dance has subsided and the long crescendo begins before the final tumult, there are several isolated accented notes from the French horns. These notes should be emphasized and even have a menacing quality, for they represent monsters suddenly appearing from out of the ground.

As far as the observance of exposition repeats was concerned (a favorite topic of many of today's critical fraternity), Monteux's basic rule was: If the composer had taken the trouble to write a lengthy first ending—as is the case in the first movements of Beethoven's Fourth, Brahms's Second, and Mendelssohn's Fourth ("Italian") Symphonies—then one must perform the repeat. This is especially true in the Mendelssohn, where the first ending contains a coda theme played by the woodwinds that, if not heard at that point, would receive its first and only presentation in the coda of the recapitulation and thus would make no sense at all. Monteux treated each movement having a short first ending, or simple repeat signs, on its own merits; on balance, he observed exposition repeats more often than not. Occasionally he would contradict himself, such as instructing his students that they *must* observe the repeat in the first movement of the Brahms Third Symphony, and then failing to do so himself in performances with the New York Philharmonic. In such a situation his decision was undoubtedly based on practical considerations, such as the overall length of the program or the timing of the broadcast. Similarly, his last two recordings of the Brahms Second Symphony contain the first-movement repeat (he was probably the first to observe it on records), but his concert performances rarely included it. As for the first movement of the *Symphonie fantastique*, he exclaimed, "We don't make that repeat. Goodness!"

In the accompanying of concertos, Monteux's feeling was that the soloist had spent quite some time perfecting his or her interpretation, and that the conductor, even if he disagreed, should accommodate himself to the soloist. After all, the conductor had a symphony or other major work on the program with which to make an impression. "You must follow the soloist" was a command frequently heard.

I recall a rehearsal at Lewisohn Stadium when Monteux was accompanying a pianist of no great repute in the Schumann concerto. After the dreamy interlude in the first movement, the pianist played the dramatic passage in octaves at a tempo so much faster than the norm that everyone was caught by surprise, Monteux included, his face registering amused shock. However, he brought the orchestra in at the pianist's tempo and the movement continued on its merry way.

A seemingly contradictory aspect of Monteux's teaching, and a frustrating one for the students, had to do with when the orchestra should be stopped for a correction. Often if a student stopped, he would be asked, "Now, what was wrong? Why did you stop?" The student would explain why, only to be told, "Oh, that is not important, don't stop so much, you lose your time." Later, when the student had not stopped for a mistake, there would be a loud clapping of hands and, in an exasperated tone, "Why did you not stop? Didn't you hear what was wrong?" The only explanation is that most likely the student did stop for an unimportant reason, and should have stopped when it was important. It was up to the student to know the difference. (Monteux occasionally asked the players seated near him to deliberately play wrong notes, to see if the conductor noticed. Usually he did not.)

Monteux did not accept women students, though some women played in the orchestra. His reason had nothing to do with antifeminism, but with the fact that in those days it was all but impossible for a woman to have a career as a conductor. Today the situation has changed; the school accepts women, and there are, if not many, at least some women conductors with major careers.

Students attended the school in Hancock to learn from Monteux, not to impress him. Occasionally he would be impressed, but he gave short shrift to anyone who paraded his knowledge, and he did not like conductors who talked a lot. One such verbally hyperactive student was pretentiously expounding the meaning of Beethoven's "Pastoral" Symphony to the orchestra—the brook, the birds, the trees, and so on. His sermonette was interrupted by the sound of a double-bass player's bow clattering to the floor. "Ah," said Monteux, "one of the branches has fallen."

While in this example Monteux was genially chiding the student, he could also be, on rare occasions, rather cruel to someone he felt was obviously showing off. One of the great stories in the lore of the school concerns a rehearsal in which the principal work for study was the "Eroica" Symphony. Mounting the podium to conduct the first movement, a rather cocky student made a great display of closing the score before beginning.

"Oh, I see you will conduct that by heart," said Monteux.

"Yes, Maître," replied the student.

"Do you really know it by heart?"
"Yes, Maître, I think I do."
"Well, you see, it is not only that you conduct by heart, but you make the *grande geste*, you close the score. Are you sure you really know it?"
Somewhat less assured, the student replied, "Yes, I think so."
At that, Monteux asked one of the other students to go to the backroom and fetch some blank score paper and a pencil. He then announced to the man on the podium, "You will not conduct now. Instead you will take this pencil and paper, you will go in the back, and you will write out the score from memory—not the whole *mouvement*, just up to the development. We will see how well you know it."
The poor fellow was on the next bus back to New York. It goes without saying that Monteux *could* have written out the score from memory.

Contemporary conductors who attended the school include Sir Neville Marriner, Lorin Maazel, David Zinman, Erich Kunzel, José Serebrier, Harry Ellis Dickson, George Cleve, Michael Stern, and Hugh Wolff, the last two after Monteux's death. While the school's publicity material lists André Previn as an alumnus, he did not study with Monteux in Maine, but privately in San Francisco.

Maazel, today one of the world's most distinguished and active conductors and music director of the New York Philharmonic since 2002, recalled that Monteux had heard him conduct at Philadelphia's Robin Hood Dell in the summer of 1944, when he was fourteen years old. Monteux was impressed enough to ask Maazel to conduct the San Francisco Symphony the following season, after which he invited him to attend the school in Hancock in the summer of 1945. Almost immediately upon arrival, Maazel came down with horrendous hay fever. He was able to attend only one or two classes and left after two weeks.

Sir Neville Marriner, of course, knew Monteux in two capacities: He was principal second violin of the London Symphony Orchestra, and he was a student in Hancock, where he studied during the summer of 1963. Monteux had become familiar with Marriner's work as director of the famous chamber orchestra he founded, the Academy of St. Martin-in-the-Fields. Marriner had led this orchestra in the baroque and classical fashion from his chair as concertmaster. After asking him, "Why don't you stand up and conduct like a man?" Monteux invited Marriner to Hancock.

Sir Neville has said that he likes to think he modeled his physical technique on Monteux, with a sort of minimal direction that was immensely effective and very accurate. "You knew where the beat stopped at all times." He recalled that Monteux insisted far more on achieving the low levels of sound (*piano* and *pianissimo*) than the high levels (*forte* and *fortissimo*), apparently feeling that the latter could take care of themselves (indeed, it is much easier for an orchestra to play loudly than softly). Marriner feels that Monteux had the strongest influence on his attitude toward the orchestra, that "technique was only a tool to get the performance you wanted."

Once the Forest Studio had been built, during the period of Joseph Barone's administration the schedule of orchestral concerts followed the pattern of weekly Sunday afternoon performances and an evening gala concert during the final week. From the students' standpoint, the only negative aspect of attending the school was that the Sunday concerts were conducted not by one or more of them, but by Barone himself. Only the gala concert was conducted by students, of whom Monteux would select ten or twelve. Each would conduct a short piece, such as an overture, or would participate in a performance of a symphony, one conductor per movement. No one could understand how Dr. Barone, as he was called, could have a monopoly on the Sunday concerts.

What the students did not realize is that, as correspondence between the two indicates, Monteux was genuinely fond of Barone and thought well enough of him as a conductor to write recommendations for him. Their correspondence also indicates that Monteux did not think most of the students were ready to conduct the weekly concerts; hence the gala concert, at which only the best would appear.

While some students attended the school for only one or two summers, the majority returned several times, a few of these for as many as ten or twelve years. One of the curiously endearing customs of the school was the occasional awarding of a discipleship to a pupil who had been a faithful attendee and whose work was judged by Monteux to have been outstanding. The ceremony would take place after the intermission of the gala concert, Doris Monteux presiding and reading the following text (in this case, pertaining to James Robertson, Conductor of the Wichita Symphony Orchestra.):

This night, James Robertson, an honor will be bestowed on you which few other men throughout the world possess. From the days of the Greatest Master of All who named those twelve Disciples of the good and beautiful, down through the ages, from Plato and Socrates, from da Vinci and Michelangelo, from Beethoven and Brahms and to the present day each Master has sent forth the product of his teaching to make his contribution to the furtherance of spiritual beauty. You have been chosen, not only because you have achieved the necessary qualifications of musical technique, but because you have also proven yourself, in the years you have been at L'École Monteux, to possess those inner sparks that produce the fires of great music. We have found you to be charitable to those with lesser sparks and kindly in your attitude to all your associates. You have listened to the words of your Master and have achieved a culture in the other arts and sciences and, therefore, enriched your own capabilities. We feel that you will bring to the city you have chosen as yours a fresh teaching in the universal language of music and that you will carry on with the same humility of spirit with which you have been taught, without which there can be no greatness.

James Robertson, step forward and receive the embrace of your Master.

Robertson, stepping forward, would then be embraced by Monteux and given the traditional Gallic kiss on both cheeks. The author of the text was either Doris or her sister Hilda Davis, or possibly both in collaboration.

Once each summer there was a soirée, for which all the pupils were invited to the Monteuxs' home ("the camp") for light refreshment and the opportunity to ask questions. Usually these were of a rather innocuous sort. I remember the following exchange particularly well:

> *Pupil*: Maître, which of the Beethoven symphonies do you think is the greatest?
>
> *Monteux*: Whichever one I play!
>
> *Pupil* (somewhat later): Maître, which do you think is greater, the Verdi Requiem or the Berlioz Requiem?
>
> *Monteux* (patiently): Well, if I conduct the Verdi, I think that one; if I conduct the Berlioz, I think that one.
>
> *Pupil*: Do you feel the same way about orchestras you conduct?
>
> *Monteux*: You want me to say that the one we have here is the one I prefer?

Once Monteux was asked his opinion of various American composers. He responded favorably concerning Samuel Barber, William Schuman, Paul Creston, and others. A student at Rochester's Eastman School of Music, of which Howard Hanson was then the director, ventured to inquire about Hanson. "He does not exist!" came the vehement reply. "He is just somebody in Rochester!" (Hanson [1896–1981], the longtime director of Rochester's Eastman School of Music, was a composer of an extremely conservative bent, a neo-romanticist, who music was rarely performed outside of Rochester, and when it was, seldom by major orchestras. His most frequently played work is No. 2, the "Romantic" Symphony.)

Aware of the absence on Monteux's programs of anything by the fine French composer Albert Roussel (1869–1937), I ventured to ask him what he thought of Roussel's music. He replied by likening the composer to a chef who had prepared a meal that featured a wonderfully piquant sauce, but no meat.

Actually, Monteux almost never conducted the Hancock Philharmonic, as the students gleefully dubbed the orchestra. However, for a concert on 9 August 1950, the official dedication of the Forest Studio, he conducted, appropriately, Beethoven's *Consecration of the House* Overture. In 1953, in a benefit concert for local charities, he led the orchestra in Beethoven's *Egmont* Overture and the Scherzo from the Brahms Fourth Symphony. Needless to say, he got good results from a mediocre orchestra. On 31 August 1957 he conducted again the *Egmont* Overture and an orchestral version of Beethoven's Septet. Two performances of Beethoven's Violin Concerto constituted the remainder of Monteux's Hancock conducting, on 23 August 1959 with Tossy Spivakovsky as soloist, and on 16 August 1962 with Naoum Blinder, his longtime San Francisco concertmaster.

Former students have recalled that while Monteux told them they must always have the score in front of them when conducting the accompaniment of a concerto, he conducted these Beethoven performances without one.

Because the proceeds from all the concerts, gala and otherwise, went to local charities, such as the Eastern Memorial Hospital in Ellsworth and the Hancock Point Library, to save money there were no printed programs. Rather, Doris would announce the programs, holding court in her inimitable manner, often saying whatever came into her head. As with Minnie Guggenheimer, people came from miles around as much for her comments as for the actual concerts. She often had her own inimitable pronunciations of foreign titles, a mixture of English and French accentuations. For example, "The Marriage of Figaro" became "The Marreeahge of FeeGAro," and the Brandenburg Concertos became the "Brandenbourgeois Concertos," which is their title in French. Usually her commentary was extemporaneous, but there was one memorable occasion when she read some remarks that Barone had prepared for her.

Doris's pupil, the mezzo-soprano Freda Gray-Massé, was about to sing an aria from Gluck's *Orfeo ed Euridice*, which Pierre was going to conduct at the Met the following season. Doris began reading in her melodiously sonorous and imposing voice, "Next we shall have an aria from Gluck's *Orfeo*, which my husband will conduct at the Metropolitan Opera next season—*whose husband, yours?* (gesturing at a flustered-looking Barone). Well, you wrote this." (Audience laughter.) "That sounds mighty queer to me!" (More laughter.)

An absolutely inexplicable incident involving Doris occurred at the school during the 1952 session. In fact, it seems so far-fetched that many think it is apocryphal, yet it is described in Harry Ellis Dickson's book *Gentlemen, A Little More Dolce Please* and has been reported by others who were there. In the midst of a rehearsal, while a student was on the podium and Monteux was observing carefully, Doris obtrusively entered the hall, banging the door behind her and bringing the lesson to a halt. Advancing to the front of the hall, she proclaimed in a stentorian voice, "Pierre, I am leaving you and never coming back!" A hushed silence followed, during which Monteux slowly advanced to the front of the stage, looked down at Doris, and replied, "Leave the check book."

As Doris obviously did not leave Pierre, whom she loved dearly and passionately, one can only wonder at her purpose in disrupting the class in this manner. Nancie Monteux has told of asking Pierre on several occasions, "How can you put up with mother's behavior?" to which he replied, "With your mother I am never bored." That was one of his salient characteristics—he could not stand being bored, which explains his frequent withdrawals into himself when surrounded by chattering conversations in which he had no interest. A case in point is a visit with Doris to her old Hancock friends, Sylvia and Russell Young (Sylvia actually a cousin), at whose home several students boarded. There would be much dinnertable conversation, Doris holding forth and Pierre sitting quietly with his thoughts. If there was a lull in the conversation, according to Gordon Peters, one of the pupils, Pierre would say to Doris, "Darling, tell them about the time . . . ," and off Doris would go again, Pierre retreating into his private world.

If one attended L'École Monteux in the 1950s and early 1960s, one became acquainted with Keith Sutherland, a young man from East Sullivan who worked for the Monteuxs in a variety of capacities—aide-de-camp would most accurately describe his position. Pierre and Doris had offered to provide a scholarship to aid a gifted Maine boy or girl of modest means with a college education, in return for which the recipient would help out doing odd jobs at the school and for the Monteuxs personally. Under this arrangement the Monteuxs paid for Keith to attend the University of Maine, where he majored in history, as well as for his graduate studies at Columbia University and Cornell University, where he earned his Ph.D. in 1964. He also occasionally traveled with the Monteuxs and went to Europe with the Boston Symphony in 1956. As Monteux got older, Keith would accompany him to the various summer concerts he conducted, which Doris usually did not attend.

Keith was quite a colorful character, with a pronounced Maine twang in his voice. Besides doing his duties at the school, he was often a wonderfully amusing provider of gossip, to whomever would listen, concerning the Monteuxs, students at the school, or the citizens of Hancock—gossip that may or may not have been accurate but was always related and embellished in masterly fashion. Unfortunately, Keith was killed in an automobile accident on 19 March 1976 in Texas, where he had been professor of history at Texas A & M University.

Another aspect of life in Hancock was the restaurant Le Domaine. Opened in 1946 and located on U.S. Route 1, this establishment was owned and presided over by Doris Monteux's son, Donald Purslow, in partnership with his wife, French-born Marianne Rose Dumas, who served as the chef and whom everyone called Mano. Le Domaine was and still is a first-class French restaurant. It was there that the students ate breakfast and lunch, which unfortunately was not the fare provided to normal diners but rather more of an institutional variety. Occasionally we were served the classic dish that is anathema to American servicemen: creamed chipped beef on toast, for which servicemen have a delightfully unprintable appellation. It was meals of this sort that caused the students to dub the restaurant with a name that rhymes with "domain." Once a week, however, after the Sunday afternoon concert, we were served the specialty of the house, Mano's *poulet provençale*, and all would be forgiven. Mano was tragically killed in a car crash in 1973, but the restaurant continues to thrive today under the able and creative ownership of Mano and Donald's daughter Nicole. It is now a four-star restaurant that has been featured and reviewed favorably in *The New York Times*.

Barone continued to administer the school and conduct the Sunday concerts, as well as give classes in baton technique to those thought to be in need of help in this area, until the end of the 1957 session, when, abruptly, he was out, never to return. The circumstances of his departure are unclear to the present day, but one could be in with the Monteuxs one day and out the next; usually Doris would be the person to decide. A letter from Monteux to Barone, dated 18 September 1957, informed him:

We have decided to have a small school with conductors which I will choose myself. In this way, we shall not need another teacher and naturally we will not need a Director. I feel, as does Doris, that this will be more in keeping with my age and strength, and I might add, patience.

In a follow-up letter dated 23 September, Doris wrote:

The truth is dear that I, myself as well as Maitre, was simply fed up with the whole thing. Lack of talent principally, lack of temperament in the pupils, those crowds around all the time and the work of it without any compensation or joy—not even money—which was the last thing taken into consideration as far as we were concerned, as Maitre would have done it for nothing if there had been two pupils with talent to exult and cheer him after those long hours. That's all—truly—It had nothing to do with you at all.

To this letter Monteux appended the following lines:

I want to add a word to tell you that I am *very very* grateful for what you have always done for the school and for me personally, for your devotion, your *fidelité*, and your friendship. As I always said to you: you are a born conductor and I am sure that you will make a career, and I admire you also for your unselfishness of making young conductors make their debuts with your orchestra in your concerts and giving a chance also to young instrumentalists, singers and composers. I hope we will always remain good friends. But frankly, I decided to stop teaching because I really lose my time with all these *nullités*. . . . I have no vacation. I must rush now my organization of two seasons, learn new scores in no time and for what? Everybody is unsatisfied. Donald complains, the pupils complain, I complain, Mum complains, and also what I don't admit is that some pupils dare to even think that Mum runs the restaurant!! I suppose they think that we get a commission on their rooms and boards?? When it comes to that, I prefer to stop the whole thing, and also I resent them going all over the country saying they are my pupils!! What good is that for the reputation of the school?

No, believe me, we have only to *thank* you and nothing absolutely nothing against you or the way you have run this school and the development you have given it, but I can no longer take it, it is too much for me and I am sure you understand. Mum does not know that I am adding this word to her letter (especially I never told her about her supposed running the restaurant!!) but believe me, *I am your friend* and anything I can do for you, let me know, it will never repay you for all your work and devotion.

The foregoing notwithstanding, Monteux had indeed decided to alter the format of the school to allow for a "Master's Class" made up of only the top students, who would receive a greater amount of instruction than the others, and to make provisions for young musicians who would attend solely to play in the orchestra to learn repertoire, thereby improving the quality of the Hancock Philharmonic.

During the winter of 1957–58 all the students received a letter from Barone lamenting the fact that L'École Monteux was no more, as Maître had decided not to continue teaching. This was not the case at all, for soon a letter arrived from Doris Monteux instructing everyone to disregard Barone's letter—the school would continue under a new management. (In a sense it was true that L'École Monteux was no more, for the name was now changed to the Domain School.) Jean Ferry, a Hancock native, was now in charge of the nonmusical aspects of administration, and a longtime pupil, Ladislas Helfenbein, was responsible for coordinating the schedule of classes under Monteux's supervision, deciding who would conduct when, who would conduct what, and so forth.

As students at L'École Monteux, we were made well aware of Monteux's "Rules for Young Conductors," posted at the back of the Forest Studio where we could not fail to see them upon leaving. There is nothing philosophical or metaphysical about them; they are simply just practical advice that any conductor could benefit by following, regardless of his or her basic musicianship, charisma, or lack thereof. Monteux, having grown up as an orchestral musician, knew what worked and what did not when it came to conducting. Here are his rules:

Eight "Musts"
1. Stand straight, even if you are tall.
2. Never bend, even for a pianissimo. The effect is too obvious behind.
3. Be always dignified from the time you come on stage.
4. Always conduct with a baton, so the players far from you can see your beat.
5. Know your score perfectly.
6. Never conduct for the audience.
7. Always mark the first beat of each measure very neatly, so the players who are counting and not playing know where you are.
8. Always in a two-beat measure, beat the second beat higher than the first. For a four-beat bar, beat the fourth higher.

Twelve "Don'ts"
1. Don't overconduct; don't make unnecessary movements or gestures.
2. Don't fail to make music; don't allow music to stagnate. Don't neglect any phrase or overlook its integral part in the complete work.
3. Don't adhere pedantically to metronomic time—vary the tempo according to the subject or phrase and give each its own character.
4. Don't permit the orchestra to play always a boresome mezzo-forte.

5. Don't conduct without a baton; don't bend over while conducting.
6. Don't conduct solo instruments in solo passages; don't worry or annoy sections or players by looking intently at them in "ticklish" passages.
7. Don't forget to cue players or sections that have long rests, even though the part is seemingly an unimportant inner voice.
8. Don't come before the orchestra if you have not mastered your score; don't practise or learn the score "on the orchestra."
9. Don't stop the orchestra if you have nothing to say; don't speak too softly to the orchestra, or only to the first stands.
10. Don't stop for obviously accidental wrong notes.
11. Don't sacrifice ensemble in an effort for meticulous beating—don't hold sections back in technical passages where the urge comes to go forward.
12. Don't be disrespectful to your players (no swearing); don't forget individuals' rights as persons; don't undervalue the members of the orchestra simply because they are "cogs" in the "wheels."

A few words about Monteux's seating of the string section of an orchestra, which the Hancock Philharmonic certainly observed. He was of a generation in which most conductors divided the violins, with the first and second sections on opposite sides of the podium. He believed, with Toscanini, that the violins were the shoulders of an orchestra. This seating arrangement is especially valuable in the many classical and romantic works in which the violins have antiphonal passages. At the same time, the cellos and violas fan out to the left and right of the conductor, respectively, with the double basses also on the left behind the cellos, or sometimes stretched at the rear of the orchestra facing the audience.

As Monteux advanced in his career, many conductors began grouping the first and second violins together to the left of the podium, with the cellos and basses on the right. The violas managed always to be on the right side, sometimes on the edge of the stage with the cellos inside, sometimes inside with the cellos on the edge. The rationale for grouping the violins together is that all the instruments' "f" holes are facing the audience, so that the second violins are also projecting their sound out into the hall. Also, the two sections can function more as a unit if they are together rather than separated. Overlooked is the fact that when the seconds are on the same side as the firsts, they are farther away from the audience and thus are heard merely as a shadow of the firsts. When the seconds are on the right side, regardless of the direction of their "f" holes, they are heard more distinctly.

When Monteux conducted orchestras that normally grouped the two violin sections together, such as the Boston Symphony in the 1950s and 1960s, he always separated them. This meant that the violas played on the left side, next to the first violins. The cellos and basses he left on the right because, as he said, "You cannot turn the whole orchestra upside down."

Chamber music was and still is an important aspect of the school. Monteux loved to play chamber music, and while he did not do so with students as part of the school, he often participated in or attended evenings of chamber music in Ellsworth at the home of Dr. Eiji Suyama, who was on the staff of the Ellsworth Memorial Hospital. Occasionally Monteux coached some student groups. I remember participating as a double bassist in Schubert's "Trout" Quintet at Suyama's home in August 1961. Other student string players took part, as well as the pianist Corinne Lacomblé, who had a summer home in nearby Sorrento, Maine. We rehearsed under Monteux's supervision, and what remains in my memory today is the tempo he wanted in the Scherzo. Normally this is played at quite a rapid pace, so we were all surprised at the rather deliberate tempo he espoused. Of course, we did it his way.

Anyone expecting to gain insight into Monteux's interpretations by examining his scores to see what he had written in them, what markings he had inserted, would be sorely disappointed, for other than the printed notes and the dynamic and tempo indications, they are completely devoid of annotations, in either pencil or ink. In contrast to most other conductors, Toscanini included, Monteux simply did not mark his scores. He studied his scores, he learned them, and he memorized them, but he left no markings.

Monteux's death in 1964 resulted in the cancellation of classes for that year. In each of the next three years, 1965–67, there was a memorial festival for which Doris invited various pupils to conduct the specially formed orchestra, as well a few non-pupils. Among the latter was Max Rudolf, then music director of the Cincinnati Symphony Orchestra, who always summered nearby.

Rudolf, who had always been friendly with the Monteuxs, conducted an all-Brahms program in 1965, after which Doris invited him for another concert the following year. Rudolf told her that he could not immediately accept, since the Cincinnati Symphony might be undertaking a world tour during the summer of 1966. When the tour was definitely scheduled, Rudolf informed Doris that he would be unable to conduct in Hancock that summer. He never heard from her again.

By 1968 Doris felt it was time to resume the school. She invited a onetime student, Klaro Mizerit, conductor of the Atlantic Symphony Orchestra in Canada, to teach the classes. However, from 1970 until his death twenty-five years later, the training of conductors was in the hands of none other than Charles Bruck, who had been one of Monteux's very first pupils in Paris and was the first person to be awarded the special prize enabling him to conduct a concert with the Orchestre Symphonique de Paris. He had gone on to have a career conducting several orchestras in France, including his last position as principal conductor of the Philharmonic Orchestra of French Radio and Television in Paris.

The Hungarian-born Bruck was an extremely knowledgeable and capable conductor who, like Monteux, had gone through the French conservatory system and possessed all the attributes such training implies in the way of aural perception, solfège, ability to read complex scores at sight, and other skills. Additionally, he had acquired a reputation as a specialist in contemporary music. But where Monteux's teaching, though firm, was laced with humor, Bruck's was stern and laced with extreme impatience. There was much yelling and screaming on his part, with some students reduced to tears at the end of a lesson. Yet obviously he had much to teach, and many students returned year after year in spite of the verbal abuse to which they were subjected. Among them were Michael Stern and Hugh Wolff. The former has been chief conductor of the Saarbrücken Radio Symphony Orchestra in Germany and at the time of writing directs the IRIS Chamber Orchestra in Tennessee. The latter's posts have included the music directorship of the New Jersey Symphony and the St. Paul Chamber Orchestra; his current post is as chief conductor of the Frankfurt Radio Symphony.

During the last years of her life Doris Monteux was assisted by her daughter, Nancie, in the school's administration. Upon Doris's death in 1984 Nancie assumed the entire burden of administration, although members of the board of directors of the Pierre Monteux Memorial Foundation assist in some aspects of the operation.

By 1995 Charles Bruck was in poor health, and in the middle of that year's session he died. Rather than cancel the remainder, it was decided that Bruck's pupil and assistant, Michael Jinbo, would complete the classes. It was later announced that Jinbo would succeed Bruck as director, a decision that was not greeted enthusiastically by many of the old-timers from the Monteux days, who felt that someone with greater experience should have been appointed, though not necessarily one of them. Jinbo was then assistant conductor of the North Carolina Symphony and, at the time of this writing, is music director of the Nittany Valley Symphony in Pennsylvania.

There was also controversy over the method of Jinbo's appointment, for at least one member of the board, who has since resigned, maintains that the full board was not consulted on the matter. Nevertheless, the school continues to flourish under Jinbo's direction. I have observed his instruction to be thorough and to the point, without Bruck's temper tantrums.

If one may venture a criticism, not necessarily of Jinbo's teaching but of much contemporary teaching of conducting and the students thus produced, it is that there is too much concentration on technical matters. Clear baton technique, getting the orchestra to play well together and in tune, controlling dynamics, and conducting complex passages correctly are important elements of conducting, and every conductor should have these skills. But that should not be the end of it. Missing is any significant attention to interpretation, to the inner meaning and style of the music. That is what Pierre Monteux had to offer, and it is why, in his day, students traveled to Hancock.

INTERLUDE

Family Life

Pierre Monteux's son from his first marriage, Jean Paul, the jazz percussionist, often performed with his group at the famous nightclub Moulin Rouge. When his schedule permitted, Pierre enjoyed going there to see and hear his son in action, especially as the sign out front proclaimed the appearance of "Monteux et ses Boys."

We also know, of course, of Pierre's children Denise and Claude, from his marriage to Germaine, and of Doris's children, Donald and Nancie. Once Pierre married Doris, and even before, there was some intermingling of the two sets of offspring: Claude and Denise visited Pierre and Doris, though Donald and Nancie did not usually visit Germaine.

Each of the children established himself or herself in a particular profession. Nancie was probably the first to do so. She had been studying classical and interpretive dancing at the Dalcroze School of the Dance in Brussels, and her European debut with Monteux and the OSP has already been noted. Depending upon how one reckons these things, her American debut took place either in Los Angeles on 7 December 1935 or in San Francisco on 15 February 1937.

The first date was a Young People's Concert with her father and the Los Angeles Philharmonic. Nancie's publicity material lists the second date as her American debut. On this program, for an adult audience, she was accompanied by the pianist Jörgen Nielsen, as well as by the harpist Virginia Morgan and the Pasmore String Quartet in Debussy's *Danses: sacrée et profane*. The newspaper reviews were unanimously favorable.

Nancie also had dramatic training, for from 18 to 23 April 1938 she appeared in the role of Bettina in the play *L'Abbé Constantin*, presented in San Francisco by Ferrier's French Theatre of Art. The comedy, by Hector Crémieux and Pierre Decourcelle, was adapted from Ludovic Halévy's novel of the same name. She gave another dance recital in the Casino d'Evian in France on 11 August 1938, accompanied at the piano by Charles Bruck. Back in San Francisco, Nancie also performed for a time as a chanteuse of popular French songs at the Rose Bowl Room of the Palace Hotel. Marriage in 1941 to the jewelry merchant Simon Barendse and the rearing of four sons effectively brought an end to her performing career.

Of Pierre Monteux, Nancie has said:

He was the only man I ever met, or was in contact with, who was so at ease with himself, who knew who he was, who, I believe, liked what he was, and had no "hang-ups." He was content to be what he considered a fine musician. He was sorry he couldn't compose, but he'd learned very early that he couldn't—it resembled everything he'd ever played, and it is why he became a teacher, because he said, "I have nothing to leave, only a few records that I don't particularly like, so I have to produce something, or to give what I have so it continues," and the only way he thought to do that was to have students. (comments made at the Conductor's Guild symposium on Pierre Monteux, 7 January 1989)

Nancie also said that one of the things she always remembers is Monteux's kindness to everyone. She told of being in a Brussels restaurant when she was nine years old. A waiter dropped a tray full of dishes, and she was about to turn to see what happened. "Don't turn around," said her father. "He is already embarrassed enough." On another occasion, when she was thirteen, Nancie came to Pierre with some gossip she had heard, that "so-and-so is sleeping with so-and-so." "Oh," said Monteux, "you were invited to the bedroom?"

Probably the most well known of the Monteux children is Claude, who has had a career as both a flutist—he appeared in numerous recitals and chamber music performances and also made a recording with his father—and a conductor. During the 1950s Claude participated in L'École Monteux in both capacities. On the 1955 gala concert he conducted "Asie" from Ravel's *Shéhérazade*, with Ginia Davis as soloist. Rumor had it at the time that Pierre did not approve of his son's conducting aspirations, either because he felt one conductor in the family was enough or because he did not feel that Claude's talent was sufficient to warrant a career as a conductor, especially with the name of Monteux.

If one accepts the latter as Pierre's reason, then one could say that as far as he was concerned, almost no one at the school merited such a career. In spite of Monteux's general benevolence, most of us were quite intimidated by conducting just a few feet away from someone who possessed such an awesome amount of knowledge and experience. With few exceptions, I would not wish to judge anyone on the basis of how he conducted at L'École Monteux.

And yet, quite a few of the students went on to careers, not necessarily of international renown, such as Erich Kunzel, Sir Neville Marriner, and David Zinman, but of local importance, such as Victor Feldbrill and James Robertson, or in academe. As for Claude Monteux, he did become the music director of several orchestras: the Columbus Symphony; the Hudson Valley Philharmonic in Poughkeepsie, New York; and the San Diego Chamber Orchestra. Now that he has retired from conducting, an unfortunate nervous affliction prevents him from playing the flute; he is, however, in charge of chamber music at the Pierre Monteux School.

Claude's sister, Denise, became the wife of the violist Thomas Lanese, who was for many years the conductor of the orchestra and professor of music theory and string instruments at Lebanon Valley College in Annville, Pennsylvania. During the 1950s Denise developed a talent in wood sculpture, for which she was the subject of an article in *The Christian Science Monitor* of 24 June 1959. She terms her medium "weathered wood sculpture," for the wood employed has already been formed by nature. She then carves the piece in such a way as to alter its shape to the degree she deems necessary to produce a figure or other object. In this respect her work differs from driftwood, which has already been shaped by the sea. She has stated that she could not start out with a square block of wood, but by modifying and refining what nature has provided she has produced some beautiful and striking pieces, which she has exhibited.

Nancie's brother, Donald Purslow, with Doris's connivance or at least clairvoyance, married Marianne Rose (Mano) Dumas of Les Baux, France, and the two of them owned and operated a restaurant in town. They remained in France during the early years of World War II, causing their families great anxiety over their safety. After arriving in the United States in 1941 they settled in Hancock, and during the war Donald served in the United States Merchant Marine. After his return home the two opened Le Domaine.

The family life of the Monteuxs includes, of course, Hilda and Meyer Davis and Charlotte and David Michlin. All three couples often spent vacations with each other. Virginia (Ginia) Davis had a career singing in operatic and concert performances, but before that materialized, she also was active as a cabaret singer of popular music.

Ginia's brother Emery Davis was a clarinetist who played for a time in the Pittsburgh Symphony and often in the orchestra at L'École Monteux, as well as in chamber music sessions with Pierre. He eventually became involved in the family business and, after his father's death in 1976, became the director of the Meyer Davis Orchestras. Another brother, Garry Davis, attracted international attention when, on 26 May 1948, after much deliberation and preparation, he renounced his United States citizenship to become a self-declared Citizen of the World, making him the object of much media attention in the United States and Europe for quite some time thereafter.

The Davises' eldest son, Meyer Jr. (Bud), was a member of the U.S. Naval Reserve during World War II. He lost his life when his ship, the U.S.S. *Buck*, was torpedoed and sunk in the Tyrrhenian Sea on 9 October 1943. For one year Bud was considered missing in action, but on 10 October 1944 the navy officially declared him dead. The Davis children also include daughter Margie, the youngest, who devoted her energies to raising her own children.

Among the vacation activities of the Monteuxs and the Davises was the production of home movies, not just randomly shot affairs but with story lines and titles in the manner of silent films. Several of these can be found at the Northeast Film Library in Camden, Maine, though I have seen video copies through the courtesy of Ginia Davis and Henry Barendse. The most interesting, as far as the participation of Pierre Monteux is concerned, is one entitled *All Is Not Gold That Glitters*, filmed in 1929 in Jamestown, New York. Here Pierre and Doris portray a wealthy couple, the Ritz-Carltons, while Hilda and Meyer are a poor couple, the Gumpskeys. The plot involves the Ritz-Carlton children getting into a fight with the Gumpskey children, after which the respective fathers confront each other. We then actually see Pierre Monteux and Meyer Davis squaring off and throwing punches at each other, the pugilism evolving into a rather wild wrestling match. At the end Pierre, who was known as "Chummy" to family members, is seen with a bloody nose.

All good, clean family fun of the type one would not expect of a dignified symphony conductor. It is hard to imagine, say, Bruno Walter or Wilhelm Furtwängler engaging in such frivolity.

CHAPTER 23

Return to NBC and the Met

During the administration of Rudolf Bing, the Metropolitan Opera was often criticized in the press for its failure to engage first-rank conductors. It had a capable staff of house conductors, but appearances by the certifiably great maestros of the time were rather scant. An exception was Fritz Reiner (1888–1963), who in 1948 had left his post as conductor of the Pittsburgh Symphony Orchestra to become a regular at the Met, where for five seasons he led brilliant performances of operas by Mozart, Richard Strauss, Verdi, and Wagner, and also conducted the American premiere of Stravinsky's *The Rake's Progress* in 1953.

In the midst of the 1952–53 season, Max Rudolf (1902–1995), the music administrator of the Metropolitan Opera and one of its conductors, learned from a reliable source that Reiner had signed a contract to take over the conductorship of the Chicago Symphony Orchestra in the fall of 1953, an engagement that had not yet been officially announced. Rudolf broke the news to Bing, at the same time mentioning that the press would now again complain that the Met had no first-rate conductor. He advised him to consider two great conductors who might be available, Pierre Monteux and George Szell. "But Monteux doesn't know opera," was Bing's response, according to Rudolf, who replied, "I happen to know that Monteux knows opera very well." Obviously Bing was unaware of Monteux's previous engagement at the Met (1917–19) or of his operatic conducting in Dieppe and Amsterdam.

Bing trusted Rudolf's judgment, so a luncheon was arranged at the Park Hotel during Monteux's next visit to New York, with Bing, Rudolf, and the Monteuxs in attendance. Again according to Rudolf, Doris left the table to go to the powder room, during which time the waiter arrived and Monteux ordered his luncheon, everything he liked. Just at that moment Doris returned to the table and asked, "What did the maestro order?" On being told, she replied, "This is not what the maestro wants, I know what he wants," whereupon she ordered a completely different meal for him (she was concerned about his diet). This was Max Rudolf's first impression of Pierre and Doris Monteux. Pierre, who had a wonderful sense of humor and equilibrium, was used to taking such incidents in stride.

During the luncheon Monteux expressed interest in returning to the Met, and Bing and Rudolf proposed that he conduct *Faust* and *Carmen*. Monteux, on the other hand, said that he was anxious to conduct *La traviata*, which the Met had no intention of having him perform. Not that he could not have done it, but the roster already included several conductors for Italian opera. What was needed was an outstanding French conductor, so that the press would not criticize the Met for failing to have French opera performed in an authoritative manner. (One is reminded of the remark Dimitri Mitropoulos made in a letter to a friend commenting on the Met's restriction of repertoire according to a conductor's nationality—that because he was Greek he was good for everything.)

Shortly before the Met season, however, another situation intervened. One often finds examples of coincidences and ironies in both everyday and artistic life. As we know, it was Monteux who conducted the first three concerts of the NBC Symphony Orchestra in 1937. Except for a single concert in the summer season of 1950, he had not since appeared with the orchestra in its more prestigious winter seasons. As usual, Arturo Toscanini was scheduled to conduct the opening broadcast concerts of the 1953–54 season, concerts that now took place in Carnegie Hall. Less than a week before the season opened Toscanini became ill with the flu and was forced to cancel his first two broadcasts. On very short notice, Monteux was invited to replace him. Originally ninety minutes in length, since the 1941–42 season the broadcasts had been of one hour's duration. Monteux did not adhere to Toscanini's announced programs, but rather devised his own (or perhaps Doris had a hand in them). On 8 November he led Beethoven's *Leonore* Overture No. 3 and the Second Symphony of Brahms, and on 15 November an all-Beethoven program consisting of three excerpts from the *Prometheus* ballet music and the Seventh Symphony.

Prior to Monteux's first rehearsal for the second program, the NBC announcer, Ben Grauer, read to the orchestra and Monteux a telegram from Toscanini in which the maestro informed the musicians that he had heard the broadcast conducted by his old friend, Monteux, and that he was proud of the magnificent performance that came into his living room. He then thanked Monteux and the orchestra for helping him in such a friendly manner.

The Italian firm of Longanesi Periodici, in its series *I Grandi Concerti*, issued the Beethoven Seventh performance on LP. It is a marvelously taut and vital account, superior in playing and control to Monteux's London Symphony rendition, fine though that is, with a particularly dynamic finale. What was coincidental or ironic about this engagement for Monteux is that he had now conducted the opening concerts of what proved to be the NBC Symphony Orchestra's final season.

The Metropolitan Opera's 1953–54 season opened on 16 November. The opera was *Faust*, the conductor Pierre Monteux, who had made his Met debut in 1917 leading the same opera. It was a new production staged by Peter Brook in his Met debut, in fact the first new production of this opera at the Met since 1917, and the stellar cast included Jussi Björling in the title role, Victoria de los Angeles as Marguerite, Nicola Rossi-Lemeni (also in his Met debut) as Mephistopheles, and Robert Merrill as Valentin.

Writing in *The New York Times* the next day, Olin Downes proclaimed the cast the finest to have appeared in this opera in recent seasons. Monteux was praised for his "sensitive and authoritative direction," under which "the score was given a reading that was an outstanding feature of a lively and fresh-spirited performance." When de los Angeles, in the Jewel Scene, required a somewhat slower tempo than was customary, Monteux "gave her wonderful understanding and support from the orchestra."

Some aspects of Peter Brook's staging were criticized, such as the garden scene, which finds Marguerite at her spinning wheel. Max Rudolf recalled that Monteux had not seen the sets until the first orchestral stage rehearsal. When the curtain went up on that scene (which should not be a garden at all but a modest chamber in Marguerite's house), and the luxurious garden was revealed, Monteux was heard to remark, "Oh, elle est millionaire!" In the street scene, when the burghers arrived in their fancy uniforms, he remarked, "Oh, c'est le comité de reception!" But Monteux was not interested in the staging and costumes, not even the fact that Mephistopheles was dressed in top hat and tails rather than in the traditional devil's costume; his sole concern was with the music and the proper realization of it. (In this respect he contrasted markedly with Toscanini, who, for example, railed at the production team at the 1935 Salzburg Festival, which he felt had not designed a true representation of a Tudor house for Verdi's *Falstaff*; the set was modified to suit him. But railing was not part of Monteux's personality.)

For Virgil Thomson in the same day's *Herald-Tribune*, "It was Pierre Monteux's evening." The glamorous first night audience, usually a show in itself, seemed aware that "there was an unusually fine musical performance going on" and that

> it all stemmed from the conductor. Nor was it a mere orchestral perform-
> ance with incidental yelping from the stage. Mr. Monteux, for all the
> refinement of his instrumental care, kept the music centered at all times on
> the stage, cared for his vocal artists, supported them tenderly and without
> forcing, paced them firmly and without brutality, gave them confidence,
> encouraged them to sing.

After discussing the pros and cons of individual singers and of the production, he concluded:

> Always there was Monteux, Olympian, serene and tenderly sensual. . . .
> His pacing of the music's grand line and his care for its every lively detail
> was one of the great theater experiences as well as a musical joy. The opera
> was beautifully sung and more than reasonably staged. And for all that, it

was Monteux's evening. He seemed to be the one who had made every excellence possible.

Perhaps the most verbally inventive critic of that time, and for many years thereafter, was Irving Kolodin of the *Saturday Review*. In the issue of 28 November he wrote:

> If any fact about the season-opening "Faust" at the Metropolitan Opera House is incontrovertible it is that two French heads are better than one, especially when one is the bushy-black, wisdom stuffed one belonging to the portly but light-handed Pierre Monteux. The product of Charles Gounod's head and heart has so long been on its own at the Metropolitan that the intercession of Monteux—at Rudolf Bing's behest—would have been thrice welcome, whatever the circumstances of cast or production.
>   About the only things older than the opera house at the beginning of its seventieth year were a) Monteux and b) "Faust." Would that one could say that the bricks and mortar have worn as well as the flesh of the seventy-seven-year-old conductor and the spirit of the verging-on-a-century-old music! No matter. . . .
>   Let it not be supposed . . . that Monteux's "Faust" was of the over-refined sort, deft and impalpable. He is an orchestral general with a sure sense of attack, of the value of a salvo of percussion when such artillery is wanted, of the flanking movement of brass, of the *coup de grace* provided by a choral outburst.

In his autobiography, *The Bluebird of Happiness*, the tenor Jan Peerce wrote:

> I had just turned fifty when I started playing the title role in Gounod's *Faust* at the Metropolitan in 1954. Our conductor, Pierre Monteux, was approaching eighty. In the opening scene, Faust is an old man who wishes to be a young man. After a rehearsal, Monteux called me over and said, "Jan, why in the first scene do you walk so stooped? Why do you tremble so?
>   "Well, Maestro, Faust is an old man."
>   "Just how old do you think he is?"
>   "Oh, I'm not sure, but certainly, er, sixtyish."
>   "And is that old?"
>   "In those days it was," I replied quickly. "Sixty was a very old man."
>   "I will be eighty next year," said Monteux. "I am more old than Faust was. Do I stoop and shake like that?"
>   "Of course not, Maestro! But look at Faust's beard!" I argued.
>   "They made a mistake! They should make it shorter. He's not supposed to look like Father Time." Monteux gave me a good-natured dressing down

—or rather a shaping up. He implanted in me the idea that Faust wasn't so old and decrepit that he was falling apart. A man in such a condition might be too feeble to even consider a deal with the devil. So my conception changed a little. My Faust never stooped again. He could be an old man who walked straight—the way my father did, the way I try to do, the way a lot of old men I see do. He doesn't have to shake—and his voice certainly shouldn't! I retailored my approach to Faust: he's not old old; he's medium old. (Peerce 1976, 227–28)

Monteux's next opera at the Met was *Pelléas et Mélisande*, which opened on 27 November, its first performance there in five seasons. Pelléas was sung for the first time by the young American Theodor Uppman, who made the best impression on Kolodin of anyone in the cast, which also included Nadine Conner as Mélisande, Martial Singher (a former Pelléas) as Golaud, Jerome Hines as Arkel, and Martha Lipton as Geneviève. Later in the season Victoria de los Angeles appeared as Mélisande.

The composer-conductor Gunther Schuller was at that time principal French horn of the Metropolitan Opera Orchestra. When I interviewed him, he recalled Monteux as having "a fabulous ear, which really means the brain and knowledge, an ear so discerning regarding intonation problems." Especially remembered is a rehearsal of *Faust* in which a particular passage requires seven different instruments to play the same F-natural in unison. Monteux was able to determine instantly which single instrument was out of tune, a feat that Schuller, himself the possessor of an extremely keen ear, considers virtually impossible.

When it came to *Pelléas et Mélisande*, Monteux, who obviously knew the opera from memory, nonetheless conducted with the score in front of him, never looking down at it but always turning the pages because he knew the page turns from memory as well. Before each turn he would lick the fingers of his left hand, then make the turn. When Schuller had an opportunity to look at Monteux's score he saw that all the corners of the pages were brown from the turning. Schuller further stated that Monteux "got along fabulously with the orchestra. He felt we were all equals."

When Max Rudolf expressed concern to Monteux over the fact that the *Pelléas* performances were not well attended, he replied, "That's all right, it is the same in Paris." When asked if he thought *Pelléas* would ever be a popular opera, he said, "It was not meant to be." Next up for Monteux was *Carmen*, opening on 12 December. The title role was sung by Risë Stevens, who had made a specialty of it, with Richard Tucker as Don José, Frank Guarrera as Escamillo, and Lucine Amara as Micaela. For the 1954–55 season Monteux's responsibilities were Jules Massenet's *Manon* and Gluck's *Orfeo ed Euridice*, the former again with de los Angeles, the latter again with Stevens. *Orfeo* was thought by many to be an ill-conceived production, though Monteux was praised for his part in it, especially the scene in the Elysian Fields. For *Manon* he was, of course, to the manner born, though in his book *The Metropolitan Opera* Kolodin complained of a practice all too prevalent at the Met during the 1950s, the constant changing of casts for any given opera, either whole or in part. Even Monteux did not conduct all the performances of operas he had been assigned. The custom was often to have a major conductor lead the first few performances, those that would be reviewed by the critical press, and then have a somewhat (or even more than somewhat) lesser figure take over.

The 1955–56 season opened on 14 November with Monteux in charge of a new production of Jacques Offenbach's *Les contes d'Hoffmann*, the Met's first new production of that opera in thirty years and its first performance of it in ten. Richard Tucker sang the title role and Martial Singher the trio of evil geniuses, while the four women were divided among Roberta Peters as Olympia, Risë Stevens as Giulietta, Lucine Amara as Antonia, and Mildred Miller in the trousers role of Nicklausse. It was generally thought that Monteux and Tucker made the evening musically, Singher dramatically. Again there were numerous cast changes as the season progressed, with Monteux conducting the first five of the eight performances. It was a particularly good Met season for major conductors; besides Monteux there were Dimitri Mitropoulos and Bruno Walter.

The 3 December performance of *Hoffmann* has been preserved by the Met in its series of historic broadcast recordings. With the above-named cast, Monteux conducts stylishly, with no want of energy and elegance as required, and the orchestra plays beautifully.

The last of Monteux's Met operas was Saint-Saëns's *Samson et Dalila*, but it had only four performances, none of which was broadcast, beginning on 29 December. Ramon Vinay and, once again, Stevens were the title protagonists, with Singher as the High Priest. Even with so few performances, the cast did not remain constant.

Bing wished to re-engage Monteux for the 1956–57 season, and there is every indication that Monteux was in accord. However, Monteux's acceptance was conditional on his being allowed to conduct *La traviata*, on which he had set his heart back in 1953. Again Bing told him this would not be possible, so as far as Monteux was concerned, that was that. When the new production of *La traviata* debuted on 21 February 1957, Fausto Cleva was in the pit. Pierre Monteux did not return to the Met.

CHAPTER 24

Monteux at Eighty

The rapport that Monteux had established with the Boston Symphony since his return in 1951 continued with his repeated re-engagements with that orchestra. His conducting at Tanglewood in 1952 has already been mentioned, as has the cross-country tour that brought him back to San Francisco. In 1952 his programs included the Boston premiere on 25 November of Bloch's *Concerto symphonique*, with his San Francisco friend Corinne Lacomblé as soloist, and the New York concert premiere of the same work on 1 November. ("Concert premiere" because Lacomblé had given the actual American premiere with Ernest Ansermet and the NBC Symphony on 21 January 1950, but for some reason a radio premiere, even one with an audience of a thousand, does not count as a concert premiere.) The critics in both cities were in agreement in finding the work rather turgid and overblown.

At Tanglewood in the summer of 1953 Monteux led an all-Tchaikovsky program in which Jorge Bolet performed the Piano Concerto No. 1, while the programs in Boston in 1954 included Leon Fleisher performing his specialty at that time, the Brahms Piano Concerto No. 1, on 29 and 30 January; and Tossy Spivakovsky playing the Bartók Violin Concerto on 5 and 6 February, the latter also in New York on 10 February. Not often conducted by Monteux, for many years it was considered "the" Bartók Violin Concerto. However, the subsequent discovery of an earlier such work has now relegated it to No. 2 status, though it is still first in stature and content.

That particular New York visit concluded with a Saturday afternoon concert at Carnegie Hall on 13 February. Earlier that day Monteux received word of the death of his first son, Jean Paul, in Paris. By a strange coincidence, his program was scheduled to conclude with Strauss's *Death and Transfiguration*, his favorite work to play in such personal circumstances, as he had done in memory of his brother in 1945. On this occasion it could only have been more heartfelt and shattering than ever. Later Monteux received a telegram from Harry Ellis Dickson on behalf of the Boston Symphony, in which he stated that the members of the orchestra sent their deepest feelings of sympathy and great admiration for the wonderful spirit in which he conducted the concert so magnificently in spite of his great bereavement.

At Tanglewood that summer Monteux offered on 17 July an unusual program of Franck and Debussy (originally announced as an all-Franck program, an idea of which someone obviously thought better), which included a rarity by Franck: the symphonic poem for piano and orchestra *Les djinns*, in which Vera Franceschi was the soloist. The Debussy works were excerpts from *The Martyrdom of St. Sebastian* and *La mer*, while one need not ponder too long to realize which symphony concluded the program.

Monteux's two weeks in Boston during 1954–55 included an unusual program. It was all Tchaikovsky, which might not seem all that unusual. But Monteux was a little more adventurous than most of his colleagues in exploring the lesser-known works of the great composers. For this occasion he offered the overture-fantasy *Hamlet*, the Variations from the Fourth Orchestral Suite ("Mozartiana"), and that rather odd but perversely endearing work for piano and orchestra, the Concert Fantasy, again with Vera Franceschi as the soloist. So the audience would not go away hungry, he concluded with the "Pathétique" Symphony. Performed in Boston on 4 and 5 February 1955, the program was repeated in New York on 9 February.

In 1955 Pierre Monteux reached the age of eighty. This is not considered a remarkably advanced age for conductors, for Stokowski lived to be ninety-five, Toscanini eighty-nine, Bruno Walter eighty-five, and Beecham eighty-one—to name just a few examples of many octogenarians (and a nonagenarian) in the profession. It has been said that a conductor's gestures, involving frequent movements of the upper torso, are a factor in strengthening the heart muscle. This is not necessarily so, for Eduard van Beinum died at fifty-nine, Dimitri Mitropoulos at sixty-four, and Charles Munch at seventy-seven, all of heart attacks. (However, they all smoked heavily.)

Since the date of 4 April was approaching, the management of the Boston Symphony Orchestra, headed by Thomas D. Perry, asked Monteux how he planned to celebrate his milestone birthday. His response was that he wished to conduct a special concert on that date for the benefit of the orchestra's pension fund. This was an extremely selfless gesture on his part, for he would be contributing his services.

And so the concert was arranged. A week or so before the performance Monteux was interviewed on a Boston radio station. Asked what would be on the concert, he replied, "Since I am known for conducting modern music, I choose Beethoven!" He then outlined the program:

Beethoven: Overture to *Egmont*
Beethoven: Piano Concerto No. 4 in G major; Leon Fleisher, soloist
Beethoven: Symphony No. 3 in E-flat major ("Eroica")

This program is almost identical to the *first half* of Monteux's debut concert with the Colonne Orchestra in 1912.

Monteux added, "I think there will also be some 'Happy Birthday to You'—I don't know what."

There was indeed some "Happy Birthday to You," for, at the conclusion of the "Eroica," after an extended standing ovation, Charles Munch came on stage to conduct the first performances of two short pieces that had been composed especially for the occasion by old friends of Monteux's: *Pensée amicale* by Darius Milhaud and *Greeting Prelude* by Igor Stravinsky. Milhaud's piece does not seem to have survived the event, whereas Stravinsky's clever treatment of the "Happy Birthday" theme has taken on a great life of its own, having been played at all sorts of musical anniversary celebrations, among them the composer's own birthday. (For the *Egmont* Overture, Arthur Fiedler played in the viola section.)

After the concert a birthday reception was held at the Fensgate Hotel, at which Monteux was further feted. With the connivance of Doris Monteux, the Boston Symphony violinist Harry Ellis Dickson, one of Monteux's conducting pupils, had unearthed a piece for string quartet that Pierre had composed while still a student. Dickson and three colleagues had rehearsed it to perform at the reception, and he introduced it by saying, "Maître, we are going to play for you a piece by a promising young composer, and we would like to have your opinion of it." Monteux's comment after the performance was, "It is better that the composer remain unknown."

By way of further entertainment, one of the BSO's cellists, Jacobus Langendoen, who had joined the orchestra when Monteux was its conductor, played his own fantasy on "Happy Birthday," which included a variation in the style of *The Rite of Spring*, as well as musical impressions of the barking Fifi and the bleating sheep on Monteux's property in Hancock.

One of the guests at the reception was the tenor Roland Hayes, who spoke eloquently and with gratitude of Monteux's engaging him as a soloist with the Boston Symphony in 1923, the first African American to appear with the orchestra. At the end of the evening Monteux, as quoted in the May 1955 *Musical America*, declared, "I am deeply moved and I am very grateful, for all this was a surprise to me. This evening I shall remember all my life."

On the following Saturday, 9 April, Monteux was at the Metropolitan Opera House for the matinee broadcast of Gluck's *Orfeo ed Euridice*, the final broadcast of the season. As he entered the pit to begin Act III, to enthusiastic applause, Rudolf Bing stepped before the curtain to address the audience. He said he had not come to interrupt the applause, but to join it, and then explained that Monteux had just celebrated his eightieth birthday in Boston and that the Metropolitan wished to extend its warmest good wishes to the man who had provided so many hours of wonderful music.

Bing went on to say that the probable secret of Monteux's apparently eternal youth was that he had conducted *Faust* so often that he had learned the trick of turning an old philosopher into a young one. The house lights were then turned up as the audience gave Monteux a standing ovation.

Of the nonmusical celebrations for his eightieth birthday, none was more meaningful to Monteux than the gift he received from the citizens of Hancock, one that demonstrated their great affection for him, their feeling that he was now truly one of them. It was a flagpole made from the finest Maine pine tree that could be found; it still stands on the Monteux property. On its base is a bronze plaque with the following inscription: "With admiration, appreciation and affection from his fellow citizens of Hancock to Pierre Monteux on his 80th birthday."

As a further demonstration of affection, knowing of Monteux's great passion for fire engines, the townspeople designated him Honorary Fire Chief. (He said he would work his subordinates hard.) Additionally, his many students contributed toward the commissioning of a portrait, which was painted by Charles Frederick Ellis of Boston after the famous photograph by Yousuf Karsh.

In the summer of 1955 he was back at Tanglewood, an all-Brahms program on 31 July (Isaac Stern playing the Violin Concerto), and a mixed program of Wagner, Brahms, Debussy, and Strauss on 13 August.

In common with many other musical organizations, the New York Philharmonic likes to observe anniversaries, usually those celebrating the births or commemorating the deaths of composers, but occasionally the anniversary of a performing musician is acknowledged. In 1944 the Philharmonic had invited Pierre Monteux to conduct two subscription weeks in honor of his seventieth birthday year (which actually occurred in 1945), concerts that also marked his debut with that orchestra in the winter season. Successful as those performances were, Monteux did not again conduct the Philharmonic until the fall of 1955, when he was invited for two weeks in honor of his eightieth birthday. Why he did not appear with the orchestra in the interim (except for the summer Stadium concerts) is not clear; one would think seventy-five would also have been an appropriate birthday.

His 1955 programs were a bit less varied than those of 1944, primarily because the orchestra was beginning to consolidate its programming. They were:

17 and 18 November
Weber: Overture to *Euryanthe*
Brahms: Symphony No. 3 in F major
Bruch: Violin Concerto No. 1 in G minor; Mischa Elman, soloist
Debussy: *La mer*

19 November
Brahms: Symphony No. 3 in F major
Schumann: Piano Concerto in A minor; Henri Deering, soloist
Debussy: *La mer*

20 November
Beethoven: *Coriolan* Overture

Brahms: Symphony No. 3 in F major
Mendelssohn: Violin Concerto in E minor; Mischa Elman, soloist
Debussy: *La mer*

24 and 25 November
Berlioz: Overture to *Benvenuto Cellini*
Berlioz: Orchestral Excerpts from *Romeo and Juliet*
Chopin: Piano Concerto No. 2 in F minor; Alexander Brailowsky, soloist

26 November
Bach: Suite No. 3 in D major
Mozart: Piano Concerto No. 24 in C minor; Robert Casadesus, soloist
Berlioz: "Feast at the Capulets" from *Romeo and Juliet*
d'Indy: *Symphony on a French Mountain Air*; Robert Casadesus, soloist

27 November
Same as 26 November except that Beethoven's Overture to *Egmont* was
substituted for Bach's Suite No. 3

Mischa Elman was a longtime friend of Monteux's and a frequent soloist with him, in spite of a certain capriciousness in his performances that made him a difficult artist to accompany. Monteux, known as an excellent accompanist, had his talent put to the test on many occasions with Elman, including the 17 November performance listed above. I was present at this concert (and at the final rehearsal that morning) and remember Elman, in the finale of the Bruch concerto, making a large unrehearsed *luftpause* ("breath pause") just as Monteux was about to bring in the orchestra with a *fortissimo* tutti passage. Monteux's right arm froze during his upbeat, and he finally gave the downbeat as Elman finished his solo. The Philharmonic men were all experienced accompanists as well, and not one of them entered even a millisecond early.

In January 1956 Guido Cantelli (1920–1956) canceled the first half of his Philharmonic engagement so that he could prepare and conduct Mozart's *Così fan tutte* for the opening of Milan's Piccola Scala theater, a new adjunct to the La Scala opera house. Because of Cantelli's defection, Monteux was engaged to conduct one of his weeks. (Cantelli, a protégé of Toscanini and one of the most gifted conductors of his generation, died in a plane crash at Paris's Orly Field on 25 November 1956, en route to an engagement with the New York Philharmonic.) For the concerts of 19 and 20 January his program was:

Creston: Symphony No. 2
Mozart: Violin Concerto No. 5 in A major; John Corigliano, soloist
Strauss: *Ein Heldenleben*

Corigliano, the orchestra's concertmaster for many years (and father of the composer of the same name), also played the solo passages in the Strauss work.

For 21 and 22 January, Nathan Milstein was the soloist in the Brahms Violin Concerto; the program repeated the Creston symphony and opened with Rossini's Overture to *L'italiana in Algeri*. The superb 22 January performance of the Creston symphony is included in the Philharmonic's CD set of American music. In a letter dated 26 January 1956 Creston wrote to Monteux:

> I have thanked you before for your many presentations of my Second Symphony, but now I can genuinely express my deep appreciation from personal experience of your magnificent performances of this work and your continued interest in it. At last I realize how justified are the reports I have received regarding your interpretation of my Second Symphony. The great service rendered my music does not come from the mere presentation, but from the lucid and sincere exposition as evidenced in your conception of it.

It should be remembered that Monteux was conducting at the Metropolitan Opera in the same weeks he was conducting the Philharmonic, for example having a Philharmonic rehearsal in the morning, a Met performance in the evening, and another Philharmonic rehearsal the next morning.

Again Monteux spent two weeks in Boston in the winter of 1955–56. One program was of the three-symphony variety—Haydn's "Surprise" (No. 94), Creston's Second, and Schubert's Ninth, the "Great" C Major Symphony.

Monteux conducted the Schubert again at Tanglewood on 22 July, in company with Bartók's Concerto for Orchestra. He had given this work once in San Francisco but was not known to have performed it frequently, though he did play it in London in 1951. The reason it was included in the Tanglewood program may have to do with the fact that the Boston Symphony was soon to embark on its second tour of Europe. As the BSO had given the work's world premiere in 1944 (under Koussevitzky, who had commissioned it), it was perhaps thought fitting for the orchestra to perform it in Europe as an example of a classic work it had brought into being. The Tanglewood rendition was broadcast nationally by NBC. Surely someone, somewhere, taped it, but to date it remains the most sought-after of unavailable Monteux performances.

Also that summer at Tanglewood, Monteux offered his friend Isadore Freed's *Festival Overture* and the Suite No. 1 by Georges Enesco, which he had given at Lewisohn Stadium in 1927. Enesco had died in 1955, and a tribute to him was planned in Paris, where he had lived.

In order to accommodate Monteux's schedule on tour with the Boston Symphony, the 1956 session of L'École Monteux was advanced two weeks, beginning on 15 July. On the tour Monteux led concerts in Edinburgh (27 and 29 August), Copenhagen (31 August), Leningrad (7 September), Moscow (9 September), Zurich (16 September), Berne (17 September), Paris (20 September), Leeds (23 September), and London (25 September). Other concerts were conducted by Charles

Munch. (On the opening concert, in Cork, Ireland, on 24 August, Munch offered a piece from the Arthur Fiedler repertoire, Leroy Anderson's *Irish Suite*, in company with works by Haydn, Dukas, and Brahms.) The orchestra gave five concerts at the Edinburgh Festival, during which it presented most of its tour repertoire. Writing of the festival appearances in the *Observer*, the critic Peter Heyworth, while generally speaking well of the orchestra, lamented that the programs did not offer a better representation of American music than what he considered to be the vapid works of Copland (*Symphonic Ode*), Creston (Symphony No. 2), and Piston (Symphony No. 6).

When the tour reached Paris, Monteux spoke ecstatically about the audiences in Russia. He found their reception of the orchestra phenomenal; seldom had he heard such enthusiastic applause, the crowds shouting and stamping their approval, demanding encore after encore. Upon leaving by the stage door he was greeted by several hundred music lovers who followed him to his hotel, congratulating him all the while. The situation was the same for Charles Munch.

Two weeks in Boston in 1957 brought Stravinsky's *Pulcinella* Suite, Preludes and Interludes from *Pelléas et Mélisande*, and the *Enigma Variations* on 18, 19, and 20 January (as well as "The Death of Clärchen" from Beethoven's *Egmont*, performed in memory of Arturo Toscanini), and, on 12, 13, and 14 April, Tchaikovsky's Fifth Symphony and *The Rite of Spring*. The latter program was repeated at Tanglewood on 20 July, absolutely stupendous performances of both works (as well as Mendelssohn's *Hebrides* Overture). For the Stravinsky, Monteux actually had the score in front of him, probably one of the very few times he did. Harry Ellis Dickson said at the time that Monteux was feeling a bit tired, and Dickson suggested he use the score to ease his mind a bit (and perhaps the orchestra's as well). My recollection is that Monteux barely looked at the score.

There was more Stravinsky in 1958, with performances of the complete *Petrushka* on 3, 4, and 5 January in Boston, 17 January in New York, and 20 July at Tanglewood. Monteux was rightly praised for performing in concert Stravinsky's original ending, Petrushka's death scene, usually avoided by most conductors in those days in favor of the composer's rather abrupt but at least *fortissimo* concert ending. Quiet endings are anathema to many conductors, for they do not elicit vociferous ovations the way loud ones do.

In 1959 Monteux offered Strauss's *Don Quixote* on 23 and 24 January, the solo parts taken by the BSO's principal cellist, Samuel Mayes, and principal violist, Joseph de Pasquale. This ingratiating performance is part of the BSO's CD set celebrating the centennial of Symphony Hall.

Monteux was not scheduled to lead the New York Philharmonic during the 1958–59 season, the orchestra's first with Leonard Bernstein as music director. However, when a heart attack forced its former music director, Dimitri Mitropoulos, to cancel his four-week engagement, Monteux was asked to substitute for the first two weeks. Fortunately, he was available. Bernstein had planned that season around several national themes. His own concerts included a survey of

American music; those of Thomas Schippers featured Italian music; of Herbert von Karajan, German and Austrian music; of Sir John Barbirolli, English music; and of Mitropoulos, French music. Whom better to call upon to save the day than Monteux? (Jean Morel and Paul Paray filled out the four weeks.)

Not every work scheduled by Mitropoulos had been French, and the first week's programs included Rudolf Serkin as the piano soloist in Beethoven's "Emperor" Concerto (No. 5). This work and soloist Monteux was happy to retain on his programs of 26, 27, and 28 February, and 1 March, but otherwise he selected his own repertoire, opening with the Overture and Allegro from *La sultane* by François Couperin, in the orchestration by Darius Milhaud, and concluding with Berlioz's *Symphonie fantastique*. The Couperin-Milhaud piece was fairly popular at one time, a twentieth-century French composer's treatment of a chamber work by a compatriot of the late seventeenth and early eighteenth centuries. Even then it was considered a bit overblown for its subject matter, and it is rarely heard today.

As for the Berlioz symphony, while Monteux had by that time made four of his five commercial recordings of this key work in his repertoire, he had rarely performed it in New York since his early Boston days—once at Lewisohn Stadium and now at Carnegie Hall. (It was now Munch's piece with the Boston Symphony.) The Philharmonic was an ideal orchestra for this work, playing with just the right amount of extroverted flair to do justice to the more flamboyant moments and, with Monteux in front of them, the requisite sensitivity and feeling for nuances. This was a masterly performance. Serkin, of course, was closely associated with the "Emperor" Concerto and gave it his customary galvanic rendition, after which he paid Monteux the compliment of sitting in the audience to listen to the Berlioz.

Joseph Szigeti (1892–1973) was the violin soloist for the first three concerts, on 5, 6, and 7 March, of Monteux's second week. He played a Bach concerto and a short work by Berlioz, and Monteux conducted three works of Ravel in a program that could be described as a musical club sandwich:

> Ravel: *Le tombeau de Couperin*
> Bach: Violin Concerto in D minor
> Ravel: *Rapsodie espagnole*
> Berlioz: *Reverie and Caprice*
> Ravel: *Daphnis et Chloé* Suites No. 1 and 2

The Bach concerto is more familiar in its version for keyboard. It was (and by some still is) thought to be originally a violin concerto, and this version is a sort of backward reconstruction for violin of the keyboard part. Berlioz's delicate and charming piece was little known at that time and is hardly more so today. It was Szigeti who brought it to the attention of Monteux, who was, strangely, unfamiliar with it.

For the Sunday program of 8 March, the young American pianist William Masselos performed the Concerto No. 2 by Saint-Saëns. Rarely can that work's scintillating Scherzo and propulsive Finale have been played with such absolute brilliance and panache as Masselos displayed on that occasion. It was a truly staggering performance that brought the audience to its feet cheering. Monteux, who had never heard of Masselos before, was duly impressed.

Replacing the *Rapsodie espagnole* on Sunday were Debussy's *L'après-midi* and d'Indy's Prelude to *Fervaal*. The 7 March performance of *Le tombeau de Couperin* appears in the Philharmonic's first CD set of historic broadcast performances.

Monteux's 1959 Tanglewood concerts featured, on 1 August, Rudolf Serkin in Mendelssohn's Piano Concerto No. 1 and Schumann's rarely heard Introduction and Allegro appassionato. The next week brought an all-Beethoven program of the *Fidelio* Overture and the Symphonies No. 6 and 5, in that order.

After the Boston Symphony, the Philadelphia Orchestra was the ensemble with which Monteux appeared most frequently during the subscription seasons in his guest-conducting years. Eugene Ormandy was not fearful, as some conductors are, of having great maestros appear with his orchestra as guests while he was on vacation. Among those he invited at various times were Ernest Ansermet, Sir Thomas Beecham, Leonard Bernstein, Paul Paray, Fritz Reiner, George Szell, Arturo Toscanini, and Bruno Walter. But Monteux seemed to have a special place in his heart, as well as that of the orchestra, for he appeared more regularly at the Academy of Music and at Carnegie Hall than any of the others.

Monteux's Philadelphia engagements of 1945 and 1947 have already been accounted for. He returned for two weeks in January 1953, during the first of which he presented a decidedly esoteric program that kept many of the subscribers away. (One is reminded of the remark attributed to the impresario Sol Hurok: "If people don't want to come to a concert, there's no way you can stop them.") Not that the program was in any way adventurous, merely that it was composed, for the most part, of rather unfamiliar music.

> Beethoven: Overture to *King Stephen*
> d'Indy: Symphony No. 2 in B-flat major
> Strauss: *Don Quixote*

We know of Monteux's fondness for Beethoven's quirky overture and of his special affection for d'Indy's symphony, of which he made the first recording. Strauss's tone poem was also one of his favorites, though it is not what one could term an "audience piece"—at least not at that time. For the Strauss, the important solo parts were taken by the orchestra's principal players, the cellist Lorne Munroe and the violist Samuel Lifschey.

As it happened, the Beethoven overture had been played only once before by the Philadelphia Orchestra, when Monteux programmed it in 1928. The d'Indy symphony had also been played only once before, in 1904. It is safe to say that it was a new piece for most of the audience. As far as Linton Martin of *The Philadelphia Inquirer* (17 January) was concerned, the neglect of those two works was not unmerited.

For his second week, 23 and 24 January, Monteux offered a program more apt to appeal to the public:

> Wagner: Overture to *The Flying Dutchman*
> Schumann: Symphony No. 2 in C major
> Badings: Ballade
> Mussorgsky-Ravel: *Pictures at an Exhibition*

Henk Badings (1907–1987) was one of the generation of Dutch composers who had come to prominence (at least in Holland) since Monteux's tenure with the Concertgebouw Orchestra. Since Monteux had begun returning to Holland, it was only natural that he became acquainted with some of their music. Badings's Ballade is a set of variations on an old Dutch song, "They Were Two Royal Children." In the *Bulletin* of 24 January, Max de Schauensee found it to be a charming, original, and skillful piece. With Mussorgsky's showpiece, Monteux left in a blaze of glory.

In an interview in the *Sunday Bulletin* of 10 July 1955, prior to his concerts at Robin Hood Dell, Monteux was reminded of the incident of 1928, which presumably he had long been trying to forget. He replied:

> Those remarks I made—oooh, how I would like to forget all about them! But what I said applied to all audiences, not solely Philadelphians. It is still true that the number of persons in a musical audience who generally appreciate and understand music are relatively small. And it is still true that some of the audience like a conductor who has showmanship. That is how it is.

He continued that he was pleased that the United States was increasingly responsive to great music. "The growth of the symphony orchestras alone proves it."

In January 1957 Monteux returned to the Academy of Music for a single week with a program tailor-made to his sympathies:

> Stravinsky: Suite from *Pulcinella*
> Brahms: Symphony No. 2 in D major
> Debussy: Preludes and Interludes from *Pelléas et Mélisande*
> Wagner: Overture to *Tannhäuser*

Monteux's final appearances with the Philadelphia Orchestra were on 4, 5, 7, and 8 March 1960. The last of these was in New York, and he presented a thoroughly Germanic program:

Brahms: *Tragic Overture*
Hindemith: Symphony, *Mathis der Maler*
Schubert: Symphony No. 9 in C major

Without exception, the Philadelphia and New York critics expressed disbelief that a man soon to be eighty-five could present performances of such vitality, tempered as they were with the wisdom achieved through his many years on the podium. He was perceived as a link with a great tradition.

Correspondence shows that Ormandy wished to invite Monteux for the 1964–65 season. By that time, though, it was too late.

CHAPTER 25

Return to San Francisco

During his tenure in San Francisco Monteux managed to do a certain amount of guest conducting, usually before or after the symphony season and occasionally during it. Engagements with the New York Philharmonic, Philadelphia Orchestra, and Chicago Symphony have been discussed. Leaving San Francisco, however, at age seventy-seven opened up the possibility of many more such engagements, and with a wide variety of orchestras, most of which he had never conducted before. And he did not seem to be terribly fussy about which orchestras he worked with, for these engagements included several of secondary and even tertiary rank.

Monteux returned to Amsterdam in 1953, another extended visit with twelve concerts between 18 February and 4 March. The programs included various Wagner excerpts, along with Berlioz's *Harold in Italy*, with the principal violist Klaas Boon as soloist; Brahms's First Piano Concerto, with Leon Fleisher; Lalo's *Symphonie espagnole*, featuring the violinist Ida Haendel; Nicole Henriot playing the Ravel Piano Concerto; and the Second Symphonies of Creston and d'Indy. Also featured were *La mer* and the *Daphnis et Chloé* Suite No. 2. Concerning the Creston symphony, it was one thing for Monteux to play this favorite American work with an American orchestra; programming it with the Concertgebouw Orchestra in Amsterdam really demonstrated his faith in the piece.

Monteux's 1954 visit was very special, a reflection of the esteem in which he was held by the directors of the Holland Festival. For this he programmed a Beethoven cycle. Between 22 April and 6 May all the symphonies were performed, as well as the "Emperor" Concerto, with Rudolf Serkin as soloist, and the overtures to *Coriolan, Egmont, Fidelio*, and *Prometheus*. While it is true that Monteux's Beethoven interpretations did not plumb the depths in the manner of Wilhelm Furtwängler in the Third, Fifth, and Ninth Symphonies, nor did they haul the tempos about in the manner of that great German maestro. (No two Furtwängler performances of the same work were identical; there was a great improvisatory feeling to his work, with frequent accelerandos and ritardandos not indicated by the composer, or, if indicated, then greatly exaggerated. For example, in

259

the scherzo of Beethoven's Fifth Symphony, where the score indicates "poco ritard.," Furtwängler's ritardandos are molto.) Monteux's performances were nevertheless notable for their clarity and kinetic energy, and Monteux had an especially touching approach to the Third Symphony's Funeral March. The Seventh was particularly dynamic in Monteux's hands, most of all in the exuberant finale. On the whole, however, one could say that Monteux was at his best in the even-numbered symphonies, especially No. 8, and in the First Symphony. While these symphonies are not necessarily lighter in nature, as is often claimed, they do contain many moments of humor that often elude the so-called serious conductors, whereas Monteux, with his innate good humor and *bonhomie*, was able to capture them perfectly. The "Pastoral" Symphony was especially well suited to his approach.

More-varied repertoire was given in 1955, when Monteux appeared for only four concerts from 23 to 26 June. Three performances of the complete *Daphnis et Chloé*, with the assistance of the Netherlands Radio Chorus, highlighted his programs. The performance of 23 June can be heard in two CD releases, by Audio Classics and Music and Arts, respectively. The former is part of a series produced in Holland that presents historic performances by the Concertgebouw Orchestra. Recorded in mono, the rendition is undeniably a great one, but one that would be surpassed a few years later in London.

One could reasonably wonder why, in seventeen years in San Francisco, Monteux never conducted opera, especially as he had become friendly with the conductor Gaetano Merola (1881–1953), director of the San Francisco Opera. Apart from the possibility that suitable dates could not be found, Monteux really did not wish to mix opera with symphony in the same city. He promised Merola, however, that he would conduct opera for him once he had left the orchestra.

Unfortunately, Merola died before Monteux could make good on his promise. Perhaps the new director, Kurt Herbert Adler (1905–1988), was aware of the promise to Merola, or perhaps he acted on his own initiative, for he invited Monteux to conduct several performances of three operas in the fall of 1954. Not surprisingly, two of the works were French, but Monteux was able to break out of the usual typecasting briefly, as we shall see.

Monteux's debut with the San Francisco Opera, at age seventy-nine, took place on 28 September with Massenet's *Manon*, in which, Monteux was quick to inform interviewers, he had played the viola in the orchestra of the Opéra-Comique in Paris when the American soprano Sybil Sanderson had appeared there in the title role. Sanderson (1865–1903) was a great favorite of Massenet's, who wrote two operas, *Esclarmonde* and *Thaïs*, especially for her. Appropriately, she was a Californian who had studied voice in San Francisco. Monteux led three performances of *Manon*, the first with Dorothy Kirsten, Giacinto Prandelli, and Lorenzo Alvary in the cast; the second, on 3 October, with Rosanna Carteri and Nicola Moscona replacing Kirsten and Alvary. The third performance was in Los Angeles, with the same cast as the 28 September performance.

Alexander Fried, writing in the 29 September *Examiner* of Monteux's San Francisco operatic debut, exclaimed that he showed promise. He went on to speak of the sustained energy and quick control of detail that Monteux, at seventy-nine, manifested throughout the four-hour performance (which Fried found too long because Monteux had restored some cuts, including the Cours-la-Reine scene).

The second French work was, strictly speaking, not an opera at all; though it lends itself to stage presentation, Arthur Honegger's *Joan of Arc at the Stake* was composed in 1934–35 as a concert piece. Charles Munch had led the American premiere in 1948 with the New York Philharmonic, but the San Francisco performance of 15 October 1954 marked the first American performance of the work in staged form. The two principal roles, Joan of Arc and Brother Dominic, are speaking parts, which in this instance were taken by the actors Dorothy McGuire and Lee Marvin. Two further performances were given, on 21 and 27 October, the latter in Los Angeles.

It is interesting to note that, of the group of French composers known as Les Six, Monteux most often performed works by Milhaud. Occasionally he programmed pieces by one of the group's lesser-known members, Germaine Tailleferre. These Honegger performances appear to be among his very few presentations of music by that composer; he certainly never conducted any of his symphonies. And the one composer of the group with whom one would have thought Monteux to be in sympathy, what with his noted sense of humor and early background at the Folies Bergères, was Poulenc, who does not appear on any of Monteux's programs after he left Paris.

The one non-French opera Monteux conducted was Beethoven's *Fidelio*, given in San Francisco on 19 October and in Los Angeles on 30 October. The role of Leonore was sung by the German soprano Inge Borkh, who had made her American debut in San Francisco the year before. Also in the cast were the tenor Roberto Turrini as Florestan and the bass Hans Hotter as Don Pizzaro.

In April 1955 Monteux was in Montreal for a concert performance on the nineteenth with that city's orchestra of Debussy's *Pelléas et Mélisande*. He brought with him his favorite interpreter of Mélisande: his niece, Ginia Davis, who was found by the critic of *La patrie* (20 April) to have a limpid and ravishing voice. The Metropolitan stalwarts Theodor Uppman and Martial Singher also performed, as well as the Canadian bass Joseph Rouleau. The event was thought to be a perfect conclusion to the orchestra's season.

All of this was but a prelude, however, to the events of the month of May, when Monteux was in Brussels for fully staged performances of *Pelléas* at the Théâtre Royale de la Monnaie. Ginia Davis, who was singing regularly with the company at that time, was again Mélisande. At the opening performance of 19 May she was judged by the critic of *La libre belgique* to have an agreeable and pure voice, as well as the ability to project the quasi-mysterious aspect of her character. Also in the cast was the American contralto Jean Madeira in the role of Geneviève, well known to Monteux through her work at the Metropolitan and

because her husband, Francis Madeira, conductor of the Rhode Island Philharmonic, had been one of his pupils in Hancock. Critics found her to be an accomplished artist with a magnificent voice of great warmth and profundity, embody-
ing the role with distinction. Monteux, at this stage of his life and career and with
this music, was impossible to fault.

Also given in Brussels was Gluck's *Orfeo ed Euridice*, which opened on 22
May. Jean Madeira and Ginia Davis were in the title roles, with Vilma Georgiou,
who had been Yniold in *Pelléas*, as Amor. All were acclaimed, as was Monteux,
whose erudition, experience, and talent were combined, the reviewer noted, in his
care of and service to the music.

On 9 June 1955 Monteux was in Paris and, in spite of his aversion to French
orchestras and their cavalier manner during rehearsals, conducted what was billed
as a *concert exceptionnel* by the cumbersomely named Orchestre National de la
Radiodiffusion-Télévision Française. In the Théâtre des Champs-Élysées, he led
performances of Wagner's Overture to *The Flying Dutchman* (*Le vaisseau fan-
tôme*—The French title does not include the word "Dutchman," or "flying," for
that matter), Beethoven's Seventh Symphony, Debussy's *Jeux*, and the Suite from
Petrushka.

On 10 and 11 February 1956 Monteux was in Cincinnati for his first-ever
(and only) concerts with that city's symphony orchestra. Cincinnati is a notably
Germanic city, though its symphony conductors included, up to the time of Mon-
teux's visit, the English-born Leopold Stokowski, the Belgian Eugène Ysaÿe, the
Hungarian Fritz Reiner, the Englishman Eugene Goossens, and the American
Thor Johnson. (It had also had the German Ernst Kunwald.) Here Monteux's
program included Beethoven's "Pastoral" Symphony (No. 6), *La mer*, and *Till
Eulenspiegel*. Originally Roger Sessions's Suite from *The Black Maskers* and
Strauss's *Death and Transfiguration* had been scheduled, but, as the 4 February
Cincinnati Post-Dispatch reported, Monteux, when asked about the program
change, replied that someone had requested *La mer* and he did not know what
had happened to *Death and Transfiguration*. "When I arrived it had been changed
and nobody told me. What if I did not know *Till Eulenspiegel?*"

On 16 January 1957 Arturo Toscanini died at the age of eighty-nine. He had
retired from conducting after his all-Wagner program with the NBC Symphony
on 4 April 1954, following which NBC, in its infinite wisdom, disbanded the
orchestra it had formed for Toscanini seventeen years before. The undaunted
orchestra members then re-formed themselves as a cooperative entity, the Symphony of the Air, and as such gave their first concert on 27 October 1954 in Carnegie Hall. As a tribute to Toscanini, the hundred-member ensemble made its
debut without a conductor. Although the podium was literally empty, the maestro's spirit was definitely present in performances of great precision and vitality.

When Toscanini's death was announced, tributes from prominent musicians
the world over appeared in the newspapers. Typically these messages were concerned with what Toscanini had meant to the world of music and to the art of con-

ducting. Also typically, the tribute from Pierre Monteux was concise and to the point: "The world has lost its greatest conductor."

On Sunday evening, 3 February 1957, the Symphony of the Air performed in Carnegie Hall a concert in memory of Toscanini, for which it invited three of the world's leading conductors each to direct a work closely associated with the maestro. Bruno Walter opened the program with Beethoven's "Eroica" Symphony; after intermission Charles Munch conducted Debussy's *La mer*, and Monteux, Elgar's *Enigma Variations*. While the audience was asked not to applaud, the impact of the performances made the request difficult to observe, so a smattering of applause broke out at the conclusion of each piece. I wondered at the time how much rehearsal there had been for the program, for while each conductor's conception of his allotted piece was demonstrably a great interpretation, there were enough moments of faulty ensemble to make one wonder what Toscanini would have thought of the proceedings. Afterward, a backstage visitor was able to overhear George Marek, director of artists and repertoire for RCA Victor, asking Monteux if he would like to record the Elgar work, to which Monteux said yes.

It was a busy weekend for Monteux, for he had also been rehearsing the group known as the Little Orchestra Society for his guest appearance the very next day. The Little Orchestra had been formed in 1947 by the conductor Thomas Scherman, whose family had founded the Book-of-the-Month Club. The ensemble, which presented an annual concert series in New York's Town Hall on West Forty-third Street, specialized in seldom-heard works both by great composers and by lesser lights, as well as contemporary music.

The Little Orchestra Society almost never had guest conductors; in fact, on 4 February 1957 Pierre Monteux became its first ever for an entire concert (Benjamin Britten had led two of his works in 1949), directing a program of the type just mentioned:

> Méhul: Hunting Overture to *The Young Henry*
> Paisiello: Piano Concerto in C major; Vera Franceschi, soloist
> Brahms: Serenade No. 2 in A major
> Schuller: Symphony for Brass and Percussion
> Hindemith: Overture to *News of the Day*

Monteux had met and worked with Gunther Schuller at the Metropolitan Opera. It is likely that as he came to know and respect Monteux, Schuller spoke to him about his music, perhaps even showed him a score or two. Additionally, Dimitri Mitropoulos, musical director of the New York Philharmonic and also one of the Met's conductors, had taken an interest in Schuller's music and probably recommended it to Monteux. Mitropoulos performed the Symphony for Brass and Percussion with the Philharmonic in the fall of 1956 and recorded it for Columbia Masterworks.

However it came to Monteux's attention, the Symphony for Brass and Percussion was unique in his repertoire. While Monteux was generally not sympathetic to the expressionist music of the so-called Second Viennese School (Arnold Schoenberg, Alban Berg, and Anton Webern), and especially to the twelve-tone music that eventually emerged from it, he had performed in San Francisco Schoenberg's Five Pieces for Orchestra and the Second Symphony of Roger Sessions, which had been influenced by Schoenberg and Berg. Schuller's Symphony for Brass and Percussion, however, was the only work purely in the twelve-tone idiom Monteux ever conducted. According to Schuller, Monteux "did it with a loving touch."

On 18 February 1957 Monteux was in Dallas, where he led that city's orchestra in Beethoven's Eighth and Creston's Second Symphonies, concluding with the *Enigma Variations*. Jack F. Kilpatrick was the critic of *The Dallas Times Herald*, and in his review of 19 February he made some perceptive statements concerning Monteux's selflessness and humanity:

> Pierre Monteux exceeds all other conductors in the ability to make the music make itself. The feat must not be simple—otherwise, there would be other Pierre Monteuxs. . . . If there is any contribution to the recreation of a composition that can be identified as being personally Pierre Monteux's, it is some sort of attitude that seems to say: "As human beings, let us listen with charity to the message of a fellow human being." . . .
>
> If the Beethoven was beautifully proportioned, then the intention was Beethoven's to have it that way. . . . If the formal originality and winning lyricism of Paul Creston's work made friends, that was as it should be. If the "Nimrod" Variation in the Elgar, to cite a detail, struck listeners as being supernal music, then that was because its creator so made it. (Reprinted with permission of the *Dallas Morning News*)

Later in 1957 Monteux was back in Vienna to record the *Symphonie fantastique* with that city's Philharmonic Orchestra, with whom he had had such a difficult time with *Petrushka* many years before. In her notes (which she did not include in her book), Doris Monteux wrote of "the dull Vienna Philharmonic" and that the recording was "a complete fiasco." She stated that the orchestra lacked "the temperament for the intense hallucination and passionate imagery" of the work, that the recording was "inferior to (the) Paris recorded years ago," and that the "San Francisco orchestra (was) also much better than Vienna." While not really "a complete fiasco," the recording was otherwise accurately described by Doris; the requisite chemistry, at least for Berlioz, was just not there between Monteux and that orchestra, which he felt would be much better if it did not think it was so good. Monteux returned to Vienna, this time to perform the Berlioz symphony on 19 April 1959. That was how things were often done, at least in Europe: a work would be recorded, then performed at a later date to promote the recording. In this case it shared the program with the two suites from *Daphnis et Chloé*. The *Vienna Express* of 20 April commented on the rarity of Monteux's unostentatious conducting style and hoped he would return frequently.

It has been noted that only a year after leaving the San Francisco Symphony, Monteux returned to the Bay city at the helm of the Boston Symphony Orchestra, and that in 1954 he was back again, this time as a guest of the San Francisco Opera. He waited somewhat longer to return and conduct his former orchestra again—eight years, in fact. Perhaps he felt that, having resigned his position, it would be silly to return to the orchestra immediately. Also, there had been those on the board and in the audience who had felt that it was time for a change, that the programs had contained too much modern music, too much French music.

Following Monteux's departure, the San Francisco Symphony played for two seasons under guest conductors, with the idea that one of them would be selected as the new conductor. Finally the post went to the Spaniard Enrique Jordá (1911–1996), who had been the very first of the guests. Jordá's tenure was not particularly smooth, and audience and critical opinion was divided between those who greatly admired his work and those who felt that he lacked the discipline necessary to maintain the quality of the orchestra.

By the 1959–60 season Monteux felt the time was right to accept an invitation to return as a guest conductor. (In today's musical life he would have been given the title of conductor laureate or conductor emeritus, but such titles had not yet been conceived.) When he returned in January 1960, those waiting for him and Doris at the airport were startled to see him arrive with a white bandage on his head and dark glasses covering his eyes. The day before, in Bangor, Maine, he had been in a minor automobile accident in which his head had hit the windshield. He now asked that any photographs of him be taken showing the left side of his face. The Municipal Band was part of the welcoming party, and Monteux could not resist conducting it as they played *For He's a Jolly Good Fellow* and other rousing numbers.

The symphony management scheduled a press conference after Monteux's first day of rehearsals. In response to questions, Monteux stated that what he missed most about San Francisco was the orchestra, which he found to be excellent. However, various local newspapers quoted him as saying, "I don't feel it is my orchestra. It does not sound like my old orchestra. . . . It was my orchestra and I could do anything I wanted with them. . . . That is the most difficult thing for a conductor, to obtain exactly what he wants." He also asserted that he had conducted enough modern music in his day, and that it was up to his younger colleagues to carry the torch. Now he would conduct Brahms.

It is interesting that the program page listed him simply as Monteux, a listing that began to be used by other orchestras as well. (Whether this was an idea of Monteux's, of Doris Monteux's, or of his management is not known. Jascha Heifetz is another artist who was eventually listed only by his surname. One might also cite the English pianist known as Solomon, but that was actually his given name.)

On the evening of 13 January 1960, Monteux was greeted by a standing ovation as he entered the stage to begin the concert, the program of which was
devoted to some of his old favorites:

Beethoven: *Leonore* Overture No. 3
Wagner: *Siegfried Idyll*
Debussy: *La mer*
Brahms: Symphony No. 1 in C minor

At the end came another standing ovation, with rave reviews the next day.
The program was repeated on 15 and 16 January, after which Monteux remained
for a second week of concerts on 20, 21, and 22 January, when the program was:

Beethoven: *Coriolan* Overture
Hindemith: *Nobilissima visione*
Strauss: *Death and Transfiguration*
Sibelius: Symphony No. 2 in D major

Hindemith's piece, a suite from his ballet *Saint Francis*, became one of Monteux's favorite twentieth-century works in his later years. It was during this two-
week engagement that he and the orchestra made two further recordings for RCA
Victor, a beautiful rendition of the *Siegfried Idyll* and a shattering version of
Death and Transfiguration. Though made in 1960, these recordings were not
issued until 1965, a year after Monteux's death. Apparently there were reservations at the time about the Strauss, having to do with technical matters concerning the sound and the orchestral balance. Heard today, such limitations are barely
noticeable, if at all, and Monteux's conception of the piece, his favorite Strauss
tone poem, is truly exceptional, a performance of great sweep and emotional
impact, all pointing to the work's one true climax, magnificently realized. Eight
years had elapsed since Monteux's last recording with the San Francisco Symphony, and the Wagner and Strauss works stand as his only stereo recordings
with that orchestra. The latter was reissued on CD in 1994, coupled with the
monaural recording of *Ein Heldenleben*.

Roland Kohloff, timpanist of the New York Philharmonic, was at that time in
the same position with the San Francisco Symphony. In my interview with him, he
remembered that, as with most great conductors, Monteux did not say very much
at rehearsals, for his beat was so clear and expressive that he could convey his
wishes simply through his gestures. Kohloff does recall, however, that when Monteux did stop for something he often said to a player, "I want that you should play
that *juste* on time," sometimes adding, "without *sentiment*" (pronounced in the
French manner). Kohloff felt that it was a very simple and very powerful instruction to give.

During this visit an extramusical interest, if not passion, of Monteux's was recognized: his great love of fire engines. In a ceremony at the office of San Francisco's fire chief, William F. Murray, Monteux was made an honorary chief of the San Francisco Fire Department.

From time to time Monteux would receive an invitation from one of his favorite pupils to appear as a guest conductor with his orchestra. Usually that ensemble was not in the top rank of orchestras, but one of a certain creditable level that employed its musicians mostly on a part-time basis. For Monteux to conduct such an orchestra would definitely be a feather in its cap, as was the case on 11 February 1960, when he appeared in Canada with the Winnipeg Symphony Orchestra. He had been invited there by Victor Feldbrill, who had studied in Hancock from 1949 to 1951 and had gone on to become one of Canada's most respected conductors.

In Winnipeg Monteux conducted works by Berlioz, Schumann, Ravel, Debussy, and Strauss, with Schumann's Second Symphony as the major work. At the time the Winnipeg Symphony, though a perfectly respectable orchestra, was not ranked on the same level with those of Montreal and Toronto, so Monteux was perhaps taking a chance in programming, with an orchestra unfamiliar to him, the Schumann symphony, with its perpetual-motion violin passages in the scherzo; Ravel's *Alborada del gracioso*, with its extremely difficult brass parts involving triple-tonguing in an extremely high register; and *Till Eulenspiegel*, with its notorious French horn solos. Yet, from all accounts, the orchestra acquitted itself extremely well.

In the 6 February edition of *The Winnipeg Tribune*, Monteux was quoted as saying, concerning his good health and his heavy schedule:

I just do what I have to do. I do not go out, do not socialize at all; for this I am excused because of my age. So I am left to conduct. I confess it is strange, as I am officially retired, but you know what happens? Symphony boards, they say to each other: Monteux, we must have him before he dies. So I work.

An invitation from his longtime pupil James Robertson to conduct the Wichita Symphony Orchestra, of which Robertson was music director, on 27 February 1960 was also accepted. Robertson was a meticulous conductor and a fine orchestral trainer who had developed a very responsive group in Wichita, and Monteux was justifiably quite fond and proud of him. He brought with him Ginia Davis to sing Ravel's *Shéhérazade*; Mozart's "Jupiter" Symphony (No. 41) and Tchaikovsky's Fifth Symphony were also on the program.

In the last week of 1960 and the first of 1961, Monteux paid his first visit to Chicago's Orchestra Hall since 1948. Why he had not appeared there in twelve years remains a mystery, for he continued to conduct the Chicago Symphony Orchestra each summer at the Ravinia Festival. (It should be mentioned that the Chicago Symphony and Ravinia have separate managements.) Rather than conjecture possible reasons for his absence from the Loop, better to just record the facts of the engagement. His program for 27 and 29 December was of a type he sometimes offered—three symphonies, in this case Mozart's "Haffner", Creston's Second, and Brahms's Fourth. But it is the second program, that of 5 and 6 January, that is significant. One might wonder what was significant about a program that featured yet another performance of the Franck symphony. Yet this was not just "another" performance of the Franck, for it led to Monteux's only recording with the Chicago Symphony, a recording that makes one regret there are no more with this great orchestra. The two San Francisco recordings of the Franck, and a broadcast recording from there as well, are absolutely transcended by this magnificent realization, which brings out a facet of the score that is lost on most conductors and hence on many listeners: its great nobility (from a conductor who once said that he was "tired to death" of this piece). In *The Chicago Daily News* of 6 January, reviewing the performance that preceded the recording, Donal Henahan (soon to join *The New York Times*) wrote:

> Only a top-notch man can make the Franck bearable, let alone fresh. By holding down the organ-like sonorities of the brasses and letting the strings sing out, Monteux gave Franck's turgid orchestration a transparency and brightness not often heard. In this work, most conductors favor the sort of sound that can be suggested quite accurately by blowing across the top of a cider jug.

Henahan had referred to the January program as "all-French," even though it had music by an Italian (Cherubini's Overture to *Anacreon*), a Belgian (Franck), and a Russian (Stravinsky's *Petrushka*). But, as he noted, "All three were Parisian by adoption and by temperament."

Between the two programs Monteux conducted a short concert unique in his career at that time. For about ten years, off and on during the 1950s and 1960s, the Chicago Symphony presented hour-long televised concerts performed in a variety of locations—a television studio, a hotel ballroom, even Orchestra Hall itself, sometimes with an audience, sometimes without. Several of these concerts have been released on video, including the broadcast of 1 January 1961. On that one Monteux conducted Beethoven's Eighth Symphony, Wagner's Prelude to Act III of *Die Meistersinger*, and Berlioz's *Roman Carnival* Overture. This, then, is the only video of Monteux's conducting available to the public.

For one who knows Monteux's two audio recordings of the Beethoven, it is a familiar interpretation, except for the fact that Monteux, eighty-five at the time, displays a bit less energy in his gestures than formerly. The Wagner is sensitively done and the Berlioz fairly exciting, though it must be said that it lacks the intensity of George Szell's performance in the same series.

Having enjoyed a great success with his first return visit to San Francisco, it was only natural that Monteux appear again the following season. Accordingly, on 15,

17, and 18 February 1961 he returned with the following program, identical to his first in Chicago a few weeks earlier:

> Mozart: Symphony No. 35 in D major ("Haffner")
> Creston: Symphony No. 2
> Brahms: Symphony No. 4 in E minor

The next week, 22, 23, and 24 February, he offered:

> Cherubini: Overture to *Anacreon*
> Debussy: *Jeux*
> Strauss: *Till Eulenspiegel's Merry Pranks*
> Berlioz: *Symphonie fantastique*

No recordings were made on this visit. It would certainly have been desirable to have on disc Monteux's interpretation of the Brahms Fourth, not to mention *Jeux* and *Till Eulenspiegel*, though recordings of broadcast performances of the last two with other orchestras have circulated.

On 9 January 1962 Monteux appeared for the first time with Washington's National Symphony Orchestra, estimated to be the 105th orchestra he had conducted. The count is only approximate because there is some question as to whether, for example, the New York Philharmonic and the Stadium Symphony Orchestra should be counted as one or two orchestras; the same is true for the NBC Symphony and the Symphony of the Air. Referring to Doris in a pre-concert interview in *The Washington Post* of 6 January, he said, concerning his many concerts, "She knows everything. She remembers all the dates. I don't even remember the program." Contrasting Doris's love of order with his lack of same, he said, "I like disorder. But in that disorder I know where everything is."

Commenting on other musicians, he spoke of Leonard Bernstein as "the most all round talented musician today" and spoke highly of him as a composer, with Rudolf Serkin as the best pianist. As for Van Cliburn, both he and Doris felt he should increase his repertoire. The comment about Bernstein brought a most appreciative handwritten response dated 29 March 1962:

> Dearest Maître:
> I was deeply touched the other day to read some wonderfully warm remarks you made about me in your Washington interviews. I had no idea you valued me so highly as a *composer*! This was a thrill to read. And you are so right about the lack of time: I have written literally nothing in five years, since West Side Story!! Alas . . .
> I miss seeing you. Won't you call on us when you are in New York? We would adore to see you both, and send our love to you and Doris.
> Bless you, and many healthy years,
> Lenny

Doris's pupil Freda Gray-Massé was the soloist on the Washington concert, singing arias from Henry Purcell's *Dido and Aeneas* and Carl Maria von Weber's *Oberon*; the purely orchestral works were Brahms's Third Symphony and the two suites from *Daphnis et Chloé*.

Monteux was to revisit San Francisco one more time, though the occasion was poignantly affected by the death of Leonora Wood Armsby, to whom he owed his coming to San Francisco in the first place. As a memorial tribute to Mrs. Armsby, the concerts of 25 and 26 January 1962 began with Enrique Jordá conducting an orchestral arrangement of the soprano aria "I Know That My Redeemer Liveth" from Handel's *Messiah* and Monteux directing "The Death of Clärchen" from Beethoven's *Egmont*. The program itself—Monteux conducting—contained the orchestral excerpts from Berlioz's *Romeo and Juliet* and Elgar's *Enigma Variations*.

For what proved to be his final appearances in San Francisco, on 31 January and 1 and 2 February, the program was:

Brahms: *Tragic Overture*
Schoenberg: *Verklärte Nacht*
Strauss: Salome's Dance from *Salome*
Beethoven: Symphony No. 3 in E-flat major ("Eroica")

Again no recordings were made, though again it would have been good to have the Schoenberg and Strauss pieces.

Other American orchestras that Monteux conducted during the 1950s and early 1960s include the Atlanta Symphony, the Baltimore Symphony, the Houston Symphony, the Los Angeles Philharmonic, the Minnesota Orchestra, the New Orleans Philharmonic Symphony (of which Monteux's pupil Werner Torkanowsky was the music director), the Pittsburgh Symphony, the Rochester Philharmonic, the Utah Symphony, and the Seattle Symphony.

As Monteux traveled around the United States from one guest engagement to another, he always granted interviews to the local papers. One particular topic recurred quite often, and the following quote from *The New Orleans Times-Picayune* of 22 January 1958 is typical. Said Monteux:

This business of not applauding between movements of a symphony is absolutely ridiculous. Absolutely. It is now almost universal, but why? People say they don't want to destroy the musical line by interrupting it with applause. This is stupid. If a composer wanted a line, he would not indicate a pause between movements. Of course, I do not think the audience should applaud unless it wants to.

I remember Monteux conducting the Boston Symphony in a Carnegie Hall performance of Tchaikovsky's Sixth Symphony on 9 February 1955. As usual, the audience burst into applause after the dynamic ending of the third movement. Monteux motioned for the orchestra to rise, turned and bowed to the audience, then once again faced the orchestra, which had reseated itself, and, once the applause had subsided, continued with the doleful finale. (I have been told of a performance at Tanglewood where he bowed and left the stage after the third movement, then returned for the finale. Not only that, but he delayed his return until those who thought the symphony was over were well on their way to the parking lot.)

An orchestra one might think Monteux would have appeared with more often was that of Cleveland. The Cleveland Orchestra at that time did not have a summer series, so there was no opportunity for annual festival visits such as those at Ravinia, Lewisohn Stadium, and Tanglewood. The result was that Monteux appeared with that great orchestra on only two widely separated occasions: the first on 13 and 15 December 1951, when Debussy's *Images* and the *Symphonie fantastique* were the major works, and the second on 28 February and 2 March 1963 at Severance Hall and 5 March at the Oberlin Conservatory.

For the latter, Cleveland's music director, George Szell, especially wanted Monteux to conduct *The Rite of Spring*, and the engagement almost came to grief because of Monteux's refusal to do so. Just about every orchestra requested *The Rite*, and he was frankly tired of conducting it, just as conducting it was tiring for him; it took too much out of him.

Szell, though disappointed not to have *The Rite*, then requested—naturally—an all-French program, to which Monteux agreed and which he conducted to great acclaim: the overture *Le corsaire* by Berlioz, Franck's Symphony in D minor, and the two suites from *Daphnis et Chloé*. As we shall see, however, Monteux did have one more performance of *The Rite* left in him.

CHAPTER 26

Finally, *Traviata*

Recordings in the 1950s

Once Monteux began appearing regularly with the Boston Symphony, it was only natural, considering the success of his *Rite of Spring* recording, that he continue to record with the orchestra. On 8 December 1952, in Carnegie Hall, he conducted for the RCA Victor microphones two works that had not appeared on his recent engagement with the orchestra, Liszt's symphonic poem *Les préludes* and Scriabin's *Poem of Ecstasy*. The Liszt was an extremely popular warhorse at the time, though it has since, for some reason, received considerably fewer performances, while Scriabin's sensuously exotic piece has maintained its foothold at the fringe of the repertoire. As might be expected, Monteux delivered a straightforward account of the Liszt, which really needs very little help to put its bombastic point across, and in the Scriabin he gave us ecstasy with clarity and an impressive climax.

The very next day, 9 December 1952, Monteux made one of his rare recordings with a pick-up orchestra, the RCA Victor Symphony. Actually, it was not so suspect a group as the term implies, for RCA regularly engaged members of the New York Philharmonic and the NBC Symphony under that *nom de disque*. On this occasion the work recorded was Chausson's *Poème de l'amour et de la mer* (Poem of Love and the Sea). Like most of Chausson's music, this is a ravishingly beautiful score that was little known at the time. In this, the work's first recording, the well-loved American mezzo-soprano Gladys Swarthout was the soloist.

Back in Boston, on 12 and 13 April 1953 Monteux recorded two Mozart piano concertos with his old friend Lili Kraus as soloist. He was successful in persuading the Boston Symphony management (unlike the Concertgebouw years earlier) to engage her for a pair of concerts and for RCA to record their collaboration. Of course, by this time Kraus was a fairly well known artist. They had performed the Concerto No. 18 in B-flat major, K. 456, at the concerts of 10 and 11 April and recorded the Concerto No. 12 in A major, K. 414, both works not frequently performed at that time.

Of the recording of the A major concerto one can say that the orchestral performance is a bit brusque, as is the piano rendition; it is overpedaled, lacking in grace, and rather heavy. The B-flat major is better, with alert and vigorous direction by Monteux, though Kraus rushes quite a bit.

On 2, 4, 30, and 31 December 1953 Monteux was back in New York, at the Manhattan Center this time, to record suites from two of the most scintillating nineteenth-century French ballets, Léo Delibes's *Coppélia* and *Sylvia*. There is no evidence that Monteux ever conducted the complete ballets in the theater—they were not in a style that appealed to Diaghilev—but he conducted the suites with a marvelous buoyancy and irresistible rhythmic vitality.

The Manhattan Center was a large ballroom in the New Yorker Hotel on West Thirty-fourth Street that was often used as a recording studio by both RCA and Columbia Records. The ensemble for the Delibes recordings was designated as "members of the Boston Symphony Orchestra." For all intents and purposes, this was the Boston Pops Orchestra, which is the BSO without its principal players. RCA used the sessions as experiments in what would become their "new orthophonic" sound. So vivid are the recordings that they could almost be mistaken for stereo.

Experiments with stereo were already under way as early as 1954–55, though the recordings were originally issued in mono. Monteux's first stereo venture was a recording made of Debussy's *La mer* at Tanglewood, where he had just performed it, on 19 July 1954. This was another act of generosity by Charles Munch, because *La mer* was really "his" piece with the Boston Symphony; however, he made himself wait a few years before recording the work so that Monteux would have an opportunity to do so.

We must remember that Monteux was a member of the Colonne Orchestra when Debussy conducted *La mer* with the group in 1908. Poorly though that orchestra behaved during rehearsals, Monteux could still recall the details of the composer's own conception of this work. Thus we get from him tempos that are a bit brisker than what is considered the norm, his timing for the piece being twenty-two minutes when most conductors today stretch it out to twenty-four or twenty-five minutes or even longer. Particularly captivating is Monteux's performance of the second movement, "The Play of the Waves."

Monteux included the brass fanfares toward the close of the work, as Toscanini and Koussevitzky did not. Debussy had deleted them from the original score, but it is possible that he told Monteux he intended to reinstate them. Monteux said that Debussy was always changing his mind about his scores, adding and subtracting details on the basis of rehearsals he had conducted or attended. Thus, according to Monteux, there is no definitive version of a Debussy score. *La mer*, in fact, exists in at least three different printed versions. Ravel, however, was exactly the opposite—the score you received from him was the one and only version.

After an all-Tchaikovsky program with the Boston Symphony on 4 and 5 February, Monteux made his first recording of that composer's music, the "Pathétique" Symphony. (He recorded the last three symphonies in reverse order.) For the most part, the great non-Slavic conductors of that time did not have much to do with Tchaikovsky's music. Toscanini performed and recorded a few works (including the "Pathétique"); Bruno Walter played fewer and did not record any. One would think that Monteux, as a Frenchman, would not be sympathetic to this composer, but he stated on more than one occasion that he loved Tchaikovsky and bore the remark out by performing his music frequently. Many were the all-Tchaikovsky programs conducted at Lewisohn Stadium, and now there was one in the Boston Symphony's subscription series, something even Koussevitzky rarely offered, though he played much music by Tchaikovsky.

It is one thing to be in sympathy with a composer, another to deliver convincing performances of his music. This Monteux did with Tchaikovsky, though he did not play him in the tortured, exaggerated manner favored by so many conductors. As always, Monteux brought a sense of proportion to his music making, and if the last ounce of emotional turmoil is missing from his Tchaikovsky, the performances were nevertheless tremendously exciting and faithful to the score. In fact, he took more liberties with the music than did the great Russian conductor Evgeny Mravinsky in his classic recordings with the Leningrad Philharmonic. Monteux's "Pathétique" displays great passion without tearing the music to shreds. It is true that in the third movement, when the march theme is played by the full orchestra toward the end, he adopted a slightly slower, more maestoso tempo not called for in the score. Concerning this liberty, favored by many conductors in those days, one could say that it is a case of observing not what is in the score, but what is in the music. And in the first and fourth movements, Monteux demonstrated that perhaps he alone (and Toscanini, of course) knew the meaning of the Italian terms *incalzando* and *ritenuto*, markings that *are* found in the score. (The former, literally "pursuing hotly," implies a moving forward, quasi stringendo, while the latter means "held back suddenly," as opposed to ritardando, which is a gradual slowing of the tempo.)

For all his conducting of opera at the Met and elsewhere, it is perhaps strange that until this time Monteux had not actually recorded an opera. That opportunity came to him in 1955, when he was engaged by the English-based firm HMV (His Master's Voice) to record Massenet's *Manon* in Paris with the Orchestra of the Opéra-Comique, as a member of which he had once played that opera. No doubt the prime reason for this recording was the desire to have the great Spanish soprano Victoria de los Angeles in the title role, which she had already performed with Monteux at the Met the year before. This she performed beautifully, with a surrounding cast that was entirely French: the other principal singers were Henri Legay as the Chevalier des Grieux, Michel Dens as Lescaut, and Jean Borthayre as the Count des Grieux.

The recording took place in Paris's Salle de la Mutualité from 30 May to 22 June. According to the program notes issued with the recording, de los Angeles was very well treated by the chief HMV producer, David Bicknell (though René Challan is listed as the producer for this recording), in that if she told him she did not feel well on a scheduled recording day, that she could not do her best, he would give her the day off and portions of the score where she was not needed would be recorded instead. Opera recordings are never made in sequence anyway, so in fact de los Angeles's entire part was recorded in one day, in three sessions. It is a tribute to the artistry of those involved that a performance of great continuity could result under such conditions. Monteux was provided with a bed in a room of the hall, where he would retire for a nap between sessions. Whatever the reason, this is a recorded performance of remarkable freshness on the part of all the performers, with the undeniable authority of Monteux at the helm. The recording is now available on CD on the Testament label.

Back at Tanglewood in the summer of 1955, Monteux recorded Debussy's Three Nocturnes with the Boston Symphony, with women of the Berkshire Festival Chorus in *Sirènes*. Recorded on 15 August, the first nocturne, *Nuages* (Clouds), is marvelously and subtly evocative, the second, *Fêtes* (Festivals), quite brisk, its trumpet fanfares slurred rather than tongued as usually heard, the climaxes almost terrifying. *Sirènes* (Sirens) is appropriately mysterious, the wordless chorus haunting in its evocation of those seductresses of the sea. Monteux also brings out the fact that the piece contains some Spanish rhythms, a detail often overlooked.

Not generally known is that Monteux was not well at the time of this recording and its preceding concert. The recording date was the middle of August, when the conducting school was in session in Hancock. Monteux often left the school for weekend concerts at Tanglewood. In this instance he had cut short the Friday morning class while a student was on the podium. Monteux, who appeared a bit pale, left the hall quietly and was driven home. There was some question about his health. Was it indigestion? Or something worse? Whatever it was, it was not a heart attack, as feared, for Monteux left that afternoon for Tanglewood and conducted a rehearsal Saturday morning and a demanding program that evening consisting of Wagner's Overture to *The Flying Dutchman*, Brahms's Third Symphony, Debussy's Nocturnes and Strauss's Suite from *Der Rosenkavalier*. The Nocturnes were recorded the following Monday, and there is no sign that Monteux was "under the weather." (It is possible that his indisposition was a harbinger of what would befall him in later years. He was only eighty at this time, after all.)

When the Nocturnes were issued by RCA, the LP coupling was, of course, *La mer* from the year before. The original release was in mono. Some years later the Nocturnes were reissued in stereo, with a different coupling. No one could understand why *La mer* was not also brought out in stereo, since it had been so recorded. And in 1994, when RCA released its twelve-CD Pierre Monteux Edition, there were the Nocturnes in stereo, but *La mer* still in mono. In a conversation I had with the late John Pfeiffer, producer of the edition, he admitted that the stereo tapes of *La mer* had been misplaced by RCA many years before and could not be found! (The Nocturnes have been included in the Pierre Monteux ser in EMI/ IMG's "Great Conductors" series.)

It was three years before Monteux made another recording with the Boston Symphony. He was, however, not idle in the recording studio during that time. From 26 May to 9 June 1956 Pierre and Doris were in Rome. Although the Metropolitan Opera would not let Monteux conduct *La traviata*, RCA apparently had no objection to his conducting a recording of one of his favorite operas. This he did with the orchestra and chorus of the Rome Opera House, with Rosanna Carteri as Violetta, Cesare Valletti as Alfredo, and Leonard Warren as Germont.

One wonders if Monteux's great love for this beautiful opera stemmed from the fact that while it is an Italian opera, it is also a French one. The story on which it is based is by Alexandre Dumas *fils*, and the action takes place in and around Paris. Perhaps he was also attracted by its intimate, almost Mozartian atmosphere and textures, from which the big moments and dynamism of such works as *Aida* and *Otello* are absent.

One does not need an excuse to love *La traviata*, however, and Monteux's affection for the score shines through this recording in spite of moments when it is apparent that the competent Italian orchestra is not entirely used to him. While all the principal singers are first-rate, the performance that remains in the memory is the magnificent Germont of the great Leonard Warren. At the time of this writing, the recording has not appeared on CD.

From 26 October to 11 November 1956 the Monteuxs were in Paris. Much as Pierre disliked working with French orchestras, it was planned for him to record Stravinsky with the Paris Conservatory Orchestra. Perhaps the fact that the music had been premiered there was sufficient reason for RCA and English Decca to collaborate on this venture in Paris.

Prior to the sessions the Monteuxs spent an enjoyable evening attending a performance by Maurice Chevalier, an artist they had long known, enjoyed, and admired. According to Doris, the show was boring except when Chevalier was onstage.

The works of Stravinsky that were recorded were the *Firebird* Suite, the complete *Petrushka*, and *The Rite of Spring*. Hearing this *Firebird* makes one wish it had been recorded in Boston or London. The string sound is weak, and the recording, made in the Salle Wagram, is not particularly outstanding. (I base this last comment on my listening to the original RCA mono release and the much later stereo release by Decca in its budget "weekend" series.) In general the performance lacks energy, although details are heard in the Infernal Dance that are normally obscured.

Monteux almost always performed the original 1910 version of the *Firebird* music, which calls for a larger orchestra than either of the composer's subsequent suites. Perhaps the most obvious difference between the earlier orchestration and the later ones is that the famous trombone glissandos in the Infernal Dance are absent from the original version. The 1910 version also contains two movements not included in 1919 but restored in 1945, the pas de deux and the scherzo, Dance of the Princesses. These Monteux included when he played the suite in concert, but they are not on this recording. As the 1910 suite ends with the Infernal Dance, Monteux then concluded with the Berceuse and Finale from the 1919 suite. The recording information states that Monteux plays the 1919 version when, in reality, it is mostly the 1910 version.

Petrushka, with Julius Katchen playing the piano part, is better, and the work's irregular meters are actually done a bit more crisply here than in the later recording with the Boston Symphony. The strings are better than in *The Firebird*, though *Petrushka* does not require the lush string sound that portions of the earlier work need. On the whole, however, this performance is a bit pedestrian.

If that is the case with *Petrushka*, what is to be said about *The Rite of Spring* from these sessions? This, Monteux's only stereo recording of the work, is a very weak and cautious performance, without passion or drive. In no way does it compare favorably with either the San Francisco or Boston renditions. It is as though the musicians could play the piece, but did not really want to. If B. H. Haggin's remarks, quoted earlier, were applied to this recording, one could say that he had a point. (Haggin had said that, compared with Stravinsky's recording, "Monteux's performance hasn't the power it should have." Actually, he was referring to Monteux's earlier performances, for which his comments were less apt.) Had RCA been more patient and waited until Monteux performed the work in Boston and Tanglewood in 1957, they would have had a splendid stereo recording.

Monteux returned to Rome in 1957 to record Gluck's *Orfeo ed Euridice* from 15 to 26 June, again with the Rome Opera forces. Risë Stevens sang the role of Orfeo, which she had performed with Monteux at the Met the year before; Lisa Della Casa was Euridice; and Amor was sung by Roberta Peters. This is frankly not the best of Monteux's opera recordings. The Massenet is his best, followed by the Verdi.

Monteux loved *Orfeo ed Euridice*, but his direction here lacks the tautness of Toscanini's NBC recording of Act II (a live concert performance). Again the Rome orchestral work is competent, but little more. The two principal singers perform their roles well, but with no particular distinction. Roberta Peters comes off best in her cameo role. Reissued in RCA's "Living Stereo" series, this was Monteux's last operatic recording.

Monteux's first encounter with the Vienna Philharmonic Orchestra, back in the Diaghilev days, was rather unpleasant. Over forty years later Decca/RCA, if they even were aware of the earlier incident, felt that the combination of Monteux and that orchestra would produce some good recordings. It did, to a certain extent, but this pairing of conductor and orchestra proved to be an odd one, and they never really achieved the desired chemistry. Mostly Germanic repertoire was recorded; the sole exception was the *Symphonie fantastique*.

The first recording with the Vienna Philharmonic, Monteux's third version of the Brahms Symphony No. 2, was made in the spring of 1956. This is a lovely performance, more expansive and more relaxed than the two San Francisco recordings, but also not as exciting. A distinguishing feature is the observance of the first movement's exposition repeat; this may actually be the first recording to have included that repeat.

Monteux recorded four Beethoven symphonies in Vienna from 1957 to 1960, Nos. 1, 3, 6, and 8. The "Eroica" is frankly disappointing and not well recorded, with a rather "boxy" sound. Monteux was to do this better in Amsterdam, but it is a work he really should have recorded in Boston, where he performed it in 1957. The more genial Nos. 1 and 6 ("Pastorale") are very fine, Monteux bringing out their moments of humor and humanity. The Eighth, always a Monteux specialty, is more polished than the San Francisco version but not quite as dynamic.

Taped in 1958, excerpts from Mendelssohn's *A Midsummer Night's Dream* and Schubert's *Rosamunde* are well done, but the former lacks the requisite magic. The *Rosamunde* Overture is quite ebullient, rather overshadowing the incidental music, which is less powerful to begin with, but nevertheless quite lovely. These two recordings have never appeared on CD.

But the jewels of Monteux's Vienna recordings, where everyone seems to have been on the same wavelength, are the two Haydn symphonies, No. 94 ("Surprise") and No. 101 ("The Clock"). Recorded in April 1959, these are wonderful performances, full of life and healthy vigor, with appropriate tempos and inflections. There are only two points to question: Monteux's failure to observe the exposition repeat in No. 94 when he does so in No. 101, and his use of a supposedly discredited text for the trio of No. 101's minuet. In this section, according to scholarly editions, such as that of H. C. Robbins Landon, the strings play the wrong harmony under the flute solo the first time it is heard, then correct it the second time. This is apparently one of the many musical jokes that abound in Haydn's symphonies, in this case implying that the strings have not paid attention the first time but realize their mistake and correct it the second time. Monteux, in common with Beecham and others of his generation (but not Toscanini in his last recording), played from an old edition in which the editor "corrected" Haydn's wrong chords. On the other hand, Erich Leinsdorf, a rather scholarly conductor, once told me that Landon's edition was "insanity" at that point. (The "insanity," if any, is surely Haydn's, not Landon's. A classical minuet and trio each contain two sections that are to be repeated, such instruction being indicated by simple repeat marks. For the first section of the "Clock" Symphony's trio, however, Haydn has not provided the repeat marks, but has completely written out the section twice. This is how it appears in all the printed editions. There is no difference between the two in the so-called corrected editions, in which case why not print it once with repeat marks? The sole difference between the two in Landon's edition, which is based on Haydn's manuscript, is that the chord is wrong the first time and right the second time.)

In 1958 Monteux resumed his recordings with the Boston Symphony. During a two-week engagement two were made. The first was Tchaikovsky's Fifth Symphony on 8 January, a tremendously exciting rendition with very flexible tempos. Some of the flexibility was requested by Tchaikovsky himself when, in the famous Andante cantabile second movement, he added the words *con alcuna licenza* ("with some license" [or "liberty"]). As was customary, and perhaps still is, Monteux prepared for the first movement's soaring second theme by ritarding into it, then playing that theme at a markedly slower tempo, something in which the strict Mravinsky did not indulge. But a slowing at that point has always been traditional and effective, and Monteux certainly made the most of it.

In the second week of Monteux's engagement his soloist was the Russian violinist Leonid Kogan (1924–1982), who was making his American debut in the Brahms concerto. RCA wanted to record Kogan and Monteux together, but not in the Brahms concerto, which Monteux was scheduled to record in London with Henryk Szeryng later that year. After casting about for an appropriate piece for the occasion, it was decided to record the Khachaturian concerto, which Monteux had never conducted before. Not a very well known concerto at the time, though it has since become a bit more so, it is an attractive, even viscerally exciting work in a lightweight popular idiom. Monteux, who certainly performed his share of lesser works in his career, learned the score in a few days and directed a sterling accompaniment to Kogan's (and Khachaturian's) pyrotechnics. An addendum on the LP release was one of Saint-Saëns's short *morceaux* for violin and orchestra, the delightful *Havanaise*, which Monteux did know.

Monteux's final two recordings with the BSO were made in January 1959. Apparently RCA and Monteux were dissatisfied with the Paris version of *Petrushka*, and it was decided to remake it in Boston. (Would that they had felt the same about *The Rite of Spring*!) This time they got it right, a very clear performance with some leisurely tempos, but one must remember that Monteux always conducted the great ballet scores according to the tempo at which they could be danced, and probably were danced by the Ballets Russes. So what we have here is not a high-powered *Petrushka*, but one that brings out the basic sadness of the story, especially in Petrushka's death scene. This is certainly preferable to the Paris recording, even if some of the irregular meters are a little tighter in that performance. Again, I must emphasize that Monteux's recordings, regardless of the number of takes required, have the effect of actual performances.

Finally, to finish in a blaze of glory, Monteux taped Tchaikovsky's Fourth Symphony on 28 January 1959. While this may not be the most Slavic, authentically Russian performance on disc, it is certainly one of the most exciting. The first movement is propulsive and impassioned throughout, the second faster than most, not dragged out. Its middle section sounds like a true Russian dance; there is no wallowing here.

The famous pizzicato Scherzo really moves, and if it is even faster the second time around it is because Monteux wanted it that way, as I can confirm from having attended rehearsals of the piece at Lewisohn Stadium. Monteux was consistent in his interpretation over the years. While it has become a cliché to use the word "exciting," that is the perfect word to describe the finale, again propulsive and calculated to bring down the house.

The playing of the Boston Symphony cannot be underestimated in these re-cordings; it was an orchestra that worked regularly with Monteux, knew him well, and loved him. From time to time it has been mentioned that in his later years—and he was now almost eighty-four—his conducting gestures lacked the energy of former years. When conducting an orchestra that was not used to him, the results, while still very good, tended to reflect the less-energized direction the musicians received from him. But the Boston Symphony, and later the London Symphony, knew what he wanted, even if he did not always indicate it, and they played their hearts out for him.

CHAPTER 27

The LSO

Monteux at Eighty-Five

Like Paris, London boasts a plethora of orchestras—five full-time symphony orchestras, two opera orchestras, and several chamber orchestras. Unlike in Paris, they do not all perform at the same time on the same day. (Nor do they in Paris any longer.) In order of seniority they are: the London Symphony Orchestra (LSO; founded in 1904), the BBC Symphony Orchestra (founded in 1930), the London Philharmonic Orchestra (LPO; founded in 1932 by Sir Thomas Beecham), the Philharmonia Orchestra (founded in 1945 by Walter Legge, initially as a recording orchestra), and the Royal Philharmonic Orchestra (RPO; founded in 1946, also by Sir Thomas Beecham).

The first of these, the London Symphony Orchestra, was founded by the players themselves as a self-governing organization. They had been members of the Queen's Hall Orchestra, whose conductor, Sir Henry Wood, had banned the Parisian-style deputy system that had existed in his orchestra. When they left in protest, they formed their own orchestra, in which they continued with the deputy system until friction within the group caused it to be abolished.

As shareholders in a self-governing organization, the musicians themselves, through a board of directors, select the conductors and guest soloists with whom they work. Early principal conductors were Hans Richter and Arthur Nikisch, with guest appearances by Thomas Beecham (not yet knighted at the time) and Leopold Stokowski, who (one must not forget) was a native Londoner.

Within a few short years the LSO established itself as the leading orchestra in English musical life, bearing in mind that the other four major London orchestras did not yet exist. Once the field became more crowded it was inevitable that one orchestra or another would be considered "the top" orchestra, depending on circumstances of the moment, such as wartime and its aftermath, economic situations, who was on the podium, and so on.

English orchestras, or at least London orchestras, for the most part do not have music directors in the sense that American orchestras do. Rather, they have principal conductors. The principal conductors lead more concerts than any of the guest conductors, of which there are many, but in general have no say in selecting the guest conductors and soloists, or even in determining the personnel of the orchestra. They may advise, of course, but they work at the pleasure of the board of directors and may even not have full say over their own programs. The LSO had, in fact, gone for long periods without a principal conductor.

At the end of World War II all the London orchestras were in a rebuilding period during which none held prominence over another. In 1950 the LSO appointed as principal conductor the highly respected Viennese-born Josef Krips (1902–1974), who continued in the position until 1954. He had succeeded in raising the quality and prestige of the orchestra but resigned after a dispute with the directors. The nature of this dispute is not known, but Krips, like many conductors of his generation, could be a bit cantankerous and immovable in certain situations involving personal convictions, and a board of orchestra musicians could, and can, be equally so.

Pierre Monteux first appeared in London in 1911 as conductor of Diaghilev's Ballets Russes. On 27 January 1927, in the Queen's Hall, he conducted under the auspices of the Royal Philharmonic Society (not to be confused with the Royal Philharmonic Orchestra), which presented a series of concerts performed by an ad hoc orchestra. For this performance the German soprano Elisabeth Schumann was his soloist in works of Mozart and Richard Strauss; the program also included Berlioz's *Symphonie fantastique* and the English premiere of *Hymn to Apollo* by Arthur Bliss.

Monteux returned in 1934 for a single concert with the London Philharmonic Orchestra on 15 March, an all-French program for which his former Paris Conservatory classmate, Jacques Thibaud, was the violin soloist in Lalo's *Symphonie espagnole*. On 18 May 1951 he conducted the BBC Symphony Orchestra in the newly opened Royal Festival Hall, with the English pianist Solomon playing Beethoven's Concerto No. 2. Mozart's Symphony No. 40 and Bartók's Concerto for Orchestra completed the program. As these were Monteux's only appearances in London until 1956, it is safe to say that he was at that time not a familiar figure in the English capital. He was not entirely unknown, however, for his recordings from Paris, San Francisco, and Boston were available there and were often played over the BBC.

Difficult though it may be to believe, a contributing factor to Monteux's long absence from London, at least following World War II and into the 1950s, was the British quarantine law, which forbids the bringing of animals into the country until they have spent six months in quarantine. Doris loved their French poodle, Fifi, so much that she could not bear to have it quarantined. And as Pierre would not travel to England without Doris, the English were deprived of Monteux's artistry for many years. (Incidentally, the students at L'École Monteux found the beloved Fifi to be a rather ill-tempered, unpleasant animal.)

It was with the BBC Symphony Orchestra that he conducted concerts on 9 and 11 May 1956, again in the Royal Festival Hall. The first of these was a sort of festival in C major, consisting of Mozart's "Jupiter" Symphony and Schubert's

Ninth, with music from Bizet's *L'Arlésienne* sandwiched between, while the second was an almost-all-French program of the Chausson Symphony, Ravel's *Shéhérazade*, and Debussy's *Images* for Orchestra. The non-French item was Ralph Vaughan Williams's *Fantasia on a Theme by Thomas Tallis*. (Vaughan Williams, it is true, did study with Ravel, but not before he wrote this piece.) The soprano soloist in *Shéhérazade* was Ginia Davis, whom Monteux had coached in the piece and whom the critics found very engaging, singing with a firm line and beautiful tone quality.

Monteux's recording contract was with RCA Victor, which in the late 1950s began a partnership with English Decca (then known as London Records in the United States) whereby the two companies would collaborate on recordings with each other's artists. Under this arrangement, in June 1957 Monteux made his first recording with the LSO, excerpts from Tchaikovsky's *Sleeping Beauty*. Long out of print, this beautiful recording finally appeared on CD in 2002 in the Perrre Monteux set in EMI/IMG's series "The Great Conductors." In January 1958 Monteux recorded that quintessential English masterwork, Elgar's *Enigma Variations*, also with the LSO. This is one of the truly great recordings of that work, along with those of Toscanini and Beecham. English orchestras are known for their ability to play very softly, and the string playing at the beginning of the "Nimrod" Variation has to be heard to be believed, a *pianissimo* of near inaudibility, and not achieved through recording trickery.

With English orchestras, recordings beget concerts. That is, if an orchestra has made recordings with a conductor with the prospect of many more to come, there is a good likelihood that the conductor will be engaged for some concerts. Recordings and film and television soundtracks constitute the major activity and source of income for London orchestras, providing them the means with which to present their own concert series. In the case of Monteux, one would like to think that the LSO engaged him because they genuinely enjoyed working with him and because he was a conductor of great reputation by that time, even if his London appearances had been rather scant.

In any case, Monteux was engaged for three concerts in the Royal Festival Hall, 13, 15, and 23 June 1958, each with a distinguished guest soloist. The program for 13 June was:

Weber: Overture to *Euryanthe*
Elgar: *Enigma Variations*
Brahms: Violin Concerto in D major; Zino Francescatti, soloist

(*Euryanthe* was one of Monteux's favorite overtures.)

Somehow the English had the impression that this was Monteux's first performance of the Elgar work, but he had already programmed it in San Francisco and conducted it in New York the year before at the Toscanini memorial concert. He had also given it in Boston in 1957 and in several seasons at Ravinia.

For the 15 June concert Francescatti was again the soloist, this time in the Tchaikovsky Violin Concerto; the program also featured Debussy's *Images*. On 23 June the great English pianist Clifford Curzon was heard in Tchaikovsky's Concerto No. 1, with the Second Symphony of Sibelius the principal orchestral work. *Images* and the Sibelius symphony would soon receive stellar recordings by Monteux and the LSO.

During this visit two further recordings were made, the Brahms Violin Concerto, but with Henryk Szeryng rather than Francescatti (since the latter was under contract to Columbia Records at the time), and Brahms's *Variations on a Theme by Haydn*, which would be issued together with the *Enigma Variations*. Both recordings reveal Monteux's great sympathy with the music of Brahms.

Monteux was re-engaged for more concerts and recordings in March and April 1959. Earlier in the year he rerecorded one of the classics from his San Francisco years, Rimsky-Korsakov's *Scheherazade*, with the LSO's leader, Hugh Maguire, playing the violin solos. (In English musical parlance, the leader is the equivalent of the concertmaster in the United States.) Maguire recently recalled that Monteux was "not always the most inspiring conductor" but was technically impeccable.

In a conversation I had with the French pianist-conductor Philippe Entremont, he mentioned that on the same day that *Scheherazade* was recorded, he recorded Tchaikovsky's Piano Concerto No. 1 with Monteux and the LSO, a version that was never released and that still remains in Decca's vaults. Entremont was under contract to Columbia Records at the time, but he was dissatisfied with the arrangements and was given permission to make this recording for Decca. He later recorded the work with Leonard Bernstein and the New York Philharmonic. A Monteux LSO concert performance with John Ogdon was released posthumously, so a Tchaikovsky Piano Concerto is not lacking from either Entremont or Monteux. Still, it would be good to have this one, if it actually still exists.

The major work performed in Monteux's 1959 London concerts was the complete score of Ravel's *Daphnis et Chloé*, with the Chorus of the Royal Opera House participating. The senior producer for Decca at the time was John Culshaw (1924–1980), who, in his book *Putting the Record Straight*, has described his pleasure in working with Monteux, who told him "how much he would like to record a complete *Daphnis and Chloé* in London." He had chosen to do exactly the opposite of most conductors: he had never recorded the Suite No. 2, and had, in San Francisco, recorded the Suite No. 1.

Culshaw relates that "RCA was only too glad to hand over some of its obligation to Monteux" to Decca, for RCA felt that his records did not sell well, "by which," says Culshaw, "I think it meant that they did not sell in such quantities as those conducted by Stokowski, Ormandy and Reiner, to say nothing of Arthur Fiedler and the Boston Pops."

The Decca salespeople were not keen on the *Daphnis* project and stated that they would agree only if the nearly-sixty-minute work could be accommodated on one LP. This was accomplished, and, said Culshaw:

It is, and always will be, one of my favorite records, not simply because it happens to be conducted by the man who had been responsible for its *première*, but because of the way he treated the music, which was to relate each part to its context and to see the work as a whole. Thus he did not allow the climax of the great *Lever du jour* to become so powerful that there was nothing in reserve when he came to the climaxes at the end of the work.

Culshaw speaks of comparable results in the *Enigma Variations*, where Monteux

would not allow the Nimrod variation, of which most conductors make such a meal, to overshadow the finale; and as a result that finale, which for years has been dismissed as cheap, vulgar and unworthy of the rest of the work, became a fitting climax to the work. (Culshaw 1981, 208–9)

Other recordings in 1959 were of Brahms's Piano Concerto No. 1, with the young American Julius Katchen as soloist; Dvořák's Seventh Symphony; and Sibelius's Second Symphony. The Dvořák is an especially captivating performance, one that simply flows naturally from beginning to end. Monteux was originally scheduled to record and perform Sibelius's First Symphony, but for some reason the Second was done instead. Additionally, recordings of Mozart's "Jupiter" Symphony and Overture to *The Magic Flute* were planned, but did not come to fruition. At the time of this writing, Monteux's fine Sibelius No. 2 has not appeared on CD.

For the first two years of Monteux's LSO engagements, it was the orchestra's general secretary, John Cruft, who handled the arrangements. The title of general secretary is equivalent to that of general manager or managing director in the United States. It is the one major post of a cooperative orchestra's management not held by one of the musicians.

In a letter dated 6 August 1959, Cruft discussed the programs Monteux would conduct for his next LSO engagement on 29 April and 6 May 1960. The repertoire included Brahms's Third Symphony, Sibelius's First Symphony, Hindemith's *Nobilissima visione*, and several French works, including *La mer*. Cruft informed Monteux that his directors very much wanted Monteux to substitute Stravinsky's *Song of the Nightingale* for the Hindemith work. *Nobilissima visione* had already been played a few times in London, whereas the Stravinsky piece was practically unknown. The demands of his conducting school prevented Monteux from replying until 8 September, when he wrote:

I am really not in the mood of playing "Le Chant du Rossignol," a work that I don't like and that I have not played for a long, long time (even if I am the creator of Le Rossignol as an opera). I would suggest in place of Nobilissima: "L'Ascension" of Olivier Messiaen.

In November 1959 John Cruft left the LSO, to be succeeded as general secretary by Ernest Fleischmann, who was himself a musician. Born in Germany, he had lived in South Africa before moving to London, had degrees in music and business, played various instruments, and had studied privately with the noted English conductor Albert Coates. In South Africa he had been active as a conductor and was also the artistic director of two major festivals there before he was invited to take over the administrative leadership of the LSO. One of Fleischmann's first tasks was to inform Monteux, concerning the two concerts in question, that they would now be part of a "French Fortnight" in London. This would necessitate a change to all-French programs, a proposal for which Monteux had little enthusiasm. The LSO suggested for the first night an all-Ravel program, including the complete *Daphnis et Chloé* (which Monteux had already conducted the year before) and a concert performance of the one-act opera *L'heure espagnole*.

Writing to Fleischmann on 26 November 1959, Monteux stated, "As to the changes in my programs, I never make a program of French works and it seemed to me there were quite enough French works in the two programs to be part of a French Fortnight!" (Monteux had ceased conducting all-French programs by 1959, but he often gave such programs in earlier years.) He did, however, agree to the all-French plan and continued:

> The suggestion of L'Heure Espagnole is really out of the question in concert form. If ever a work needed the stage it is this one. I absolutely refuse to do this work in concert form and suggest for the second part excerpts from Pelléas—including the wonderful interludes and giving a good idea of Debussy's masterwork. For this work I will choose a Pelléas, Mélisande and a Golaud, artists who have worked with me.

This last sentence could be categorized under the heading "famous last words."

Fleischmann's reply of 9 December agrees with the substitution of excerpts from *Pelléas* for the Ravel work and points out that the French government is prepared to send singers from the Opéra-Comique in Paris to participate. He asks Monteux to let him know what singers he has in mind, so that he may give their names to the French Embassy in London. He states that the embassy will not pay travel expenses for the singers to come all the way from America, but he is certain that they would like to have the very best team representing the Opéra-Comique at the Royal Festival Hall with Monteux.

It was soon decided that, instead of presenting excerpts from *Pelléas et Mélisande*, the first concert would be devoted to an abridged version of the complete opera, and the second an all-Ravel program of *Le tombeau de Couperin, Shéhérazade, Alborada del gracioso*, and the complete *Daphnis et Chloé*. On 26 December Monteux wrote to Fleischmann that he was waiting to hear from Camille Maurane and Michele Roux, the artists he wished to sing respectively the roles of Pelléas and Golaud. He continued, "As for Mélisande, I have already asked Miss

Ginia Davis who has accepted. In addition, she will sing also Shéhérazade by Ravel that I have included in the Ravel program."

Fleischmann had already written to Monteux on 21 December. In the letter, which crossed Monteux's of 26 December in the mail, Fleischmann stated that the French Embassy and the Paris Opera were arranging for Maurane and Roux to participate in *Pelléas*, as well as, in the role of Mélisande, Nadine Sautereau.

An indignant Monteux replied on 11 January from San Francisco, where he was conducting the orchestra,

> I am surprised that the French Embassy could *engage* singers for *my* concert without understanding with me.
>
> I have written to you that *I* [underlined twice] already engaged Miss Davis for Pelléas and Shéhérazade. If the French Embassy is paying for the singers they can as well pay for the ones I have chosen. After all, I changed my programmes to please them, they cannot also impose on me what artists I must work with.
>
> When it was a question of Pelléas, I specified absolutely that I would choose my artists who already sang the opera with me. If I must depend on the French Embassy, I prefer to change this programme.

In a letter of 14 January 1960, Fleischmann agreed that the French embassy should have consulted with Monteux concerning the singers. He then mentioned that the BBC was considering recording the *Pelléas* performance for future broadcast, thus providing much extra income for Monteux and the orchestra. But the BBC, which approved the participation of Camille Maurane and Michele Roux, emphatically stated that Ginia Davis would not be acceptable. Fleischmann stated that while the LSO did not wish to offend Monteux and would certainly like to respect his wishes, the orchestra did have a certain obligation to the French embassy and, more important, felt it must consider the financial implications of a BBC recording.

An even more indignant Monteux replied on 27 January, making the following points:

> I. When I accepted these 2 concerts, it was no question of French week or French programs or French Embassy. My programs were made in accord with the committee of the orchestra in view of recordings. I never would have accepted a French program because I do not approve of nationalist programs!
>
> II. To please you (the orchestra) I accepted these two French programs and when I proposed a selection of Pelléas + Mélisande with understanding that *I* would choose my singers, it was because I wanted to give my own interpretation with soloists that I know, especially Mélisande, who is supposed

to sing in addition, some parts of Geneviève and the whole of Yniold!!
Now, the French Embassy *engaged* another artist that I don't know and
I must say to Miss Davis that she is *not acceptable*!! Somebody in BBC
knows better than I who is "acceptable" or not!!!

III. This puts me in an impossible position knowing full well my affection
for the L.S.O. I cannot let them lose money.

IV. So I will accept the soloists that B.B.C. esteem "acceptable" for Pelléas.
But, for the second concert I insist that Shéhérazade be sung by Miss Davis.
If the French embassy don't want to pay her fee, I will pay it myself and
I would have paid it for Mélisande also.

He concludes by saying that he hopes the French embassy will be satisfied.

In the end, Ginia Davis was accepted for the Ravel program, with the French
singers performing in *Pelléas*. An addition to the cast was the French bass André
Vessières in the role of Arkel. Writing in the *Financial Times* of 30 April, Andrew
Porter spoke of the *Pelléas* performance as

> delicately luminous. . . . The greatness in Monteux's reading lay in his reve-
> lation of what was distinct and what was unknown, in bringing together, as
> Debussy did, precision and awe. The London Symphony Orchestra play as
> a super-fine instrument under his hands. . . . It was a completely integrated
> performance in which Maeterlinck, Debussy, Monteux, took one into a
> world of enchantment—mysterious, beautiful, tragic, violent—that lies at
> the heart of the world around us.

In the *Manchester Guardian* of the same date, the dean of British music critics,
Neville Cardus, observed that seldom had this kind of artistry been experienced
on the concert stage, artistry that enchanted the listener into Debussy's world.
All the soloists were praised for their performances, and Monteux's superb and
unobtrusive mastery of the score kept everything in proportion when a climax
came. The London Symphony Orchestra played Debussy's masterwork with a
truly astonishing range of expression and refinement, especially considering that
the work is not in the regular concert repertoire. Cardus deemed the event "a
night to remember gratefully."

As for the Ravel evening, the uncredited writer in *The Times* of 7 May spoke
first of Ravel, of how there is a wizardry in this composer's makeup, and that one
could say the same of Monteux, whose conducting technique was effortless and
without unnecessary gesture, minutely calculated to release every subtlety of
dynamics, tonal balance, and rhythmic propulsion, and to delineate every aspect
of the score. Monteux's "Danse générale" in *Daphnis* was very different from
Carlo Maria Giulini's frenzy because it came as the climax of the entire work and
not as an isolated section of the concert suite.

In *Shéhérazade* Ginia Davis was found to be excellent in *parlando*, and when her voice opened up she projected a line, like that of a violin, in the overall sound picture. There had been "no concert quite like this for years."

Recordings made by Monteux and the LSO in 1960 were of Beethoven's Second and Fourth Symphonies, plus his overtures *Leonore* No. 3, *Fidelio*, and *King Stephen*. The last, while a decidedly minor work of the master, is nevertheless rollicking good fun and was a special favorite of Monteux's. All these recordings were, for some reason, kept in Decca's vaults for several years and eventually released posthumously, with the exception of *Leonore* No. 3, which has never been issued.

On his eightieth birthday, 4 April 1955, Monteux had conducted the Boston Symphony in an all-Beethoven program for the benefit of the orchestra's pension fund. As 4 April 1960 approached, the orchestra's management asked him what he would like for his eighty-fifth birthday, to which Monteux's reply was a performance of Beethoven's Ninth Symphony. This work had always been very special to him—witness his almost annual season-closing performances of it in San Francisco—and it was certainly the ideal work with which to celebrate another milestone birthday. As reported in Ross Parmenter's interview of Monteux in the 3 April *New York Times*, Monteux specifically requested that there be no party afterward because an eighty-fifth birthday was not an important enough occasion for such a fuss. "They can give me a party on my ninetieth birthday."

The concert was scheduled for 6 April, again for the Boston Symphony's pension fund. His actual birthday was spent rehearsing the orchestra alone in the morning, the four soloists—Eleanor Steber, Freda Gray-Massé, John McCollum, and David Laurent—in the afternoon, the Chorus Pro Musica in the evening. When he appeared at the orchestral rehearsal, dressed in his Maine lumberjack shirt, the members rose in unison, cheered him, and played the first few bars of "Happy Birthday." In spite of the musicians' good intentions, their initial response to Monteux's conducting was a bit sluggish. He stopped them and asked to start over. "I don't want to follow you, so you have to follow me." This remark produced not only laughter, but the desired result. Later Monteux commented, "It's a kind of suggestion. You take the minds of the people in your hands, and they will understand you."

In the interview with Parmenter Monteux repeated that he resented being labeled a "French" conductor, which is why he was happy to be conducting Beethoven on this occasion. "After all, Debussy didn't exist when I was educated [that is, most of the great works by which the composer was known had not yet been written when Monteux was a student]. Neither did Ravel. I was brought up on Haydn, Mozart, and a little Brahms. I have learned the French since. But I'm not a French conductor. I'm just a conductor." He added that the music of Brahms has been the closest to him. "His music is nearer me. It is our rapport."

On 5 April Monteux rested during the day and rehearsed the combined forces in the evening. On the sixth came the concert before a packed Symphony Hall. As the Ninth Symphony is not long enough to comprise an entire program (though it has come to be often so considered), Monteux selected Mozart's delightful "Haffner" Symphony (No. 35) to open the evening.

The lovely performance of the Mozart seemed only to heighten anticipation of what was to come. At the conclusion of the Beethoven, joyful pandemonium reigned for at least five minutes, the audience standing and roaring its approval with deafening shouts of "Bravo." As reported in the 7 April *Christian Science Monitor*, after bows by Monteux and the soloists had been taken, those taking the stage were the chorus master Alfred Nash Patterson, who received his share of accolades; then Henry B. Cabot, president of the orchestra's trustees, who proclaimed the event a once-in-a-lifetime occasion and praised Monteux highly; and then the longtime Monteux pupil and BSO member Harry Ellis Dickson, who presented Monteux with a scroll "for his inspired teaching," inscribed by many of his former Hancock pupils. Dickson also announced that pupils and friends had purchased a television set for Monteux, which had already been delivered to Hancock.

Alan Kayes of RCA Victor then presented Monteux with an album of first pressings of his recordings from San Francisco, Boston, Vienna, and London. (It is this album that contains the still unreleased *Leonore* No. 3.) The last person to appear was Charles Munch, whose embrace of Monteux, to whom he had always been so generous, created further tumult in the hall.

Never one to rest on his laurels, Monteux was back in action the very next day, rehearsing the BSO for its weekend Friday-Saturday concerts, which were to have been conducted by the Hungarian maestro Ferenc Fricsay (1914–1963). When Fricsay became ill Monteux was asked to take over the concerts. He agreed and conducted a program of his own choosing: Beethoven's "Eroica" Symphony, Respighi's *Fountains of Rome*, and Strauss's *Till Eulenspiegel*.

Monteux's summer schedule included his usual visits to Lewisohn Stadium, Robin Hood Dell, and Ravinia, as well as to Tanglewood, where on 31 July he repeated the program of his eighty-fifth birthday concert with the same soloists, but with the Berkshire Festival Chorus. Beethoven's Ninth was a work normally conducted at Tanglewood by Munch, but who better to conduct it this particular year than Monteux.

Jay S. Harrison, in his 1 August review in the *New York Herald Tribune*, summed up the event:

> He [Monteux] gets to the heart of the Ninth, for example, by a process I can only describe as divination. He unfolds each aspect of the score as though he had a direct means of contact with its creator; at any rate, he makes explicit precisely what the music implies. That is ever the root of Pierre Monteux's greatness.

As before, the Ninth was preceded by Mozart's "Haffner" Symphony, in which, according to Harrison, "Each phrase was shaped as though Mr. Monteux had just discovered the right way it should go."

On 23 and 24 April 1960 Monteux was back in Vienna for a program of music atypical for the Vienna Philharmonic:

> Messiaen: *L'ascension*
> Stravinsky: *Symphony of Psalms*
> Debussy: Three Nocturnes
> Stravinsky: Suite from *The Firebird*

The Stravinsky symphony and the third of the Nocturnes included the participation of the chorus of the Wiener Gesellschaft der Musikfreunde (Vienna Society of Friends of Music). As usual, Monteux performed the 1910 *Firebird* Suite with the addition of the Berceuse and Finale from 1919. I attended this concert and can vouch for the fact that the Vienna Philharmonic played throughout with the delicacy and nuances of an ideal French ensemble, the aggressive moments tempered with lightness and clarity.

A letter from Monteux to the management of the Vienna Philharmonic shows that he was unhappy with the program that had been devised, feeling that it lacked substance. He preferred that instead of the Nocturnes and *Firebird*, the second half be devoted to "a big symphony from the repertoire," and he even left the choice of that symphony to the orchestra. By that time the program had been announced and the orchestra did not wish to change it, so Monteux acquiesced. On the dates in question there was no evidence that he was unhappy with the program.

In October 1960 Sir Thomas Beecham was to have conducted his Royal Philharmonic Orchestra on a tour of Germany, but he became ill. In his stead Monteux was engaged, an eighty-five-year-old maestro replacing one of eighty-one. I was nearing the end of my army service in Germany and attended the concert in Stuttgart's Liederhalle. The program consisted of Cherubini's *Anacreon* Overture, Mozart's "Haffner" Symphony, Ravel's *Daphnis et Chloé* Suite No. 2, and Beethoven's "Eroica" Symphony. It was an excellent concert in spite of some imprecise string playing in the Mozart and Beethoven works. The orchestra was frankly not used to Monteux. During the interval I spoke with Monteux and, as a New Yorker, asked him if he would be conducting again at Lewisohn Stadium the following summer. He replied, "Yes, but you know it is so *désagréable* there, and that woman [Minnie Guggenheimer], each year I ask her for more money, hoping she say no, and each year she say yes!"

While Monteux and the RPO were in Wuppertal, he received a telegram from Beecham expressing his appreciation for Monteux's kindness in stepping in to replace him. He stated that the orchestra was equally grateful to him and would long remember and appreciate his gracious gesture. Beecham died the following year. .

In the spring of 1960 the Concertgebouw Orchestra's artistic director, the composer Marius Flothuis, who had succeeded Rudolf Mengelberg, had made plans for Monteux's fall concerts, his first in Amsterdam in five years. Two performances of *Petrushka* were scheduled in November, and Flothuis wished to add a few more in other cities. In response to this request he received a letter from Doris Monteux, dated 28 April 1960, in which she said, "My husband wishes me to tell you that he is absolutely fed up with Petrouchka and prefers to give up the engagement if it is a question of playing it more than twice. . . . I personally feel he should play the things which give him joy at this late date. Of course the decision is up to you."

The records show that in the end Monteux conducted three performances of *Petrushka*, on 30 October and 7 November in Amsterdam and on 5 November in 's Gravenhage. The engagement also included a pair of performances, on 2 and 3 November, of Dvořák's Cello Concerto, with Mstislav Rostropovich as soloist. (In the same letter to Flothuis, Doris had said that the Dvořák work "has only a wonderful adagio to recommend it!!!")

If Monteux was indeed "fed up" with *Petrushka*, it is also possible that he never really liked *The Rite of Spring*. When he was a guest conductor of the Rochester Philharmonic Orchestra in 1958, the Eastman School of Music arranged a session for the students to meet Monteux and ask him questions. Former students who were present recall that there were the inevitable questions about *The Rite*, one of which dealt with his feelings when he first saw the score. "*Sacre bleu!* I thought he was crazy!" And what did he think about Stravinsky and the piece now? "*Sacre bleu!* He is still crazy!" Of course, Monteux liked to respond to questions with remarks that could be considered humorous, but in this case his comments reflected his true feelings.

For the 1960–61 season Monteux was again engaged for two concerts with the LSO, as well as for two with the London Philharmonic, these last preceding the LSO engagement. The first, on 6 April, featured Lili Kraus as soloist in Beethoven's Third Piano Concerto and the orchestra performing Ravel's orchestration of Mussorgsky's *Pictures at an Exhibition*. On 2 May Monteux presented an unusual program of twentieth-century works: Milhaud's *Protée*, Debussy's *Jeux*, Pijper's Third Symphony, and Hindemith's *Mathis der Maler*. Felix Aprahamian in the Sunday *Times* of 7 May thought this "the season's most enterprising programme," for which "the London Philharmonic were rewarded, not with a full Festival Hall, but with the rarer satisfaction of playing unhackneyed music under a great conductor, and with the enthusiastic acclaim of those privileged to hear it." He concluded that Monteux's "sparing gestures " succeeded in

> coordinating the *pointilliste* flecks of Debussy's "Jeux" into a continuum of marvellous sound, as lithe and flexible as the imagined tennis-players of its scenario. With equal mastery they welded the more solid materials of Hindemith's "Mathis der Maler" into an imposing edifice which reaffirmed its position among the finest symphonies of the thirties. A memorable concert.

If the hall was not full, it was because London concertgoers, like their counterparts in other cities, tend to shy away from programs devoted to relatively unfamiliar music, no matter who is performing it.

"A night to remember gratefully"; "no concert quite like this for years"; "a memorable concert"—these are just a few of the typical critical summations that Monteux's concerts would receive from the London press. A love affair had been established that also included the public and the members of the orchestra.

If Monteux had intended to rest a bit after the LPO concert, his plans were dramatically altered when he agreed to substitute, on short notice, for an indisposed Josef Krips, who had made his peace with the LSO and was scheduled for a concert on 5 May. Krips had planned a program of Wagner and Bruckner, the Wagner portion of which was retained by Monteux—excerpts from *The Flying Dutchman*, *Die Walküre*, and *Götterdämmerung* with the great Canadian-born bass-baritone George London as soloist. The Bruckner work was the Seventh Symphony, which Monteux had conducted in San Francisco years before but was not part of his regular repertory. He said he could have conducted it, but would have had to learn it all over again, and there just was no time. In its place he conducted one of his specialties, the *Symphonie fantastique*.

Noël Goodwin, writing in the *Express* the next day, commented that age had caused Monteux to attenuate some of the more vivid moments in the *Symphonie fantastique*, but he still found greater detail and beauty in the music than did many conductors fifty years his junior—with a complete absence of showmanship and entirely from memory.

Monteux's two scheduled concerts were on 19 and 22 May, and Berlioz figured mightily on the latter date with a complete performance of his dramatic symphony *Romeo and Juliet*. Rarely heard in its entirety at that time, and even today for that matter, this performance aroused great interest in London. Again Monteux had requested a specific soloist, this time the mezzo-soprano Freda Gray-Massé. There was little or no resistance to engaging her, and the other soloists were Camille Maurane and André Vessières, both of whom had participated in *Pelléas* the year before. The BBC Chorus and Choral Society also took part.

The unnamed *Times* critic wrote, "It would be sad indeed if one of the record companies did not capture so fine an interpretation for us." Soon after, one of the record companies did: Monteux and his forces recorded the score for Westminster Records, but with different soloists. Recently reissued on CD by Deutsche Grammophon, Monteux's superior interpretation is marred by the peculiarity of the recording, in which harps are made to sound louder than the full orchestra and the miking of the strings tends to make them sound like a chamber orchestra. (These comments apply to the original Westminster release. The Deutsche Grammophon reissue ameliorates the technical shortcomings somewhat.)

Sir Neville Marriner, at that time principal second violin of the LSO, has recalled that, after the *Romeo and Juliet* performance, Doris Monteux asked her husband, "Darling, were you thinking of me during the love music?" He responded, "No, Eleanor Roosevelt!"

Following these concerts the orchestra embarked on a brief tour, the high point of which was three performances in Vienna during the prestigious Wiener Festwochen (Vienna Festival Weeks). The Viennese authorities had been reluctant to engage the LSO because, following the Krips period, its reputation in Europe had been that of a rather desultory ensemble. However, Ernest Fleischmann had a few cards up his sleeve. According to Maurice Pearton in *The LSO at Seventy*, Fleischmann contacted the Festwochen director and asked, "If I produce for you Stokowski, Monteux, and Solti, will you take us?" The answer was a resounding yes (Pearton 1974, 161).

Monteux's LSO concert in Vienna was on 4 June 1961. The program was:

> Cherubini: Overture to *Anacreon*
> Berlioz: Orchestral Excerpts from *Romeo and Juliet*
> Debussy: "Gigues" and "Rondes de printemps" from *Images*
> Elgar: *Enigma Variations*

Vienna's *Die Presse* stated the next day that Monteux's appearance, that of a master conductor at the head of the London Symphony Orchestra, produced a high degree of intonation and technical perfection that was greeted by storms of applause.

After the concert, the Monteuxs and Ernest Fleischmann returned to Monteux's hotel, the Imperial, for a late supper. In the room next to theirs another late supper was in progress, one in which the principals were the U.S. president, John F. Kennedy, and the Soviet premier, Nikita Krushchev, who were in the midst of some rather unproductive meetings.

According to Fleischmann, in a television interview broadcast after Monteux's death, Monteux was in great good spirits and asked, "Is there anything, *anything*, that I can do for this orchestra, because I love them so much?"

Fleischmann replied, "Obviously there is something, but I hesitate to say. We'd love you to become our principal conductor, but obviously you can't accept that." The eighty-six-year-old Monteux responded, "I said I would do anything, but there is one condition: I want a twenty-five-year contract with a twenty-five-year option."

Later, upon receiving a letter from Fleischmann officially inviting him to become principal conductor of the London Symphony Orchestra under the terms specified above, Monteux, by now back in America, replied by cable, "Tell them I promise to be a good father to my children." In his letter, dated 16 June 1961, Fleischmann had explained that it was not the policy of the LSO to have a principal conductor (and they had not had one since Krips's departure in 1954), but that each member of the orchestra had such great admiration and affection for him that they were anxious to change this policy. The official announcement was

made in August 1961, when Monteux was in the midst of teaching his conducting class in Hancock. Profuse congratulations from the students brought forth
the comment from Monteux, "That means I conduct five concerts a year instead
of four." Among the many congratulatory messages that Monteux received was
the following from Erich Leinsdorf, then music consultant at the Metropolitan
Opera, whose own new position as music director of the Boston Symphony
Orchestra had recently been announced:

It is delightful news that you have accepted the invitation from the London
Symphony Orchestra. Not that you need the distinction because you are
bringing more distinction to them than any orchestra can bring to you.
Delightful because it proves what I and your many admirers can see clearly:
that you feel wonderfully and that you will be active for the greater glory
of music for many years to come.

CHAPTER 28

Principal Conductor

W hen Monteux said "five concerts instead of four" he was joking, but principal conductors of British orchestras really do not appear much more often than that during a season, though they do tend to conduct the orchestras' tours. Actually, he led a few more than five, and his first concert as principal conductor of the LSO was Sunday, 9 December 1961, a benefit for the orchestra's benevolent fund. As such, a popular program was called for:

> Wagner: Prelude to *Die Meistersinger*
> Bizet: *Carmen* Suite No. 1
> Ravel: *Pavane pour une infante défunte*
> Ravel: *Rapsodie espagnole*
> Rimsky-Korsakov: *Scheherazade*

Upon receiving his schedule for the season, Monteux wrote Fleischmann on 19 February 1962:

I have my schedule for our rehearsals and concerts coming now, and I am very upset to see that I should have a rehearsal the morning of each concert!! The orchestra must realize that it is impossible for me, for example, to play the Damnation of Faust twice in the same day!! The same thing for Heldenleben and Daphnis!! If it is necessary to have two sessions in one day it should not be the day of the concert. So I am writing today so you will have time to make these changes. No rehearsal the day of any concert!!

This letter points up a fact of life of London orchestras. Because they are so dependent on recording activity, it is not uncommon for them to have a general rehearsal in the morning, a recording in the afternoon, and a concert at night. The LSO valued its work with Monteux, so changes were made in the rehearsal schedule to accommodate him, even though it may have meant some loss of income for the orchestra.

On 8 March 1962 there was a complete performance of *The Damnation of Faust*, then a rarity for London, with the LSO Chorus and soloists Régine Crespin, André Turp, Michel Roux, and John Shirley-Quirk. This marvelous performance, broadcast live by the BBC and taped by them, has been issued on CD by the BBC. There is very little in it that would warrant retakes, were it a studio recording.

On 22 March 1962 Monteux and the LSO gave a blockbuster of a program if ever there was one: Richard Strauss's *Ein Heldenleben* and the complete *Daphnis et Chloé*, with the LSO Chorus in the latter. The critics noted Monteux's feat of conducting the entire program from memory; they also relegated Strauss's massive score, as a composition, to second place.

Monteux returned to Amsterdam for concerts in the Holland Festival between 13 May and 7 June 1962. Featured were two Beethoven-Brahms programs, Leon Fleisher playing the Brahms Piano Concerto No. 1 on 13 and 14 May, and the Concerto No. 2 on 20 and 22 May, with Brahms's *Tragic Overture* and Beethoven's Sixth and Eighth Symphonies filling out the programs. The *Symphonie fantastique* and the Pijper Third Symphony were also heard in the later concerts.

Although by the later years of his life and career Monteux could play virtually anything he wished, he was consolidating his repertoire; the same works appear repeatedly on his programs. Perhaps this was due to his willingness to accommodate the requests he continually received to play certain favorite pieces with which he was associated, but it can just as likely be attributed to Doris Monteux's feeling that "he should play the things which give him joy." In this respect, he was very similar to Toscanini and Bruno Walter, who, in their last years, continued to play their basic core repertoire at the expense of the many works they had performed previously and now abandoned. Of the great conductors, only Stokowski and Koussevitzky continued to play a widely varied repertoire, including much new music, until the end of their days.

The centennial of Debussy's birth was celebrated on 10 June 1962 with a program of *Ibéria*; the Clarinet Rhapsody, played by Gervase de Peyer, principal clarinetist of the LSO; the Three Nocturnes; the *Danses: sacrée et profane*, with the principal harpist, Ossian Ellis; and *La mer*. Writing the next day in the *Telegraph*, Martin Cooper stated that Monteux was the most authentic of all living conductors of this music and the orchestra played for him as if each member were held captive by his extraordinary insight and unpretentious authority. Correspondence from Westminster Records shows that there were plans to record *La mer*, the Nocturnes, and the Clarinet Rhapsody, but these did not materialize. Monteux and the LSO repeated the Debussy program in Paris on 22 June at the Théâtre des Champs-Élysées and a portion of it the next day in the Festival de Strasbourg, with Beethoven's *Fidelio* Overture and Elgar's *Enigma Variations*.

The several London orchestras are all, in fact, relative newcomers in comparison with those in what are often referred to as "the provinces." Oldest of these is the Royal Liverpool Philharmonic Orchestra, the history of which dates back to 1840. On 7 November 1962 it became a new addition to the total of orchestras he had conducted when Monteux led that ensemble in a program at the Royal Festival Hall, with Yehudi Menuhin the soloist in the Brahms Violin Concerto. This was preceded by Wagner's Overture to *The Flying Dutchman* and Beethoven's Fourth Symphony. On 13 November he conducted the orchestra in its home city, without Menuhin but with works by Franck and Strauss instead.

In the fall of 1962 Monteux conducted concerts in Stockholm on 31 October and 1 and 4 November, and in Bergen, Norway, on 18 November. The programs contained a standard assortment of pieces by Beethoven, Brahms, Debussy, Rossini, Strauss, and Vaughan Williams. A photograph taken in Bergen shows the Monteuxs surrounded by several of his pupils, who either traveled with him or simply appeared at the appropriate location on the appropriate day. His pupils were very loyal to him.

One of the most gifted pupils at L'École Monteux in the late 1950s and early 1960s was David Zinman. Once the principal conductorship of the LSO was announced, Monteux invited Zinman to become his assistant conductor and travel with him and Doris to London, Amsterdam, and other cities. In this capacity Zinman would attend all the rehearsals and concerts, have private lessons with Monteux when convenient, and even from time to time conduct one or two rehearsals for Monteux so he could save his strength, having become physically weakened through age and illness. If necessary, he was expected to be ready to deputize for his teacher in an emergency.

Zinman has told of one occasion when he almost did stand in for Monteux. It was the evening of 13 December 1962; Monteux was conducting a Beethoven and Strauss concert at the Royal Festival Hall, and Zinman was at home in bed with the flu. At about 8:20 P.M. the phone rang. Zinman's wife, Leslie, answered; it was Ernest Fleischmann. "You'd better tell David to get down here right away," he said. Monteux had collapsed shortly after beginning the second movement of Beethoven's Fifth Symphony.

Zinman dragged himself out of bed and got dressed as quickly as possible, which is not very quickly when one is half dazed with the flu. Unable to find a taxi, he eventually arrived by tube at Festival Hall, several miles from his flat. When he entered the backstage area he was astonished to hear the finale of Beethoven's Fifth in full sway, with Monteux on the podium. He had been carried offstage by several orchestra members, attended to by three doctors, revived, and, after a few minutes' rest, had returned unaided to the podium and begun the second movement again. There was some discussion to the effect that Zinman should perhaps conduct one of the works on the second half, such as Salome's Dance, so as to relieve Monteux a bit. Afterward Zinman, wandering about the backstage area, came upon one of the LSO's principal players, who was not needed in the Beethoven half of the program but would take part in the Strauss. The player gestured angrily toward the stage and exclaimed, "That man out there! Why doesn't he just quit? He won't be happy unless he dies on stage! Meanwhile, look what he's putting us through!"

Apparently conducting the rest of Beethoven's Fifth had revivified Monteux, who now felt strong enough to complete the concert—thus no Salome's Dance, or anything else, for Zinman that night. David Cairns of *The Times* (14 December) wrote of the performance of *Don Juan* that it was "unforgettably played. . . . Monteux simply played it as a brilliant and fascinating piece of music, letting it surge forward with electric vitality. It was glittering virtuoso playing which never forgot to be, first and last, musical." (This from an eighty-seven-year-old man who had fainted a few minutes before.) According to another report, at the end of the concert Doris Monteux spoke to the audience from the side of the stage, saying, "Ladies and gentlemen, I want you to know that my husband is suffering from an attack of gastric flu—and I gave it to him."

Monteux conducted Beethoven's Ninth Symphony on two occasions with the LSO, 14 June 1962 and 6 April 1963, but it was in recording sessions independent of either performance that Westminster Records recorded Monteux's interpretation, with the London Bach Choir and the soloists Elizabeth Söderström, Regina Resnik, Jon Vickers, and David Ward, a version reissued in 2001 by Deutsche Grammophon. Monteux's interpretation is very straightforward and faithful to the score; there is nothing "philosophical" about it, yet it is both exciting and sensitive.

It is worth repeating that Monteux never indulged in obvious retouching of Beethoven's orchestration or that of other composers. The original release of the Ninth Symphony included a sequence of rehearsal excerpts in which, during the Scherzo, the French horns can be heard adding their sonority to a passage Beethoven wrote only for the woodwinds. This revision, followed by many conductors, was originated by the Austrian Felix Weingartner (1863–1942), who was the first to record all the Beethoven symphonies and who published a treatise on their interpretation. In the rehearsal, when Monteux hears the horns in that passage, he stops the orchestra and exclaims quite firmly, "That is not Beethoven. That is Weingartner, and I don't like it at all!" (He used to tell his students that the Ninth's Adagio movement, with its prominent first-violin passages in the variations, was a "concerto for the first violins.")

The operative word in the first sentence of the preceding paragraph is "obvious." Henry Greenwood, the LSO's librarian at the time, has recalled that Monteux often asked him to insert subtle dynamic markings and instrumental additions in the orchestral parts so as to strengthen a musical line and allow an instrumental voice to be heard that might otherwise remain obscured. These changes were such as to be unnoticeable to the listeners, yet they succeeded in clarifying textures. (In truth, they are simply the type of markings any practical and responsible conductor would insert.)

In the spring of 1963 the LSO took off for a tour of Japan that included five concerts in the Osaka International Festival. Monteux conducted three of them, Antal Doráti and Georg Solti one each. Monteux opened the festival on 13 April with the *Meistersinger* Prelude, *Enigma Variations*, and Sibelius Second Symphony, continuing on 15 April with Beethoven's *Coriolan* Overture and Eighth Symphony and the Second Symphony of Brahms, and concluding on 19 April with Tchaikovsky's *Romeo and Juliet*, Strauss's *Don Juan*, and Schubert's "Great" C major Symphony. The Japanese, known for their love of Western classical music, erupted in tremendous ovations for the orchestra and all the conductors, but especially for Monteux. Reviewing the opening concert in the *Asahi Evening News* of 14 April, Klaus Pringsheim repeated what many had written before him when he spoke of Monteux's subtle blending of the orchestral choirs, the subtlety of his dynamic shadings, and the equilibrium of conceptions—nothing exaggerated, everything unfolding naturally—all backed by his great authority and knowledge. He thought Monteux was little short of a miracle. Pringsheim's colleague, Heuwell Tircuit, reviewed Monteux's next two concerts with similar praise and reported that never in his six and a half years in Japan had he seen an audience so reluctant to leave the hall. Tircuit wrote that he was forced to ask himself whether Monteux *ever* gave a bad performance.

The most extraordinary concert of Monteux's late years took place in London on 29 May 1963. This was a performance on the fiftieth anniversary to the day of the premiere of *The Rite of Spring*, the work that had changed twentieth-century music and brought Monteux his first great *réclame*. For the occasion the LSO booked the Royal Albert Hall rather than its normal venue, the Royal Festival Hall, to accommodate the larger audience anticipated for such a gala event, which was to be in aid of the London Symphony Orchestra Trust. To top it all off, Stravinsky would be there. On the first part of the concert, attended by an audience of at least six thousand, Monteux conducted Wagner's Prelude to *Die Meistersinger* and Brahms's Piano Concerto No. 2, with Van Cliburn as soloist. Cliburn had skyrocketed to world attention five years before as the winner of the first Tchaikovsky International Piano Competition in Moscow, an outcome that enthralled and galvanized the United States at the height of the cold war. On returning to New York, Cliburn was given a ticker-tape parade on Broadway. Cliburn and Monteux together made an amusing sight, the one six-feet-four and thin as a rail, the other five-feet-five and plump, though less so than in former years.

While Cliburn was treated respectfully by the press, interest focused on Monteux and Stravinsky. The newspapers reported that there was no violence this time, merely six thousand people cheering their heads off. Monteux conducted *The Rite* from memory, and without exception the critics of the many London papers hailed the performance as masterful, the work not as shocking as it once was but still a masterpiece. For Donald Mitchell in *The Daily Telegraph* the next day, Monteux's extraordinary ear was responsible for the revelation of many musical subtleties. He felt that few conductors could perform the mysterious introduction to Part II with such clarity. Finally, in no way did Monteux subject the piece to a display of his own conducting brilliance; he was, in the best sense, completely without showmanship.

In the midst of the fifteen-minute ovation that followed the final crashing chord, Monteux accepted the applause (to which the orchestra members contributed wildly), left the stage, and proceeded to wend his way to the box in which Stravinsky sat. The two octegenarians, once "partners in crime," embraced to further eruptions from the audience. In its own way, this concert was as historic an occasion as the original event. Said Percy Cater in the 30 May *Daily Mail*, "In a long experience of London's music, I do not recall a scene to surpass this."

Stravinsky actually did not arrive at the Albert Hall until about halfway through the performance of *The Rite*. At that time the circular hall was notorious for its peculiar acoustics (since remedied) whereby, depending on where one sat, one would hear not excessive reverberation but an actual echo. In a work such as *The Rite*, with its many rhythmic intricacies, such a situation could prove disastrous. That it did not was a tribute to Monteux's and the orchestra's powers of concentration. Nevertheless, according to Robert Craft, "we arrive at Albert Hall during the *Danse de la terre* to find half of the orchestra following Monteux's actual beat and half what they, and probably *le maître*, know the beat should be" (Stravinsky and Craft 1966, 253). Craft also writes that in the end, Stravinsky was not at all moved by the significance of the occasion. "On the contrary, it has incited him to loud criticism, and only late at night as we are re-entering the hotel does he cool off about the wrong *tempi* long enough to call *le maître* a '*très brave homme*'." Years earlier Stravinsky had stated, "Let me say here that Monteux, almost alone among conductors, never cheapened *The Rite* or looked for his own glory in it, and that he continued to play it all his life with the greatest fidelity" (Stravinsky and Craft 2002, 92).

In mid-October 1963 Monteux was in Liverpool for a concert on the fifteenth with that city's Philharmonic Orchestra. The ever-popular (with Monteux) *Euryanthe* Overture, Brahms's Fourth Symphony, *L'après-midi*, and *La mer* made up the program. One of Monteux's American conducting pupils, John Covelli, who was with him at the time, remembers Monteux saying, "I don't want to die in Liverpool." (This remark was surely not meant to be a disparagement of Liverpool. Rather is it an indication that Monteux, at this stage of his life, was feeling vulnerable, and that he did not think Liverpool an appropriate place for him to die, as opposed to, say, Boston, London, Paris, or Hancock.)

On 30 and 31 October 1963 Monteux appeared in Manchester at the head of the Hallé Orchestra, founded in 1858 by Charles Hallé, who, in the tradition of Parisian orchestras, named it after himself. The ensemble has had a distinguished history, especially in the mid-twentieth century: from 1920 to 1933 its conductor was Sir Hamilton Harty (of Handel-Harty fame—Harty was noted for his updated reorchestrations of works of Handel, such as the *Water Music* and the *Royal Fireworks Music)*, from 1933 to 1943 Sir Thomas Beecham and Sir Malcolm Sargent often conducted it, and from 1943 until his death in 1970 Sir John Barbirolli was in charge.

Monteux's program featured the Brahms First Symphony and also included his beloved *King Stephen* Overture by Beethoven, excerpts from Fauré's incidental music to *Pelléas et Mélisande*, and Hindemith's *Nobilissima visione*. Writing in *The Guardian* of 1 November, Michael Kennedy stated that Mancunians had heard Barbirolli and Boult at their best, and now it was Monteux's turn to take Manchester by storm. In a city that had heard many great Brahms performances in the past two decades, Monteux conducted one of the greatest of Brahms's First Symphony. He continued that Monteux, at age eighty-eight, did not attempt to find new meaning in the music. Rather, "he gave us the music, fresh as on the day it was written." At the end, he "looked quite capable of giving the whole of *Rite of Spring* as an encore."

The Royal Philharmonic Society was founded in London in 1813, although the "Royal" prefix was not appended until 1912. The society's stated purpose is to encourage symphonic and solo instrumental concerts, and it presents its own annual series of concerts in which various British orchestras participate independently of their own series. From time to time the Gold Medal of the Royal Philharmonic Society is presented to musicians deemed worthy of receiving it. On 5 December 1963 it was presented to Pierre Monteux, and that evening he conducted the LSO in a program of Beethoven's "Pastorale" Symphony, the three orchestral excerpts from *La damnation de Faust*, and the Third Symphony of Brahms. At the concert's conclusion Sir Adrian Boult, then the dean of British conductors and himself a recipient of the honor, entered the stage along with Monteux and presented him with the medal. As reported by Paul Bowen in the 6 December *New Daily*, Sir Adrian, in a brief speech, referred to Monteux as "not just a great conductor of French music, but a great conductor, one of the greatest living, and that is all there is to it!" Monteux replied by saying he was "very moved, very touched, very honored, grateful and happy."

In his autobiography, *My Own Trumpet*, Boult recalled the occasion:

That evening we had an alarming moment as we left the platform after the presentation. Mr. Monteux gave two little groans as we walked down the passage, and I suddenly found my arms full of violins and bows. The orchestra had recognized the signs. Their beloved chief was fainting. Some of them supported him to the couch in the conductor's room, and then took their fiddles again and left him to Mrs. Monteux. I was afraid that I had spoken too long with my presentation; he had refused the chair I had offered him and had insisted on standing throughout. My wife hurried to the hotel next morning to see Mrs. Monteux, who said that he fainted on the slightest provocation. A day or two earlier . . . she had fainted, and on seeing this he followed suit and there was a fainting duet on the bedroom floor. No indeed, he was now quite well, sitting up in bed eating a hearty breakfast and playing with his Medal. (Boult 1973, 169)

For the concert three days later, on 8 December, Monteux felt it was time to present his pupil David Zinman to the London public. Monteux conducted Berlioz's *Benvenuto Cellini* Overture, Rimsky-Korsakov's *Scheherazade,* and Ravel's *Alborada del gracioso* and graciously allowed Zinman to close the program with the two suites from *Daphnis et Chloé.* Referring to Zinman the next day, Noël Goodwin in the *Express*

> was impressed and immensely exhilarated by the performance. The newcomer showed a keen ear for subtlety of orchestral colour and a firm sense of rhythm. He had the orchestra playing splendidly for him. He is a conductor of evident talent, and I should imagine that we shall soon be hearing him give a full-scale concert on his own.

Zinman has since had a distinguished career that has encompassed the direction of the Netherlands Chamber Orchestra, the Rotterdam Philharmonic Orchestra, the Rochester Philharmonic Orchestra, the Baltimore Symphony Orchestra, and, at the time of this writing, the Zurich Tonhalle Orchestra. He is also music director of Colorado's Aspen Music Festival and has been a guest conductor of most of the world's leading orchestras.

In London Monteux gave an interview that was widely distributed through the press services, in which he was asked for his opinion of various twentieth-century composers, and which ones would survive musically. Here he does not appear to have been a particularly accurate forecaster:

> I don't see anyone, except perhaps Stravinsky—some works of his. Prokofiev: I don't think so. Shostakovich: No. Berg: He will be finished in ten years. Hindemith: No inspiration. He will not live. Bartók: I give him ten years. Mahler: He will not live. He's not a creator. He's an imitator.

Concerning modern music in general, Monteux commented, "I see how it has been written. I see what is in the interior of the works of all these composers. They have just a little inspiration in one bar of music and then they develop it. They have technique and technique and technique—and that's not interesting."

Finally, he added, "Probably one or two works of Debussy and of Ravel will live. But when I play their works so many times, I see how they worked it. You should not see the work when you hear it."

During Monteux's principal conductorship he continued to record with the LSO, now mostly for the Philips label. This series began in June 1962 with what is perhaps the finest of all his recordings with that orchestra, excerpts from Tchaikovsky's *Swan Lake* (originally planned with the Concertgebouw Orchestra), a performance to make one wish he had recorded the complete ballet. In November of the same year came Monteux's fourth recording of the Second Symphony of Brahms, the first of what was hoped would finally be his cycle of the four symphonies, but it was not to be. This version, again with the first-movement repeat, is the most beautiful of the four recordings, although those from San Francisco, if less polished, have a bit more thrust. Still, one would not want to be without Monteux's final thoughts on this glorious work. The same sessions also produced recordings of the two Brahms overtures, the *Tragic* magnificent in its feeling of inevitability, the *Academic Festival* sturdy but exciting and majestic.

May 1963 brought wonderful Debussy recordings, the three *Images* and the Symphonic Fragments from *The Martyrdom of St. Sebastian*; this last was a comparative rarity, certainly at that time, and Monteux's performance sensitively captured its austere beauty. That month the LSO toured Europe, and on 31 May Monteux conducted a concert in the Vienna Festival, the same event that two years previously had brought about his engagement as principal conductor. Now an all-Tchaikovsky program was given: *Romeo and Juliet*, the Piano Concerto No. 1 with John Ogdon as soloist, and the Symphony No. 5. Recorded by Austrian Radio, the entire concert was issued in 1994 on the Vanguard label to unanimous critical acclaim the world over. In February 1964 came an exquisite version of Ravel's complete *Mother Goose* ballet music, along with his *Boléro* and *La valse*. The *Boléro* is good but not overpowering, *La valse* elegant but not as exciting as San Francisco, though here the trumpet player gets it right.

During this same period Monteux made two recordings in Amsterdam with the Concertgebouw Orchestra, Beethoven's "Eroica" Symphony in July 1962 and Schubert's "Unfinished" Symphony in May 1963. The "Eroica" is a vast improvement over the previous Vienna Philharmonic recording. One could call it a good, solid performance, though not a compelling one, while the "Unfinished," its first-movement repeat observed, is very beautiful, with nicely contrasting tempos. Monteux felt that if one accurately observed the tempo markings of the two movements, Allegro moderato and Andante con moto, they were very close to the same. Therefore, his practice, which he recommended to his students, was to play the first movement slightly faster than indicated, the second movement slightly slower to arrive at some contrast of pacing. The initial Philips LP release of the "Eroica" contained a brief rehearsal sequence from the opening of the Funeral March, in which we can hear that Monteux was extremely fastidious in terms of rhythmic detail.

Monteux's final LSO recordings, also in early 1964, were for the Decca label, a collaboration with his son Claude, who is the flute soloist in Bach's Suite No. 2, Mozart's Concerto No. 2, and the Dance of the Blessed Spirits from Gluck's *Orfeo ed Euridice*. This recording, not yet issued on CD, though rather heavy in the bass and not one that would please today's purists, who would surely object to the size of the forces employed and the constant use of vibrato, nevertheless displays great affection for the music.

CHAPTER 29

The Final Year

Monteux made his last appearances in Amsterdam in 1963, beginning with two concerts with the Concertgebouw Orchestra in the Holland Festival, 29 June and 1 July. What was unusual about these concerts is that they were all-Wagner programs. Monteux had conducted such programs in his San Francisco days and at Tanglewood, but they were rare in his career, primarily because concert managements had a prejudice against French conductors performing Wagner (even though Wagner is very popular in France and French conductors are well versed in his music). But by this time he could play just about anything he wanted, and he had little trouble persuading the Holland Festival management to let him do a couple of concerts of one of his favorite composers. What is interesting, however, is his reason for suggesting this programming. At the time Birgit Nilsson had recently begun her international career as the greatest Wagnerian soprano of the day; Monteux had heard about her but had not actually heard her, and he wanted to work with her and hear her for himself. Thrilling performances of Isolde's "Liebestod" and Brünnhilde's Immolation Scene were the result. If these have not yet been issued by one of the historical performance companies, they certainly should be.

On 23 September Monteux opened the LSO's season with a concert celebrating the orchestra's sixtieth year, for which he programmed what appeared to be an appropriate work, Vaughan Williams's *London Symphony*. Monteux had played the work many years before when he was the conductor of the Boston Symphony. In rereading the score now, some months before the London performance, he had misgivings about it; it seemed dated to him, and he wrote to Fleischmann expressing his dissatisfaction with it, saying he would prefer to offer another work. Fleischmann replied that the program had already been announced and discouraged Monteux from changing it. Monteux reluctantly agreed to retain the symphony, which even the London critics felt was out of place on such a gala program. It was generally thought that Elgar was much better at evoking Edwardian London. Nevertheless, Monteux was praised for his performance.

On the same program with the Vaughan Williams symphony, Isaac Stern was the soloist in the Sibelius Violin Concerto. Two days later, on 26 September, Monteux, Stern and the LSO were joined by the cellist Leonard Rose for a performance of the Brahms Double Concerto, after which Rose and the LSO's principal violist Simon Streatfeild, were heard in Richard Strauss's *Don Quixote*. The *Times* critic the next day was most enthusiastic about the latter, calling it one of those rare occasions when everyone concerned not only gave of his best but seemed of one mind. Rose was praised for his ravishing tone and the element of pathos he brought to "Don Quixote's Vigil."

The great Spanish cellist and conductor Pablo Casals (1876–1973) was in London at that time to conduct a performance of his oratorio *El pesebre* (The Manger) with the London Philharmonic Orchestra. Monteux and Casals had known each other for many, many years; it seems that all the great musicians of the first half of the twentieth century knew each other. Leonard Rose was instrumental, along with Isaac Stern and their trio partner Eugene Istomin, in arranging a late-night dinner for Casals and his young wife Marta at the Westbury Hotel following the performance of *Don Quixote*, which Casals had not attended. The dinner was actually intended as a surprise meeting of Casals and Monteux, who had not seen each other for quite some time. It was a great success; to the delight of their hosts, the two octogenarians reminisced about music and musicians and their own experiences far into the early hours of the morning.

Meanwhile, not to be outdone by San Francisco and Hancock, the London Fire Brigade inducted Pierre Monteux as a member, gave him a helmet, lined him up with several dozen firemen, and staged a drill for him. (He was not, however, made a fire chief.)

Later in the fall of 1963 Monteux directed five Concertgebouw concerts between 20 and 25 November. His soloist on the twentieth and twenty-first was Victoria de los Angeles, who sang an aria from Mozart's *Idomeneo* and Ravel's *Shéhérazade*, the latter preserved on the same Audio Classics and Music and Arts CDs that contain the 1955 *Daphnis et Chloé*. It remains Monteux's only available performance of this most gorgeous and sensitive of Ravel's works, which de los Angeles delivered magnificently with beautiful support from Monteux and the orchestra.

No concert was scheduled for 22 November 1963. Doris had given David Zinman a ticket for a performance that evening of Verdi's *Otello* by the Netherlands Opera. During the first intermission, as he wandered about, he noticed a group of people clustered at one end of the lobby and speaking animatedly in heavily accented English. Through the general intermission din in the lobby he could make out the words "Dallas" and "two shots." A red-faced man told him that someone had tried to kill President Kennedy, but there was as yet no definite news.

The bell rang signaling the imminent start of Act II, during which Zinman found it difficult to concentrate on the opera. By the second intermission the awful news had been confirmed: President John F. Kennedy had been assassinated in Dallas. Zinman rushed to his hotel across the street, where the lobby was filled with people watching the news reports on television. Once in his room he tried to use the phone, but all the lines were busy. Soon, however, his phone rang. It was Doris Monteux. Had he heard the news? Maître was very upset—he had loved Kennedy so. Doris then proceeded to tell David that Pierre wished to perform the "Eroica" Funeral March as a memorial to open the next day's concert, which would be in The Hague, and that David should be prepared to rehearse it with the orchestra the next morning.

The Concertgebouw Orchestra did not have a rehearsal scheduled for the morning of 23 November, but they assembled for that purpose in tribute to President Kennedy and to Monteux. Zinman was introduced to the orchestra and, as the manager had already done, the concertmaster Herman Krebbers announced, on behalf of the orchestra, "We wish to extend to you our deepest sympathy on the death of your president." Zinman could see on the solemn faces of the orchestra members not only their feeling about the current tragedy, but a reflection of all they and their country had been through during World War II.

Zinman expressed to the orchestra Monteux's appreciation for their having come in that morning. Then the rehearsal began, the first time Zinman had stood before the Concertgebouw Orchestra. As it progressed, he thought of all the points Monteux had made about that movement in his lessons in Hancock, how it should not drag, that it was a French march (Napoleon was French, after all), how the maggiore section represents all the good things the hero has done in his life, how the fugato expresses the onset and accumulation of apocalyptic tragedy, the trumpet calls represent the Last Judgment, and in the coda the family weeps alone. Zinman did not stop for corrections; the music said enough.

Monteux was very quiet on the drive to The Hague, while Doris was commenting on all the news that had arrived since Kennedy's death, about Lee Harvey Oswald and poor Jacqueline Kennedy and what she was going through. She and Pierre had spent the afternoon praying for Kennedy's soul. "It's up to us Catholics to make sure he gets to heaven, right, Pierre?" she said. Monteux sighed and said nothing.

At the concert the orchestra's artistic director, Marius Flothuis, announced the change of program and asked the audience to rise for a moment of silence in memory of President Kennedy. According to Zinman, the concert went well, with Monteux conducting the Beethoven "with an intensity and depth of feeling appropriate to the circumstances." At the end of the concert he was drained, and it was clear to Zinman that though Monteux was deeply disturbed by the assassination, he was resigned to it "as just another of the countless cataclysms that disturb the rhythm of his life as his own days speedily drain away."

Monteux's final appearances with the Concertgebouw Orchestra were on 24 and 25 November, when he presented Berlioz's *Harold in Italy* and Brahms's First Symphony. In the Berlioz the orchestra's principal violist, Klaas Boon, was the soloist. Both of these renditions have been available on records, the Berlioz in a Past Masters LP set that also includes performances by the orchestra under Mengelberg, van Beinum, Klemperer, and Paul van Kempen, while the Brahms is in a Monteux Concertgebouw CD set issued by Tahra Records. (Monteux was a great interpreter of the Brahms First Symphony, and one of his finest renditions was the performance at Tanglewood in 1963. If the Boston Symphony ever issues recordings from Tanglewood, I hope Monteux's Brahms No. 1 will be among them.)

Monteux closed 1963 with a pair of concerts in Boston. Even though Charles Munch was no longer the Boston Symphony's music director, his successor, Erich Leinsdorf, was also a great admirer of Monteux and was happy to continue what had become the tradition of inviting Maître as a guest each year. For the concerts of 20 and 21 December, Monteux directed the following program:

> Vaughan Williams: *Fantasia on a Theme of Thomas Tallis*
> Beethoven: Symphony No. 4 in B-flat major
> Sibelius: *The Swan of Tuonela*
> Elgar: *Enigma Variations*

The choice of the Sibelius was undoubtedly an act of homage to Louis Speyer, the Boston Symphony's longtime English horn player (the instrument Sibelius uses to represent the swan), who would be retiring at the end of the season. He had enjoyed a long association with Monteux dating back to the premiere of *The Rite of Spring* in Paris in 1913. Also notable—and either this is a pure coincidence or Monteux realized that these were likely to be his last performances with the Boston Symphony—is that Beethoven's Fourth Symphony had been included on the program for his return to the BSO in 1951.

The Boston Symphony has included Monteux's performance of the Vaughan Williams piece in its set of historic broadcast performances commemorating the centennial of Symphony Hall. This may be the fastest rendition on record of this basically slow-moving piece, the normal playing time of which is about fifteen minutes: Monteux gets through it in a little over twelve. There is something about this piece that enables it to be effective at a wide variety of tempos, from Monteux's to Fritz Reiner's, at about nineteen minutes in a Chicago Symphony broadcast recording. Monteux imparts a bit more urgency to it than most conductors, and it still sounds beautiful.

Concurrent with this engagement Monteux made what proved to be his final recording in the United States, though it was not with the BSO. At the time, the orchestra's associate principal trumpet player (soon to become principal) was Armando Ghitalla (1925–2001). Long an admirer of Monteux, who returned the feeling, the two had discussed for several years the idea of recording together the Trumpet Concerto by Johann Nepomuk Hummel (1778–1837). A decidedly minor master, Hummel is known today primarily for this delightful and unpretentious concerto, notwithstanding several more ambitious piano concertos and other works. It and the Haydn concerto constitute a trumpet player's basic classical concerto repertoire.

Also discussing a concerto recording with Ghitalla was Harold Farberman, percussionist of the BSO, who was then at the outset of a conducting career. He had organized the Boston Chamber Ensemble, composed mostly of members of the BSO, and had arranged for the recording to be made by the locally based Cambridge Records. When it developed that Monteux would be available for the Hummel concerto, Farberman was thrilled at the prospect of sharing an LP with Monteux. The first-ever recording of the Hummel was made on 17 December 1963.

In February 1964 the Monteuxs were in Hamburg, where Pierre was to make a series of recordings with the Sinfonieorchester des Norddeutschen Rundfunks (North German Radio Symphony Orchestra), with which he had already recorded Beethoven's Second and Fourth Symphonies in 1960. David Zinman was not present on this occasion; his place was taken by another gifted pupil, Erich Kunzel, who has since gained fame as the conductor of the Cincinnati Pops Orchestra as well as being in charge of pops concerts with many major orchestras.

Kunzel has mentioned that these recordings were, unusually, not connected with public concerts, and that he sat directly in front of Monteux during the sessions. Recorded by the Swiss firm TONO, they were subsequently released on the Concert Hall label. While the repertoire consisted of some works that Monteux had previously recorded (the *Symphonie fantastique*, and Tchaikovsky's Fifth Symphony), there was also a sizable chunk of works new to his discography. Of special interest among these are Mozart's Symphonies Nos. 35 and 39 and a group of orchestral excerpts from Wagner operas: the Overture to *The Flying Dutchman*, the Overture and Bacchanale from *Tannhäuser*, and the Prelude and "Liebestod" from *Tristan und Isolde*. The Mozart works are the only symphonies by that composer ever recorded commercially by Monteux, and very stylish his readings are, the finale of No. 35 (the "Haffner") rather impish in its touches of humor. Unusually, Monteux observed both repeats in the slow movement, something he did not do in his concert performances. As for the Wagner recordings, his only ones of that composer's music except for the *Siegfried Idyll* in San Francisco, they, too, are finely characterized, with flowing tempos and great excitement where required.

The other works recorded were the Overture and Adagio from Beethoven's *Prometheus* ballet music and a Russian collection: Borodin's Polovtzian Dances from *Prince Igor*, Mussorgsky's *Night on Bald Mountain*, Rimsky-Korsakov's *Capriccio espagnol*, and Tchaikovsky's *Romeo and Juliet*; the latter was especially ardent for someone in his eighty-ninth year. The 1960 Beethoven symphonies are the only recordings issued on CD, on the Via Classique label. They are excellent performances, though shorn of all repeats except in the scherzo movements, no doubt so that each would fit on one side of an LP. The orchestra is less than top rank, but as with San Francisco the performances transcend its limitations. What actually compromises the entire series is the quality of the recorded sound, which is the opposite of what would be obtained with a compressor, though equally objectionable. Here the loud passages are very much so, very forward, while the soft passages are very distant. Obviously someone's hand was on the controls at all times, and it is possible that at this stage of his life and career, Monteux was not overly concerned with the final results. He may not even have been consulted about them. (The Hamburg Beethoven Symphony No. 2 and Prelude and "Liebestod" are included, in greatly improved sound, in the Pierre Monteux set in EMI/IMG's series "The Great Conductors.")

From Hamburg Pierre and Doris flew to Israel, their very first visit to the Middle East, for concerts with the Israel Philharmonic Orchestra in Tel Aviv and Jerusalem. According to Doris, Pierre was profoundly moved by his visit to the Holy City and happy that he would be playing his beloved Brahms there. The Fourth Symphony provided a fitting climax to this memorable occasion.

Meanwhile, the LSO's fall 1964 American tour was in the planning stage. Monteux's proposed schedule included concerts in East Lansing, Michigan, and Toledo, Ohio, which prompted the following comments in a letter from Doris Monteux to Ernest Fleischmann, written in Israel and dated 15 March 1964:

> I don't want to add to your worries, but we *refuse* to go to East Lansing Michigan—it is the site of the State University—a fine place for Colin Davis who will appeal to the youthful males and females. But no place for Monteux. . . . I don't think much of Toledo Ohio either. The only decent thing there is a small but rather distinguished Art Museum. Please remind them [the tour's sponsors] that we *know* the U.S.A. rather well!! . . . We refuse to be relegated to the Toledos and East Lansings. You may quote me.

The next stop was Rome, for a pair of concerts with the Santa Cecilia Orchestra on 1 and 2 April 1964. Doris felt that the experience in Israel, with restful afternoons in Tel Aviv, had brought Pierre renewed energy. He was now "tanned a ruddy brown," his health seemingly restored to him after the harsh winter and tiring trips that had rather debilitated him.

The first night's concert had gone very well, and Monteux was in a particularly good mood for the second performance, the first half of which included Beethoven's Symphony No. 1. Doris felt that "the Maestro seemed full of the very spirit of youth as he conducted it." During the intermission he was relaxed and full of good humor. But while conducting Ravel's *Pavane pour une infante défunte* on the second half, he lost his balance and fell not only to the stage, but five feet farther to the auditorium floor. He was then brought backstage and attended to by doctors. After a brief interval, in spite of protests from musicians and audience alike, he returned to the stage to finish the Ravel and conclude the concert as scheduled with *La mer*. The only concession he made was to conduct seated in a chair. He received a tremendous ovation, and the next day the Italian newspapers praised him for his courage. They quoted Doris as saying that the hall had been too hot, that he had felt a bit dizzy and stepped back, his foot slipping at the edge of the podium, after which he slipped under the podium's guardrails and then to the floor.

Monteux slept soundly that night, and the following day he and Doris visited the ancient city of Ostia in the vicinity of Rome. There they enjoyed a very relaxed meal, strolled about for an hour or so, and then returned to Rome, leaving the next day by car for Assisi. It was now 4 April, Pierre's eighty-ninth birthday. Doris said that he had wanted to spend that birthday "with Saint Francis."

That night, just as he was about to go to sleep, he again fainted, and this time Doris had great difficulty reviving him. She did not want to leave him to call for help, so with a combination of "massage, medicine, and prayer," she succeeded in bringing him to, after which he immediately fell asleep. He awoke ten hours later completely refreshed, as though nothing had happened.

In Assisi the Monteuxs visited the Basilica of St. Mary of the Angels, where Pierre spent some fifty minutes within the oratory; then they were driven to Perugia. On the way there Doris asked him, "Darling, did you have so much to pray for, you who are so good?" He answered, "I was asking God to please give me just one more year with my beautiful music, just till my ninetieth birthday." If Doris's recollections are accurate, Pierre's response would indicate that while he was not an overtly religious person, he did believe in God and turned to Him in his especially private moments.

Again Monteux slept ten hours that night. The following morning he and Doris left by car for Milan, where he was to conduct a concert with the Italian Radio Orchestra, the rehearsals for which were described by Doris as "arduous and annoying," though she does not elaborate. The Overture to *The Flying Dutchman*, the Brahms Double Concerto, and the *Symphonie fantastique* made up the program, which was televised throughout middle and southern Europe. (A video of this concert has yet to turn up.) The critics the next day wrote of Monteux's "youthful, vibrant interpretations."

On the morning after the concert, 13 April, just after he had finished shaving, Monteux fell backward and hit his head on the marble floor of the bathroom, and it seemed like an eternity before Doris could revive him. The day was then spent quietly, Monteux sleeping half the time. Again he awoke refreshed, saying he had never felt better.

The next day it was time to leave for London. While paying the bill at the hotel, Doris heard a commotion behind her, and the cashier said he thought someone had fainted. It was Pierre, who was carried by porters to an armchair. Doris once again revived him, and he recovered very quickly. At the airport he walked to the plane without difficulty, and the flight to London was fortunately uneventful.

Once in London, Doris tried to persuade Pierre to cancel his concerts there and to return to Maine to be under the care of his good friend Dr. Edward

O'Meara and to rest and prepare for his summer Tanglewood concerts with the Boston Symphony. Pierre refused, exclaiming, "What! Give up my beautiful programmes, my music, my orchestra. Never! I was fine in Tel Aviv, I gave fine concerts in Rome and Milano, I shall give wonderful ones here in London with my own orchestra. . . . They count absolutely on me, now please stop worrying."

Four days later Monteux had his last rehearsal with the LSO, in which he corrected errors in the parts of Dvořák's "New World" Symphony, parts that had been used for many years without anyone making the corrections. The orchestra members were amazed and delighted. According to Doris, the men repeatedly said to her, "Now we've got our Maestro back, what do you think of him, Madame, correcting those mistakes, isn't that something?" (At that time the London Symphony Orchestra, alone among English orchestras, had no women members. It was to be many years before a woman was finally admitted.)

That night there was a severe power blackout in London because of a serious accident in the main power plant. As a result the elevator in the Monteuxs' hotel was not running, and they had no choice but to climb the six flights of stairs to their suite, which they did very slowly. When they reached their drawing room, now barely lit by three candles, Monteux once again fell on his back, hitting his head on the edge of a table as he fell. In the meantime, Doris also suffered a slight fainting spell because of the effort she had expended in climbing the stairs. Now the two of them lay next to each other on the floor for at least an hour. When they revived, Doris decided then and there to pack their luggage and leave for home on the first plane the next day. She was both surprised and relieved when Pierre agreed. Less than twenty-four hours later, they were back in Hancock.

Monteux's sudden departure meant that David Zinman took over not only the next day's concert, which featured the "New World" Symphony, but also the following one, a repeat performance of Berlioz's *Romeo and Juliet*, which Monteux had recorded the year before.

On the morning of 25 April, Pierre, now confined to his room, asked to sit in his favorite armchair before the window, where he would have a beautiful view of the garden. The profusion of lilac blossoms, tulips, and apple blossoms was mirrored by lavish pink and white clouds overhead. Doris asked him, "Darling, isn't it wonderful to see our dear garden again?" His response saddened her immeasurably. "I did not realize Green Park has so many flowers." He was still in London, oblivious of his surroundings; during the ensuing weeks he often asked Doris how she happened to have his mother's picture "here in London."

As May gave way to June he gradually receded further, frequently speaking of music, of the London Symphony, how it was now time for the rehearsal or concert, how his orchestra needed him. He had three slight strokes and, toward the end, a cerebral thrombosis. Though he was not in pain and recognized his family and students who came to visit, he continued nonetheless in a fantasy world of his own. One day he was heard to cry repeatedly, "Oh that poor Schumann, that poor, poor Schumann," then would speak of Robert Schumann's periods of depression and confinement in a mental institution.

He also spoke of Clara Schumann and Brahms, of how he was certain Schumann had composed his "Rhenish" Symphony to prove to Clara that he could write a symphony as great as one by Brahms. Another time he motioned to everyone to be quiet, for *The Marriage of Figaro* was playing. He then proceeded to sing, as best he could, passages from the overture and various arias from the opera.

While it was generally known that Monteux was ill, the severity of his condition was not common knowledge. On 2 June a telegram arrived from Washington, sent by Maine's Senator Edmund S. Muskie, who extended his best wishes for a speedy and full recovery. He told Monteux that his music had thrilled millions throughout the United States and the world and that his return to health and conducting was awaited with great anticipation.

One day Monteux was visited by his pupil Werner Torkanowsky, then music director of the New Orleans Philharmonic-Symphony Orchestra, who was amazed to hear him say, "When I see Brahms, I must apologize to him for the way I have played his beautiful music." This was not just dementia; Monteux had given extremely beautiful performances of Brahms's music throughout his life, but great artists are never satisfied with their performances.

Always attended to by Doris or one of her sisters, or by her daughter-in-law Marianne (Mano) Purslow, he would speak of various composers—Handel, Mozart, Bizet, Strauss, Tchaikovsky, and Stravinsky. They thought it strange that he never spoke of Beethoven, Debussy, or Ravel, though Wagner was often on his mind, as well as Schubert. He continued on about orchestral difficulties, swinging his left arm in conducting gestures while his right arm lay paralyzed by his side. One night he was heard loudly singing "La Marseillaise." By now Monteux had been confined to his bed for eight weeks. One night Doris and her sister Charlotte were sitting nearby when "he gave a loud, inhuman cry, a hoarse, harsh sound which filled the room. We watched in agony as our dear Maestro, his face livid and contorted, struggled with the appalling and dreadful thrombosis consuming him, his poor slight body tortured by an over-powering perturbation impossible to control." Within an hour he was sleeping, the doctor having assured everyone that he was in no pain. He remained quiet for several days, unmindful of those around him. Then, on his next to last day of life, "without warning, his eyes opened wide, shining with wondrous light, impossible to describe" (D. Monteux 1965, 203–13). He then cried out loudly, "C'est Dieu!" (It is God!) Those were his last words. At 4:30 in the morning of 1 July 1964, Pierre Monteux died. At his side were Doris, her sister Charlotte Michlin, his son Claude, his daughter Denise (Mrs. Thomas Lanese), and their daughter-in-law Mano.

Funeral services, including a requiem mass, were held on Saturday, 4 July, at St. Joseph's Catholic Church in Ellsworth. They were attended by family and friends as well as notables from the world of music, including the conductors

Eugene Ormandy and Max Rudolf and the Metropolitan Opera soprano Roberta Peters.

On the day following Monteux's death, BBC television broadcast an interview with Ernest Fleischmann, general secretary of the London Symphony Orchestra, in which he was questioned by a former Monteux pupil, Francis Coleman. The following are some of Fleischmann's comments:

> Not having Monteux with us is somehow being not quite complete anymore. It was not only the twinkle in his eye, it was his tremendous peace of mind, the sort of thing that enabled him, when we flew to Japan, for example, to be by far the most rested and alive member of our touring party, after we'd flown for over twenty hours. The rest of the orchestra was completely dead, but he was raring to go.
>
> This great peace of mind, I think, was what gave him this tremendous control over an orchestra. There was never any tension, any feeling of "will it work or won't it?" One relied on him, one knew that he knew, therefore this gave the musicians fantastic confidence. It was something very rare and wonderful that we had so much of him during these last few years of his life.
>
> He liked working in the recording studio. Again, when he was in the studio, there wasn't this mad excitement and "will the next take be all right?" The takes inevitably were all right, and the records were made in far quicker time than is usual with many other conductors. He loved this feeling of making music together, but with a great deal of authority. The orchestra all seemed to share in the experience of making music with him, but, my goodness, he *was* the boss, and although he never raised his voice, he heard everything that went on, and he managed to detect all sorts of things that even surprised the musicians. We couldn't get away with anything with Monteux, except he didn't make a fuss about it, and this is why it was so much easier to really give of our very best with him.

To open the Tanglewood season on Friday, 3 July, Erich Leinsdorf conducted the Boston Symphony and the Berkshire Festival Chorus in the Kyrie from Mozart's Mass in C minor in memory of Monteux.

Obituary notices appeared in all of the world's major and minor newspapers, often accompanied by editorials and appreciative articles by music critics. The San Francisco papers naturally were particularly expressive in their appreciation, their remembrances, and their sadness. The following editorial is from *The San Francisco Examiner*:

> Pierre Monteux had to leave San Francisco for San Franciscans to discover how firm and enduring a place he had won in their affections. He is gone for good now, at 89, after a rich and full and rewarding life of the kind

given to few men. And thousands upon thousands of Bay area citizens whose lives he enriched as "Papa," their maker of fine music for 18 years as conductor of the San Francisco Symphony, know a deep sadness.

Millions of others around the world share the same feeling. It is, as we said, sadness rather than grief. His life was too full, too rich, for any to feel that his work was not yet done.

His career was, in a way, one long symphony.

From an editorial in the *San Francisco Chronicle*:

It is not enough to say that Pierre Monteux fashioned the Symphony into one of high repute and major stature. It must be recalled that when he took over its direction . . . he took over what was hardly a symphony orchestra at all. It was at most a bedraggled and undernourished organization, one that had survived the lean and hungry depression years only through Government handouts as a WPA project.

From such beginnings the Monteux magic transformed it into one of the nation's ranking orchestras. Meanwhile, "Papa" Monteux was very much the San Francisco citizen, sharing in civic affairs, enjoying its amenities, gathering in friends by the hundred, demonstrating the personal attributes that kept him, until the last, beloved and in pressing professional demand around the world.

Writing in *The New York Times*, the critic Ross Parmenter had his own unique evaluation of Monteux's conducting:

It was one of Mr. Monteux's gifts that he could give the illusion that his orchestra was playing, not on a shallow stage, but in a great courtyard from which the sounds could come at will from various distances. He could create the sense that the listener was simultaneously hearing sounds from far off and others from up close.

From *High Fidelity* magazine, September 1964:

He saw a work not as a series of episodes to enable him to show off, but as a whole. He was able to judge true climaxes in the repertoire of symphonies, romantic overtures, and tone poems. Even an opera like *Carmen* became far more of a musical unity; under his direction an act spanned from curtain to curtain, rather than from section to section. Pierre Monteux commanded respect not only by his age, but by his invariable courtesy and absolute professionalism. He *had* to make music as the composer intended; his work was a reflection of his personal honesty.

In *The Boston Globe* of 5 July, Michael Steinberg wrote:

We must learn to live with the idea that some part of Beethoven, of Schumann, Brahms, Debussy, Strauss, Stravinsky has died with Pierre Monteux,
whose figure, so unforgettable an amalgam of dignity and humor, we shall
not see again.
The grand figures among the conductors of his generation are almost all
gone now. He stood apart from his contemporaries because his era was one
essentially of eccentrics, often inspired ones. It was an age of a distinctly
idiosyncratic approach to performance: Stokowski, Koussevitzky, Mengelberg are the archetypes. Pierre Monteux gave the music straight, at least, as
he knew how. That, to many, was his limitation, but to many it was his
glory. . . .
Monteux was fond of attributing the course of his career to indolence.
He switched from violin to viola, he insisted, because it was easier, and the
violist became a conductor for the same reason. And what was he planning
to do when he retired from conducting? "Music criticism, of course." I am
glad it never came to that point. It was, after all, so good to have Monteux
conducting.

In addition, Doris Monteux received hundreds of telegrams from musicians
and friends the world over, including Leonard Bernstein, Arthur Fiedler, Otto
Klemperer, George Szell, Maine's Governor John H. Reed, the members of the
Boston Symphony, the Concertgebouw Orchestra, the London Symphony, and
the board of governors of the San Francisco Symphony. She even received a letter
from the manager of London's Stafford Hotel, where the Monteuxs had stayed on
their last visit, expressing regret that Monteux's having to walk up six flights of
stairs during the power cut may have contributed to his untimely death.
Without wishing to minimize the sincerity of the many telegrams, if I were to
quote just one as an example, it would be that from a man who "grieved over the
loss of his oldest friend in music"—Igor Stravinsky.
The week following Monteux's death the London Symphony performed the
Berlioz Requiem in Saint Paul's Cathedral as scheduled, the opening concert of the
annual City of London Festival. Colin Davis conducted, and the performance
was dedicated to the memory of Monteux. On its American tour in the fall of
1964, the LSO performed a Pierre Monteux memorial concert in Carnegie Hall on
21 October. Pablo Casals conducted the first two works on the program, opening
with Bach's Brandenburg Concerto No. 5, in which the soloists were the pianist
Rudolf Serkin, the violinist Isaac Stern, and the LSO's principal flute, Alexander
Murray. Following this work came the aria "Erbarme dich" from Bach's *St. Matthew Passion*, sung by the contralto Maureen Forrester, with Stern playing the
violin obbligato. The first half closed with Leopold Stokowski conducting Beethoven's Choral Fantasy with Serkin again at the piano and the Rutgers Univer-

sity Choir. None of these works was particularly associated with Monteux, but they made an effective grouping as a memorial observance. Nor was the work on the second half especially associated with him, though he did perform it in San Francisco: the Fifth Symphony of Shostakovich, conducted by Stokowski, who *was* associated with it.

As reported the next day in the *Herald Tribune*, Isaac Stern spoke a few words of tribute before the Bach aria and asked the audience not to applaud at its conclusion. "As you listen, "he said, "you must each in your own way remember Pierre Monteux."

All the participants contributed their services to the event, the proceeds of which went to the newly established Pierre Monteux Memorial Foundation.

One cannot help but wonder what Monteux would have thought of the obituary that appeared in the *Herald Tribune*. The accompanying photograph had been retouched to make his hair appear white.

CODA

Closing Thoughts

The Conductors Guild, an organization of and for conductors, holds a conference in January of each year, one session of which is devoted to a retrospective of the career of a historic conductor. In 1989 the subject was Pierre Monteux, and the panelists included Leon Fleisher, Isaac Stern, and David Zinman. The discussion was taped for archival purposes and, with the permission of the surviving members, here are some of their remarks.

Leon Fleisher

Schnabel said that of all the conductors he had played with, his favorite to make music with was Monteux. That always surprised me in a way because, though Monteux never, in my recollection, spoke of music in terms of its abstractions, its concepts, its spirituality, if you will, those elements were there most powerfully in his music making. Schnabel, on the other hand, would speak mostly in those terms, of abstraction and concepts. It wasn't necessary for Monteux to speak of these elements, these ineffable elements of music, but he was mightily aware of them. I think, because of that awareness and his incredible sensitivity and sensibility, one was able to join an ongoing concept, an ongoing creation.

David Zinman

He was a living tradition and he always let you know about it, but he let you know about it in a very, very nice way, never in a preaching way. He always had something practical to say; he taught in a most practical way from the standpoint of an orchestral musician. If it worked for the musician, it was a good thing. In all the times that I worked with him, he would say, "Here the second trombone is too loud, here you should use an up-bow, here watch out, he will always come early, watch out in this place," and he just told you the places where there were traps for musicians and how to do it. And he always said one very important thing. He said, "You must respect your musicians." He had a basic respect for all the musicians in the orchestra, and he conducted an orchestra as an avuncular or father figure.

319

Isaac Stern

The first thing you learned from Monteux was the absolute necessity of authority, that could give confidence to every man in the orchestra, that no matter where they were, *he* knew where they were supposed to be. He *always* used his eyes as he went around the orchestra, and somehow sensed when a player was not certain where he was.

Monteux knew his scores, every part of the score. For a soloist he was incomparable. He had this sense of anticipation; he could tell before you did what you were going to do. He had complete sensitivity to the overall music and to what the soloist was about, and never did he impose his musical judgment or his will on the soloist. He would never argue, he would never suggest, he would never murmur, he would never look at one of the other players and make a grimace or a smirk if the soloist did something which was obviously unmusical or incorrect. He was always thoughtful. The one thing he knew most of all was how constantly terrifying it is to be a performer. The most he could do was to envelop you with this loving, appreciative, thoughtful humanity that gave you absolute freedom, but a cushion on which to rest. He was never away from you; no matter what you did, you could never lose Monteux, but you always had someone around to protect you.

Even at an early age, one knew that what you were listening to were authoritative performances of the repertoire, whether it be German, French, contemporary, it didn't matter, they were authoritative. He lived well in the skin of the music, not only his own skin but the skin of the music—very rare, especially in days that have developed since, where personalities have sometimes tended to transcend the needs of music.

There was always his respect for music, not his demand for his own ego. He was a man very certain of himself; he did not lack for an ego. But he was never a brash, self-centered man—he couldn't be, because he always had respect for what he himself had yet to learn. Monteux had an enormous repertoire, but I never knew him not to be spending part of each day studying, whether it was something that he was learning or something he had played before. It didn't matter—study. Music was not a profession, or an ego trip—it was a way of life. It was a self-discipline, it was a necessity, that this was the way a civilization operated. And to those of us who were fortunate enough to have had the time to spend a little bit of his life with him, we were the richer for that little bit of civilization that we learned from him.

Pierre Monteux's
Recorded Repertoire

The numbers in parentheses indicate a work's position in the Discography.

Bach

Concerto in D minor for Two
  Violins, BWV 1043 (9)
Christmas Oratorio, BWV 248:
  Sinfonia (88)
Suite No. 2 in B minor BWV 1067
  (254)

Bach-Respighi

Passacaglia and Fugue in C minor,
  BWV 582 (89)

Beethoven

Piano Concerto No. 4 in G major,
  Op. 58 (172)
The Consecration of the House, Op.
  124: Overture (90, 105)
The Creatures of Prometheus, Op.
  43: Adagio (32)
The Creatures of Prometheus, Op.
  43: Overture and Adagio (246)
Egmont, Op. 84: Overture (117, 212)
Fidelio, Op. 72: Overture (28, 191)
King Stephen, Op. 117: Overture
  (192)
Leonore Overture No. 3, Op. 72a
  (124)

The Ruins of Athens, Op. 113:
  Overture (87)
Symphony No. 1 in C major, Op. 21
  (187)
Symphony No. 2 in D major, Op. 36
  (86, 189, 194)
Symphony No. 3 in E-flat major
  ("Eroica"), Op. 55 (158, 218)
Symphony No. 4 in B-flat major, Op.
  60 (129, 190, 195)
Symphony No. 5 in C minor, Op. 67
  (63, 210)
Symphony No. 6 in F major
  ("Pastorale"), Op. 68 (168)
Symphony No. 7 in A major, Op. 92
  (138, 211)
Symphony No. 8 in F major, Op. 93
  (98, 188, 199)
Symphony No. 9 in D minor, Op.
  125 (221)

Berlioz

Benvenuto Cellini: Overture, Op.
  23 (4, 126)
Le corsaire Overture, Op. 21
  (123)
Roman Carnival Overture, Op. 9
  (60, 201)

Les Troyens à Carthage: Prelude (5, 38, 50)
The Damnation of Faust, Op. 24 (214)
The Damnation of Faust, Op. 24: Orchestral Excerpts (33)
The Damnation of Faust, Op. 24: Rakóczy March (116)
L'enfance du Christ, Op. 25: Prelude to Part II (74)
L'enfance du Christ, Op. 25: Trio of the Young Ishmaelites (67)
Symphonie fantastique, Op. 14 (2, 42, 76, 96, 159, 239)
Symphony, *Harold in Italy*, Op. 16 (235)
Romeo and Juliet, Dramatic Symphony, Op. 17 (216)
Romeo and Juliet: Orchestral Excerpts (34)

Borodin

Prince Igor: Polovtzian Dances (119, 247)

Brahms

Piano Concerto No. 1 in D minor, Op. 15 (193)
Violin Concerto in D major, Op. 77 (106, 167)
Academic Festival Overture, Op. 80 (223)
Tragic Overture, Op. 81 (79, 215, 224)
Alto Rhapsody, Op. 53 (43)
Song of Destiny, Op. 54 (85)
Symphony No. 1 in C minor, Op. 68 (234)
Symphony No. 1 in C minor, Op. 68: 2d movement, Andante sostenuto (118)
Symphony No. 2 in D major, Op. 73 (47, 115, 152, 222)

Symphony No. 3 in F major, Op. 90 (196, 226)
Variations on a Theme of Haydn, Op. 56a (170)

Brahms-Hertz

Five Waltzes, Op. 39 (84)

Bruch

Violin Concerto No. 1 in G minor, Op. 26 (39)

Chabrier

Le roi malgré lui: Fête polonaise (3, 69)

Chausson

Poème for Violin and Orchestra, Op. 25 (52)
Poème de l'amour et de la mer, Op. 19 (135)
Symphony in B-flat major, Op. 20 (99)

Coppola

Interlude dramatique (8)

Creston

Symphony No. 2, Op. 35 (148)

Debussy

Images for Orchestra (114, 227)
Images for Orchestra: "Gigues" and Rondes de printemps" (20)
Images for Orchestra: "Gigues" and "Ibéria" (150)
Images for Orchestra: "Ibéria" (202)
Jeux (144)
Le martyre de Saint-Sébastien: Symphonic Fragments (228)
Le martyre de Saint-Sébastien: Excerpts (163)
La mer (141)

Three Nocturnes for Orchestra (146)
Nocturnes for Orchestra: *Nuages* and
  Fêtes (205)
Prélude á l'après-midi d'un faune
  (107, 204)
Pelléas et Mélisande: Preludes and
  Interludes (156)

Debussy-Ravel

Sarabande (58)

Delibes

Coppélia: Suite (139)
Sylvia: Suite (140)

Dukas

The Sorcerer's Apprentice (121)

Dvořák

Symphony No. 7 in D minor, Op. 70
  (183)

Elgar

Enigma Variations, Op. 36 (108,
  166)

Falla

The Three-Cornered Hat: Two
  Dances (208)

Franck

Psyché: Two Excerpts (31)
Rédemption: Symphonic Interlude
  (130)
Symphony in D minor (18, 59, 95,
  209)

Franck-O'Connell

Pièce héroïque (19)

Franck-Pierné

Prelude, Chorale, and Fugue (30)

Glazunov

Scènes de Ballet (26)

Gluck

Iphigenia in Aulis: Overture (35)
Orfeo ed Euridice (161)
Orfeo ed Euridice: Dance of the
  Blessed Spirits (255)

Gounod

Faust: Ballet Music (68)

Gruenberg

Violin Concerto, Op. 47 (51)

Haydn

Symphony No. 88 in G major (36)
Symphony No. 94 in G major
  ("Surprise") (180)
Symphony No. 101 in D major ("The
  Clock") (181)

Hindemith

Symphony, *Mathis der Maler* (220)

Hummel

Trumpet Concerto in E major (237)

Ibert

Escales (54)

d'Indy

Fervaal, Op. 40: Prelude (40)
*Symphony on a French Mountain
  Air*, Op. 25 (17)
Symphony No. 2 in B-flat major, Op.
  57 (21)
Istar Variations, Op. 42 (41)

Khachaturian

Violin Concerto (164)

Lalo

Le roi d'Ys: Overture (22)
Symphonie espagnole, Op. 21 (37)

Liszt

Hungarian Rhapsody No. 2 (82)
Les préludes (102, 133)

Mahler

Kindertotenlieder (97)

Massenet

Manon (143)

Mendelssohn

The Hebrides Overture, Op. 26 (77)
A Midsummer Night's Dream:
  Overture, Op. 21, and Excerpts,
  Op. 61 (169)
Ruy Blas Overture, Op. 95 (71, 83)
Symphony No. 4 in A major
  ("Italian"), Op. 90 (64)

Messiaen

L'ascension: Three Movements (75)

Milhaud

Protée (Symphonic Suite No. 2) (48)

Mozart

Piano Concerto No. 12 in A major,
  K. 414 (136)
Piano Concerto No. 12 in A major,
  K. 414: Andante and Allegretto
  (103)
Piano Concerto No. 18 in B-flat
  major, K. 456 (137)
Flute Concerto No. 2 in D major, K.
  314 (256)
The Abduction from the Seraglio, K.
  384 Overture (49)
Don Giovanni, K. 527: Overture (94)

The Magic Flute, K. 620: Overture
  (120)
Symphony No. 35 in D major
  ("Haffner"), K. 385 (53, 240)
Symphony No. 39 in E-flat major, K.
  543 (241)
(attr.): Violin Concerto in D major
  ("Adelaide") (10)

Mussorgsky

Night on Bald Mountain (244)

Nováček

Perpetuum mobile, Op. 5, No. 4
  (12)

Offenbach

Les contes d'Hoffmann (147)

Paganini

Violin Concerto No. 1 in D major,
  Op. 6 (11)

Rachmaninoff

Symphony No. 2 in E minor, Op. 27:
  Movements 3 and 2 (14)

Ravel

Alborada del gracioso (72)
Boléro (251)
Daphnis et Chloé (145, 178)
Daphnis et Chloé: Suite No. 1 (57)
Ma mère l'oye (253)
Ma mère l'oye: "Petit poucet" (7)
Pavane pour une infante défunte
  (206)
Rapsodie espagnole (207)
Shéhérazade (233)
Le tombeau de Couperin (176)
La valse (6, 15, 252)
Valses nobles et sentimentales (56)

Rimsky-Korsakov

Capriccio espagnol, Op. 34 (122, 245)
Christmas Eve: Suite (27)
Le coq d'or: Introduction (46) and
  Bridal Procession (16)
Russian Easter Overture, Op. 36
  (132)
Sadko, Op. 5 (44)
Scheherazade, Op. 35 (23, 177)
Symphony No. 2 ("Antar"), Op. 9
  (55)
The Tale of the Tsar Saltan: March
  (25)

Rossini

L'italiana in Algeri: Overture (128,
  225)

Saint-Saëns

Havanaise, Op. 83 (165)

Schubert

Rosamunde: Overture and Excerpts
  (170)
Symphony No. 8 in B minor
  ("Unfinished") (236)

Schumann

Piano Concerto in A minor, Op. 54
  (24)
Symphony No. 4 in D minor, Op.
  120 (127, 213)

Scriabin

Poem of Ecstasy (70, 134)

Sibelius

Violin Concerto in D minor, Op. 47
  (109)
Kuolema: Valse triste, Op. 44 (81)
Symphony No. 2 in D major, Op. 43
  (179)

Sousa

The Stars and Stripes Forever (73)

Still

Old California (29)

Strauss

Death and Transfiguration, Op. 24
  (131, 184)
Don Juan, Op. 20 (92, 182)
Don Quixote, Op. 35 (173)
Ein Heldenleben, Op. 40 (66, 219)
Der Rosenkavalier, Op. 59: Suite
  (112, 149)
Till Eulenspiegel's Merry Pranks, Op.
  28 (125, 186)

Stravinsky

The Firebird: Suite (153)
Petrushka (154, 174, 197)
The Rite of Spring (1, 45, 110, 155,
  157)
Symphony of Psalms (203)

Tchaikovsky

Piano Concerto No. 1 in B-flat minor,
  Op. 23 (231)
Romeo and Juliet (100, 230, 243)
Sleeping Beauty, Op. 68: Excerpts
  (160)
Swan Lake, Op. 20: Excerpts (217)
Symphony No. 4 in F minor, Op. 36
  (175)
Symphony No. 5 in E minor, Op. 64
  (162, 232, 242)
Symphony No. 6 in B minor
  ("Pathétique"), Op. 74 (142)

Thomas

Mignon: Overture (78)

Vaughan Williams

Fantasia on a Theme by Thomas Tallis (238)

Verdi

La traviata (151)

Wagner

The Flying Dutchman: Overture (111, 249)

Götterdämmerung: "Siegfried's Rhine Journey" (113)

Die Meistersinger: Prelude to Act I (65, 229)

Die Meistersinger: Prelude to Act III (200)

Die Meistersinger Three Excerpts from Act III (104)

Parsifal: Prelude and Good Friday Spell (101)

Rienzi: Overture (93)

Siegfried Idyll (185, 198)

Siegfried: Forest Murmurs (62)

Tannhäuser: Overture and Bacchanale (248)

Tristan und Isolde: Prelude and "Liebestod" (80, 250)

Die Walküre: "Wotan's Farewell" and "Magic Fire Music" (61)

Weber

Euryanthe: Overture, Op. 77 (91)

Konzertstück in F minor, Op. 79 (13)

Discography

This is a chronological listing of Pierre Monteux's recordings, both commercial and otherwise. Those that are taken from live performances are so indicated. As many of these have existed in multiple incarnations, the record number information refers to the most recently available release. All are on CD unless otherwise indicated.

Key to orchestra identifications

BBCNSO	BBC Northern Symphony Orchestra
BBCSO	BBC Symphony Orchestra
BCE	Boston Chamber Ensemble
BSO	Boston Symphony Orchestra
COA	Concertgebouw Orchestra of Amsterdam
CSO	Chicago Symphony Orchestra
DSRSO	Danish State Radio Symphony Orchestra
GSO	Grand Orchestre Symphonique
LSO	London Symphony Orchestra
MOO	Metropolitan Opera Orchestra
NBCSO	NBC Symphony Orchestra
NYP	New York Philharmonic
NDR	Norddeutscher Rundfunk Orchestra
ONF	Orchestre National de France
OSP	Orchestre Symphonique de Paris
PCO	Paris Conservatory Orchestra
POCO	Paris Opéra-Comique Orchestra
RCAVSO	RCA Victor Symphony Orchestra
ROO	Rome Opera Orchestra
RPO	Royal Philharmonic Orchestra
SFSO	San Francisco Symphony Orchestra
VPO	Vienna Philharmonic Orchestra
VSO	Vienna Symphony Orchestra

1. Stravinsky: *Le sacre du printemps*. GOS. 23–25 January 1929. Dante LYS-374. Pearl GEMM CD-9329
2. Berlioz: *Symphonie fantastique*, Op. 14. OSP. 20, 23, 27–28 January, 3 February 1930. Dante LYS-368. Pearl GEMM-CD-9012. Music & Arts CD-762
3. Chabrier: *Le roi malgré lui*: "Fête Polonaise." OSP. 29 January 1930. Dante LYS-374. Pearl GEMM CD-9012
4. Berlioz: *Benvenuto Cellini*: Overture, Op. 23. OSP. 30 January 1930. Dante LYS-368. Pearl GEMM-CD-9012. Music & Arts CD-762
5. Berlioz: *Les Troyens à Carthage*: Prelude. OSP. 30 January 1930. Dante LYS-368. Pearl GEMM-CD-9012
6. Ravel: *La valse*. OSP. 31 January 1930. Dante LYS-374
7. Ravel: *Ma mère l'oye*: "Petit poucet." OSP. 3 February 1930. Dante LYS-374
8. Coppola: *Interlude dramatique*. OSP. 3 February 1930. Dante LYS-374. Pearl GEMM-CD-9012
9. Bach: Concerto in D minor for Two Violins, BWV 1043. Yehudi Menuhin, Georges Enesco. OSP. 4 June 1932. EMI CDH 567-201-2. Dante LYS-374
10. Mozart (attr.): Violin Concerto in D major (*Adelaide*), KVAnh 294a. Yehudi Menuhin. OSP. 18 May 1934. EMI CDH 763-718-2. Biddulph LAB-051. Dante LYS-479
11. Paganini: Violin Concerto No. 1 in D major, Op. 6. Yehudi Menuhin. OSP. 18-19 May 1934. EMI CDM 565-959-2. Biddulph LAB-051. Dante LYS-479
12. Nováček: *Perpetuum mobile*, Op. 5, No. 4. Yehudi Menuhin. OSP. 18 May 1934. Dante LYS-479
13. Weber: *Konzertstück* in F minor, Op. 79. Lili Kraus. COA. 17 October 1939. Audiophile Classics 101.560 (live)
14. Rachmaninoff: Symphony No. 2 in E minor, Op. 27: Movements 3 and 2. SFSO. 27 February 1941. Music & Arts CD-978 (live)
15. Ravel: *La valse*. SFSO. 21 April 1941. RCA/BMG 09026-61895-2
16. Rimsky-Korsakov: *Le coq d'or*: Bridal Procession. SFSO. 21 April 1941. RCA Camden CAL-215 (LP)
17. d'Indy: Symphony on a French Mountain Air, Op. 25. Maxim Schapiro. SFSO. 21-22 April 1941. RCA/BMG 09026-61888-2
18. Franck: Symphony in D minor. SFSO. 22 April 1941. RCA Camden CFL-104 (LP)
19. Franck-O'Connell: *Pièce héroïque*. SFSO. 22 April 1941. RCA/BMG 09026-61967-2
20. Debussy: *Images* for Orchestra: "Gigues" and "Rondes de printemps." SFSO. 2 March 1942. RCA Camden CAL-161

21. d'Indy: Symphony No. 2 in B-flat major, Op. 57. SFSO. 2–3 March 1942. RCA/BMG 09026-61888-2
22. Lalo: *Le roi d'Ys*: Overture. SFSO. 3 March 1942. RCA/BMG 09026-61895-2
23. Rimsky-Korsakov: *Scheherazade*, Op. 35. SFSO. 3–4 March 1942. RCA/BMG 09026-61897-2
24. Schumann: Piano Concerto in A minor, Op. 54. Artur Schnabel, NYP. 13 June 1943. Music & Arts CD-1111 (live)
25. Rimsky-Korsakov: *The Tale of the Tsar Saltan*: March. SFSO. 4 March 1942. RCA WDM-920 (45 rpm)
26. Glazunov: *Scènes de ballet*. SFSO. 12 December 1943. Music & Arts CD-978 (live)
27. Rimsky-Korsakov: *Christmas Eve*: Suite. SFSO. 19 December 1943. Music & Arts CD-978 (live)
28. Beethoven: *Fidelio*: Overture, Op. 72. SFSO. 16 January 1944. Music & Arts CD-978 (live)
29. Still: *Old California*. NYP. 5 November 1944. New York Philharmonic American Celebration. NYP-9902 (live)
30. Franck-Pierné: Prelude, Chorale, and Fugue. SFSO. 3 December 1944. Music & Arts CD-978 (live)
31. Franck: *Psyché*: Two Excerpts. SFSO. 3 December 1944. Music & Arts CD-978 (live)
32. Beethoven: *The Creatures of Prometheus*, Op. 43: Adagio. SFSO. 17 December 1944. Music & Arts CD-978 (live)
33. Berlioz: *La damnation de Faust*, Op. 24: Orchestral Excerpts. SFSO. 26 November 1944. Music & Arts CD-978 (live)
34. Berlioz: *Romeo and Juliet*, Op. 17: Orchestral Excerpts. SFSO. 26 November 1944. Music & Arts CD-978 (live)
35. Gluck: *Iphigenia in Aulis*: Overture. SFSO. 21 January 1945. Music & Arts CD-978 (live)
36. Haydn: Symphony No. 88 in G major. SFSO. 21 January 1945. Music & Arts CD-978 (live)
37. Lalo: *Symphonie espagnole*, Op. 21. Yehudi Menuhin, SFSO. 26–27 January 1945. RCA/BMG 09026-61395-2
38. Berlioz: *Les Troyens à Carthage*: Prelude. SFSO. 27 January 1945. RCA/BMG 09026-61894-2
39. Bruch: Violin Concerto No. 1 in G minor, Op. 26. Yehudi Menuhin, SFSO. 27 January 1945. Biddulph LAB-129
40. d'Indy: *Fervaal*, Op. 40: Prelude. SFSO. 27 January 1945. RCA/BMG 09026-61900-2
41. d'Indy: *Istar Variations*, Op. 42. SFSO. 27 January 1945. RCA/BMG 09026-61900-2

42. Berlioz: *Symphonie fantastique*, Op. 14. SFSO. 17, 28 February, 15 April 1945. RCA/BMG 09026-61894-2
43. Brahms: Alto Rhapsody, Op. 53. Marian Anderson, SF Municipal Chorus, SFSO. 3 March 1945. RCA/BMG 7911-2-RG
44. Rimsky-Korsakov: *Sadko*, Op. 5. SFSO. 3 March 1945. RCA/BMG 09026-61897-2
45. Stravinsky: *Le sacre du printemps*. SFSO. 10 March 1945. AVID Master Series AMSC-6000
46. Rimsky-Korsakov: *Le coq d'or*: Introduction. SFSO. 19 March 1945. RCA 12-0502 (78 rpm)
47. Brahms: Symphony No. 2 in D major, Op. 73. SFSO. 19 March 1945. RCA/BMG 09026-61891-2 (erroneously listed as 1951 recording)
48. Milhaud: *Protée* (Symphonic Suite No. 2). SFSO. 14 April 1945. RCA Camden CAL-385 (LP)
49. Mozart: *The Abduction from the Seraglio*, K. 384: Overture. SFSO. 21 April 1945. Music & Arts CD-978 (live)
50. Berlioz: *Les Troyens à Carthage*: Prelude. SFSO. 18 November 1945. Music & Arts CD-978 (live)
51. Gruenberg: Violin Concerto, Op. 47. Jascha Heifetz, SFSO. 17 December 1945. RCA/BMG 09026-61754-2. Naxos 8-11094-2
52. Chausson: *Poème*, Op. 25. Jascha Heifetz, SFSO. 17 December 1945. Testament SBT 1216
53. Mozart: Symphony No. 35 in D major ("Haffner"), K. 385. SFSO. 24 March 1946. Music & Arts CD-978 (live)
54. Ibert: *Escales*. SFSO. 2 April 1946. RCA/BMG 09026-61895-2
55. Rimsky-Korsakov: Symphony No. 2 ("Antar"), Op. 9. SFSO. 2 April 1946. RCA/BMG 09026-61897-2
56. Ravel: *Valses nobles et sentimentales*. SFSO. 3 April 1946. RCA/BMG 09026-61895-2
57. Ravel: *Daphnis et Chloë*: Suite No. 1. Univ. of Calif. Chorus, SFSO. 3 April 1946. RCA/BMG 09026-61895-2
58. Debussy-Ravel: Sarabande. SFSO. 3 April 1946. RCA-BMG 09026-61900-2
59. Franck: Symphony in D minor. SFSO. 7 April 1946. Music & Arts CD-978 (live)
60. Berlioz: *Roman Carnival* Overture, Op. 9. SFSO. 8 December 1946. Music & Arts CD-978 (live)
61. Wagner: *Die Walküre*: "Wotan's Farewell" and "Magic Fire Music." SFSO. 19 January 1947. Music & Arts CD-978 (live)
62. Wagner: *Siegfried*: "Forest Murmurs." SFSO. 19 January 1947. Music & Arts CD-978 (live)
63. Beethoven: Symphony No. 5 in C minor, Op. 67. SFSO. 16 February 1947, 10 December 1950. Music & Arts CD-978 (live)

64. Mendelssohn: Symphony No. 4 in A major ("Italian"), Op. 90. SFSO 23 February 1947. Music & Arts CD-978 (live)
65. Wagner: *Die Meistersinger*: Prelude to Act I. SFSO. 16 November 1947. Music & Arts CD-978 (live)
66. Strauss: *Ein Heldenleben*, Op. 40. SFSO. 20 December 1947. RCA/BMG 09026-61889-2
67. Berlioz: *L'enfance du Christ*: Trio of the Young Ishmaelites. SFSO. 21 December 1947. Music & Arts CD-978 (live)
68. Gounod: *Faust*: Ballet Music. SFSO. 22 December 1947. RCA/BMG 09026-61975-2
69. Chabrier: *Le roi malgré lui*: "Fête Polonaise." SFSO. 22 December 1947. RCA/BMG 09026-61899
70. Scriabin: *Poem of Ecstasy*. SFSO. 22 December 1947. RCA DM-1270 (78 rpm)
71. Mendelssohn: *Ruy Blas* Overture, Op. 95. SFSO. 22 December 1947. RCA 12-0657 (78 rpm), 49-0883 (45 rpm)
72. Ravel: *Alborada del gracioso*. SFSO. 22 December 1947. RCA/BMG 09026-61895-2
73. Sousa: *The Stars and Stripes Forever*. SFSO. 7 March 1948. Music & Arts CD-978 (live)
74. Berlioz: *L'enfance du Christ*: Prelude to Part II. SFSO. 28 March 1948. Music & Arts CD-978 (live)
75. Messiaen: *L'Ascension*: movements 1, 2, and 3. SFSO. 28 March 1948. Music & Arts CD-978 (live)
76. Berlioz: *Symphonie fantastique*, Op. 14. COA. 20 May 1948. Tahra TAH-177 (live)
77. Mendelssohn: *The Hebrides* Overture, Op. 26. SFSO. 9 January 1949. Music & Arts CD-978 (live)
78. Thomas: *Mignon*: Overture. SFSO. 6 February 1949. Music & Arts CD-978 (live)
79. Brahms: *Tragic Overture*, Op. 81. SFSO. 20 February 1949. Music & Arts CD-978 (live)
80. Wagner: *Tristan und Isolde*: Prelude and "Liebestod." SFSO. 20 February 1949. Music & Arts CD-978 (live)
81. Sibelius: *Kuolema*: Valse triste, Op. 44. SFSO. 13 March 1949. Music & Arts CD-978 (live)
82. Liszt: Hungarian Rhapsody No. 2. SFSO. 13 March 1949. Music & Arts CD-978 (live)
83. Mendelssohn: *Ruy Blas* Overture, Op. 95. SFSO. 27 March 1949. Music & Arts CD-978 (live)
84. Brahms-Hertz: Five Waltzes, Op. 39. SFSO. 27 March 1949. Music & Arts CD-978 (live)

85. Brahms: *Song of Destiny*, Op. 54. Stanford Univ. Chorus, SFSO. 19 April 1949. RCA/BMG-09026-61891-2
86. Beethoven: Symphony No. 2 in D major, Op. 36. SFSO. 19 April 1949. RCA LM-1024 (LP)
87. Beethoven: *The Ruins of Athens*, Op. 113: Overture. SFSO. 19 April 1949. RCA/BMG-09026-61892-2
88. Bach: Christmas Oratorio: Sinfonia, BWV 248. SFSO. 19 April 1949. RCA DM-1340 (78 rpm)
89. Bach-Respighi: Passacaglia and Fugue in C minor, BWV 582. SFSO. 19 April 1949. RCA/BMG 09026-61892-2
90. Beethoven: Overture for *The Consecration of the House*, Op. 124. SFSO. 4 December 1949. Music & Arts CD-978 (live)
91. Weber: *Euryanthe*: Overture, Op. 77. SFSO. 29 January 1950. Music & Arts CD-978 (live)
92. Strauss: *Don Juan*, Op. 20. SFSO. 29 January 1950. Music & Arts CD-978 (live)
93. Wagner: *Rienzi*: Overture. SFSO. 5 February 1950. Music & Arts CD-978 (live)
94. Mozart: *Don Giovanni*, K. 527: Overture. SFSO. 5 February 1950. Music & Arts CD-978 (live)
95. Franck: Symphony in D minor. SFSO. 26 February 1950. RCA LM-1065 (LP)
96. Berlioz: *Symphonie fantastique*, Op. 14. SFSO. 27 February 1950. RCA LM-1131 (LP)
97. Mahler: *Kindertotenlieder*. Marian Anderson, SFSO. 26 February 1950. RCA/BMG 09026-61891-2
98. Beethoven: Symphony No. 8 in F major, Op. 93. SFSO. 28 February 1950. RCA/BMG 09026-61892-2
99. Chausson: Symphony in B-flat major, Op. 20. SFSO. 28 February 1950. RCA/BMG 09026-61899-2
100. Tchaikovsky: *Romeo and Juliet*. SFSO. 12 March 1950. Music & Arts CD-978 (live)
101. Wagner: *Parsifal*: Prelude and "Good Friday Spell." 9 April 1950. Music & Arts CD-978 (live)
102. Liszt: *Les préludes*. SFSO. 16 April 1950. Music & Arts CD-978 (live)
103. Mozart: Piano Concerto No. 12 in A major, K. 414: Andante and Allegretto. William Kapell, SFSO. 23 April 1950. Music & Arts CD-978 (live)
104. Wagner: *Die Meistersinger*: Three Excerpts from Act III. SFSO. 23 April 1950. Music & Arts CD-978 (live)
105. Beethoven: Overture for *The Consecration of the House*, Op. 124. COA. 12 October 1950. Audiophile Classics APL 101.559 (live)

106. Brahms: Violin Concerto in D major, Op. 77. Nathan Milstein, COA. 12 October 1950. Tahra TAH-176 (live); Audiophile Classics APL 101.559 (live)

107. Debussy *Prélude à l'après-midi d'un faune*. COA. 12 October 1950. Audiophile Classics 101.559 (live)

108. Elgar: *Enigma Variations*. Op. 36. COA. 12 October 1950. Audiophile Classics APL 101.560 (live)

109. Sibelius: Violin Concerto in D minor, Op. 47. Jan Damen, COA. 1 November 1950. Tahra TAH-178 (live); Audiophile Classics APL 101.560 (live)

110. Stravinsky: *Le sacre du printemps*. BSO. 28 January 1951. RCA/BMG 09026-61898-2

111. Wagner: *The Flying Dutchman*: Overture. SFSO. 11 February 1951. Music & Arts CD-978 (live)

112. Strauss: *Der Rosenkavalier*, Op. 59: Suite. 25 February 1951. Music & Arts CD-978 (live)

113. Wagner: *Götterdämmerung*: Siegfried's Rhine Journey. SFSO. 4 March 1951. Music & Arts CD-978 (live)

114. Debussy: *Images* for Orchestra. SFSO. 3 April 1951. RCA/BMG 09026-61900-2

115. Brahms: Symphony No. 2 in D major, Op. 73. SFSO. 4 April 1951. RCA LM-1173 (LP)

116. Berlioz: *La damnation de Faust*: Rakóczy March. SFSO. 4 April 1951. RCA/BMG 09026-61894-2

117. Beethoven: *Egmont*, Op. 84: Overture. SFSO. 23 December 1951. Music & Arts CD-978 (live)

118. Brahms: Symphony No. 1 in C minor, Op. 68: second movement. SFSO. 23 December 1951. Music & Arts CD-978 (live)

119. Borodin: *Prince Igor*: Polovtzian Dances. SFSO. 23 December 1951. Music & Arts CD-978 (live)

120. Mozart: *The Magic Flute*, K. 620: Overture. SFSO. 3 February 1952. Music & Arts CD-978 (live)

121. Dukas: *The Sorcerer's Apprentice*. SFSO. 3 February 1952. Music & Arts CD-978 (live)

122. Rimsky-Korsakov: *Capriccio espagnol*, Op. 34. SFSO. 2 March 1952. Music & Arts CD-978 (live)

123. Berlioz: *Le corsaire* Overture, Op. 21. SFSO. 9 March 1952. Music & Arts CD-978 (live)

124. Beethoven: *Leonore* Overture No. 3, Op. 72a. SFSO. 30 March 1952. Music & Arts CD-978 (live)

125. Strauss: *Till Eulenspiegel's Merry Pranks*, Op. 28. SFSO. 30 March 1952. Music & Arts CD-978 (live)

126. Berlioz: *Benvenuto Cellini*: Overture, Op. 23. SFSO. 6 April 1952. RCA/
     BMG 09026-61894-2
127. Schumann: Symphony No. 4 in D minor, Op. 120. SFSO. 6 April 1952.
     RCA LM-1714 (LP)
128. Rossini: *L'italiana in Algeri*: Overture. SFSO. 6 April 1952. Music &
     Arts CD-978 (live)
129. Beethoven: Symphony No. 4 in B-flat major, Op. 60. SFSO. 7 April
     1952. RCA/BMG 09026-61892-2
130. Franck: *Rédemption*: Symphonic Interlude. SFSO. 13 April 1952. Music
     & Arts CD-978 (live)
131. Strauss: *Death and Transfiguration*, Op. 24. SFSO. 13 April 1952.
     Music & Arts CD-978 (live)
132. Rimsky-Korsakov: *Russian Easter* Overture, Op. 36. SFSO. 13 April
     1952. Music & Arts CD-978 (live)
133. Liszt: *Les préludes*. BSO. 8 December 1952. RCA/BMG 09026-61890-2
134. Scriabin: *Poem of Ecstasy*. BSO. 8 December 1952. RCA/BMG. 09026-
     61890-2
135. Chausson: *Poème de l'amour et de la mer*. Gladys Swarthout, RCAVSO.
     9 December 1952. RCA/BMG 09026-61899-2
136. Mozart: Piano Concerto No. 12 in A major, K. 414. Lili Kraus, BSO. 12
     April 1953. RCA France GM-43276 (LP)
137. Mozart: Piano Concerto No. 18 in B-flat major, K. 456. Lili Kraus, BSO.
     12 April 1953. RCA France GM-43276 (LP)
138. Beethoven: Symphony No. 7 in A major, Op. 92. NBCSO. 17 November
     1953. Longanese Periodici GCL-28. (LP, live)
139. Delibes: *Coppélia*: Suite. BSO (members). 2, 4 December 1953. RCA/
     BMG 09026-61975-2
140. Delibes: *Sylvia*: Suite. BSO (members). 30, 31 December 1953. RCA/
     BMG 09026-61975-2
141. Debussy: *La mer*. BSO. 19 July 1954. RCA/BMG 09026-61890-2
142. Tchaikovsky: Symphony No. 6 in B minor ("Pathétique"), Op. 74. BSO.
     26 January 1955. RCA/BMG 09026-61901-2
143. Massenet: *Manon*. POCO & Chorus, Victoria de los Angeles, Henri
     Legay, Michel Dens. 30 May–22 June 1955. Testament SBT 3203
144. Debussy: *Jeux*. ONF. 9 June 1955. Discocorp 313 (live)
145. Ravel: *Daphnis et Chloé* (complete ballet). COA, Netherlands Radio
     Choral Union. 23 June 1955. Audiophile Classics APL 101.549 (live);
     Music & Arts (live)
146. Debussy: Three Nocturnes. BSO, Berkshire Festival Women's Chorus. 15
     August 1955. RCA/BMG 09026-61900-2; EMI 7243 5 75474 2 0
147. Offenbach: *Les contes d'Hoffmann*. MOO & Chorus, Lucine Amara,
     Mildred Miller, Roberta Peters, Risë Stevens, Richard Tucker, Martial
     Singher. 3 December 1955. MET 14 (live, LP)

148. Creston: Symphony No. 2, Op. 35. NYP. 22 January 1956. New York Philharmonic American Celebration. NYP-9902 (live)

149. Strauss: *Der Rosenkavalier*, Op. 59: Suite. BSO. 17 February 1956. Symphony Hall Centennial Celebration. BSO CD-100 (live)

150. Debussy: *Images* for Orchestra: "Gigues" and "Ibéria." ONF. 3 May 1956. Discocorp 313 (LP, live)

151. Verdi: *La traviata*. ROO & Chorus, Rosanna Carteri, Cesare Valletti, Leonard Warren. RCA LM-6040 (LP)

152. Brahms: Symphony No. 2 in D major, Op. 73. VPO. 1956. Decca/London 430-214-2

153. Stravinsky: *The Firebird*: Suite. PCO. 1956. Decca/London 421-635-2

154. Stravinsky: *Petrushka*. PCO. 1956. Decca/London 421-635-2

155. Stravinsky: *Le sacre du printemps*. PCO. 1956. RCA LSC-2085 (LP)

156. Debussy: *Pelléas et Mélisande*: Preludes and Interludes. BSO. 19 January 1957. Discocorp RR-313 (LP, live)

157. Stravinsky: *Le sacre du printemps*. BSO. 13 April 1957. Discocorp RR-312) (LP, live)

158. Beethoven: Symphony No. 3 in E-flat major ("Eroica"), Op. 55. VPO. 1957. Decca/London 440-627-2

159. Berlioz: *Symphonie fantastique*, Op. 14. VPO. 1957. Decca/London STS-15423 (LP)

160. Tchaikovsky: *The Sleeping Beauty*, Op. 68: Excerpts. LSO. 3–6 June 1957. EMI 7243 6 75474 2 0

161. Gluck: *Orfeo ed Euridice*. ROO & Chorus, Risë Stevens, Lisa Della Casa, Roberta Peters. 15–26 June 1957. RCA/BMG 09026-63534

162. Tchaikovsky: Symphony No. 5 in E minor, Op. 64. BSO. 8 January 1958. RCA/BMG 09026-61901-2

163. Debussy: *The Martyrdom of St. Sebastian*: Excerpts. BSO. 11 January 1958. Discocorp 313 (live)

164. Khachaturian: Violin Concerto. Leonid Kogan, BSO. 12, 13 January 1958. RCA/BMG 09026-63708-2

165. Saint-Saëns: *Havanaise*, Op. 83. Leonid Kogan, BSO. 13 January 1958. RCA/BMG 09026-61890-2

166. Elgar: *Enigma Variations*, Op. 36. LSO. 24, 25 January 1958. Decca/London 452-303-2

167. Brahms: Violin Concerto in D major, Op. 77. Henryk Szeryng, LSO. June 1958. RCA 6716-2 RG

168. Beethoven: Symphony No. 6 in F major ("Pastorale"), Op. 68. VPO. 1958. Decca/London 440-627-2

169. Mendelssohn: *A Midsummer Night's Dream*, Op. 21 and 61: Excerpts. VPO. 1958 RCA LM-2223 (LP)

170. Schubert: *Rosamunde*: Excerpts. VPO. 1958. RCA LM-2223 (LP)

171. Brahms: *Variations on a Theme of Haydn*, Op. 56a. LSO. June 1958. Decca/London 452-893-2
172. Beethoven: Piano Concerto No. 4 in G major, Op. 58. Paul Badura-Skoda, VSO. 1958. Discocorp RR-558 (LP, live)
173. Strauss: *Don Quixote*, Op. 35. Samuel Mayes, Joseph de Pasquale, BSO. 24 January 1959. Symphony Hall Centennial Celebration. BSO CD-100 (live)
174. Stravinsky: *Petrushka*. BSO. 25, 26, 28 January 1959. RCA/BMG 09026-61898-2; RCA/BMG 09026-63303-2
175. Tchaikovsky: Symphony No. 4 in F minor, Op. 36. BSO. 28 January 1959. RCA/BMG 09026-61902-2
176. Ravel: *Le tombeau de Couperin*. NYP. 7 March 1959. New York Philharmonic Historic Broadcasts. NYP 9708/09 (live)
177. Rimsky-Korsakov: *Scheherazade*, Op. 35. LSO. 1959. Decca/London 421-400-2
178. Ravel: *Daphnis et Chloé* (complete ballet) LSO, Royal Opera House Chorus. 27, 28 April 1959. Decca/London 425-956-2
179. Sibelius: Symphony No. 2 in D major, Op. 43. LSO. 1959. RCA LSC-2343 (LP)
180. Haydn: Symphony No. 94 in G major ("Surprise"). VPO. April 1959. Decca/London 452-893-2
181. Haydn: Symphony No. 101 in D major ("The Clock"). VPO. April 1959. Decca/London 452-893-2
182. Strauss: *Don Juan*, Op. 20. BSO. 24 July 1959. Music & Arts CD-269 (live)
183. Dvořák: Symphony No. 7 in D minor, Op. 70. LSO. 19, 20 October 1959. Decca/London 433-4032
184. Strauss: *Death and Transfiguration*, Op. 24. SFSO. 23 January 1960. RCA/BMG 09026-61889-2
185. Wagner: *Siegfried Idyll*. SFSO. 24 January 1960. RCA VICS-1102 (LP); RCA VICS-1457 (LP)
186. Strauss: *Till Eulenspiegel's Merry Pranks*, Op. 28. BSO. 9 April 1960. Music & Arts CD-269 (live)
187. Beethoven: Symphony No. 1 in C major, Op. 21. VPO. 1960. Decca/London 440-627-2
188. Beethoven: Symphony No. 8 in F major, Op. 93. VPO. 1960. Decca/London 440-627-2
189. Beethoven: Symphony No. 2 in D major, Op. 36. LSO. 1960. Decca/London 443-479-2
190. Beethoven: Symphony No. 4 in B-flat major, Op. 60. LSO. 1960. Decca/London 443-479-2
191. Beethoven: *Fidelio*: Overture, Op. 72. LSO. 1960. Decca/London 443-479-2

192. Beethoven: *King Stephen*: Overture, Op. 117. LSO. 1960. Decca/London 443-479-2

193. Brahms: Piano Concerto No. 1 in D minor, Op. 15. Julius Katchen, LSO. 1960. Decca/London STS-15209 (LP)

194. Beethoven: Symphony No. 2 in D major, Op. 36. NDR. 1 October 1960. Via Classique 642302-WM-321; EMI 7243 5 75474 2 0

195. Beethoven: Symphony No. 4 in B-flat major, Op. 60. NDR. 1 October 1960. Via Classique 642302-WM-321; EMI 7243 5 75474 2 0

196. Brahms: Symphony No. 3 in F major, Op. 90. COA. 30 October 1960. Tahra TAH-176 (live)

197. Stravinsky: *Petrushka*. COA. 30 October 1960. Tahra TAH-178 (live)

198. Wagner: *Siegfried Idyll*. RPO. 18 November 1960. BBC Legends BBCL4096-2 (live)

199. Beethoven: Symphony No. 8 in F major, Op. 93. CSO. 1 January 1961. Video Artists International 69604 (live, video)

200. Wagner: *Die Meistersinger*: Prelude to Act III. CSO. 1 January 1961. Chicago Symphony in the 20th Century. CSO CD 00-10 (live). Video Artists International 69604 (live, video)

201. Berlioz: *Roman Carnival* Overture, Op. 9. CSO. 1 January 1961. Chicago Symphony, the First 100 Years. CSO 090/12 (live). Video Artists International 69604 (live, video)

202. Debussy: *Images* for Orchestra: "Ibéria." BBCSO. 8 December 1961. BBC Legends BBCL 4096-2 (live)

203. Stravinsky: *Symphony of Psalms*. BBCSO, BBC Symphony Chorus. 8 December 1961. BBC Legends BBCL 4096-2 (live)

204. Debussy: *Prélude à l'après-midi d'un faune*. LSO. 11–13 December 1961. Decca/London CS-6248 (LP)

205. Debussy: Nocturnes: *Nuages* and *Fêtes*. LSO. 11–13 December 1961. Decca/London CS-6248 (LP)

206. Ravel: *Pavane pour une infante défunte*. LSO. 11–13 December 1961. Decca/London 425956-2

207. Ravel: *Rapsodie espagnole*. LSO. 11–13 December 1961. Decca/London 425956-2

208. Falla: *The Three-Cornered Hat*: Two Dances. LSO. 15 December 1961. BBC Legends BBCL 4096-2 (live)

209. Franck: Symphony in D minor. CSO. 7 January 1961. RCA/BMG 09026-61967-2; RCA/BMG 09026-63303-2

210. Beethoven: Symphony No. 5 in C minor, Op. 67. LSO. 1961. Decca/London 443-479-2

211. Beethoven: Symphony No. 7 in A major, Op. 92. LSO. 1961. Decca/London 443-479-2

212. Beethoven: *Egmont*: Overture, Op. 84. LSO. 1961. Decca/London SPA-585 (LP) (The performance of the *Egmont* Overture included in Decca/London 443-479-2, and attributed to Pierre Monteux and the LSO, is actually by the Vienna Philharmonic Orchestra, conducted by George Szell.)
213. Schumann: Symphony No. 4 in D minor, Op. 120. BBCSO. 18 October 1961. BBC Music BBCL 4058-2 (live)
214. Berlioz: *La damnation de Faust*, Op. 24. LSO, Régine Crespin, André Turp, Michel Roux, John Shirley-Quirk, LSO Chorus. 8 March 1962. BBC Music BBCL-4006-7 (live)
215. Brahms: *Tragic Overture*, Op. 81. COA. 14 May 1962, Tahra TAH-175 (live)
216. Berlioz: *Romeo and Juliet*, Op. 17. LSO, Regina Resnik, André Turp, David Ward, LSO Chorus. June 1962. Westminster 289-471-242-2
217. Tchaikovsky: *Swan Lake*, Op. 20: Excerpts. LSO. June 1962. Philips 442-546-2
218. Beethoven: Symphony No. 3 in E-flat major ("Eroica"), Op. 55. COA. July 1962. Philips 442-545-2
219. Strauss: *Ein Heldenleben*, Op. 40. BSO. 29 July 1962. Music & Arts CD-269 (live)
220. Hindemith: Symphony, *Mathis der Maler*. DSRSO. 11 October 1962. EMI 7243 5 75474 2 0 (live)
221. Beethoven: Symphony No. 9 in D minor, Op. 125. LSO, Elisabeth Söderstrom, Regina Resnik, Jon Vickers, David Ward, London Bach Choir. November 1962. Westminster 289-471-216-2
222. Brahms: Symphony No. 2 in D major, Op. 73. LSO. November 1962. Philips 442-547-2
223. Brahms: *Academic Festival Overture*, Op. 80. LSO. November 1962. Philips 442-547-2
224. Brahms: *Tragic Overture*, Op. 81. LSO. November 1962. Philips 442-547-2
225. Rossini: *L'italiana in Algeri*: Overture. BBCNSO. 21 November 1962. BBC Music BBCL 4058-2 (live)
226. Brahms: Symphony No. 3 in F major, Op. 90. BBCNSO. 21 November 1962. BBC Music BBCL 4058-2 (live)
227. Debussy: *Images* for Orchestra. LSO. May 1963. Philips 442-595-2
228. Debussy: *The Martyrdom of Saint Sebastian*: Symphonic Fragments. LSO. May 1963. Philips 442-595-2
229. Wagner: *Die Meistersinger*: Prelude to Act 1. LSO. 29 May 1963. BBC Legends BBCL 4096-2 (live)
230. Tchaikovsky: *Romeo and Juliet*. LSO. 31 May 1963. Vanguard DVC 8031/2 (live)

231. Tchaikovsky: Piano Concerto No. 1 in B-flat minor, Op. 23. John Ogdon, LSO. 31 May 1963. Vanguard DVC 8031/2 (live)
232. Tchaikovsky: Symphony No. 5 in E minor, Op. 64. LSO. 31 May 1963. Vanguard DVC 8031/2 (live)
233. Ravel: *Shéhérazade*. Victoria de los Angeles, COA. 20 November 1963. Audiophile Classics APL 101.549 (live); Music & Arts (live)
234. Brahms: Symphony No. 1 in C minor, Op. 68. COA. 20 November 1963. Tahra TAH-175 (live)
235. Berlioz: *Harold in Italy*, Op. 16. Klaas Boon, COA. 24 November1963. Past Masters PM-37 (LP, live)
236. Schubert: Symphony No. 8 in B minor ("Unfinished"). COA. November 1963.
237. Hummel: Trumpet Concerto in E major. Armando Ghitalla, BCE. 17 December 1963. Crystal CD-760
238. Vaughan Williams: *Fantasia on a Theme by Thomas Tallis*. BSO. 20 December 1963. Symphony Hall Centennial Celebration. BSO CD-100 (live)
239. Berlioz: *Symphonie fantastique*, Op. 14. NDR. February 1964. Concert Hall SMSC-2357 (LP)
240. Mozart: Symphony No. 35 in D major ("Haffner"), K. 385. NDR. February 1964. Concert Hall SMS-2359 (LP)
241. Mozart: Symphony No. 39 in E-flat major, K. 543. NDR. February 1964. Concert Hall SMS-2359 (LP)
242. Tchaikovsky: Symphony No. 5 in E minor, Op. 64. NDR. January 1964. Concert Hall SMS-2333 (LP)
243. Tchaikovsky: *Romeo and Juliet*. NDR. January 1964. Concert Hall SMS-2361 (LP)
244. Mussorgsky: *Night on Bald Mountain*. NDR. January 1964. Concert Hall SMS-2361 (LP)
245. Rimsky-Korsakov: *Capriccio espagnol*, Op. 34. NDR. January 1964. Concert Hall SMS-2361 (LP)
246. Beethoven: *The Creatures of Prometheus*, Op. 43: Overture and Adagio. NDR. January 1964. Concert Hall SMS-2761 (LP)
247. Borodin: *Prince Igor*: Polovtzian Dances. NDR. January 1964. Concert Hall SMS-2761 (LP)
248. Wagner: *Tannhäuser*: Overture and Bacchanale. NDR. January 1964. Concert Hall SMS-2362 (LP)
249. Wagner: *The Flying Dutchman*: Overture. NDR. January 1964. Concert Hall SMS-2362 (LP)
250. Wagner: *Tristan und Isolde*: Prelude and "Liebestod." NDR. January 1964. Concert Hall SMS-2362 (LP); EMI 7243-5-75474-20
251. Ravel: *Boléro*. LSO. February 1964. Philips 442-548-23.
252. Ravel: *La valse*. LSO. February 1964. Philips 442-548-2

253. Ravel: *Ma mère l'oye* (complete ballet). LSO, February 1964. Philips 442-548-2
254. Bach: Suite No. 2 in B minor. Claude Monteux, LSO. February 1964. Decca/London CS-6400 (LP)
255. Gluck: *Orfeo ed Euridice*: Dance of the Blessed Spirits. Claude Monteux, LSO. February 1964. Decca/London CS-6400 (LP)
256. Mozart: Flute Concerto No. 2 in D major, K. 314. Claude Monteux, LSO. February, 1964. Decca/London CS-6400 (LP)

Significant World Premieres
Conducted by Pierre Monteux

Antheil: Symphony No. 6; San Francisco, 10 February 1949
Bliss: *Hymn to Apollo*; Amsterdam, 28 November 1926
Bloch: *Evocations*; San Francisco, 11 February 1938
Debussy: *Jeux*; Paris, 15 May 1913
Gilbert: *The Dance in Place Congo*; New York, 23 March 1918
Griffes: *The Pleasure Dome of Kubla-Khan*; Boston, 28 November 1919
Malipiero: Violin Concerto; Amsterdam, 5 March 1933 (Viola Mitchell, violin)
Milhaud: Viola Concerto; Amsterdam, 15 December 1929 (Paul Hindemith, viola)
Milhaud: *Opus Americanum* No. 2; San Francisco, 11 December 1943
Pijper: Symphony No. 3; Amsterdam, 28 October 1926
Poulenc: *Concert champêtre*; Paris, 3 May 1929 (Wanda Landowska, harpsichord)
Prokofiev: Symphony No. 3; Paris, 17 May 1929
Ravel: *Daphnis et Chloé*; Paris, 8 June 1912
Ravel: *Tzigane*; Amsterdam, 19 October 1924 (Samuel Dushkin, violin)
Schmitt: *The Tragedy of Salome*; Paris, 12 June 1913
Sessions: Symphony No. 2; San Francisco, 9 January 1947
Stravinsky: *Petrushka*; Paris, 13 June 1911
Stravinsky: *Le rossignol*; Paris, 28 May 1914
Stravinsky: *Le sacre du printemps*; Paris, 29 May 1913

Selected Bibliography

Armsby, Leonora Wood. 1960. *We Shall Have Music*. San Francisco: Pisani.

Bing, Sir Rudolf. 1972. *Five Thousand Nights at the Opera*. New York: Doubleday.

Bloomfield, Arthur. 1997. Program Notes for Music and Arts' *Sunday Evenings with Pierre Monteux*.

Bookspan, Martin, and Ross Yockey. 1981. *André Previn: A Biography*. New York: Doubleday.

Boult, Sir Adrian. 1973. *My Own Trumpet*. London: Hamish Hamilton.

Brymer, Jack. 1979. *From Where I Sit*. London: Cassell.

Buckle, Richard. 1979. *Diaghilev*. New York: Atheneum.

Canarina, John. 1986. "Pierre Monteux: A Conductor for All Repertoire." *Opus*, April.

Collester, Jeanne Colette. 1995. *Rudolph Ganz: A Musical Pioneer*. Metuchen, New Jersey: Scarecrow Press.

Craft, Robert, ed. 1982. *Stravinsky: Selected Correspondence*, vol. 1. New York: Alfred A. Knopf.

———. 1984. *Stravinsky: Selected Correspondence*, vol. 2. New York: Alfred A. Knopf.

Culshaw, John. 1981. *Putting the Record Straight*. London: Secker & Warburg.

Davis, Hilda Emery. 1996. *In Time with the Music*. Sullivan, Maine: Privately published by Ginia Davis.

Dickson, Harry Ellis. 1974. *Gentlemen, More Dolce Please!* Boston: Beacon Press.

Doráti, Antal. 1979. *Notes of Seven Decades*. London: Hodder & Stoughton.

Downes, Irene, ed. 1957. *Olin Downes on Music*. New York: Simon & Schuster.

Frank, Mortimer H. 2002. *Arturo Toscanini: The NBC Years*. Portland, Oregon: Amadeus Press.

Freed, Richard D. 1994. *Pierre Monteux Edition*. [Program notes.] RCA-BMG.

Haggin, B. H. 1964. *Music Observed*. New York: Oxford University Press.

Hart, Philip. 1979. *Conductors: A New Generation*. New York: Charles Scribner's Sons.

———. 1994. *Fritz Reiner: A Biography*. Evanston, Illinois: Northwestern University Press.

Howe, M. A. DeWolfe. 1931. *The Boston Symphony Orchestra, 1881–1931*. Boston: Houghton Mifflin.

Iancu, Danièle, and Carol Iancu. 1995. *Les Juifs du Midi: Une histoire millénaire*. Paris: Éditions A. Barthélemy.

Jackson, Paul. 1997. *Sign-Off for the Old Met: The Metropolitan Opera Broadcasts, 1950–1966*. Portland, Oregon: Amadeus Press.

Kelly, Thomas Forrest. 2000. *First Nights*. New York: Yale University Press.

Kennedy, Michael. 1987. *Adrian Boult*. London: Hamish Hamilton.

Kolodin, Irving. 1966. *The Metropolitan Opera, 1883–1966: A Candid History*. New York: Alfred A. Knopf.

Landowski, Marcel. 1994. *Pierre Monteux Edition*. [Program notes.] RCA-BMG.

Leinsdorf, Erich. 1976. *Cadenza: A Musical Career*. Boston: Houghton Mifflin.

———. 1981. *The Composer's Advocate: A Radical Orthodoxy for Musicians*. New Haven, Connecticut: Yale University Press.

Levant, Oscar. 1940. *A Smattering of Ignorance*. New York: Doubleday, Doran.

Levy, Alan. 1976. *The Bluebird of Happiness: The Memoirs of Jan Peerce*. New York: Harper & Row.

Lipman, Samuel. 1984a. "A Conductor in History." *Commentary*, January.

———. 1984b. "Mme. Pierre Monteux." *New Criterion*, May.

———. 1989. "Pierre Monteux and the Criterion for Success." *New Criterion*, February.

Monteux, Doris. 1965. *It's All in the Music*. New York: Farrar, Straus & Giroux.

Monteux, Pierre. 1958. "Early Years." Liner notes for *The Rite of Spring*. RCA Victor, LSC-2085.

Mousnier, Jean-Philippe. 1999. *Pierre Monteux*. Paris: L'Harmattan.

The NBC Symphony Orchestra. 1938. New York: National Broadcasting Company.

Nijinsky, Romola. 1934. *Nijinsky*. New York: Simon & Schuster.

O'Connell, Charles. 1947. *The Other Side of the Record*. New York: Alfred A. Knopf.

Pearton, Maurice. 1974. *The LSO at Seventy: A History of the Orchestra*. London: Victor Gollancz.

Phippen, Sanford, ed. 1978. *A History of the Town of Hancock, 1828–1978*. Ellsworth, Maine: Downeast Graphics.

————. 2000. *The Sun Never Sets on Hancock Point: An Informal History.* Ellsworth, Maine: Downeast Graphics & Printing.

Previn, André. 1991. *No Minor Chords.* New York: Doubleday.

Rodzinski, Halina. 1976. *Our Two Lives.* New York: Charles Scribner's Sons.

Rubinstein, Arthur. 1980. *My Many Years.* New York: Alfred A. Knopf.

Sachs, Harvey. 1978. *Toscanini.* Philadelphia: J. P. Lippincott.

Schneider, David. 1983. *The San Francisco Symphony: Music, Maestros, and Musicians.* San Francisco: Presidio Press.

Schonberg, Harold C. 1967. *The Great Conductors.* New York: Simon & Schuster.

Smith, Moses. 1947. *Koussevitzky.* New York: Allen, Towne & Heath.

Snyder, Louis. 1979. *Community of Sound: Boston Symphony and Its World of Players.* Boston: Beacon Press.

Speyer, Louis. 1972. *A Life of Music* [Boston Symphony program book].

Stravinsky, Igor, and Robert Craft. 1959. *Conversations with Igor Stravinsky.* New York: Doubleday.

————. 1960. *Memories and Commentaries.* New York: Doubleday.

————. 1966. *Themes and Episodes.* New York: Alfred A. Knopf.

————. 2002. *Memories and Commentaries.* London and New York: Faber and Faber.

Thomson, Virgil. 1966. *Virgil Thomson.* New York: Alfred A. Knopf.

————. 1981. *A Virgil Thomson Reader.* Boston: Houghton Mifflin.

Untermeyer, Sophie Guggenheimer, and Alix Williamson. 1960. *Mother Is Minnie.* Garden City, New York: Doubleday.

Walsh, Stephen. 1999. *Stravinsky: A Creative Spring: Russia and France, 1882–1934.* New York: Alfred A. Knopf.

Index